THE BACKSTAIRS DRAGON

ROBERT HARLEY, EARL OF OXFORD

ELIZABETH HAMILTON

The Backstairs Dragon

A LIFE OF

ROBERT HARLEY, EARL OF OXFORD

TAPLINGER PUBLISHING COMPANY

NEW YORK

First published in the United States in 1970 by

TAPLINGER PUBLISHING CO., INC.
29 East Tenth Street
New York, New York 10003

SBN 8008 0587 9

Library of Congress Catalog Number 75-97190

Printed in Great Britain

To DICK

CONTENTS

LIST OF ILLUSTRATIONS

ENDPAPERS

A*

ACKNOWLEDGEMENTS

I SHOULD LIKE TO THANK the following for permission to consult and quote from unpublished manuscripts: the Duke of Portland, the Duke of Marlborough, the Marquess of Bath, Lady Monica Salmond and Mr Peter Walne, County Archivist at the Hertford County Record Office where the Panshanger MSS are lodged, Colonel Lloyd Baker, and Mr Christopher Harley. Miss Jancey, of the Herefordshire County Record Office, who has worked through the Brampton Bryan estate papers, was able to give me valuable information, and also drew my attention to letters of the Foley sisters in the Morgan (Mill Street) collection at Shrewsbury. The Shropshire County Archivist, Miss Mary Hill, kindly provided photostat copies. I am grateful to Miss K. M. Gell and Mrs E. A. Cooke for their courtesy and help during my visits to Blenheim and Longleat, to Mr Francis Needham, to the staff of the London Library, the Bodleian Library, the British Museum Manuscripts room, and the Warwickshire County Library. Mrs Hill, of the National Portrait Gallery, took a great deal of trouble over the choice of portraits. Mr Christopher Harley has shown great kindness in allowing the reproductions of his family portraits, and both he and Mrs Harley have been most hospitable and helpful.

Of the many scholars whose work I have consulted, I owe a particular debt to Mr Geoffrey Holmes, of the University of Glasgow, for his advice and guidance. I appreciate his generosity in allowing me to make use of his exciting discovery that the Code in the Portland Loan at the British Museum provides the key to previously undeciphered letters written by Harley to Abigail Masham—'Cousin Catherine Stephens'—in the autumn of 1708.

I owe a debt of gratitude to all those who have helped me at home, to Mrs June Hawkins for secretarial work, to my husband for his help and advice, and to all the family for being so tolerant.

NOTE

IN GENERAL, dates are given in the 'Old Style' of the Julian Calendar which was still in use during Harley's lifetime, but the new year is dated from January 1, and not March 25 as was customary at that time. Spelling and punctuation, with some exceptions, have been modernized. Notes at the end of the book are given by reference to page numbers.

CHAPTER I

FIRST BEGINNINGS

ROBERT HARLEY was born on December 5, 1661, in Bow Street at his parents' London home. His father, Sir Edward, was a country squire of Puritan stock, with considerable estates in Herefordshire and across the border in Radnor. He was a man of upright character, with a quickness in the eyes which commanded respect, and although he was only thirty-seven, his hair was liberally sprinkled with grey. 'I have tasted of many troubles,' he wrote, 'but my God hath given me always a cup running over with mercy.' He had suffered for his opinions in the turbulent times of civil war; the Harley castles and estates had been devastated, and he still carried in his body a shot received while leading a regiment of horse against the Royalists. Later he had spoken out in Parliament with courageous frankness against Cromwell's tyranny, and as a result had been forced to live as a proscribed person until the Restoration. Now, times were happier. King Charles II had rewarded him for his good service and loyalty by creating him a Knight of the Bath, and although his virtuous nature made him recoil from the corruption of Charles's court, he was able to serve his country as a conscientious M.P. and was free to repair the damages done to his estate. In addition, God had granted him a son to inherit his name and lands.

Robert's mother, Abigail Stephens, also came from a Puritan family. She was a woman of exemplary piety, 'absolutely free,' her younger son was later to write, 'from all those passions with which the female sex do so commonly disturb themselves.' From the first, Robert was surrounded by an aura of sanctity.

In April 1662, Lady Harley took her infant son with his two elder sisters, Brilliana and Martha, to the paternal seat in Herefordshire on the Welsh–Shropshire border. Sir Edward was unable to follow until Parliament adjourned. 'I thank God you and your little caravan passed so well,' he wrote to his wife on April 11. At Brampton Bryan, seat of the Harley family for several centuries, builders were working on a new house close to the ruined castle, set in a broad, peaceful valley among finely wooded hills. Less than twenty years before, in 1643, Sir Edward's mother, Brilliana, with the help of only eight soldiers, her servants, a barrel of powder and a small quantity of match, had defended the castle for six weeks against the King's men. Her antagonists found her stubborn and determined. 'I have your petition instead of an answer, which in my opinion is too long by twenty lines and too full of the spirit of contradiction and expostulations,' raged Sir John Scudamore, showing his disapproval by slinging cannon-balls into the castle from the roof of the nearby church. His threats had little effect on Brilliana; she wrote serenely to her husband, Sir Robert, who had ridden off to join the Roundheads: 'Dear Sir, be not too much troubled for me or your children. We are all very cheerful and not afraid.' Her refusal to surrender brought ruin and destruction to the little town of Brampton and its people, whose pitiful cries when they heard of her decision did nothing to soften the determined lady's heart. All the papists in the neighbourhood hurried to join the siege, with as many guns and engineers as they could lay hands on. 'Dear Sir, pray for me, for I have great need of it,' wrote Brilliana, shortly before the end of her ordeal. 'All the children are well but I have taken an exceeding great cold which much troubles me.' She lived long enough to see the castle burned, the town sacked and the church destroyed, but her health was undermined by the strain of the preceding weeks and she was seized with apoplexy, lethargy and convulsions. The faithful family doctor, who had stood by her throughout the siege, could do nothing to save her, and on a Sunday 'the sweet lady's soul' was sent to keep the eternal Sabbath in heaven where, it was pointed out, she would run no further risk of being besieged.

Sir Robert was too preoccupied to spend much time mourning for his wife. He was a man of narrow, bigoted ideals who had been appointed Chairman of the Commons Committee formed to destroy all evidence of idolatry in churches and cathedrals. He arranged for, among other things, the removal of stained glass windows from Westminster Abbey, St Margaret's and Hampton Court, the large-scale destruction of images of the Virgin Mary, the burning of the embroidered altar cloth at Canterbury, and the removal from the Duke of Richmond's chapel of a picture of God the Father with Christ in his bosom. One Jane Bagley received £1. 5s. as a result of his misguided zeal, for cutting pearls off mitres and copes. Fortunately, his son Edward rejected such stern prejudices and was open-minded enough to attend Anglican church services, although he always stood out against measures for persecuting dissenters. He concentrated on living a Christian life rather than arguing about doctrine, and kept a firm and watchful guard over his children to make sure that they grew up in the right faith. An atmosphere of intense religion prevailed in the family circle, with frequent appeals to the Almighty for mercy and protection. To the end of his life Robert Harley laced his letters to relations with pious references, and his genuine belief in divine indulgence enabled him to face difficulties and dangers with a calm indifference that was the envy of his enemies. From his grandmother, he inherited considerable courage, not to mention an unshakeable belief in the rightness of his own actions. His father bequeathed him a spirit of tolerance and mercy.

Robert Harley spent most of his childhood in Herefordshire, troubled neither by serious illness, nor by such political turmoils as had bedevilled his father's youth. When he was just under a year old, Sir Edward noted: 'Robin newly furnished with a fore tooth below . . . He is very merry, his face is full of heats, I suppose more teeth are coming. We have cause to bless God he toothes so well.' When he was eight years old, his tutor reported that he had a good memory and learnt quickly. 'The boys are in good hopes of drums, or guns, or swords, when you come as they learn their books so well,' wrote Lady Harley to her husband. At times, the intensity of adult religion weighed a trifle heavily on the little boy's mind. When he was nine years old, he was found in the middle of the night awake and in tears. He had heard his elders declaim about sinning against the Holy Ghost; not knowing what the sin was, and afraid to ask in case he found he had already committed it or might be tempted by the devil to do so, he was busily praying God to rebuke the tempter. According to his mother, 'the poor child with tears told me he was afraid if he died he should go to hell'.

Early the following year the austere Lady Harley decided that it was time for the elder boys to be sent away and she put a strong case for the benefits of boarding school in a letter to her husband:

My judgment is not for the boys being kept at home, for it is not possible to keep them from associating with servants and getting a strange clownish speech and behaviour, which our boys have already, and the longer they live at home the worse it will be. Besides, I think learning alone makes them have a greater aversion to their books, having nothing of emulation to spur them on. I dare say too that Ned will never be anything of a scholar if he goes not abroad. I know not for Robin, because they tell me he is apprehensive and willing, but he is sometimes extremely lazy so that I have been near whipping him.

The choice of a school was none too easy, for the Harleys with their dissenting background were barred from the traditional seats of learning. There were, however, many well-run academies framed to cater for the sons of non-conformists, one of the most excellent of these being Mr Birch's at Shilton near Burford in Oxfordshire, a school so favoured by the non-conformist gentry that it had become overcrowded and many boys had to share a bed. Robin was sent there when he was nine, and his first letter home was carefully preserved:

Please to accept my most humble duty to you and my Lady mother, presented in this line from a learner. I hope through the Grace of God, with your blessings and prayers, which I earnestly beg, my endeavours may in time send you fairer fruits than these first beginnings.

The wide curriculum at Shilton helped the pupils to prepare for public life. They learnt less Latin and Greek than their Church of England contemporaries and studied more 'modern' subjects—English, mathematics and geography. Both the Harley brothers, Robin and Edward, grew up to take a keen interest in the nation's economics, and Robin was to grasp the importance of the press, public opinion and trade. Thirteen of Robin's schoolmates at Mr Birch's later entered public service, ten were elected to Parliament, Harcourt became Lord Chancellor and Thomas Trevor Lord Chief Justice. Sir Edward, who was himself educated at Shrewsbury, deprecated his son's lack of classical learning, and counselled him sternly to study the Greek Lexicon and Erasmus's *Adages*. The 'schoolers', as Lady Harley called them, were by no means entirely dedicated to their studies, and liked to go home to Brampton when their father was there so that he could take them out hunting. At Whitsuntide in 1675 they went to stay with their uncle, Richard Stephens, who lived at Chavenage in Gloucestershire, because their sisters, Brill, Martha and Abigail, were ill with a mild form of smallpox. 'After the pox is scaled off they rise up in bumps,' noted Lady Harley. 'I believe it is occasioned by their picking them off before they are ripe.' Robin himself began to show signs of the delicate health which was to trouble him throughout his life, suffering two alarming agues, which were treated with Indian bark ground up, and called Jesuit's powder in the medical jargon of the time. He also had ear trouble, for which his father sent him balsam of Peru (he was later to suffer from deafness) and a rupture, for which the only remedy was patience. 'God's time is the best for healing,' pontificated Sir Edward adding, a little heavily: 'Redeem the time you have in some measure lost at home. Be a pattern of studious diligence to your brothers and cousin.'

The universities did not open their doors to young men of dissenting stock, and rather than risk rejection, Sir Edward decided to send his son to a finishing school set up by the French Huguenot, Monsieur Foubert, who had been driven out of France on account of his religion. At his Academy, which was near the Haymarket, Foubert taught riding, fencing, dancing, handling arms, and mathematics. When he was nineteen, Robin spent a year there, mastering these various arts. Thomas Coningsby, a member of the influential Herefordshire family, visited him and sent Sir Edward an encouraging report:

I have been to wait upon your most sober son. Mr. Foubert gives him so good a character that I believe no young man in England ever had a better.

Robin's mother was rather less sanguine about his progress. 'I hope Robin does not lose his time,' she wrote anxiously, and a letter which he received from a friend soon after he left the Academy shows that the atmosphere was hardly what the saintly Puritan would have wished for her son:

Mr. Foubert . . . held forth in the dining hall and told us we most miserable academists had been guilty of many disorders of late and that very good friends of his had told him of the looseness of his academy. Jason lives as he used, contriving lewdness five days in the week.

After leaving Foubert's, Robin studied French and read for the Bar. He began to take an interest in politics and sought out the society of lesser public men. Though small in stature, with an awkward gait, he appeared a pleasant young man with an easy charming manner which attracted many friends. He soon developed a taste for good wine and witty conversation, and the poet Prior was later to say that he would rather hear once a month from Harley than be talked to once a day by the Grand Monarch. He was level-headed and calm, not a man, it was said, 'to tear up his own bowels from despair'. His austere relations were slightly disconcerted by his conviviality, and, realizing that he could not altogether live up to his parents' high moral expectations, he began to veil his affairs with a cloak of secrecy, extricating himself from awkward situations with oily protestations of innocence. Sir Edward continued to watch over his sons with 'holy jelosie', as Robin described it, determined to shield them from the temptations of London life. 'I do not approve of your brother lodging in a coffee house,' he told Robin flatly, in July 1684.

Apart from the occasional signs of worldliness, Robin was shaping well, and his father began to introduce him gradually to public service in his own county. In 1685, when he was twenty-four years old, a suitable match was arranged with Elizabeth, eldest child of Thomas Foley of Witley in Worcestershire. The Foleys were influential politically both in their own and neighbouring counties; they had made a fortune in iron and were putting their money to good use in building up a strong electoral interest for themselves and their relations. Such considerations weighed heavily in the choice of a bride. Lady Harley, realizing that the girl had been brought up in the luxury of a home where everything was 'handsome and plentiful', wondered apprehensively how she would enjoy being 'cubed upe' in the little house at Brampton, but soon decided that the more she saw of her future daughter-in-law the more she liked her, for the girl was extremely pious. The marriage took place in May at Witley, and was very quiet, with no company. 'No time is yet agreed for bringing her home,' wrote Lady Harley. 'I hope it will be a month. I do not know how we shall get the house in any order.'

Lady Harley had more time than she imagined to straighten up the newly finished house, and outside events cast a shadow over the married bliss of Robin and his seventeen-year-old wife. Charles II had been succeeded that year by James II, and in June Charles's bastard son, Monmouth, urged on by his ambitious mistress, Lady Wentworth, who fancied herself as queen, appeared with a small force off the Dorset coast. There were fears of a general uprising, especially among the non-conformists who mistrusted James's Catholicism. All over the country dissenters were disarmed, and Sir Edward suffered the indignity of being called before the Justices at Hereford to hand over any weapons he possessed; these amounted to a birding gun and two javelins—hardly an armoury to frighten the government. He was ordered to remain in Hereford during the emergency, but was able to thank God that he was not taken away to Chepstow Castle or thrown into gaol, as some had been in other counties. He also considered himself lucky that he was offered no affronts, and that he was allowed to walk about, talk to his friends and even go to church. Altogether, the tender mercies of the Lord were 'most graciously vouchsafed to a poor worm'.

Robin remained with the Foleys at Witley, where all the women-folk were 'very fearful'. Soon, however, everyone was rejoicing to hear that the rebels had been defeated at Sedgemoor. Sir Edward was allowed to go home, and the young couple went off on a health-giving, if unromantic, trip to Tunbridge Wells. The waters, far from making Robin well, brought on a serious illness:

There was no physician nearer than London [he wrote] and though Providence cast me upon a wilderness, for such Tunbridge is at this time of year, yet his loving kindness did not fail, for my Aunt Ernly was with us and my grand-mother sent every day, being nineteen miles, to see me, with such things as she thought proper.

Elizabeth was greatly alarmed, but, kept on a diet of strained water gruel, Robin recovered slowly, though he was left with a weakness of the eyes. Many of his friends, rather strangely, advised him to cut off all his hair. 'I hope it will wear off without that,' he wrote.

It was not until April 1686, nearly a year after the marriage, that Elizabeth's belongings, complete with the family joiner to put the furni-ture together when it arrived, were finally taken on a waggon from Witley to Brampton. Robin took the opportunity of sending on the waggon a very large rolling-stone, ready fitted except for a frame, for use on the Brampton bowling green. He was a keen bowls player, and in future years, when the political scene was at its murkiest, he sometimes thought longingly of the smooth green lawn he had laid down with such care, and which he rarely had a chance to use.

The defeat of Monmouth did not bring the nation's troubles to an end, for James II's Catholicism grew more militant after the Rebellion and it became a time of great anxiety for the dissenting community. Sir Edward's house was several times searched for arms, his letters were opened and he was in danger of imprisonment. In spite of this he con-tinued to go to church and spent one day a week praying that the country might be saved from barefaced popery. In August 1688 it seemed that the decisive blow had been struck for Catholicism when James's Queen gave birth to a son. The child began to sicken in the first few days of his life, when he was fed on a highly unsuitable diet of water gruel, sugar and canary, but the town gossip, according to Robin, was that 'upon sucking a brickmaker's wife', the prince recovered, even though his wet-nurse was a heretic. Most good Protestants viewed the little prince's parentage with scepticism. The popular theory was that the midwife, an avowed Catholic, had undertaken to smuggle the boy into Queen Mary's bed in a warming pan, a feat entailing considerable sleight of hand considering that five countesses and at least a dozen other sharp-eyed ladies were in the room at the time, not to mention more peers of the realm than any woman would care to have at her bedside at the moment of giving birth. The Lord Chancellor and Lord Middleton testified that the infant steamed and was as 'foul' as only a new-born child could be, but the Queen was still distressed by rumours about its parentage. Many people were sure that the ageing King could never have fathered the child, and the deed was attributed to the more virile and attractive young Papal Nuncio called, appropriately enough, Count d'Adda. It was ironical that the little Prince James Edward should thrive so well when other more welcome royal heirs sickened and died.

On November 5 William of Orange landed at Torbay. He met with very little opposition and journeyed to London, according to Edward Harley, more like a traveller than a conquering general. The King and Queen, with their infant son, fled ignominiously to France.

As soon as William's arrival was known to be imminent, Sir Edward despatched his son Ned to buy arms in London, while he and Robin raised a troop of horse at their own expense. They were joined at Worcester by the Foleys and other gentlemen, and Sir Edward was declared governor of the town. Ned described the scene in his *Memoirs*:

Some parties having brought in the plunder of horses and other things, he ordered all that could be seized to be restored, except a blasphemous image of the Holy Trinity, which he ordered to be broken to pieces in the open street ... But by his great care and prudence, that very populous city was kept in absolute quiet, which perhaps was the only one throughout the kingdom that did not feel the shocks of this consternation.

Sir Edward was chosen Member for the county of Hereford in William's first Parliament, but although he sent his sons to pay their respects to the new King, he demanded no favours for his good service at Worcester.

After some consultations amongst the relations and in-laws, it was decided that Robin should now be given a chance to enter Parliament. Thanks to the Foleys' connections with the Boscawen family he was, in April 1689, returned by a hundred obedient electors in the small town of Tregony in Cornwall. 'I pray God . . . to enable you with every good and perfect gift, that you may . . . be faithful and serviceable.' wrote the prayerful Sir Edward. The young Harleys now had three children, Elizabeth, Edward, and Abigail, who were very 'pert and merry'. Elizabeth, always her father's favourite, was on good terms with her grandfather, who was now a widower. 'Betty often goeth to the study door to see for her grandfather, and knocks,' wrote Robin, adding, in a later letter, 'Betty improves in language very much, continually talking of her "Dampader".' In the summer of 1689, Edward was taken ill and the doctor diagnosed a rupture. A plaster was applied and a heavy truss ordered from Worcester, but this proved so tight that the poor child was thrown into convulsions. Towards the end of the year the children and their mother were all ill, but on December 9 Elizabeth Harley wrote to her sister: 'I thank God we are all pretty well now, the swelling is almost gone down on my face . . . my little ones are very well, Neddy goes all alone himself.'

Elizabeth soon learnt the drawbacks of being married to a busy M.P., for she remained in Herefordshire most of the time while Robin, in London, threw himself enthusiastically into political life. He gravitated naturally towards a compact group of young Members from Stafford-shire, Worcestershire and the border counties. Most of them were of dissenting stock, and therefore in the Whig camp, but the old fiery puritanical principles were now sobered down in a political doctrine based on loyalty to the nation and its constitution. The group came to be called the New Country Party, or the Country Whigs, and championed, in particular, the cause of incorruptibility and economy in government spending.

The first surge of loyalty and enthusiasm for William soon died down. Abigail Pye, a cousin on their mother's side, who was always ready to provide her Harley relations with some of the latest gossip, reported that Queen Mary was 'a lovely woman and very obliging', but few people were prepared to enthuse about William. The English found him austere and unsympathetic, and disapproved of his foreign advisers. He was in poor health and was inclined to shun company as too much conversation brought on violent attacks of coughing. His Calvinistic background and obvious contempt for Church of England ceremony made him unpopular with churchmen. Hooper, one-time chaplain to the Princess of Orange, recorded William's reaction to the private chapel which was made for Mary in a converted dining-room:

The Prince came and as there was a step or two at the communion table, and another for the chair where the Princess was to sit, he kicked at them with his foot asking what they were for, which being told in a proper manner he answered with a hum.

Such boorishness was not likely to appeal to ardent Anglicans, although the dissenting Whigs were sure that William would prove a man after their own heart—a monarch who would show due gratitude for their part in the Revolution. To their surprise and chagrin they saw the new monarch turn to the Tories as the men most likely to champion his cause and to uphold the ideal of kingship, while he viewed the Whigs with obvious distrust as republicans at heart and heirs to the executioners of Charles I. The Whigs were eager to revenge themselves indiscriminately on Tories and churchmen, but William gave them no encouragement; on the contrary, as soon as possible he recommended an Act of Grace to provide an amnesty for all past political crimes. Even so, he could not prevent the two parties indulging in vicious quarrels which sprang from long-established feuds. Doctrinal disputes, class distinctions, subtle differences in party creed and affiliation, all this made William impatient. He complained that English politicians did nothing but intrigue from morning to night, and it was not surprising that sometimes he longed for his native Holland. 'Oh, for the wings of a bird,' he exclaimed.

The year 1690 opened badly with a fierce storm which the pious Harleys attributed to the nation's wickedness. 'Poverty and confusion, the just deserts of a prophane nation that has despised the Gospel, seem to make haste towards us,' noted Robin's brother Ned darkly. There was a feeling of instability with continual rumours of Jacobite plots. Many Tories, apprehensive about Whig intentions, began a long flirtation with the exiled court at Saint-Germain to insure against a possible Restoration. Paul Foley, Elizabeth's uncle, and all his followers, began to harry the government, criticizing William's expensive commitments on the continent, and resisting his attempts to run the nation into a costly European war. They kept a close eye on government expenditure, standing out not only against the Court Whigs but also against the moneyed Whigs in the City, who, they feared, might all too easily gain a financial stranglehold on the nation. The King, unnerved by the opposition he met with in Parliament, decided on a dissolution, hoping that an election might bring him a Commons more sympathetic to the throne. His first experience of an English election was not encouraging. He was shocked by the cabals and intrigues, the corruption and slander. In the City, people talked of nothing but the election, according to Abigail Pye:

I am sorry to see so great a violence of spirit as is in both parties which shall get uppermost. I hope whichever is predominant, they will mind the public good and not fall to private pique and quarrels.

In the country the situation was no better. The Tories, encouraged by William's favour, were full of confidence. 'The Herefordshire Tories talk big,' Ned reported to his father. From the pulpits the clergy inveighed against the Whigs, and the Tory bishops soon entered the fray. Corruption of every kind was rampant, and the puritanical Ned Harley was shocked by rumours that at Weobley men were imported from Hereford to lie with the townsmen's wives in the hope that these good women, having fallen, would then prevail upon their husbands to vote for their seducers' master. Robin's patron in Cornwall, Mr Boscawen, was reviled by the Bishop of Exeter, and in Herefordshire the gentry turned against

Sir Edward, who lost his seat. His family and friends were indignant and accused them of treachery and baseness. Robin, too, was in trouble. The electors of Tregony decided that they favoured a local candidate rather than a 'stranger', and it was decided that he should stand at New Radnor where his family connections would help. But he was notorious for his vocal support of the Foley group, and had earned himself a place on the Whig blacklist. Local opposition was organized by Thomas Coningsby, a Court Whig and member of a Herefordshire family which had been at odds with the Harleys ever since a dispute about a broken marriage settlement in 1604. It was Fitzwilliam Coningsby who had despatched a Captain and ten trumpeters to demand Brilliana's surrender of the castle, and Thomas Coningsby was eager to pay off scores both old and new. Being an experienced campaigner, he knew all the customary ruses that could be used to rig an election, from bribery of the returning officer to the suppressing of legal electors. When the results were known, Robin, convinced that his defeat was due to deception and fraud, decided that he would petition Parliament.

In the weeks following an election, Members always had to spend many tedious days considering innumerable election petitions, examining endless witnesses and listening to dismal tales of corruption. The whole process was something of a farce, since almost every case was decided regardless in favour of the candidate whose party was in a majority in the House. Since the Tories had been returned in strength, there was considerable doubt as to whether Robin's petition would be successful. But in October he brought up a coachload of witnesses, drawn by six able horses, and on November 8 the case was heard. 'Everything was carried beyond expectation without the least slur on any of the witnesses,' wrote Ned Harley to his father. 'Whatever was offered on the other side turned to their prejudice or was the occasion of laughter.' He reported that there were no more than three votes against when the question was finally put. The affair caused a great deal of interest, and many influential men who did not usually bother to attend the Committee turned out on a wild night for the hearing. It was a considerable triumph for Robin Harley.

But public success was accompanied by private sorrow. In the summer, Robin and Elizabeth lost an infant son, Robert, who died after sixteen 'strangling fits'. Robin's re-election entailed a long separation for the young couple, since Elizabeth was unable to bring her children up to London during the winter months. At Brampton she began to take on the responsibility of running the household, and on April 18, 1691, Robin wrote to Sir Edward:

I know she will be always ready to obey what you shall command, and what method you will please to order she will study to observe . . . She is but young; it is her first entrance upon business of this nature.

Well away from the patriarchal atmosphere of Brampton, Robin began to make his mark. His interest in financial affairs and the troubled question of government spending had not gone unnoticed, and soon after his re-election he was appointed one of the nine Commissioners for Public Accounts as well as an arbitrator for the two Indian companies. The Commissioners entrusted him with the task of finding a meeting place and he arranged for them to take a house in York Buildings off the Strand, where he himself was later to live. On March 7, 1691, he wrote to his father:

Next day we all met in the Speaker's Chamber, thence adjourned to view a house in York Buildings, where some hot words did pass between some. But all is calmed and I hope it will be a warning to prevent all sallies of passion.

At first the Commission sat very late, hotly debating methods of procedure, but after a few days Robin was able to report: 'Business now has taken off the edge of our passions and we are fallen to it with calmness and diligence.' He became a keen student of parliamentary procedure and it was rumoured that he used up half his meagre income of £500 a year paying clerks to copy out all the papers that were handed in to the House. He was soon so knowledgeable that few people dared to argue with him over matters of procedure. 'His plain familiar Behaviour, Flexibility and unaffected Dexterity,' as Boyer put it, 'and his unwearied application to House of Commons affairs, made him noticed early in his career.' He learnt, by keen observation, all the tricks of parliamentary management, and found out how to play on men's subtle loyalties and feelings.

Ned Harley appears to have been the model of propriety and good behaviour. He was the heir to his parents' Puritanism, and showed great approval of proclamations for suppressing debauchery and profanity. Robin's character was more of an enigma, and in the summer of 1691 his convivial habits called forth a rebuke from the father-figure, Sir Edward, who accused him of overmuch visiting in public houses. Robin replied in a spirit of unctuous self-justification:

In the first place I desire to look up to Heaven, without the permission of which neither a hair falls to the ground nor a cubit taken from our reputation, and I do most humbly bend my knees to the Father of mercies. . . . As to the matter charged I beg leave to say with sincerity and singleness of heart, I trust I have that in me that I dare confess my faults rather . . . than add to them by the covering of a lie. I can most solemnly declare I have not been in any public house—except just the time of dining—since I came out of the country.

In November he took a further step forward when he was made chairman of the Committee for Examining the Estimates of the Fleet. He was absorbed in this new task when the news came that his wife had fallen ill at Brampton with smallpox. 'My earnest prayers are that God will carry her through this valley of the shadow of death,' Robin wrote distractedly. After a day or two she seemed better, but on November 30 she died. 'This is a bitter cup,' wrote Robin to his father. 'I dare not, I would not wish her back again, for I doubt not her holy soul is in the fruition of the joy of her Lord, with whom she walked upon earth. . . . She is now beyond all fear of parting with my dear mother whom she loved so well, and with our little Robin that is gone before. She is gone to the city of the living God, to an innumerable company of angels.'

Fortunately the infection did not spread through the family, and the children were spared. After his wife's death, Robin threw himself still more vigorously into politics, even to the detriment of his health, for in the new year he suffered from stomach trouble and fainting fits. But his hard work was bringing its reward. 'The favour and esteem my brother has in the House of Commons is very extraordinary,' Ned told his father, in January 1692. At the age of thirty the young widower was well known and respected, and recognized by many as a rising star. The Whigs feared him, but some of the more influential Tories were beginning to look on him favourably, wondering whether they could not utilize his energy and knowledge, his flair for dealing with all kinds of people, from 'angry men' to 'men of trick'. He was already emerging as a born moderator who could calm passions and bring agreement out of discord. His aim was to stand out as a man of integrity and honesty in a false world, and as a great lover of his country.

CHAPTER 2

FAIRER FRUITS

IN THE FIRST MONTHS of 1692 everyone was talking about the quarrel then raging between Queen Mary and her sister, Princess Anne. As so often happened, the court attached to the next in line to the throne became a focal point for all those who disliked the existing regime. In particular Anne entertained at her apartments at the Cockpit, just across the road from the Palace of Whitehall, the brilliant, ambitious John Marlborough. Marlborough, in common with many others, was keeping discreetly in touch with Saint-Germain through his wife's sister, the Duchess of Tyrconnel, and his nephew, the Duke of Berwick, natural son of Arabella Churchill and James II at the time he was Duke of York. Although William was wise enough to ignore Jacobite tendencies, which even his most trusted servants indulged in, Marlborough's case was different. With the army behind him, he was the one man who had the power to oust William, and there was even a danger that he might try to set up the stolid Anne as an English rival to the unpopular Dutchman. William was determined that he should go. 'The cause of the Earl of Marlborough's removal is not known,' reported Ned Harley to his father. 'It is said that great intrigues are discovered at the Cockpit, and letters intercepted from the Prince and Princess of Denmark;' and Robin added, 'King William says the Earl of Marlborough has used him so that were he not a prince he must ask satisfaction with his sword.' Further friction developed when Princess Anne went to visit her sister at the new palace at Kensington with the disgraced Earl's wife in attendance. 'There are supposed to have passed some sharp letters to Princess Anne for the removal of Lady Marlborough, which had not yet been complied with,' wrote Robin. The Duke of Somerset offered the Princess a refuge at his own Sion House, whereupon she removed from the Cockpit without further ceremony, although she was expecting a child at any moment.

England had been at war with France since 1689, but the main sphere of interest had so far been centred on Ireland. A large Jacobite army led by James himself could not be tolerated on Ireland's shores, and William had the country behind him when he launched an expedition to remove his rival. His victory at the Boyne, which sent James scurrying back to France, made him for the while a national hero, but he knew himself that this was merely a prelude to what lay ahead. William's mission in life was to subdue the might of France in the battlefields of Europe, and in March 1692 he crossed to the continent, leaving Mary to deal with a threatened French invasion. Two months later the French fleet was soundly defeated at La Hogue. The English Admiral, Russell, who was largely responsible for the victory, was a notorious Jacobite, and it was a cause for optimism that his loyalties were clear in the heat of action. 'They make strange noises about the burning of a few ships,' Louis XIV remarked when he heard the news, but the English were naturally over-joyed. At Brampton Bryan the occasion was celebrated with guns and bonfires.

Sir Edward spent some weeks in London with his son that summer, returning home soon after hearing the news of the naval battle. 'King Street appeared but a lonesome place,' Robin wrote, after his father's departure. In August, as soon as Parliament was prorogued, Robin followed, and while staying at Brampton, was able to pay a visit to the electors of New Radnor, where Sir Edward from time to time sweetened the poor with gifts of beef and corn. Towards the end of September he became ill with an abscess and was unable to return to London as soon as he had hoped, to the regret of his fellow Commissioners and the impatience of the New Country Whigs. 'I believe London air will agree better with you and I hope you will quickly find it so,' suggested his wife's cousin, Thomas Foley. After a week, the 'impostumation' broke. 'I doubt not that the evacuation of humours by it will be a good security for his future health,' wrote Sir Thomas Clarges, a fellow member of the Commission, adding, to Robin: 'All your friends here were much dejected to hear of your sickness and are heartily glad to hear the danger is passed.' He was not well enough to make the journey until October 29, but he had a far less eventful trip than his brother Edward who, travelling a few weeks later, almost lost the way as he came over the downs near Woodstock in the dusk, and complained that highwaymen infested the roads as badly as pirates did the sea, having the impudence to parade about publicly, like soldiers, carrying carbines and blunderbuses.

In December the weather in London was very cold, with many 'stinking fogs,' but the bitterness of the weather contrasted with the warmth of parliamentary debate, for Members were growing hot about William's expensive estimates for the continuance of the war with France. Paul

Foley warned Robin, before he came down to London, that some men were already preparing 'to please by change of faces' while others were playing a double game, or hoping to make some profit for themselves out of the situation. Tempers grew short over the navy estimates and the Ministers responsible had to endure considerable mud-slinging. The lengthy sittings proved hard and tiring for Robin after his recent illness, but he had the satisfaction of waiting on the King with his fellow Commissioners to present the Accounts. William received them graciously and thanked them for their pains.

1693 proved to be another successful year of political apprenticeship, starting off propitiously when the Foley group helped to pressure through the Triennial Bill, which aimed at the introduction of three-yearly elections. Although Robin feared that the opposers of the Bill would resort to a common form of sabotage by 'clogging' it with so many amendments as to make it quite useless, the yeas had it, after a very solemn debate, during which Sir Edward Seymour, a hard-hunting Tory gentleman, declared that it was a Bill 'against the Crown and against the Commons and ought not to be countenanced'.

In the spring, after a by-election, Sir Edward was re-elected to the House, where, as he told Ned, he was admitted with great respect—'which is mentioned in all humility to the glory of God,' he added hastily. He was too advanced in years now to enter into politics at all actively, and he did not stay in London long. This was perhaps just as well as he might have been shocked to discover that Robin, in spite of parental warnings, still kept company with young men-about-town as notorious as Henry Boyle. All the same, as a family man, Robin stood aloof from the main group of bachelor 'rake-hells', as a letter from a Welsh friend, Francis Gwynn, reveals:

My wife this morning brought me another brave boy and both are very well. You are the father of children and therefore can give grains of allowance to those who trouble their friends with news of this kind but if one should write such a letter as this to Harry Boyle or such rake-hells, they would wonder what was the satisfaction a man could take in things of this sort.

Although Harley enjoyed gay company, he was not drawn towards a dissolute life, and he was far too ambitious to neglect his career for trivial friendships. He was careful to make a good impression with his political associates—Foley, Musgrave and Clarges. Halifax, the great 'trimmer', the man of the centre, whose character was described as the temperate zone between the extremes, recognized in this moderate, balanced young man the natural heir to his own ideals and beliefs. 'I am now little less impatient than a lover would be to meet his mistress,' he wrote when Harley had been out of town, 'therefore let me know whether you can come to my lodging at Whitehall, or if you had rather, at Somerset House.'

During the summer recess, Robin went down to Brampton as usual. On October 7 he visited Radnor on business, and while there was set upon by men with drawn swords. He was fortunately able to defend himself with his cane until he had a chance to draw his own sword. Monsieur Foubert's tuition stood him in good stead, for he was able to survive even though his attackers made thirty passes at him. His sister Abigail assured Martha that he might several times have killed either of them: 'It never will be a grief of heart that he has not avenged himself'. Strangely enough Lord Coningsby thought fit to visit the family at Brampton that very day, staying from ten o'clock till three in the afternoon, and appeared 'very merry and complaisant'. The Harleys were sure that the murder attempt had been engineered by Coningsby and that he had only made the visit to Brampton to dissociate himself from blame. He had not easily forgiven Robin Harley for winning the election petition.

In 1694, Robin married again. As usual he was secretive about his affairs and Sir Edward was not kept informed. 'I wish you would be more large concerning your great affair,' his father wrote peevishly. Ned negotiated the marriage settlement, and although the bride's relations demanded that her estate should be settled on the heirs of the survivor, it was agreed that she should herself reverse this by a secret document. The bride-to-be was Sarah Middleton, widow of a city merchant, who made a dutiful and unexceptionable step-mother for Betty, Edward and Abigail, and an unobtrusive wife content to keep well away from the jostling ambitious ladies of the court. 'She is a silly mere old woman,' Swift wrote of her unkindly in later years, but she had the negative virtue of remaining well in the background. Robin, who apparently loved secrecy for its own sake, made sure that the marriage was thoroughly clandestine. 'In the fear of the Lord, humbly begging his direction and blessing, it was finished this morning just after nine, and I returned to the office without any notice taken. It will be endeavoured to keep it private until my return out of the country, therefore she will not be known but by her former name.' Those who were lucky enough to be in the secret declined to trouble him with extra business for a few days, knowing him to be pre-occupied with 'accounts and amours', and less than a fortnight after the marriage he went down to Brampton. His wife did not go with him.

Harley's friends assured him that he was very much missed in the House and he hurried back to London as soon as he could, to find his wife afflicted with a cold. The King landed at Margate some days later, and although his autumn compaign on the continent had been unspectacular, he was given a great welcome by the people of London, who always enjoyed an excuse for bonfires and illuminations. All the same, according to Harley, the new parliamentary session began angrily.

It was a bad year for smallpox. Just before Christmas, the family was thrown into great anxiety when brother Edward contracted the disease. He suffered the usual torments of blood-letting and purging, and the relations rallied round with their own pet remedies. 'My Aunt Foley sayth a chain of gold about the neck is good to keep the throat clear,' Robin told his father. Robin's wife proved her worth by personally making up a concoction called the Countess of Kent's powder which included among its ingredients crabs' claws and viper's skin jelly. Perhaps because of, or more likely in spite of, this remedy, Edward recovered, and was advised to spend six weeks in the country drinking asses' milk.

On the same day that Edward fell ill, the Queen was stricken with the same complaint. As so often happened, and indeed had been the case with Robin's first wife, Queen Mary appeared to be much better on the third day. The King, who had been sleeping on a camp bed in her room and weeping copiously, moved next door and there was some premature rejoicing at her recovery. But on Christmas day her condition worsened, and on December 27 she died. When the news was read out in the Commons, Members wept, and the country as a whole went into mourning for the death of their English Queen.

Princess Anne was at the time in an advanced stage of pregnancy, and William did not encourage her to come for fear of harming her unborn child. The Princess had been subjected to every kind of slight; the King had even forbidden her chaplains to bow to her as they went up to the pulpit. Anne, for her part, made no secret of her hatred for her sister and, even more so, for the King, to whom she referred as Caliban and other derogatory names. But when the Queen lay dying, Anne experienced a change of heart, and it soon became known that she was reconciled. On the day after Mary's death, the Prince of Denmark paid a dutiful visit, and although the King, worn out with sorrow, was asleep, he received the Prince later with due ceremony and allowed Anne to live at St James's Palace with all her guards in attendance.

Sir Edward, recovered from his illness, came up to London for the ceremonies which followed the Queen's death and found his son busily embroiled in political matters. On March 4 Robin wrote:

It was so late after I came from Kensington that I could not wait upon you . . . I have sent your ticket. There will be officers of the House to see none but members deliver tickets at the Banquetting House. I desire John Child may bring my black cloak and my long periwig tomorrow morning by seven at the furthest.

Abigail Pye told the family at Brampton that 'the coronation was not thought so fine as the funeral, though a very melancholy pompous sight.'

In March 1695, the Foley group really came into prominence when Paul Foley, Elizabeth Harley's uncle, was elected Speaker of the House of Commons. The King, who had been supporting another candidate, was amazed to hear of the election of a man he had never even met, but this was all part of what seemed to him the madness of English politics. The Foleys, a close and devoted family, now had a formidable force of friends and relations in Parliament. Their link with the Harleys was consolidated when Robin's brother Ned married Sarah Foley, Elizabeth's younger sister. Apart from her political connections, Sarah was extremely pious, which, as far as Ned was concerned, was the only thing that mattered. The strong family feeling and built-in religious outlook of the Foleys is well illustrated in a somewhat ill-spelt letter which Sarah wrote to one of her sisters:

Since my Sister Harley's wedding we have never been all together no never shall till the day of judgment when the great trumpet of our holy God shall call us out of the grave. Pray God we may be found at the write hand and then we shall spend a blessed eternity together which will make amends for all our separation here; I think I mistake we were all together once after my dear mother went to heaven, whose holey life dear sister let it be our indever to follow that we may be eternally with her.

Sarah sometimes resented the male preoccupation with politics. 'My brother is so great a politishon I never hear one word from him,' she complained.

Robin, with five years of hard work on the Commission behind him, was now one of the most experienced of the younger generation. He had proved himself an efficient committee-man and a good chairman. He was an expert not only in parliamentary method but also in the financial workings of government. Paul Foley singled him out to be his right-hand man and soon began to find him indispensable. 'His presence is much wanted here,' he wrote to Sir Edward when Robin was down at Brampton recuperating from an attack of the stone. 'All things stand still till he comes.'

When the King returned from the continent in October, he decided to call an election in the hope of gaining a Parliament more enthusiastic about the war with France. The town emptied rapidly as Members hurried out into the country to fight their local battles. The King, for once, allowed himself a holiday, visiting various seats in the Midlands and the north and enjoying a few days hunting with the Duke of Newcastle in Sherwood Forest. On the whole the tour was a success, and did something to revive William's flagging popularity, but in Warwickshire and some other places people were disappointed when the royal route was changed and crowds waited without seeing him.

Paul Foley was one of the few Members who remained in London, where he was detained with a swollen face and had to undergo the usual tortures of bleeding, blistering and fomenting, while his relations attended to his election for him. Sir Edward was returned without opposition, and Robin's electors at New Radnor, whom Sir Edward had so carefully nursed with gifts, returned him without undue trouble or expense. In many places there was the usual ferment and high spending, but from the King's point of view it was all worth while since the new Parliament, when it assembled, meekly voted him over five millions for the war.

It was one thing to vote the money, quite another to provide it, and no great insight was required to see that the country was on the verge of an economic crisis. War had brought the usual inflation, and bad harvests helped to exacerbate the situation. The silver coinage had been debased by 'clipping'—a popular occupation with the criminal classes—and shilling pieces, in bulk, dropped to about half their original weight. Golden guineas had risen in value to thirty shillings, and the more sophisticated crooks were making substantial capital gains by exchanging silver coins on the continent for gold which they turned into guineas at a fat profit. For Foley and his followers, such financial problems were of greater moment than the religious differences for which ancestors had shed their blood. Puritanism and a good business sense often go together, and the dissenting Members from the Marches had some practical and original ideas for saving the nation's economy. William, however, was not keen to have Parliament meddling in financial affairs. He would have liked to issue a proclamation introducing a new coinage at the old standard, even though Treasury experts advised devaluation. The King was restrained from making any arbitrary announcements, but the Whigs, led by Montagu, supported his ideas and pressed for new coin and no devaluation. On this issue the split between the Whigs and Foley's Country Members became very obvious. They advocated devaluation and also

Photo : National Portrait Gallery

QUEEN ANNE

JOHN, DUKE OF MARLBOROUGH
Photo : National Portrait Gallery

SARAH,
DUCHESS OF MARLBOROUGH
Photo : National Portrait Gallery

believed that it would be wise to avoid the expense of issuing new coin during this period of financial stringency.

The tax system was rudimentary and there seemed to be no way of raising money for the war except by increasing the Land Tax levied on the country gentlemen's verdant but already groaning acres. There was a danger of new divisions appearing in the nation between the merchant and landed classes, divisions as bitter and inflammable as the old religious feuds. The gentry felt that the money raised on their land too often went into the pockets of contractors who made spectacular fortunes out of supplying the forces in the field with food, clothing and arms; they were suspicious of the Bank of England which they viewed as a Whig machine contrived to effect their ruin. The Foley group had a new and imaginative scheme to free the nation from financial enslavement to the big business-men in the City. All through the summer of 1695 there had been dis-cussions about the forming of a Land Bank in which money would be lent on the security of land. Robin was vocal in these deliberations, and in the spring of 1696 he helped to bring in a Bill for the foundation of the scheme.

Meanwhile the Whigs pressed on with the new coinage, and it was announced that after May 1696 old coins would not be allowed to circu-late. The measure caused a great deal of hardship amongst those who still had clipped money and old guineas on their hands and, worst of all, very little new money had been issued by the time the old was withdrawn. Trade and commerce was soon almost at a standstill and the poor near to rioting. On the continent the situation was even more precarious. The Dutch refused to accept English bills of exchange, and there was no way of supplying the troops. For a while the only solution seemed to be to disband the army and accept French offers of a truce. William almost accepted the necessity of devaluation and had he done so the Land Bank might well have succeeded, since the landowners would have been pre-pared to lend their guineas at thirty shillings apiece. Harley told William Bromley, an ardent Tory, that he hoped supporters of the Bank would give encouragement to their friends 'by subscribing at midsummer sessions in their several counties'.

I am sure you will sacrifice more than that to the preserving the whole and keeping the nation from the power of a party who can have no strength but what is given them by such a refusal. Therefore I hope we shall be preserved by you from having stripes by scourges cut out of our own skins.

The country landowners, never too eager to lend money at the best of times, were understandably reluctant to subscribe to the scheme at such an

B

unpropitious moment. They eyed each other, holding back to see whether there were any signs of their neighbours 'signing and acting', but in general the frugal instinct prevailed, and as the threat of devaluation was diverted, there was no great incentive to lend guineas at the old standard of value. Thus the Land Bank failed at the start, and Foley and his friends suffered a considerable setback, losing the respect both of the King and of the public.

William's stock had risen since the discovery of the Fenwick plot to murder him as he returned from hunting at Richmond. Members of Parliament were so shocked by the news that they could think of nothing else, and plans for saving the economy were pushed aside. Non-jurors and Jacobites were in disgrace, and the Whigs, having weathered the coinage crisis, were triumphantly in the ascendant. But it was difficult for a House of Commons man *par excellence* like Robin Harley to feel well disposed towards a King who apparently looked on Parliament as a body of cantankerous men to be wooed only because they could vote money and supply soldiers for the war. His defection from the Whig party was caused by his disapproval of its backing for William's warlike aims. Systematically and courageously, knowing that he was jeopardizing his chances of promotion, he opposed the King's schemes for high taxation and oppressive treason laws. And after the Peace of Ryswick was concluded in 1697 he came out even more openly against court and King when he opposed William's plan to keep a large army in readiness just in case hostilities should break out again.

The English had a deep-rooted fear of maintaining an army in times of peace; the whole idea smacked of military dictatorship. William, for his part, saw this attitude simply as a typical example of English stupidity. He had studied his enemy for years, and he saw Louis as a wily megalomaniac with a lust for power who was on no account to be trusted. Matthew Prior shared the King's distrust of the French, whom he had learnt to know well during the Ryswick peace negotiations. 'These people are all the same,' he wrote from Paris, 'civil in appearance and hating us to hell at the bottom of their heart; they assure us one day of the continuance of their friendship and tell King James next they will never forsake him.' The Sun King was not a pretty sight; he had lost his upper teeth, and Prior noted that he was given to picking the bottom row with a great deal of affectation. But despite the onset of age, he was as vain and proud as ever. The English persistently underestimated him, and William despised them for their lack of good sense.

Harley understood both the danger and the English fear of a military dictatorship. His sympathies lay with the country gentlemen who, he knew, would have to bear the cost of maintaining the army. Even his Whig friends were beginning to realize that he was at heart a Tory squire:

Your making excuses for your very entertaining letters has a great deal of the country fashion in it [wrote Henry Boyle] . . . I have already told you how much you are a country gentleman, and therefore I won't expose any ignorance in writing about the harvest which is so good that nothing but the skill and integrity of the managers you speak of could reduce the people to want and necessity in the midst of so much plenty.

All the same, although he would not concede William's demands for a large force, Harley knew that it would be in the nation's interest to accept the principle of keeping a small nucleus of trained men under arms. He therefore embarked on his first great campaign to achieve a compromise.

When he arrived in London in the autumn of 1697, Harley found the town buzzing with excitement, as he explained to his father:

We came here well this evening. The vale was dangerous with frost . . . The prospect is very cloudy. Every one is full of the common topic, a standing army, and it is talked with heat on both sides. . . There is very little prospect of moderate councils.

A week later he reported that the heat against an army increased all the time, even though every effort was made to 'sweeten people'. A Bill for disbanding the army was almost rushed through the House in January 1698. 'It was designed this day to break through the vote of disbanding the army, by surprise, contrary to all order,' Harley told his father. 'The thing was laid, but after eight hours debate was defeated.' A year later the Bill was brought in again. After a debate in which Harley played a leading part it was decided that William must be content to face the saturnine Louis with a token force of 7,000 men; as it was stipulated that these must all be Englishmen, William's beloved Dutch Guards had to be sent back to Holland. 'It is said the King is very uneasy,' Edward reported to his father, but this was an understatement. William was furious. He refused to acknowledge that the outcome was a moderate and skilful compromise. He was tired of the English and their self-delusion. They complained that they were bankrupt, and yet all round him he saw extravagance and luxury. In November 1699 Princess Anne gave a ball and she herself spent five hundred pounds on the trimmings of her petticoat; the Duke of Norfolk appeared resplendent in scarlet embroidered with gold, and there was a wealth of rich liveries. 'Some says the King seems to dislike the extravagant fine clothes that appear in his suite, and says sure there is none of money wanting in England,' commented one of Sir John Verney's female relations.

Robin Harley was out of favour with the King because of his part in the army debate, and the Whig lords too were treated coolly. The proud ambitious men who had come to be called the Junto, Somers, Montagu, Wharton, Orford—and particularly the two last—were aggressive and domineering, difficult enough to deal with singly and distinctly over-powering in the mass. William had no illusions about them; he suspected that they were just the kind of men who would have been happy to substitute oligarchy for monarchy. They possessed, he said, a 'natural sourness' which made them quite impossible to live with, and he believed that they would always put their own private interests before the public good. William wanted Shrewsbury and Sunderland, but Sunderland was old and tired and confused by all his various changes of heart. 'The creature can live but in an element suitable to its nature,' he wrote sadly to Harley. 'I have been used too much to courts, but I know not how to live in this, which I am now I doubt too old to learn.' Shrewsbury, although a much younger man, also lacked determination and energy. He was continually in trouble with his health, which always broke down under stress, and on one occasion he contrived to give himself a blow with his horse's head as he leaped a ditch. Shrewsbury was handsome and charming, but he lacked fibre and shied away from responsibility in a manner that amazed more ambitious men. And the Junto disliked the feeling that it was being 'managed' by these two inadequate lords.

Although lack of favour with the King meant that Harley was cut off from the most important source of power, he was not idle during the last two years of the century. He continued to harry the government, joining in the attack on the Irish grants, and wherever possible using his influence to tone down the excessive passions of party. He cultivated influential friends and gradually gained the confidence of leading Tories. The Whiggish Henry Boyle was as faithful as ever; 'I am sure I want your company extremely, both for pleasure and improvement,' he wrote, and invited Harley to join him in the gay round of 'handsome treats', where, as he put it 'all the while one is feasting, the good people of the house never fail to ask pardon for putting us in danger of being starved'. On the more serious side, Harley was taking an interest in books and manuscripts. He encouraged scholars by giving subscriptions for first editions and lending transcripts of old manuscripts. His family was now growing up and the time had come to find a tutor for his son Edward. Although no children were born to Harley by his second marriage, Sarah proved a dutiful step-mother, and after 1697 when the couple moved house, probably to York Buildings where they were to remain for the rest of Harley's active career, she paid several visits to Brampton and brought the children up to London with her. Plans were always subject to Sir Edward's approval, and Robin was still the dutiful and obedient son, even though he was nearly in his forties. 'I had hoped to hear what you were pleased to command in relation to my wife and sisters coming up for a few weeks, and the little ones,' he wrote in 1699, and in March 1700:

I trust that a few weeks will put an end to the session and then I might come down with them after the children have seen London for a fortnight or three weeks. For I would hasten down immediately and would not stay now, were it not that this is the critical time of the session. All their arts are using towards ruining all hath been done by derision, lies, and other usual methods.

He was very glad that his wife and children had not been in London the previous week when he had faced a crisis that had brought out all his enviable calmness and sang-froid:

On Tuesday a great rabble of pretended soldiers and seamen were got together to the House door, Court of Requests, Westminster Hall, &c on pretence of a Bill about their pay—tho' not a farthin is due to them. While we were in solemn debate about the revenue, a member as they say, came to them and told them they must fall upon Mr. Harley, and this with other vilaini to stir them up, set them in a tumult, they would have forced their way in. The Justices of the Peace were sent for; they instead of dispersing the mob seized the members' footmen. The House rose about six or seven. And I went through them all, drawn up from one end of the Hall to the other, rather than go the back way, I thank God without any hurt or word spoken. They pretended to threaten to pull down my house.

It was while on a visit to London that Harley's little daughter Abigail— 'Tabby' as she was affectionately called—was attended by the King's doctor, the famous Dr Radcliffe. The doctor thought at first that she had smallpox, but Harley was relieved to be able to report that it was only measles, though 'very full':

God is very gracious to poor Tabby. She is very cheerful. They begin to die upon her. Dr. Radcliffe is very glad it is the measles, the symptoms being bad for the small-pox.

Harley also consulted Dr Radcliffe about his father's health which was giving cause for concern. Sir Edward had for some time been troubled with vertiginous fits and 'fumes'. In the summer of 1700 he had a bad cough for which the doctor recommended conserve of roses and the frequent use of ground ivy leaves made and drunk as tea and sweetened with sugar candy, and, more horrible, the swallowing of a clove of garlic over night 'to preserve the stomach against goutish humours'. The Almighty was requested to rebuke the distemper, but as autumn came he grew weaker, and in December he died. Robin was bereft of the stern but much-loved parental presence just as he was beginning to break out with his 'usual splendour' from his retirement behind a cloud, to the satisfaction and pleasure of his friends, his own honour, and the country's safety—as his old school friend, Simon Harcourt, was pleased to put it. Sir Edward lived long enough to find great pride in his son's achievements. Earlier doubts about Robin's character were quietened. The frequent letters giving the coffee-house talk and 'flying stories' of the day always proved a cordial and a tonic to the old man throughout his long sojourns in the country. But, best of all, he had been able to hear his son intervene in debates: 'I bless God that vouchsafed me a son to speak and also the mercy to me to hear him.'

Other triumphs lay ahead. In November 1699 the Speaker, Paul Foley, died; he had been in bad health for some time, but it was rumoured that his death was precipitated by buckling one of his shoes too tightly. Harley at once stepped into his place as the leader of the now very considerable Country Whig group. 'It has pleased God to lay a great load upon me,' he wrote, 'and the heavier since the loss of so good a friend. This week has been very difficult. I think I have not exceeded four hours sleep. I bless God I am well.' There were new moves to reconcile the Junto and country elements. In 1700 Sunderland began to make approaches to Harley, hoping to gain him and all the ranks of his supporters in a new administration to be headed by Somers, the most civil and personable of all the Junto lords. 'Eyes will be on you when you come into the Senate,' Harley had been told before the army debate, and this was certainly true now. He had become a key figure in politics.

Harley was by nature a moderate man, and to take a central position was instinctive with him. The session of 1698–99 proved that as a middle-of-the-road politician he could wield a great deal of power. William was trying to work with the dregs of a Ministry, Sunderland and Shrewsbury were inadequate on their own and the Junto lords more unpopular than ever. Harley had deprived the Whigs of so many good men that they were now no longer able to command a majority, and so he was in the happy position of holding the balance of power. If the government wished to pass its vital money Bills, it must come to him humbly, begging for support. The session was a stormy one and nobody scrupled to harry the unfortunate government. Everything that the King supported was automatically opposed. Bills to reform the calendar and to effect a union with Scotland were soon in difficulties. To add to the King's discomfiture, the troubled question of forfeited lands in Ireland came up again, and a Bill introduced for the resumption of the forfeitures was an overt criticism of the use William had made of the lands in the past. To make sure that this measure should have an easy passage through the Lords, it was 'tacked' to the Land Tax Bill—a particularly unpleasant ruse, since money Bills were the only ones which the Lords were unable to reject outright. The debates, though tempestuous, were skilfully 'managed' by Harley, who frankly joined with the opposition Tories to make life difficult for the Ministry. There was plenty of drama for the town gossips to mull over—'the saying in town is, that three B's are for rejecting the bill, and embroiling the nation, viz. the bishops, beggars and bastards'— with the Bishop of Salisbury crying out in a fever of excitement 'stuff, stuff' at his opponents, and the hard-hunting Tory, Seymour, jesting about the Union with Scotland and saying that 'whoever married a beggar could only expect a louse for her portion'. Harley made it quite clear where he stood. 'Mr. Harley,' Vernon wrote to Shrewsbury, 'laid open the deplorable state the nation was brought to, that the army was disbanded, that credit was broke, that the Exchequer Bills must swallow up the Civil List.' But although Harley was a vocal critic of the government, he refused to use the power he wielded to the full. He could have obstructed every government Bill if he had cared to, even the money Bills, but he held back, reluctant to harm the national interest. 'Mr. Harley . . . could have made things worse than they are,' Vernon went on. 'Whether he can make them better I know not.'

There was a strong move afoot in the summer of 1700 to find out whether Harley could prove as useful to the government as he had been in opposition. Lord Coningsby was alarmed; the thought of his local rival rising to such heights was more than he could stand, and on his way to Herefordshire in May he called in at Heythrop, Shrewsbury's country seat, for consultations. The Tories, in their turn, were frightened by this visit, and soon began to 'smell a design of piecing up again with the Whigs'. In May and June the town was full of secret comings and goings, typical of a time of political crisis. Influential men were whispering and wooing, and news of important meetings flew about the city.

There were two Secretaries of State at the time, dividing their duties into the Northern and the Southern Departments. Vernon was already a Secretary, and there was talk of making Harley the second one. Vernon was opposed to this. He thought that the Seals should be given, not to another Commoner, but to 'some person of quality, for preserving the office from contempt'. 'And how if Mr. Harley should be the man?' inquired Lord Jersey. Vernon replied that he thought Harley was not ready yet for such high responsibility. The truth was that the Whigs still hoped to re-form a Ministry headed by Somers and backed by Harley's group, which was to be bribed with various offices. Harcourt, for example, was to be made Solicitor-General. But Harley was resisting the whole idea. He had no intention of serving under Somers, or any of the Junto for that matter.

On June 22, Vernon met Harley by chance, and found him very exasperated with Somers. Vernon warned him strongly of the dangers of opposing the Junto; he need not expect any compassion from them. The next day Harley visited Vernon and asked him flatly whether the intention was to turn the Commons into a 'cockpit', with the usual fights and arguments rising to even greater fury than usual. For the first time for years, William had a chance to form a moderate government and free himself from all the petty feuds of faction. 'Mr. Harley professes himself to be of no party,' Vernon noted. 'What this third invisible power should be I can't imagine.'

Harley found it difficult to understand why the King was so anxious to hang on to the remnants of Whig power. 'The King's business must miscarry if blasted men had the conduct of it,' he said, adding that

if the King's business were in other hands, it could not but go on smoothly; that there was such a weight in a Court, that if things were not grossly mismanaged they would never lose a question; and it required but little skill to foresee what would pass in a House of Commons and what would not, so that those must be unpardonable who run a government upon rocks and shallows.

He already had in his mind the picture of an ideal government which he spent most of his life trying to bring down to reality. A moderate government, headed by a man skilled in all the parliamentary tricks, and smiled on by the monarch—this was his rather over-simplified recipe, which did not allow for mankind's odd passions, jealousies and shifting loyalties. But at least he seemed a step nearer achievement when, at the beginning of July, the King, who was just about to leave for Holland, called him to the Palace for a discussion about the future. William also interviewed Rochester—his wife's uncle and one of the leading Tories. It looked as if at last he was turning away from the Whigs.

At the end of July the particularly virulent form of smallpox which was rampant in the hot summer weather struck down the Duke of Gloucester,

Princess Anne's only surviving child. He had never been strong; in infancy he had suffered from water on the brain, but he had ridden a pony no bigger than a mastiff and loved to play at soldiers with his friends. 'I can't brag of his beauty,' wrote his mother. But although he was a strange-looking child, he had a sweet nature and was one of the few people who succeeded in melting the stern heart of William. On his eleventh birthday, he had a party at which he danced, which made him very hot, and ate some fruit, in those days considered very unwise. The next day he was ill and was immediately blooded and blistered, but spots appeared, and 'his little body', according to Harley 'turned green and yellow immediately'. On July 30 he died. The Princess, who only a week before had been staying at the Deanery in Winchester and enjoying some good hunting—she had been in at the death of a stag—was completely struck down by this sudden, unexpected sorrow. But there was more involved than personal grief. The death of the little Duke brought up all the old doubts and fears about the Protestant succession. It was essential to ensure that the Jacobites had no chance to fill the gap with their candidate, and to settle the succession quickly on the Electress Sophia of Hanover, daughter of Charles I's sister, Elizabeth of Bohemia. This erect and handsome woman of seventy was known variously as the old lady of Hanover, or the old strumpet. This hardly did her justice, as she was a shrewd and witty intellectual who was greatly attracted, in spite of her age, to the idea of becoming Queen of England. William, anxious as he was to make the future secure, knew that he needed a strong government for the task. Sunderland no longer had the energy or the authority to bring in an Act of Settlement, and Shrewsbury was seriously ill and spitting blood, his only hope of recovery a trip to southern Europe. The King was prepared to forget that Harley had played such a prominent part in the disbanding of the army; perhaps he appreciated the fact that the motives had been good and the welfare of the nation the prime consideration. The genuine Tories were less easy to forgive; they had none of Harley's temperate attitude, they might well prove as insolent and bitter as the Whigs, and besides they were isolationists committed to keeping England out of Europe. So, William invited Harley to talk to him about important affairs, although he made no very definite move towards the Tories before he went abroad.

Harley was also being non-committal, not to say enigmatic. This was a side of his character his family knew well, but which his political colleagues had not met and found irritating. 'He does not confide enough in me, to tell me what he aims at,' complained Vernon. After attending

B*

discussions and political dinner parties, and talking to everyone about moderation—a quality which hot men like Rochester found quite incomprehensible—Harley departed suddenly to Brampton, where he remained until November, one of the longest breaks in his career. While he was away, Henry Guy, Sunderland's friend and henchman, kept in touch with him, informing him of all the cabals that were going on in his absence. Guy was over seventy and one of the most experienced and skilful managers in the game of politics. He told Harley that the moderate Godolphin and the violent Rochester were reconciled, which was a good start, but that many people believed these two could do nothing on their own:

I agree with our friends [he wrote] that all depends on Harley . . . and if he be *hors de jeu* good night to all.

He repeatedly urged Harley to come up to London for consultations with his friends at the first opportunity and in any case at least three days before the King's arrival from Holland. Harley did not hurry. His lack of eagerness when power and position were so nearly in his grasp was vaguely disconcerting to an old campaigner like Guy who had been used to playing on men's ambition and lust for influence and money. Vernon, too, the dry, practical, unimaginative man who was more of a civil servant than a politician, was plainly puzzled by Harley's lack of the more normal urges:

I find his thoughts are bent upon having the superiority next session. . . He says he will use it with moderation and not begin accusations if they are not attacked.

It was unprecedented to hear a man talk like this; he seemed to think that he could rule by mildness and, more extraordinary still, he appeared to be quite devoid of the instinct for revenge.

Harley was still taking his ease at Brampton when the news came of the death of the Spanish King, impotent, unhealthy Charles II. Two years previously the nations of Europe had foreseen this moment and had tried to avert trouble by arranging the succession in advance. There had been three possible claimants—Philip of Anjou, grandson to Louis XIV, the Austrian Archduke Charles, second son of the Hapsburg Emperor, and young Joseph Ferdinand, Electoral Prince of Bavaria. Nobody was eager to see Spain linked with the power of France or of Austria, whereas a union with little landlocked Bavaria seemed relatively harmless. But Louis and the Emperor made it quite clear that, if Bavaria were to succeed, they would expect liberal compensation for standing down so nobly. Louis, partly because France was exhausted by strife and needed a rest, and partly because Madame de Maintenon, according to Matthew Prior, was doing her best to increase the 'pacific humour' in him, was in an amenable mood. He was quite ready to confer with the other powers and re-arrange the map of Europe. To his great satisfaction he learnt that Naples and Sicily were to come under his sway, and he pictured himself dominating the Mediterranean. The Archduke Charles was allotted Milan, among other prizes. All these concessions were incorporated into the first Partition Treaty of 1698, which might have proved highly satisfactory had not the little Bavarian Prince chosen to die only a few months after the treaty was signed. William and Louis had to set to at once to frame another treaty in which, incredibly enough, Louis agreed to accept the Archduke Charles as the heir to Spain, the Indies and the Spanish Netherlands, and take for himself, by way of compensation, no more than Naples and Sicily with the addition of Milan. Louis, in fact, was all mildness; it was the Emperor who proved difficult, and refused to accept the settlement unless his younger son was promised the Spanish Empire intact. He refused to sign and made it plain that he was prepared to go to war on this issue, when the time came.

Charles II, before he died, had one thought only in his decaying mind: Spain must not be divided. Willingly aided by French sympathizers in his retinue and with the realization that he was dying, he made a new will leaving everything to Philip of Anjou. When he heard this glad news, Louis hesitated, but not for long. Of what value was the second Partition Treaty since the Emperor had never recognized it? It looked as if Austria was going to fight the matter out anyway, so Louis, once more his old, truculent, aggressive self, decided to shock Europe and accept the will. William was completely cast down; he would not have believed that even Louis would treat a solemn agreement as if it were the merest scrap of paper, and he was full of self-reproach for his folly in trusting his perfidious enemy. What made the whole thing almost unbearable was that the extraordinary English seemed pleased about it. Harley expressed a prevalent viewpoint when he wrote to Lord Weymouth on November 5, 1700:

After the death of the King of Spain I fancy it will not be unacceptable to your Lordship to hear what came but this evening, that the French King renounces the treaty. This is very surprising and better than we could expect. It is plain he is not fond of entering upon a war without which Naples &c could not be his.

Harley's own view was coloured by the fact that his youngest brother Nathaniel was a merchant in Aleppo, where besides experiencing a series of stirring adventures—on one occasion tribesmen had mortally wounded the horse he was riding, but the faithful animal had carried its master home before expiring—he was engaging in a lucrative trade, which might well be jeopardized if the French commanded the bay of Naples and the strategic ports of Sicily. There were many other people who had a vested interest in the Levant trade, and who would rather have seen Philip of Anjou well occupied in Madrid than mischief-making in the Mediterranean, but this attitude William could not comprehend. His adopted country was making life difficult for him; when he returned from Holland in 1700, he was greeted by a barrage of libellous pamphlets and a particularly unpleasant piece in rhyme by John Tutchin called *The Foreigners*.

The Whigs had not given up hope of a revival. Coningsby was still whispering with Sunderland and advocating an alliance with the Junto. The best way of dealing with such secret workings, Harley thought, was to let the design be 'publicly talked of, like giving air to a mine'. He was still, himself, proving maddeningly elusive. Family affairs claimed him at the beginning of 1701, and there was his election at New Radnor to attend to. It was true that most other people were out in the country in January, election campaigning in bitter weather, but Harley took his time and Henry Guy certainly felt that he lingered at Brampton longer than necessary. His election was achieved without any trouble, but he was now master of Brampton and there were matters to be settled. The house that had been built close to the castle was pleasant and comfortable; the gardens had been laid out with some advice from the King's gardener, who had also been responsible for landscaping the Foley grounds at Stoke. The brothers in London had often sent down goods from London, including garden seeds for their sister Abigail and brass bolts for the parlour and drawing-room doors. Apart from Harley's much-loved bowling green, there was a level court in front of the house— 'very dry and handsome', according to Edward—and a green court which had a high paling round it, to ornament the house and keep out the swine. The estate had been extended, to include many important livings and properties, all tending to give the Harley family status and power within its own county. Such possessions might have tempted another man to retire from public life, but Harley was by now too much drawn into the web of politics to be anything except an absentee landlord. He had not been in the country for more than a couple of weeks before his friends were urging him to return to London. Henry Guy was soon on his old theme:

Rochester and Godolphin did yesterday again enjoin me to write to you this night to come with speed; for . . . there are several things of the greatest moment which do really want the opinion and advice of Harley. The King asked when Harley would come, and desired him to hasten him.

The Tories were confident that they would achieve sweeping gains at the polls, but Louis proved an unexpected ally for the Whigs. In February, when many elections still remained undecided, French troops marched into the Spanish Netherlands and seized the forts which made up the Dutch 'Barrier'. Even the pacific English were shaken out of their complacence by this frankly aggressive act. The Tories, great campaigners for peace as they were, could hardly fail to be adversely affected by such news, and although there was a Tory majority in the Commons, it was not so overwhelming as everyone expected.

In February Harley was elected Speaker of the House. He was the obvious choice, if only for his outstanding knowledge of the workings and everyday business of Parliament. But, besides that, his passion for moderation, which party men found embarrassing, was an asset in this connection, and his ability to see both sides of the question made him the ideal chairman. 'An able gent' was John Evelyn's verdict, and William Bromley wrote congratulating him:

Give me leave to congratulate your advancement to a dignity you so well deserve. . . We that are in the country look upon your having the chair as a very good omen at this critical juncture.

CHAPTER 3

THE GILDED MACE

THE NEW MINISTRY, with Godolphin at the Treasury, had indeed taken over at a moment of crisis. Working with a majority of Tories, many of whom, on the extreme fringes, veered towards France and King James, it was faced with the task of bringing in, as soon as possible, an Act of Settlement to ensure the Protestant Succession. And although the men who comprised it were, themselves, men of peace, they had to shoulder the responsibility of turning the country's thoughts towards war.

The credit for achieving these two vital factors went to Harley. His knowledge of procedure helped him to steer the House through the most difficult debates, and there was seldom any argument about technical points of order or wording so long as he was in the chair. His patience and skill were admired by men of all parties, and he was soon to reveal himself as the least vindictive of all the 'great men' of his time. He inherited a forgiving nature from his father; it was typical of Sir Edward that when he was due to claim legal damages from Sir Henry Lingen, who had burnt the castle and town of Brampton, he asked Lady Lingen to make an inventory of her husband's estate, and, having inquired if the list was correct, handed it back to her, renouncing all his right to claim retribution. In the same way, his son refused, all his life, to revenge himself on his political enemies, and this reluctance sometimes caused him to fall out with more implacable colleagues. It was the accepted practice to make life as difficult as possible for the defeated party—just to make sure that it did not come back again in a hurry. Standard politics required that there should be a thorough purge of all officers down to the Lords-Lieutenant, Sheriffs and Justices, and even the Army was not exempt. Harley's theory was novel and not altogether appreciated. He felt that such purges created a bad atmosphere and aroused bitter opposition to the ruling party. He thought—and the King agreed—that it was better to avoid making anybody 'desperate'. Moderation, forgiveness and patience were the Harley mottoes.

The Speaker's Chamber had a commanding view of the Thames over Lord Halifax's garden. Harley's friend, Halifax, had died in 1700, and his title passed to the Junto Whig Montagu. 'I do not envy Mr. Montagu his peerage, but I cannot help begrudging him the title of our poor friend Halifax,' wrote Francis Gwynn, Harley's Welsh crony. But although Halifax had gone from the scene, the Speaker was reminded of him daily, as he looked out across his garden walks, and he stayed faithful to his memory, walking in the middle way, and refusing to be led astray by the violent counsels of party men.

The Tories, of course, were bent on personal revenge, and they soon singled out their most powerful enemies, Somers, the new Halifax, and Orford, as the subjects of their attack. It was decided to impeach these men, because, although they had been responsible Ministers at the time, they had allowed William to negotiate the Partition Treaties without their knowledge. It was largely thanks to Harley that the impeachments were never carried to a bitter conclusion, but the harm was done; party differences were underlined and confirmed and animosities aroused which were to prolong the party battle for years to come.

The impeachment was a warning to many. It taught Harley to be doubly careful about what he wrote or said, knowing that at any turn of the weather-vane his enemies might be upon him, making use of incriminating documents or letters. He developed a style of writing so involved, so clogged with relative clauses and qualifying phrases, that the real meaning became safely, if irritatingly, veiled. In the House he was the same; his debating style was nebulous and vague. William, too, learnt to be more wary, and resolved to take his Ministers and his Parliament into his confidence as be began to build up a strong alliance to oppose the new menace from France.

Louis's attitude helped to cut a path for the Act of Settlement through the Tory House of Commons, but once again Harley's management proved a vital factor. William was pleased by the unexpectedly easy passage of the vital resolution in March 1701, even though one clause which aimed at foreign favourites and advisers, and another which stated that no future monarch should be allowed to leave the kingdom without the consent of Parliament, were not so acceptable since they were a back-handed criticism of the King's own methods. Nevertheless, the passing of the Act gave some measure of security for the future.

There were still plenty of Tories, including Rochester, who were obtuse enough to think that it was possible to remain friends with France and to keep out of the threatening conflict. But public opinion was veering away from peace-at-all-costs. The people of Kent felt that more was needed than the blue waters of the channel to protect them from invasion. The freeholders of Maidstone felt so strongly that they drew up a petition at the quarter sessions, entreating the House to grant William the means to support his allies before it was too late. The Tories were stung by the insinuation that they were unpatriotic. Defoe described the situation in his popular poem *The True-Born Englishman*:

> And now your wrath is smoking hot
> Against the Kent petition
> No man alive can tell for what
> But telling truths which pleased you not
> And taxing your discretion.

The Tories, with cavalier disregard for the law, decided to send the gentlemen who had brought the petition to prison for the rest of the session.

This arbitrary act roused the people of England, and in particular Daniel Defoe, at this time an unknown bankrupt who had lost money speculating in land, in civet cats and Oporto wine, and, more patriotically, insuring vessels during the war. He arrived at the door of St. Stephen's Chapel on the morning of May 14, guarded by sixteen gentlemen with drawn swords, and carrying his *Legion's Memorial*, which asserted the right of true-born Englishmen to petition Parliament. He sent in a message asking to see the Speaker. If Harley was surprised to find the hawk-nosed, grey-eyed Defoe waiting at the door disguised as a woman, he gave no hint of it. He spoke to the petitioners 'in his usual haughty tone', and told them they must be ready to stand outside the House to justify their petition, as this was the normal custom. He took the *Memorial* and, holding it up disdainfully by one corner, he inquired: 'Gentlemen is this your petition?', to which they, bowing respectfully, replied 'Yes, Mr. Speaker'. The enclosed note assured him that the Memorial was motivated neither by popish, Jacobite, or any party interest, but simply by honesty and truth, and commanded him in the name of two hundred thousand Englishmen to deliver it to the House of Commons, and to inform members that it was 'no banter but serious truth'.

'Our name is LEGION and we are many' the Memorial began, and it ended with an ominous postscript: 'If you require to have this Memorial signed with our names, it shall be done on your first order and personally presented.' Thanks to the Speaker's strong nerve, there was no panic in the House, although the thought of so many thousand stalwart Englishmen turning up at the House made several Tory squires fade away into the country, rather sooner than originally planned. *The Legion's Memorial* was treated with a great deal more respect than the Kentish Petition, which had been termed 'insolent'. It was seen as an unmistakable weather-sign:

> A strange memorial too there came
> Your members to affront
> Which told you truths you dare not name,
> And so the paper 'scaped the flame
> Or else it had been burnt.

Another indication of the change in public opinion was the success of *The True-Born Englishman*, which became a best-seller, and even brought a smile to William's pallid lips:

> Ye true-born Englishmen proceed
> Our trifling crimes detect,
> Let the poor starve, religion bleed,
> The Dutch be damn'd, the French succeed,
> And all by your neglect.

In September came the final spark which ignited all latent patriotism. James II, the papist ex-King, and his melancholy wife, had been looking a sorry sight for some time. 'Their equipage is mighty ragged, and their horses are all as lean as Sancho's,' Matthew Prior reported. In March James had suffered a stroke and lost the use of his right arm, which the doctors thought they could cure by 'pumping'. But at least the French still called him 'Roy d'Angleterre' and his journey to Bourbon for a cure was almost on the scale of a royal procession. On September 16, however, after a second seizure, he died, and King Louis at once declared the Jacobite Prince of Wales, now thirteen years old, James III of England.

Immediately, there was panic and confusion in England. William was still abroad, and Princess Anne was in a quandary. First of all she covered the walls of St James's with mourning draperies, then she put all the coloured ones back again. The audacity of the French King angered the English people and William found them in a militant mood when he returned. He recalled his ambassador in France and dismissed the French secretary in London. He was now reconciled with Marlborough who had been playing a valuable part in negotiating the Grand Alliance with Holland and the Emperor Leopold of Austria. William could not ignore the fact that his own health was failing, and that he would probably die before his task of humbling France had been completed, or even begun. So he began to look on Marlborough as his heir, recognizing at last the man's military genius, and noting, with satisfaction, how well the Dutch reacted to this English milord.

On his arrival in London, William immediately dissolved Parliament. Having been out of the country, he had not appreciated the extent of the Tory change of heart; he only knew that the temper of the electorate had changed, and believed that an election would bring back a Whig majority which would be able to forget the impeachments and other trivia and would concentrate all its efforts on the conduct of the war. The Tories were hurt by William's refusal to trust them. Apart from a small number of Jacobites—a number that William probably over-estimated—most of them were prepared to abandon petty principles and put the national interest before party considerations. William Paterson, one of Harley's agents, expressed the feelings of the Speaker and other 'considerable men' in a letter dated November 22:

Anything the ensuing parliament will or can do might have been justly expected from the last, and this continual altering of men and measures will make the minds of people so irritated and uncertain as to reduce the nation to the state its enemies would wish.

At such a moment the time and money involved in an election could well have been used better. 'Such frequent elections one would think should cure people from throwing away their money,' wrote Lady Pye to her cousin Abigail.

The Whigs were far less numerous in the new Parliament than William would have liked. The parties came back evenly matched, but the Whigs were reinstated, and Godolphin vanished from the Treasury. It seemed as though Harley's brief term in the Speaker's Chair was also over. The King favoured his old candidate, Sir Thomas Littleton, who had once been so surprisingly defeated by Foley:

At one the King came to the House of Lords, sent for the Commons, ordered them to return and choose a Speaker and present him tomorrow at 11 o'clock.

After a short debate, the vote was taken; the closeness of the contest mirrored the fine balance of the parties. When the count was made, it was found that Harley had been elected—by four votes:

After the usual method (I suppose) he expressed himself, and amongst the rest to this effect, (as I remember) he was sorry for the great division in the House on that occasion, the only thing he desired was the union of England.

Harley was still on the old theme.

The French were delighted to learn that such a Tory-minded man had been returned to the chair, and they happily anticipated great troubles for the King as a result. But the Speaker meant what he said, and did all he could to calm faction, promote patriotism and support William's preparations for war. Both he and the King found the balance of parties strangely favourable; neither Whigs nor Tories could afford to be dictatorial, and they could be played off against each other by a skilful manager. William was delighted; perhaps for the first time in his reign he held the balance of power, and this increased his own sway immeasurably. Harley's power too had been augmented, but he wielded it without becoming aggressive, and he still retained the respect of the House. 'Yet I fear the gilded mace carried before a rich gold laced brocade gown,' wrote one of the more puritanical relations, expressing a fear that Harley, as first commoner of the realm, might well become 'too proud and full of himself' and look down on his old friends.

Had William lived, it would have only been a matter of time before Speaker Harley was replaced by a Whig candidate. But on February 21, when the King was riding in the park at Hampton Court, his horse stumbled, he was thrown and broke his collar bone. In his usual stoical way he went back the same evening, in a jolting coach, to Kensington. For a week he kept to his room and seemed likely to recover, but on the afternoon of March 3 he fell asleep by an open window where he had sat down to enjoy the sunshine of an early spring afternoon. As he slept the sun went in and he awoke shivering. Next day he was feverish, unable to keep food down and continually vomiting phlegm and choler. He was just able to set his seal to the Act of Abjuration which required everyone holding office in Church or State to 'abjure' the Pretender and his heirs. Then on March 8 he died.

His death was announced in the Commons by Sir John Packington, the epitome of a country Tory: 'Sir, we have lost a great King: we have got a most gracious Queen.' At the palace, the courtiers bowed their heads in sorrow for their master, and anxiety for the future. Shopkeepers who had laid in a stock of coloured silks and 'other modish things', all ready for the spring market, grieved for their loss of trade. But, after a scarcely decent interval, regret gave way to general rejoicing. One observer noted a universal astonishment for a bare two hours after the King's death, and another admitted that he had never seen 'so short a sorrow'. Loyal addresses poured in from all parts of the country, the Mayor and Aldermen crowded to kiss the royal hand, and everybody who had been in opposition during William's reign hastened to fall down and worship in agreeable expectation of honour and profit.

For Robin Harley the new reign had come at just the right moment.

Everyone knew that the Queen would turn to the Tories, for they were the Church party, and she loved her Church with a deep sincere affection. Better still, she was an English queen, who would love and understand her own people. The future opened out for this new recruit to the Tory ranks who had the country and its constitution so closely at heart.

The Whigs knew that their reign was over. Vernon went quietly, enjoying the prospect of retirement with only the 'honest old authors' for company. Such a life seemed preferable to the bustle of the secretary-ship. 'The peevishness of our friends at St Stephen's Chapel is sufficient to make any man wish for a cloister,' was Matthew Prior's opinion. But withdrawal held no charms for Harley. In the smoky, overcrowded chamber of St Stephen's he was in his element. The political arena was his natural habitat. Slight and small, he mingled with the crowd in the Court of Requests, flattering men with whispered confidences and gentle innuendoes. This mild Member from Herefordshire had captured the respect of the House. His next task was to gain the affection of a Queen, and to indoctrinate her with his moderate ideals.

CHAPTER 4

THE NEW QUEEN

FOR THE FIRST FEW DAYS of Queen Anne's reign, the weather was as warm and bright as summer. Everybody was in a mood to accept this as a good omen, and a sign that the country was about to embark on a glorious period of its history. The people warmed to their new monarch. She might be middle-aged and massive, riddled with gout and subject to the vapours, but she was homely and peace-loving. Some felt impelled to compare this matronly woman with the Virgin Queen herself. Chesterfield, for instance, went, with 'the impudence of an old courtier', to tender his respects:

Without anybody to introduce me [I] sent in my name, and was soon admitted into Her Majesty's closet, where there was nobody but Prince George. And after having been received very graciously, and stayed a quarter of an hour, I took my leave. . . . My opinion is that if her Majesty would have no favourites, but choose a wise Council, and rely upon a Parliament, she might have so happy a reign as to eclipse that of Queen Elizabeth.

She did not lack willing advisers. Her uncle, Earl of Rochester and grand monarch of the High Tory party, was anxious to offer avuncular advice, even to rule for her, if she preferred. The friends who had stood by her in darker days waited for the rewards their loyalty deserved. The Marlboroughs and Godolphin, affectionately nicknamed Mr and Mrs Freeman and Mr Montgomery, were honoured at once for the service they had rendered when she was only a Princess with humble apartments at the Cockpit. Marlborough, whose military flair had been wasted for so many years, was made Captain-General without delay. His wife, Sarah, Anne's childhood friend, was put in charge of the household, rapidly receiving the honours of Mistress of the Robes and Groom of the Stole.

A wise law passed in William's reign laid down that Parliament could sit for at least six months after the monarch's death, so that affairs could go on smoothly for a period, without the immediate chaos of an election. But fortunately for Anne and for her friends, there was nothing to stop her choosing new advisers. She immediately turned to Godolphin even though, as yet, he had no official position.

Sidney, first Earl of Godolphin, was a short, dark man with a stern expression and 'an awful serious deportment'. He had a clear, tidy mind, was experienced in the routine of government, and was particularly knowledgeable about financial affairs. Reliable, incorruptible and discreet, and, according to Charles II, 'never in the way, never out of the way', he had, in fact, only two faults: he was somewhat lacking in a sense of humour, and at times of crisis he tended to fuss.

After the death of the King he found himself suddenly facing, almost alone, the responsibility of guiding the Queen. William had scarcely confided in her; she had little experience of public affairs or public speaking and was anyway in poor health. Godolphin, overwhelmed by his task, turned to Harley for help; during his brief term at the Treasury in William's reign, he had learned to value the Speaker's competent and calm approach. Never a great speech-maker himself, Godolphin soon had Harley helping with the Queen's speeches. Her first address, to the Privy Council, was a success. She had a soft, beautiful voice, which had always been one of her greatest assets; King Charles, indeed, had so admired it, that he had had her coached by a famous actress. Although she was too shy to enjoy public speaking, she had a 'sweetness of pronunciation' that charmed her hearers, and, given the right thing to say, she could make a profound effect. Godolphin, worried and anxious, leaned on Harley heavily for help and advice. On March 8 he wrote:

You were pleased to tell me today in the House of Commons that what the Queen was to speak from the throne was to be to the same purpose with that she said at Council.

I wish you could have time to make a draught of it yourself, and appoint us to come to your house to morrow night to see it. I think her speaking can't be deferred longer than Tuesday.

She is very unwieldy and lame; must she come in person to the House of Lords, or may she send for the two houses to come to her?

Harley advised that everything should go on as naturally and normally as possible to give the nation confidence. He urged Godolphin to send the Queen to the House, gout or no gout. Godolphin, always inclined to find a worry, said anxiously, 'I doubt if she has any robes'.

All difficulties were overcome; the Queen went to Parliament magnificently attired in robes that were said to be copied from a portrait of Queen Elizabeth. Resplendent in red velvet, ermine and gold galloon, with the badge of St George at her breast, she assured her listeners in her sweet thrilling voice, that she was determined to protect Church and State against the growing might of France. She expressed her loyalty for William's memory and finished with the resounding statement that her heart was truly English. The whole occasion was a masterpiece of stage management. This was the kind of thing her people wished to hear. Only a few carping Whigs complained that her last phrase was a reflection on the King; everyone else was overcome with enthusiasm and emotion.

William's funeral was so simple and unpublicized that some said it was hardly decent; by contrast, the coronation was a magnificent affair. Scaffolds were put up for spectators in the Abbey and all along the route to Westminster Hall. Peers and their wives were ordered, all excuses set apart, to make their appearance at the Abbey on April 23 'furnished and appointed as their rank and quality appertaineth'. Because of her gout, the Queen was carried in an elbow chair of crimson velvet, with four maiden ladies—earls' daughters—in attendance, all richly dressed in cloth of gold or silver. For the first time in her life, Anne was the centre of the picture. She had always been the scorned younger sister, dimmed by Mary's more attractive light. Now, a prodigious number of people turned out to see her. Wearing gold tissue, she looked stout, but not unhandsome; her best attributes were her finely shaped hands, her voice and, in particular, her luxuriant chestnut hair, dressed on Coronation Day with diamonds which, as Celia Fiennes remarked, 'at the least motion brilled and flamed'. The Queen conducted herself well and impressed the onlookers with her friendly looks and bows. Her close friend John Sharp, Archbishop of York, preached the sermon, even though he was ill with the stone, strangury and colic. The Queen's weather-luck held. 'It was a bright day,' John Evelyn wrote, 'and everybody much pleased and satisfied.'

The ceremony over and the excitement subsiding, the Queen and her friends had to face up to the details of everyday government. The Queen had dedicated herself, in her speech, to defending the Protestant Succession, and the allies wanted practical proof that she meant what she said. To put their minds at rest, immediately after the coronation she despatched Marlborough to the Hague with encouraging messages. On his return he put forward his plan to help the alliance, which was sanctioned by Parliament, and war was formally declared in early May. Louis XIV said it must be a sign he was growing old now that the ladies had taken to declaring war on him. Soon afterwards Marlborough left England to take up his command. He embarked at Margate, and watched the receding cliffs through a perspective glass, hoping for a last glimpse of Sarah.

He confessed in a letter written on board that he would have given his life to be back with her.

King William's experience had taught Marlborough that war could never be successfully waged unless there was somebody sympathetic at the head of the Treasury. He agreed to command the Queen's forces only on condition that Godolphin was made Lord Treasurer. Anne had no objection and duly invited her old friend to fill the post. He hesitated, whether from genuine reluctance or false modesty nobody knew, although Dartmouth unkindly wrote that Godolphin 'constantly refused anything that he knew would be forced upon him'. The appointment, when it was announced, caused little surprise, but there was a great deal of talk when the Marquis of Normanby was created Lord Privy Seal and Duke of Buckingham. He was a sour-looking, unpopular man, a Jacobite who, according to Macky—who described most of the court characters for the Electress Sophia's information—was violently in favour of the High Church, but seldom went to it. His experience in practical politics was negligible and his only claim to fame was that once, many years ago, he had paid his court to Anne, to the disapproval of Mary, who said she thought nothing was more prejudicial to a young woman than ill company. The Queen made up her mind that she wished to honour her one and only old flame, and nothing that anybody could say would shake her. Marlborough advised her against the appointment, but he came up against the Stuart stubbornness which he soon learnt to respect. There was some criticism on the continent, for it was well known that Buckingham was a Francophile who had been friendly with Tallard, the French ambassador, and some feared that he might be a security risk. But Marlborough had to admit to his European friends that he was quite unable to influence the Queen in everything.

There was one other point over which Anne was determined to show that she was Queen indeed. If she used her power for nothing else, she would use it to honour her husband, to whom she was devoted. They had been married for nearly twenty years now, and Prince George of Denmark was no longer the fair-haired comely person 'with few pock holes in his visage', who had first been seen at the English court. He was of an easy-going disposition, not over-gifted with intelligence. 'I have tried him sober, and I have tried him drunk, but there is nothing in him,' said Charles II, advising George, as a cure for obesity, 'to walk with me, ride with my brother, and do your duty by my niece'. In this last respect, the Prince had done all he could. Anne bore him seventeen children, mostly miscarriages and stillbirths, perhaps due to a blood incompatibility, or according to a recent suggestion, because Anne suffered from the common royal malady of porphyria, a hereditary liver complaint. The English liked him because he showed no ambition to meddle in their affairs. 'He is very fat, loves news, his bottle and the Queen,' commented Macky. Apart from hunting, which amused him, his main occupation was to stand at the top of the stairs, look out of a window and make malicious remarks about the passers-by. But although Anne used admittedly 'to grow uneasy at the figure His Highness cut in that princely amusement', she loved him deeply, and was hurt when William treated him with disdain, and would not even allow him to travel in the royal coach during the Irish campaign. There had been an undignified quarrel when Prince George, realizing that William would give him no military command, had decided in a patriotic moment to go on shipboard as an ordinary officer, and had been recalled by a peremptory order from the King. The Queen wished to compensate her husband for these unhappy experiences, and as soon as possible. She made him Lord High Admiral with the power to govern by a council, which some believed to be of doubtful legality. In deference to the Queen's feelings, such objections as there were never, according to Burnet, rose above a murmur.

Marlborough, Godolphin and Harley were all agreed that a moderate policy should be pursued without any spirit of revenge. No Whigs were actually appointed to the vacant offices, but unnecessary dismissals were not encouraged either in the household, or in the counties, where the Lords-Lieutenant would normally have been turned out at the first possible moment. The judges, who had all been waiting in some trepidation to know their fate, were relieved to find that with the exception of two, they were all quite safe. The Tories were pacified by the appointment of the Earl of Nottingham and Sir Charles Hedges as Secretaries of State. Nottingham, tall and dark, like a Spaniard or a Jew, with black beetling brows and a mournful expression that earned him the nickname of 'Dismal', was a great lover of the Church, and therefore acceptable to the Queen. Hedges made a good henchman, a sound, hardworking and reliable man who was quite happy to do the work and let others reap the credit. These, and other appointments, should have satisfied the Tories, but they were frankly disappointed. Rochester, in particular, who had been sitting back comfortably expecting to be handed the White Staff of the Lord Treasurer's office, and to become virtual prime minister of the realm, waited in vain. The Queen had no intention of being ordered about by her uncle, like any poor relation. She was a Queen, and to make sure that he realized the fact, she appointed him Lord-Lieutenant of

Ireland, an important post, but one that with any luck might keep him well out of the way.

The fine warm weather that had graced the Queen's accession gave way to hard frosts and bitter winds that blighted the fruit blossom. The first enthusiasm, which had for a few weeks united the whole country, soon began to die. The rank and file of the Tory party began to smart in sympathy with Rochester. Sir Nathan Wright, an unpleasant-looking man, with a fat heavy face deeply pitted by smallpox, had been appointed Lord Keeper in 1700 during the brief Tory rule, and had remained there ever since. The Queen, unwisely, let him stay. As Lord Keeper he wielded great power over appointments of every kind, and he was a zealot determined to hound out every Whig he could lay hands on. Marlborough and Godolphin concentrated on protecting army officers and treasury officials, and Harley's friends begged him to do what he could to take care of the law appointments. All three men were aware of the aftermath of bitterness that would result from a general clearout, particularly the dismissal of worthy Justices who had given good service, in favour of far less suitable men. It was madness to alienate the Whigs unnecessarily at this juncture, since they controlled financial resources without which the war could never be fought, let alone won. Nor was the trio of moderates anxious to have an election; as things stood, they could hold the balance and play off one faction against the other, but an election would be sure to bring back a large Tory majority and one that was likely to prove very unmanageable. Besides, there had been two elections in two years and nobody wanted the worry and expense of another straight away.

The Tories were not to be deflected. They continued to press for position, and to nag for a dissolution. All their pettiness depressed Godolphin. 'I wish with all my heart that four or five of these gentlemen that are so sharp set upon other people's places had mine amongst them to stay their stomachs,' he broke out. He was overwrought and anxious. 'When I saw your hand upon the outside of the enclosed letter it gave me a great deal of satisfaction to think you had forgiven that torrent of impertinence which dropped from me last night.' He found Harley invaluable, sometimes, it is true, venting his nervous irritation, more often asking for advice.

It was during the summer of 1702 that Harley first began to visit the Queen in the course of his duty. She gave in, finally, to the Tory clamour for an election, and the Speaker was naturally consulted about the dissolution. 'The Queen appoints half an hour after five tomorrow at her backstairs,' wrote Godolphin on July 7. 'You will please send in your name.' The Queen did not encourage her Ministers to use the more ceremonial approaches when they came to her on business. She herself had escaped by a backstairway when she fled to the north on the news of William's arrival, and while she was away her first thought was to order that the backstairs at the Cockpit might be painted 'that they may be dry against I come home but when next that may be God knows'. Certainly, in Queen Anne's reign, the key to favour was synonymous with the key to the backstairs, a fact that Robert Harley did not take long to grasp. The clandestine element appealed to him; he always preferred to go in by a secret side entrance rather than enter openly through flunkey-flanked main doors.

At length, in mid-July, Parliament was dissolved, and Members went away, thankfully, to the country. The city was sultry in the summer, and although cooling trips could be taken on the river, a fresh breeze in an open boat was inclined to play havoc with an elaborate wig. St James's Park was pleasant enough, and both common people and persons of quality could stroll there among the red deer and English kine. But in the streets, the stench was intolerable, stones were hot and hard on the feet and the cobbles jolted the limbs of gouty M.P.s as they went to the House in their coaches. Sunday observance, the legacy of Puritanism, made week-ends in London unbearably dreary. All play was forbidden, boats and hackney coaches were not allowed to ply, public houses were closed, and society hostesses would not even let their guests play on the viol-de-gamba. As one foreigner rather acidly remarked:

This is, I suppose, the only point in which one sees the English profess to be Christians, certainly from the rest of their conduct one would not suspect it of many of them.

Christian virtues were certainly not in the ascendant at election time. Political ferment in midsummer London, mingled with the smell of sewage and the dread of disease, rapidly drove Members out into the country to tickle palms and intimidate the tenantry in the purer air of the shires.

Harley made for Hereford and was able to spend a few weeks with his children, to read books and play bowls. His election passed without trouble. He did not bother to write many letters, and young St John, the promising Tory politician, complained to Paterson that he had not had a communication for three weeks. 'To mollify him I told him I was much longer before I had one' was Paterson's tactful repartee. Godolphin kept in touch; in September he was worried about the Queen's speech, which would have to be ready for the opening of Parliament, and he was still eager for Harley's backing and advice, being unsure of himself and fearful of criticism. On September 16 he sent Harley a draft, giving him a free hand to add his thoughts and amendments:

I consider that the better any thing of this nature is digested before it comes to be seen by many persons, the better one shall be able to defend it from any wild or inconvenient proposals of alteration.

The election results confirmed all Godolphin's worst apprehensions. Everywhere the rabid Tories had gained ground, and would soon be crowding back to London, thirsting to avenge themselves on the Whigs in the name of the Church of England. 'I pray God our friends act soberly and reasonably,' hoped Henry Guy. 'I am sure all is lost without it; some hot men do talk very largely.'

Godolphin pursued the Queen to Bath. The royal visit made prices rise, and lodgings were very scarce. The Queen herself was in good health, but Prince George was unwell, numbering among his symptoms 'a spice of lethargy', and the Queen, as always when he was ill, sat up with him all night and refused to leave his side. She was unaware of the difficulties that lay ahead. Marlborough's campaign was going well, and the Tories, to her, were the loyal Church party. She looked forward to the next session of Parliament, when she believed Members would grant her whatever she asked for the two greatest objects of her affection—Prince George and the General, her friend Marlborough.

CHAPTER 5

THE TRIUMVIRATE

WHEN MEMBERS RE-ASSEMBLED in the autumn of 1702, many
Whig faces were missing, while the Tory ranks were strengthened by a
new batch of country gentlemen who intended to find as good sport
at Westminster as they enjoyed on their rural estates. They rallied like
hounds to the call of their leaders; it was natural to them to hunt in a
pack. Old Sir Edward Seymour, diabetic and irascible, had come back
flushed with election success; in his western empire, where he controlled
great wealth and electoral influence, the Tories had swept all before
them, and this fact inspired his dying body with new and hectic life.
An inveterate devotee of the chase, he had not so long ago nearly lost his
life in a west-Country bog, and certainly it would have been better
for the moderates if old Sir Chuffer, as they called him, had been silenced
for all time. Rejuvenated, he came blustering back, to make what trouble
he could and to encourage warmth and heat—the very temperatures
which Godolphin and Harley particularly wanted to avoid.

The more ardent Tories would have liked to oust both the Speaker
and the Treasurer, and substitute more furious men:

> Granville shall seize the long expected chair
> Godolphin to some country seat repair.

wrote Walsh ominously in his *Golden Ages Restored*. But Harley had
gained the respect of the country gentlemen, and when Parliament met,
he was elected Speaker for the third time without opposition. The Queen's
speech, which he had helped to devise, was framed to flatter the Tories
with promises of support for the Church. In return, the Lords and
Commons presented an address full of congratulations for the success of
Her Majesty's arms on the continent.

Marlborough's summer campaign had been reassuringly successful,
which gave an excuse for a magnificent procession through the City,
and a thanksgiving service at St. Paul's. The new cathedral was still
unfinished, as the duty on coal which was supposed to be used for the
purpose was often diverted to some other cause, but it was complete

enough to form a fine setting for the ceremony. All along the route there were cheering crowds, salvoes of guns roared out from the Tower, and at Ludgate Hill the royal coach was greeted by a dazzling 'pyramidical illumination'. The Queen was smothered in jewels for the occasion, but Sarah Marlborough, who travelled with her in the coach, wore a plain dress, unadorned, which flattered her striking good looks.

The enthusiasm of the London populace was a strange contrast to the crabbed reaction of Tory Members of Parliament, who did their best to couple Marlborough with Tory heroes such as Rooke and Ormonde, who had achieved minor successes in the Mediterranean. The Whigs, too, jealous of William's memory, objected when Marlborough was said to have 'retrieved the ancient honour and glory of the nation'. Ignoring all this, the Queen told Sarah in a letter that she intended to invest the commander of her forces with a title to fit his position. She wished, in fact, to make him a Duke. Sarah, on her own admission, was so surprised that she let the letter fall from her hand, and at first both husband and wife resisted the idea. The frugal Marlborough was more interested in money than titles, but he was persuaded that the Queen's gesture would be popular with the allies, and agreed to accept the honour, provided that a suitable grant was made for himself and his heirs. Poor Godolphin had the task of persuading Parliament to settle public revenue in perpetuity on a man whom the majority regarded with a jaundiced eye. He might, in John Evelyn's words, be 'handsome, proper, well spoken and affable', he might be the Queen's best friend, but, after the success of only one campaign, it was 'bold and unadvised' to demand money over and above the £30,000 a year he already had in places and employments; besides, everyone knew that he owed his rise in society to the fact that his sister was 'a miss. to K. James the 2nd when Duke of York'. Debates on the subject became personal and malicious; Sir Chuffer headed the opposition, driving on his pack and thoroughly enjoying the sport. Godolphin was shocked, the Queen humiliated, and Marlborough, anxious to keep the Commons in a good temper to vote supplies for his army, hastily withdrew the request for a grant to his heirs.

If the Queen was impervious to reservations about Marlborough's character, she was even more so when they concerned her husband. She tried to have him appointed commander-in-chief of all the armies—a request that was quietly shelved thanks to Marlborough's tactful handling —and decided to grant him a large income which he would continue to enjoy even if she were to die before him. This time it was the Whig lords who were obstructive; the Tories voted the Prince the astonishing sum of a hundred thousand pounds a year with hardly a murmur, but the Whigs caused trouble about a clause which they made out to be a threat to the Act of Settlement. There seemed to be no limit to party pettiness.

At any rate the Queen looked forward to the task of strengthening her Church. She had been brought up in the faith by Anglican divines, and was suspicious of other doctrines. Her dislike of Catholicism had been confirmed when she stayed with Mary on the continent. 'Their images . . . are in every shop and corner of the street,' she had written. 'The more I see of those fooleries and the more I hear of that religion the more I dislike it.' She approved of any measure that might help the established Church; all the same, religious debates did seem to unleash the most un-Christian emotions, and clergymen were the least responsive group of all when it came to appeals for unity. Through the summer, the country parsons had been indoctrinating the sleepy squires from their pulpits, inciting them to fight for the Church on their return to Westminster. Henry Sacheverell set a fashion when he preached an inflammable sermon, calling on the Church to raise 'the bloody flag of defiance'. This histrionic prelate, who had a gift for cheap rhetoric and a flair for coining provocative slogans, pointed an accusatory finger at dissenters who quietly partook of the Anglican communion from time to time in order to qualify for public office. An oppressive law, framed to curb the Catholics, still officially kept dissenters too out of public life, but many an able non-conformist had come to terms with his conscience for the sake of a career. The clergy with their long powdered perruques, silk cassocks, and covetousness (John Evelyn's description), were more than ready to rally to Sacheverell's call. And as soon as Parliament met, the country squires, headed by William Bromley, a Warwickshire gentleman, and by the brilliant young Henry St John, a most unreligious rake, introduced a Bill to penalize those who occasionally conformed to Anglican rites for the sake of convenience. Since a great many Whig politicians were dissenters, the Bill was also calculated to consolidate the Tory party and chase a great many talented enemies from the public scene. The behaviour of the more fanatical Tories, who shamelessly promoted animosity at a time of national crisis, seemed incomprehensible to more level-headed men.

Godolphin was soon distracted. He had little patience with other people's folly. He was tormented out of his life by place-hunters, harried in the House and worried by unexpected alarms. All he wanted was some peace and quiet to put through the money Bills for Marlborough, and he was being continually harassed by the madness of people who ought to have known better. In the turbulent weeks before Christmas, when troubles about occasional conformity, and Marlborough, and Prince George were driving Godolphin to distraction, he turned more than ever to Harley for help and advice. 'I give you a thousand thanks for your patience last night when I had so little,' he wrote on December 14, 'and for the calm and sincere advice you gave me.' He communicated with Harley almost daily, frequently asking him to call after the House rose. Godolphin often needed to be soothed down after his encounters with the Tory zealots. 'I can submit in most things to better judgments,' he noted bitterly, 'but am at present so out of patience with Sir Edward S[eymour] that I am sure I can meet him nowhere but to scold.'

Apart from his skill in parliamentary affairs, Harley was proving an invaluable steadying influence, Like Godolphin, he disapproved of accentuating religious difficulties, but he knew it was useless to argue with zealots like Sir Chuffer, and a waste of energy to become agitated about their manœuvres. The Tories were in the majority, alienate them and they could soon make life even more difficult by rejecting money Bills and cutting off Marlborough's supplies. Even Godolphin could see the logic of this argument, and the two men lay low, neither opposing nor defending the Occasional Conformity Bill, which, as was expected, passed through the Commons and was carried up to the Lords by a party of triumphant Tories.

In the upper house it was a different story. There, the benches were packed with Whig lords and bishops created by William to ensure a sympathetic majority among the peers, and it was easy to bring in amendments which reduced the heavy fines for occasional conformity, and which rendered the whole ruse more or less harmless. Prince George, an occasional conformist himself, who did not mind receiving the Anglican sacrament from time to time, was ordered by his wife and Queen to vote for a measure that could make life embarrassing for him personally; however, as he passed by his Whig friends on his way to the lobby, he whispered to them in his heavy foreign accent, 'my heart is vid you'.

The House of Commons was mortified by the action of the Lords. The peers had no right to interfere in financial matters, and therefore should not have been allowed to tamper with fines that had been fixed in the lower House. Feelings were soon running high between the two Houses. Humble baronets were hardly on speaking terms with belted earls. Tory parsons preached bitter sermons against Whig bishops. The Queen said angrily that she had been maliciously hindered. She had prayed for peace and unity and had so far met with nothing but divisions and arguments.

KENSINGTON PALACE

SIDNEY, EARL GODOLPHIN

ROBERT HARLEY IN HI
SPEAKER'S ROBES, AND
HOLDING THE ACT OF
SETTLEMENT

*Photo: Witt Library,
Courtauld Institute of Art*

Robert Harley was wise to lie low during the Occasional Conformity debate. He was himself in an invidious position. His family were known dissenters, and many of them still went to chapel. He disliked militant churchmen of any creed, who went about 'in the habit of a clergyman, but in the spirit of a dragoon', as he himself neatly put it. To show his tolerance, he often invited both an Anglican and a dissenting clergyman to share his Sunday meal. All the same he was conscious that it was far more dangerous to be a devout dissenter than a wicked Anglican; he did his best to keep in with the churchmen, and made no great parade of his tolerance, or of the part he played in the eventual dropping of the Occasional Conformity Bill, after the Lords had mauled it in the new year.

Affairs were in a confused state as 1703 dawned. 'The Queen's servants in both Houses are vying who shall be maddest,' Godolphin penned in despair on January 14. All the same, by keeping calm, and managing the Commons with skill, Harley piloted the crucial money Bill through the House. The country gentlemen seemed sublimely unaware of the dangers to which they were exposed, and they cared far more about the occasional conformity of their neighbours than they did about Louis XIV and all his armies. 'And do they forget,' Godolphin burst out, 'that not only the fate of England but of all Europe depends upon the appearance of our concord in the despatch of supplies?' It was useless to point out that the war was being fought to protect Protestants of all kinds from the Catholic domination of France, that freedom of conscience was at stake. The hot Tories were beyond the reach of reason. But Harley did not appeal to their reason; he simply outwitted them.

Until the money Bill was through, Godolphin's nerves were stretched to breaking point. He could not do without Harley for a day, and summoned him to a meeting with Marlborough even on Sunday, February 6, which, as Godolphin admitted, 'ought to be a day of rest to all people and to you particularly'. He frequently called in at the Speaker's house in York Buildings, or invited him to wait on him at his own, leaving a rare book out for Harley to thumb through until the evening's Council meeting was finished. Godolphin viewed the mounting criticism of Marlborough's campaign with apprehension; in particular he was worried by the hot-headed Rochester, who refused to take up his appointment in Ireland, and hung about in London, determined to be at the centre of affairs, and making trouble wherever he could. St John, young and enthusiastic, was given the task of looking into the financial affairs of William's Ministers. Halifax in particular was accused of misappropriating public funds—an easy enough charge to bring when perquisites were

C

claimed by more or less everyone as a right. The Tories seemed to grow even more vindictive after the failure of their precious Bill, and, partly to spite Marlborough, they began to preach a doctrine of non-involvement on the continent, advocating that the English contribution should be limited to the war at sea. The landed gentry hinted that if they were expected to pay the hated four-shilling Land Tax, while the merchants went more or less unscathed, they should expect to have a say in the way the war was carried on.

The Queen was disappointed by the behaviour of the Tories, of whom she had expected so much. She blamed her uncle, Rochester, whose trouble-making was only too apparent, and whose campaign against Marlborough annoyed her. Finding his presence increasingly oppressive, she suggested, reasonably enough, that he should take up his Irish appointment. Angry at being ordered about by his niece, he resigned at once and went into bitter opposition, a remarkable instance, Sarah Marlborough considered, of how much self-love and self-conceit can blind even a man of sense. But if the Queen hoped that all would be easy once Rochester was banished from her councils, she was mistaken; he continued to plot in the background, encouraging the Tories to obstruct the work of Marlborough and Godolphin.

Once the money Bill was through, the session ended, but there was no respite for Marlborough, and little enough for Godolphin. Not surprisingly, after the strain of the winter, Godolphin was ill during the summer months, and he began to talk, not for the last time, of retiring. For the Marlboroughs, the year 1703 had begun badly with the death of their only son, the Marquis of Blandford, whom the Duchess had understandably kept in England, for fear of the dangers to which he would be exposed if he went on his father's campaigns. He was only sixteen, and she thought he would benefit from another year at Cambridge. But in February he was struck down by an even deadlier enemy than the French. Like his royal companion, the Duke of Gloucester, he died of smallpox.

Marlborough had little time to grieve. As soon as the green shoots began to appear in the fields of Flanders it was time to assemble the armies. Winter was always a time of truce, for it was too expensive to find fodder for the horses during the lean, bitter months. All campaigning had to be done in the dust and heat of summer, and the General frequently complained of headaches, sore eyes and lack of sleep. The Dutch were being difficult; they refused to let him execute his brilliant attacking schemes and were dilatory in the transport of supplies. But, for the sake of his Queen, his country and religious freedom, he was prepared to endure the discomforts of a military life and the sorrow of being parted from his wife when she was laid low by the death of their son. All the same, he often thought longingly of his home at St Albans, with its orchard and flowering trees.

Sarah Marlborough was completely thrown off balance by the death of her son. Her uncontrolled grief was compared unfavourably with Anne's dumb acceptance of the Duke of Gloucester's death. 'We hear the Duchess of Marlborough bears not her affliction like her mistress,' Lady Pye observed to Abigail Harley. 'If report be true it hath near touched her head.' For although the Duchess prided herself on her common sense and honesty, she was highly strung, and, after the death of her son, she became increasingly neurotic. By nature she was domineering, open and frank, and in their childhood days Princess Anne had been glad to follow the lead of her brilliant friend. But now an adjustment had to be made; the Princess had become a Queen, and it was her turn to rule. Now that she held sceptre and orb, Anne had no more desire to be dominated. The Duchess, for her part, saw no reason why anything should be different, and she took upon herself the task of telling the Queen exactly what she thought of her. Convinced that rulers were too often ruined by flattery, she went so far as to think 'it was a part of flattery, not to tell her everything that was in any sense amiss in her'. She thought herself well above the common run of courtly sycophants and did not flinch from showing her superiority with blunt comments about the royal family being ruined by obstinacy. These the Queen did not appreciate, nor did she like it when the Duchess tried to dictate to her on the subject of politics. Sarah, somewhat under the influence of her Whig son-in-law Sunderland, had decided, once and for all, that she preferred Whigs to Tories. Her husband, no great lover of party politics, was, if anything, a Tory, and the Queen, poor fool, insisted on remaining stubbornly loyal to the Church party, in spite of all its scandalous behaviour during the winter session. It grieved Sarah to find her mistress blind to those principles which for her burned with the light of unarguable reason. How could any sane person listen to Tory gibberish about passive obedience and hereditary right? The Queen refused to be bullied into changing her ideas, but she was anxious that political quarrels should not cloud an old-established friendship. 'Never let difference of opinion hinder us from living together, as we used to do,' she urged.

When Sarah was appointed Mistress of the Robes, she declared, in her straightforward way, that there would be no more buying and selling of appointments. This was an admirable theory, which like so many others, soon foundered on the rock of human frailty. The Duchess did not allow for the fact that, besides placing herself in a very powerful position, she had also made herself a prey to every ambitious man or woman anxious to find a niche in her department of the Palace. The situation soon became almost intolerable, and having dispensed the positions of starchers, sempstresses, pages, grooms and waiters, to men and women known to herself, or recommended by her friends, she began to keep away from the court in order to avoid being plagued by petitioners and place-hunters. Life in the stuffy sick-room atmosphere of Kensington soon began to pall. There was hardly any more gaiety at court than there had been in King William's time, and it was not surprising that the Duchess was often lured away to St Albans in the summer of 1703, by the cool country air and the charms of solitude or the company of her daughters. Now that her husband was a great general, she began to grow too grand for menial tasks, and she often entrusted her waiting to Abigail Hill, the humble cousin she had adopted, saved almost from starvation, and introduced to court. Abigail had been a Bedchamber Woman for several years now; she was quiet and discreet, and well able to attend to the details of humouring an ailing Queen. Although she lacked beauty and breeding, she was not without charm and had learned to proffer compliments. She could also play the harpsichord, which the Queen enjoyed. As a mere indebted, grateful relation, Abigail could be relied upon to look after affairs for her protectress when that great lady was absent.

In retrospect, it is often difficult to decide when the estrangement began. The Duchess, who, for all her honesty and frankness, was singularly self-deluded, sometimes attributed the first coolness to some trivial incident—a word or two overheard and misinterpreted. Sometimes the Queen appeared to take offence when she was only being silent and preoccupied, as was her way. 'I really look grave and angry when I am not so,' Anne had assured Lady Bathurst, her 'dear Semandra', years earlier. The Duchess was not the first to be deceived by the Queen's heavy, brooding look, and being of a far more vivacious nature herself, she was often irritated by Anne's taciturnity. 'She has an easy way . . . when she has not known what to say which is to move only her lips and make as if she had said something when in truth no words were uttered,' she wrote later, in her searing manner. Queen Anne, like many silent people, could express herself far better on paper than in conversation, and if at times she appeared to be offended by her friend's absence, annoyed by her political opinions, or hurt by her frank comments, she was able to show, warmly, in her letters, that she was still as fond and affectionate as ever. Never let anyone accuse her of indifference or believe there was any lack of 'value, esteem, or tender kindness for my dear dear Mrs. Freeman it being impossible for any one to be more sincerely another's than I am your's', she insisted. And yet, as early as 1703, there were signs that things were going wrong; only those uncertain of themselves and of their affection demand and give effusive demonstrations of what in happier circumstances can be taken as said.

It was the coldest, wettest summer within living memory, which did nothing to help anybody's health or low spirits. Godolphin grew more and more depressed. He was so tired of the Tories and their antics that he was inclined to agree with the Duchess when she suggested that the seven most influential including Nottingham, Jersey and Seymour, should be removed at a stroke. Both he and Marlborough began to harp on what was to become a recurrent theme with them—the possibility of retirement. It would be better to row as slaves in the galleys, they thought, than to wear themselves out in the service of an ungrateful nation. But this kind of talk alarmed the Queen. She too had to suffer the 'hurry and impertinencies' of public life, but for her there was no withdrawal. They had all been through so much together, and now, just when she needed them and after so short a time, they talked of abandoning her. There was one simple solution. If they went, she would abdicate. 'We four must never part, till death mows us down with his impartial hand,' she stated in her regal prose.

Marlborough knew that he would have to go on. He would try to do the best he could for the nation as a whole, be governed by neither party, and probably displease both. 'As long as I have quiet in my own mind, I shall not care,' he wrote. In his desire to free himself from the thralldom of party, he was encouraged by the Speaker, who seemed to think, quite seriously, that it was possible to govern with a group of men gifted with good sense and moderate beliefs. Unlike his friends, Harley had not succumbed to the spleen, and he spent the summer months busily preparing for the future. He still had at the back of him the solid phalanx of Foleys and other family supporters. Paul Foley's country Whigs had never been fully absorbed into the main body of the High Church Tories, and there was still a clear line of demarcation between the hot, fanatical, angry party members, and the moderates who felt uneasy about repressive measures like the Occasional Conformity Bill, and who would have liked to dissociate themselves from revengeful attacks on the old Ministry.

Likewise, on the Whig side, there were many moderates who distrusted the Junto and who might well be persuaded to join a coalition government of the centre. With this in mind, he set about courting people who might be of use to him in the future. The Duchess of Marlborough has described his 'familiar, jocular, bowing, smiling airs' which, according to her, were assumed in order to cover up what could not be covered. The direct Duchess instinctively suspected anyone who had a command of honeyed words, and who was lucky enough to be gifted with charm. Fortunately, there were other people who succumbed to the Harley technique. St John, bored with the blusterings of aged men like Seymour, was ripe for treatment, and he turned his back on Bromley and the Occasional Conformity Bill with characteristic carelessness. There were even some churchmen who might be persuaded to tone down the worst excesses of the party, and to keep in with at least one of them, Harley cultivated a friendship with the benign Dr Hooper, Dean of Canterbury, whom he often asked to dinner:

The dean was very much esteemed and valued by the speaker to the end of his life, though the beginning of the acquaintance seemed to proceed from a design in Mr. H. to appear a church-man . . . which nothing could more effectually promote than an intimacy and friendship with the dean of C: which he very carefully cultivated . . . sending for him under various pretences, and to have his opinion and when the dean took boat at York buildings where Mr. H. lived, would sometimes go with him in it to the Lambeth side, and at others would first make the waterman row about in order as he said to converse with him without interruption, and with more privacy, though the conversation they generally had did not seem much to require it. However the dean never concealed his opinion when he thought it for the service of the public to own it, whatever Mr. H. might do, who had a particular talent in talking a good deal without discovering his own in any thing.

Harley did not, however, limit his contacts to Tories and he had no scruples about befriending Whigs if he thought they might use their influence to plead the moderate cause. The first letters he received from the Whig Duke of Newcastle date from this time, and in the spring of 1703 he was putting out feelers to see whether he could interest this rich grandee in his schemes. Robert Monkton, a man of the centre after Harley's own heart, and one of Newcastle's myrmidons in the north country, did his best to act as a go-between, although he found the Speaker's reluctance to be tied down extremely trying:

I was with his Grace yesterday morning, and I doubt not you will find him disposed to concur with you to your satisfaction. But this is chiefly to tell you that you must of necessity appoint your time when you will be with him. He will otherwise think you are not so sincere with him as he desires to be with you . . . I beseech you do not neglect this caution.

In spite of Harley's initial elusiveness, the friendship with Newcastle soon became firmly established, based on Harley's mixture of political expediency and genuine personal liking.

Besides understanding the need for good personal contacts, Harley had already realized the value of successful public relations. He advised Godolphin to appoint an able writer who would be responsible for putting the government point of view. Godolphin agreed, but was far too busy, miserable, and preoccupied to do anything about it. It was left to Harley to keep a look-out for a suitable man. Strangely enough, he found one in Newgate Prison.

When the Occasional Conformity crisis was at its height, a pamphlet had appeared called *The Shortest Way with Dissenters*. Parodying the melodramatic style that many churchmen had copied from Sacheverell, the author recommended the eradication of occasional conformists who were, after all, no better than snakes and toads. For a few days the Tories enthused about the paper, and were extremely angry when they found that they had been duped. They spared no pains to discover and punish the anonymous author who, when he was found, turned out to be none other than the irrepressible Daniel Defoe. He was sentenced to stand three times in the pillory and to remain in prison during the Queen's pleasure. While in prison, he wrote a witty poem called *Hymn to the Pillory*—that 'Hiroglyphick state machin, contriv'd to punish fancy in'. Like most of Defoe's works, this was very popular and his three days in the pillory did not turn out to be at all the disgrace his persecutors had intended, on the contrary it was a kind of triumph, with the denizens of the city pelting him with flowers instead of the customary rotten eggs, and toasting him with pots of English ale.

The ordeal misfired, but the Tories, headed by Nottingham, tormented the prisoner by cross-examining him endlessly to see whether any member of the government had set him on to write *The Shortest Way*. He was bribed with the prospect of freedom if he could reveal any useful names, but since nobody had sponsored the pamphlet but himself, he was unable to buy his release. Meanwhile his wife and their numerous children were all on the brink of starvation, and it was said that, to add to her troubles, the honest Mrs Defoe was invited, by a certain Lord, to barter her virtue for her husband's release. It looked as if Defoe was in for a long spell of imprisonment, for the wily pamphleteer was far too clever to be trapped into any false confessions.

Then, in July, Harley sent a messenger to Newgate with the brief instruction: 'Pray, ask that gentleman what I can do for him.' To Defoe this was the voice of Providence itself. Taking up his pen, he quoted in reply the blind beggar in St Mark. 'Lord that I may receive my sight,' he wrote. And if Harley became, for Defoe, the embodiment of divine intervention, Defoe was to Harley the very man he had been looking for. All his pamphlets had become an immediate popular success; he was witty, he hated faction and worshipped moderation. It did not take long to find out about Defoe's financial straits and the plight of his family, and soon Harley was writing to Godolphin giving all the details:

I find Foe is much oppressed in his mind with his usage; . . . he is a very capable man, and if his fine be satisfied without any other knowledge but that he alone be acquainted with it that it is the Queen's bounty to him, and grace, he may do service, and this may perhaps, engage him better than any other rewards, and keep him under the power of an obligation.

Godolphin acted promptly. A week later he wrote from Bath, where he had been visiting the Queen:

I have found it proper to read some paragraphs of your letter to the Queen. What you propose about Defoe may be done when you will, and how you will.

Defoe was released in November. As Harley had prophesied, he was so full of gratitude that he was ready to do anything to help his liberators. Once he had considered Harley a Whig deserter; now he thought of him as the successor to William, the new disciple of the haunting ideal of moderation, the golden mean, the point of equilibrium between the extremes. So, when Harley explained to Defoe that his task was to state the facts for the government, to explain policies, create a sympathetic climate, and prevent the masses from 'being imposed upon by the stories raised by ill designing men', he responded enthusiastically.

The government needed all the help it could find. There was a bad spirit of disunity and self-seeking everywhere. 'We have had a very uncertain summer which hath much affected all the rich meadows on the Thames,' Harley wrote to his sister Abigail, 'yet the farmers near the town wish for scarcity to increase the price of their grain.' Troublesome broils, as political controversies were called, kept him in town far longer than expected, and it was not until late August that he reached Brampton. While he was there he still received letters from Godolphin, gloomily predicting that the government would be torn to pieces as soon as Parliament reassembled. St John, the new convert to the moderate cause, apologizing for disturbing a keen sportsman, advised the Speaker to enjoy all the benefits of a country life while he still could. His description of the urban scene was not much more encouraging than Godolphin's:

The chit-chat of this place will bear transcribing no more than one of Sir Chuffer's speeches. . . . There never yet was more gravity and less thought, more noise and less mirth.

The High Tories were as yet strangely ignorant of the Speaker's true position. Some of them confided in him, little realizing that all they told him went straight to Marlborough. 'The Speaker is very industrious,' said Godolphin, 'and has found out things two or three several ways.' It seemed that men of both parties were planning to make capital out of Dutch lack of co-operation, and it was certain there were going to be great complaints about the expense of the war. Marlborough was troubled; he realized that if the High Tories had their way they would quickly ruin the whole alliance:

The conversation that was between Lord Rochester and the Speaker is no doubt the language that he entertains the whole party with: and if they can once be strong enough to declare which way the war shall be managed, they may ruin England and Holland at their pleasure.

The Tories were becoming impossible to work with, and the idea of a central coalition began to take definite shape in the minds of the General and Treasurer.

The Queen, too, was thoroughly out of humour with her Church party. She was hurt by the suggestion that even under her highly Anglican rule the Church could be in danger. Worse still, there were rumours that the Tories intended to criticize publicly the management of the Fleet, a point on which she was particularly sensitive. It was exceedingly tactless to cast aspersions on Prince George, her most beloved Lord High Admiral.

With all these points in mind, Godolphin asked the Speaker to make a list of headings for the Queen's speech. In early October, the royal retinue left Bath for Windsor, visiting various peers on the way. The draft of the speech was discussed there, and the finished result contained many ill omens for the Tories, particularly a hint that the Queen would not give her support to another Occasional Conformity Bill. She was now thoroughly frightened by the bitter feelings which this subject aroused.

The Queen's plea for unity was strongly worded, but in spite of this there was even more division and argument than before. The country was split in half by the Whig–Tory controversy. Swift, who was in London that winter, observed that even the dogs seemed more 'contumelious' than

C*

usual. In December the country was hit by a tempest which wrecked buildings, brought down chimneys and nearly wiped out the English fleet, which was only saved by the skill of British seamen. The storm was seen by many as a judgment on a wicked nation:

> And every time the raging Element
> Shook London's lofty towers, at every Rent
> The falling Timbers gave, they cried—Repent

wrote Defoe in his *Essay on the Storm*.

Harley had hoped that his careful propaganda among the moderate-minded men might have prevented the introduction of a new Occasional Conformity Bill, but the zealots were not so easily deflected. St John was not yet ready to detach himself completely from his old masters, Musgrave and Bromley, and once again lent his debating skill, even though he was quite indifferent about the religious implications. The Tories tried to outwit the Lords by stating less heavy fines for offenders than they had done the year before, and once the Bill was through the Commons they rushed it up to the Lords without a moment's delay, hoping to catch the Whig peers unprepared and out of town. They did not reckon with the Whig party machine, which was highly organized for those days. The Junto lords rapidly arranged proxies for those who could not arrive in time; many others came posting up from the country, and as others had grown chary about the whole idea, the Bill was thrown out by a majority of twelve without a second reading. The Queen did not send the Prince to vote against hypocritical conformists like his own dear self, and her obvious coolness was a considerable hindrance to the sponsors of the Bill. In their fury, the disappointed Tories turned on the Queen, accusing her in newspapers and lampoons of bringing the Church into danger. This did not please her.

Marlborough and Godolphin registered their votes for the Bill, much as they disliked it, for fear of offending the High Tories irrevocably before the introduction of the money Bill in the new year. But all the time they were veering towards Harley's idea of breaking free from the troublesome zealots. They knew that somehow they must lower the political temperature. 'I am glad to hear you talk of calming people in these holidays, and should be glad to have your directions what part I should be able to take towards making men a little more moderate,' Godolphin wrote, rather pathetically, to the Speaker on January 7, 1704.

The money Bill went through, not without the usual broils, and was supported by St John, whose conversion was now complete. The rift between Godolphin and Marlborough and the High Tories was such that it was impossible to come to any kind of agreement at official Council meetings, which were now nothing more than a formality. Policy was decided at secret consultations which took place regularly between Marlborough, Godolphin and Harley. 'It is necessary . . . that the Duke of Marlborough and you and I should meet regularly, at least twice a week if not oftener, to advise upon everything that shall occur,' Godolphin informed the Speaker. The feeling that they were being deliberately excluded made the High Tories feel understandably bitter. They also believed that they were being unjustly thwarted by the Lords, who, encouraged by their success over the Occasional Conformity Bill, were delighting in their new-found power, and preparing to make use of it again.

Various suspicious characters, including Sir John Maclean, head of the Highland clan, had been arrested trying to land from France on the coasts of Sussex and Kent. The Lords attacked Nottingham for his part in the affair, accusing the Tories of negligence in their examination of the suspects. The implication was that the churchmen were too friendly with France and the Pretender to probe too deeply. A new examination was set on foot in the Lords, which put the Commons out of humour, and the session ended in an uproar between the two Houses.

Nottingham, upset by the remarks made about him by Whig Lords, and particularly by Somerset, who was still a member of the Ministry, threatened to resign unless the Queen dismissed all the remaining Whigs in her Cabinet Council. He was sure that the Queen would respect his wishes, since he knew that she liked him personally, was not unmindful of his past services, and was, like him, a lover of the Church. But he overestimated his powers. The Queen was governed by friendships more deeply rooted and she had watched for too long the discomfiture of her servants Marlborough and Godolphin. Nottingham was no favourite of Marlborough's, for he was the man who had been most eager to involve England in the struggle to place Charles of Austria on the throne of Spain, and who was even now pressing for troops to be taken away from Holland and sent to the Peninsula. Godolphin had little sympathy with the man or his principles; Nottingham's attitudes were uncompromising and without shade. He made it clear that he would never rest until the Occasional Conformity Bill was through. He could not countenance the idea of a coalition. The Queen must govern either with Tories or with Whigs; as far as Nottingham was concerned there was no middle way.

Even so the Queen was reluctant; she disliked resignation scenes and would never have chosen to part with such a good churchman. When Nottingham brought her the Seals of his office, she refused three times to accept them before she finally succumbed. More dismal than ever, Nottingham went into a long retirement, never modifying his principles in the smallest detail. Sir Edward Seymour went with him, and the Earl of Jersey, who was highly suspect on account of his French connections and his papist wife.

When the Whigs heard about Nottingham's removal they waited expectantly. For several days they were in suspense, wondering which of them was to be chosen, but they were due to be disappointed. The only Whig called upon was the Earl of Kent, a courtier rather than a career politician, an ineffective character, unlikely to alter the complexion of the Ministry. He was nicknamed 'the Bug', and Dartmouth, with his usual lack of charity, said that he was 'strong in nothing but money and smell'. It would have been difficult to find a more lukewarm successor to the hot-headed Jersey.

There was a great deal of speculation about the Secretary's post. Harley had been thought suitable and a serious candidate as long ago as 1701; in the three years that had passed he had gained greatly in experience and stature. 'He has certainly those qualities which give him exceedingly the preference to any that I have heard spoken of,' Vernon stated in a letter to Shrewsbury. 'The great doubt has been how this is consistent with the Speakership.' There was little doubt in the minds of either Godolphin or Marlborough. 'I take it for granted by the next post to hear Lord Nottingham has given up the Seal,' wrote Marlborough from Vorst on May 7, 'which makes me beg you will take no excuse from Harley but that he must immediately come in.'

It was the Speaker himself who hesitated. In his present position he was courted and admired by men of all parties. Impartial, level-headed and independent, he was ideally fitted for the chairman's role, so much so that it was the common belief the post would be entailed to him indefinitely. 'Whatever distinguishing favour you show on either side, doth not lessen your esteem in the other party,' said his friend Stanley West. ' 'Tis all ascribed to a depth of policy which they cannot comprehend . . . and in such an unprecedented manner do you manage the heads of both parties, that both sides believe, at a proper time and occasion you will show yourself entirely in their distinct interests.'

To accept the Queen's offer of the Seal was to come out into the open—something Harley always preferred to avoid. His friends warned him that once he cast in his lot with the court he would never again be so popular. But it would have been affectation to hesitate too long, especially since it seemed that his dream of a moderate coalition, with the throne at its centre, was likely to become a reality.

As expected, those party leaders who had so recently confided in him turned against him as soon as they understood the game. It was his hidden ambition, the Tories said, which was responsible for the recent upheaval and the resignation of Nottingham. They were shocked to learn that such a faithful churchman had been superseded by this 'spawn of a Presbyterian', as the Dean of Christchurch was pleased to call him. The Whigs were jealous of his success and the Duchess of Marlborough felt that she distrusted him. But much as Marlborough loved his wife, he did not set great store by her feminine intuition. He himself could think of nobody better qualified, or more trustworthy: 'I am sensible of the advantage I shall reap by it, in having so good a friend near her majesty's person to represent in the truest light my faithful endeavours for her service.'

Many moderates welcomed the news of the appointment. The Duke of Newcastle felt greatly encouraged. The Bishop of Hereford had a heart full of joy. Even the old enemy, Lord Coningsby, offered congratulations. St John agreed to lay his brilliant talents at the feet of his new master, and became an energetic Secretary-at-War. The post of Comptroller, vacated by Seymour, was filled by Sir Thomas Mansell, a gay, witty Welsh landowner who was a personal friend and political ally of Harley's. Like St John, Mansell was a convert, a violent Tory turned moderate. Hedges, who had proved rather less of a yes-man than everybody expected, was allowed to stay as Harley's fellow Secretary. He was moved to the southern department, and Harley took over the northern, which included responsibility for Scotland and the northern European states. Hedges proved an amenable and capable colleague, and the two men managed to share their responsibilities without rancour. Marlborough and Godolphin were in complete agreement with Harley's moderate theories, and shared his hatred of party tyranny. 'The Duke, the Treasurer, and yourself are called the Triumvirate and reckoned the spring of all public affairs,' wrote Stanley West. 'Your interests and counsels are so united and linked together that they cannot be broken, nor in any danger of it during this reign.'

Harley was now Privy Councillor, Secretary of State and Speaker of the House. Such a position would be unthinkable in modern times, and was abnormal then. Many wondered whether he would be able to reconcile his different tasks. 'That is only determinable when the Parliament meets, and it will be incongruous or otherwise, according to the humour they shall be in at their sitting down,' warned Vernon. Godolphin had no patience with the critics. ' 'Tis a pretty hard matter to please everybody and especially those who will neither lead nor drive,' he said. 'I never was near so industrious before in my life, and shall be very glad never to have occasion of being so again.' He had chosen wisely. Harley was loyal, hard-working and experienced, in every way well qualified for the job, and he had a formula for controlling the two overbearing parties. 'I know of no difference between a mad Whig and a mad Tory,' he wrote, and continued, quietly, to press for a government by mild-mannered, reasonable men of the centre.

CHAPTER 6

SECRETARY OF STATE

THE SECRETARIES OF STATE were responsible for both home and foreign affairs. Their offices dealt with vital negotiations abroad, as well as the most trivial domestic matters. The French that Harley had learnt during the year after he left Foubert's now stood him in good stead. 'The foreign ministers find he understands French perfectly well,' approved Vernon, 'though it is not yet easy for him to speak it as he does Latin.' But Harley was far less interested in foreign affairs than in the politics, administration and finance of his own country, and this was partly why he took over the northern department with responsibility for the less vital Scandinavian countries.

The Secretaries' responsibilities were heavy, and the system of dealing with routine affairs chaotic. There was no permanent civil service, and officials expected to come and go with the party in power. The lack of continuity was emphasized by the fact that the retiring Secretary had a right to remove all his papers and documents and treat them as his private property. The working accommodation itself was cramped and inconvenient and it was not until October 1705, nearly eighteen months after taking office, that Harley persuaded the Queen to allow him more spacious quarters at the Cockpit, with a room large enough to hold meetings in, and a pleasant outlook over the Privy Garden. The rambling buildings of the Cockpit were a mixture of antiquated offices and much-coveted private apartments. They stood on the north side of Whitehall and before the palace was burnt down in 1697, when reigning monarchs had spent much of their time at Westminster, the offices had been conveniently sited, both for St Stephen's and for consultations with the Crown. Now the Queen lived a good chair-ride away at St James's, and it was not always pleasant or convenient to turn out in the cold night air after a long day in the House. It was worse still whenever the court removed to Windsor, because Ministers were then faced with a three-hour journey after attending to business on a Saturday morning; usually they stayed all Sunday, returning on Monday to another heavy week's work. The

Crown and politics were still so closely linked that plans to rebuild the Palace at Whitehall envisaged court apartments and government offices under one roof, but since such an ambitious scheme was never embarked on, the Queen remained at homely, unimposing St James's, and Ministers accepted the trip across the park as part of their daily routine.

Certainly hardly a day passed without the need for consultation with the Queen. Her signature was constantly required, and her advice about letters to foreign monarchs or about petitioners and many other domestic affairs. Time always being short, the Secretary searched for and found the most convenient means of access to the royal presence; the Queen's friends, and those in the inner circle of power, were admitted by the backstairs entrance, which was easy enough, provided the visitor was on good terms with the pages and, more important still, with the Duchess of Marlborough. The informality of Anne's court amazed foreigners and sometimes alarmed her sworn servants, who felt that it would be all too easy for a potential assassin to enter without being challenged. 'I never saw anybody attending there but some of her guards in the outer rooms, with one at most of the gentlemen of her bedchamber,' commented a Scotsman, Sir John Clerk. When the Duchess was away from court, as she now frequently was, it could prove difficult to gain admission, but it did not take the cunning Secretary long to make the acquaintance of her substitute. Abigail Hill, by a strange coincidence, stood in exactly the same cousinly relationship to Harley as she did to the Duchess. Sarah Marlborough had 'raised her from a broom', and never let her forget the fact; Harley, although he had done nothing to help her in the past, now treated her with respect, flattered and made her his friend. Soon, she was ready to do anything he asked for, in particular to open the door to him whenever she heard his signal scratch—which was all he required, for the time being.

The Queen, too, soon succumbed to his charm. She found his visits a pleasant change from the lugubrious company of Godolphin, or the over-bearing presence of Tory zealots. She liked his political theories; how much more gratifying it was to be told that persons and parties must go to the Queen, and not she to them, than to be ordered about and forced into policies of which she did not approve. Inevitably, in a Queen's court, 'female buzz', as Defoe called it, was all too often heard, and most men were impatient of the feminine atmosphere in which the Queen lived. But Harley never forgot that she was a woman, and courted her as such. He knew that she enjoyed his company, especially when there was no need to stand on ceremony; she was cut off from normal everyday life, and left alone too often with that painful companion, the gout. He provided the link with the outside world, bringing her diverting stories of the town, and entertaining her with a little harmless gossip, or 'snush' as his daughter Tabby called it. 'On pretence of business,' wrote Abel Boyer, 'he was, at last, admitted into her pleasurable retirements, where he had opportunities, not only to study and humour her inclinations but also to insinuate such hints of persons and things, as were agreeable to his designs.' What began as an official business association ripened into friendship, until, as the French plenipotentiary Mesnager later put it, 'let her chagrin be ever so great . . . Harley always had it in his power to cheer her by his representations, and generally left her composed and happy'. Even before he was appointed Secretary, Harley had worked his way into favour, so much so that in 1703 the Queen appointed him housekeeper of St James's, a post which did not involve any duties, and brought in the small sum of £92. 3s. 4d. To go with it, Anne granted him a house adjoining the Palace which gave him a useful *pied-à-terre* and stepping stone for his increasingly frequent visits.

The Queen's official letters to her ambassadors and emissaries were taken to the Cockpit, where they were copied into the letter books before being sent off in the diplomatic bags. Defoe, visiting the Secretary at his office, was shocked to see many important documents lying untended on the tables, or carelessly put between the leaves of the letter book as they awaited copying. He advised his master to tighten up security arrangements at once. He also outlined a plan to form a government intelligence service. The system of espionage was haphazard, and mainly sponsored by individuals, particularly the Secretary-at-War. Defoe wanted to form an office that could be run 'without the help of Mr St John's backstairs'. Although this office would be in touch with agents all over the world, its real purpose would be so secret that even the clerks who worked in it would have no idea that they were part of an intelligence network. It had for a long time been accepted that the country must have its spies abroad, but both Defoe and Harley agreed that it would be valuable for the government to have agents at home as well, who could report on the climate of opinion in the provinces.

Although Defoe's original scheme proved too ambitious, he helped Harley to build up one of the most comprehensive systems of information that England had ever known; at one time he could list sixty-three agents in this country alone, some of them itinerant, like Defoe himself, who went on several news-gathering journeys in England and Scotland, and some of them 'settled', like John Drummond, who was a respected resident in Holland. Contact was kept with 'ear-witnesses' in coffee houses and inns, and the meaner instruments, as they were called, were used as intermediaries—maid-servants, sailors, or doubtful characters who lurked near the sugar houses at Battersea, like the man of middle stature who had a face 'ruddy and full of pimples'. Trusty friends were employed to keep watch on the ports, or to shadow Frenchmen who posed as priests or teachers of languages. Harley, with his love of the clandestine, entered fully into the cloak-and-dagger atmosphere, himself assuming the name of 'Robert Bryan'—a hark-back to his distant castle— and posing as a merchant, so that many of his correspondents did not know that they were working for the Secretary of State. Although the more important agents were furnished with the Secretary's pass, they were ordered not to use it except in the last extremity, and great pains were taken to ensure secrecy:

When it is a little dark you may send your porter for my wife and she will give you my letters. . . . You may cause your porter to put off his livery coat when he brings her. She lodges in Drury Lane at the sign of the Boot and Slipper.

The Secretary was inclined to use men who were indebted to him, often keeping them short of money to ensure that they remained dependent. Official secret service payments tended to be erratic, and although Harley subsidized his agents, he was never in a hurry to pay out. Defoe's letters more often than not ended with an appeal for money to stem the fury of his creditors and the cravings of his seven children. William Greg, a clever young man, whom Harley sent on a fact-finding mission to Scotland, and later used in the office, was almost destitute when the Secretary took him up, and in addition had a record of petty crime. John Ogilvie, a Jacobite conspirator, owed his very life to Harley's intervention, and to show their gratitude he and his wife carried out a dangerous assignment at the courts of Versailles and Saint-Germain. Mrs Ogilvie risked being thrown into a convent for the rest of her life, if caught spying on James's widowed Queen, but her husband did not think there was much risk of that. 'My wife is cunning abundantly and very close-minded and hates the Queen,' he wrote reassuringly. When they returned from France, they and their four children were set up in a small house 'on the other side of the park', which Mrs Ogilvie undertook to furnish very prettily for forty pounds, a sum which they extracted from the Secretary's pocket.

Defoe was far more than an intelligence agent, becoming an unofficial adviser and government spokesman as well. In the summer of 1704, after he had proved his worth by anticipating and helping to defeat a Tory Bill for muzzling the press, and by starting the *Review*, Harley signed the blank warrant for his pardon. Defoe was often invited to York Buildings to advise the Secretary about financial and other problems. Their common dissenting background and similar kind of education helped the two men to understand each other. Besides their mutual love of moderation, both believed in the mercy of God and in His ability to intervene on behalf of people like themselves, who were worthy, industrious and self-reliant. Their association was veiled in secrecy, and Defoe accepted the need for his services to go unacknowledged; he could well understand that it was hardly suitable for a Tory Minister to employ a Whig dissenter as a mouth-piece. His loyalty to the man who had liberated him from New-gate never wavered. Week by week in the *Review* he pressed the moderate viewpoint, providing edifying reading for the dissenting middle-classes. Even when he was on tour, or, in later years, imprisoned for old debts, he never failed to offer advice from the 'Scandalous Club' to the merchants and shopkeepers who enjoyed its gentle satire on the foibles of the age. The *Review* paved the way for the more famous *Tatler* and helped to establish the idea of a continuous publication, which many readers pre-ferred to the vicious essays, lampoons, pamphlets and squibs which so often troubled the politician and shocked the sensitive Puritan.

Harley's intervention on Defoe's behalf was one of the most acute moves he ever made, and he showed the same insight when he appointed as one of his secretaries a Welsh schoolmaster from Carmarthen, Erasmus Lewis. Lewis had served a term as secretary to Lord Macclesfield, the Ambassador in Paris, and he proved to be the ideal assistant, discreet, reliable and loyal. Later he became an intimate friend of Swift's, and was equally at home with politicians and men of letters. He strengthened the team of Welshmen and borderers that Harley was gradually building up at Westminster, and was able to help attend to a mass of minor detail. The domestic letter book, now in the Portland Loan at the British Museum, forms a record of the strangely various business the office had to deal with—prayers for introductions at foreign courts, instructions for the firing of guns at the Tower to celebrate naval and military vic-tories, arrangements to help the wounded or wrongfully imprisoned. The letter book, into which all outgoing letters were meticulously copied, shows that it was the Secretary to whom people applied when they were in doubt about the security of the realm; it was his responsibility, for example, to take into the Royal Mews some horses, including a gelding with three white feet, which, it was said, a Frenchman had bought for the use of Her Majesty's enemies. When an ostler rode through Hereford one Good Friday on an ass, it was the Secretary who ordered the Mayor to see that 'so enormous a crime' should be duly punished.

For Godolphin it was a relief to have a Secretary who was both reliable and loyal. He was depressed as usual in the summer, and there were rumours abroad in June that he talked of 'laying down', but as time went on and the more aggressive Tories drifted away to their country estates, the political atmosphere became, for a while, rather less frenzied than usual, and the Treasurer summoned enough courage to continue. Marlborough had been at his lowest ebb in the spring, tormented by his wife who went into a mad fit of jealousy and accused him of infidelity. He was doubtful of his allies, disgusted with politicians, and in a bad state of health. But, fortified by doses of liquorice and rhubarb, he carried out his plan despite lack of co-operation from almost everybody, and led his army down the Rhine in the lightning campaign that culminated in the victory of Blenheim. In August the Queen received his famous note, giving news of the victory, written with a black lead pencil, on horseback from the scene of the action. There were joyful demonstrations all over the country, and even the Tory squires who, as Thomas Coke put it, had 'groaned so long under the weight of four shillings in the pound, without hearing of a town taken or any enterprise endeavoured', were delighted to hear that at last their money was being put to good use.

The victory was a blow to High Church pride. Anyone would have thought, Sarah Marlborough complained, that the Duke had beaten the Church instead of the French. In the autumn the zealots held meetings at the Fountain Tavern and, under the influence of strong October ale, they made their plans to harry the government and minimize Marlborough's victory. They were not discouraged by the removal of Nottingham; on the contrary, the Tory dismissals had made them even more determined. Harley's brother-in-law, Thomas Foley, reported that Sir Edward Seymour had appeared at Warminster Sessions in August 'very gay, new shaved, with a fine long periwig'. By the autumn he was all ready for the fray. He encouraged his cronies to enthuse about a very indecisive battle in the Mediterranean between Sir George Rooke and the French, which prompted Defoe to express the unpatriotic thought that it would have been better if Rooke had been soundly defeated, since his exploit had given such a handle to his Tory friends at home.

In spite of the lift that the news of Blenheim had given to many hearts, it was uncomfortably obvious to Godolphin and Harley that trouble was brewing among the fanatics. Godolphin's vexation deepened; in October he was troubled with one of his frequent attacks of gravel and stone and was forced to defer his journey to Newmarket, for his friends a sure sign that he was in very bad health. Harley, whose happier temper Godolphin greatly envied, went quietly on, forestalling danger, and assuring the moderates that the angry men would alienate everyone by their tactics, except 'their own dear selves' as he put it. He warned Marlborough that Sir Chuffer and all his hounds would be on to him as soon as he returned, and advised him to ensure that the backward Dutch despatched promised supplies to Portugal without delay if he wanted to avoid being sneered at. Harley himself was not immune from criticism; Defoe, who was out in the country testing public opinion, reported that he had to sit by and hear his master damned. Some people were even jealous because Marlborough had included Harley in the list of people he wrote to immediately after Blenheim, and the fact that the General addressed all his letters to Harley rather than Hedges, who was considered the 'senior' Secretary, also caused unfavourable comment. Most ominous of all, for men of good sense, was the news that the High Tories intended not only to bring in their beloved Occasional Conformity Bill once again, but this time to 'tack', or join, it to the Land Tax Bill. Knowing that the Lords must either accept a money Bill, or reject it outright, the High Tories hoped to put the upper House into a dilemma; either they must accept the Occasional Conformity Bill, or else throw out the urgent money Bill.

There were many level-headed Tories who were patriotic enough to resist a ruse that was likely to harm the war effort. Harley realized that a dangerous schism was appearing in the Tory ranks, and he and his friends encouraged the moderates to part company with their leaders on this issue. 'For God's sake do not at the furthest stay longer than Sunday,' wrote St John on October 16 to his crony Coke, who was lingering in the country, 'because it is most certain our patriots design some gallant thing to open the session with.' Even the Queen did her best by summoning Hooper and asking him to use his influence with the gentlemen of the House of Commons, who, she assured him, would certainly listen to his opinion. She had created Hooper to the see of Bath and Wells after Bishop Kidder and his wife were killed in their Palace during the great storm of 1703, but he was still staunchly High Church in spite of Harley's mid-river indoctrination, and quietly told the Queen that he thought the Bill was a very good one. 'His reasons she approved, but insisted only on the unseasonableness of the time,' commented Hooper's daughter. The Bishop also claimed that Godolphin had made it a condition of his accepting the bishopric that he should vote against the Bill. A great many Tories proved more receptive, and as Harley prophesied, party discipline was not strong enough to persuade men to vote against their consciences. Many who had supported previous Bills now refused to come out in favour of 'the Tack' which was defeated by a large majority. The zealots did themselves great harm by resorting to a device which many Members, regardless of party, believed to be quite unconstitutional. They also alienated the Queen, who had made an explicit plea that Parliament should refrain from re-introducing the Bill at such an unpropitious moment.

Still undaunted, the High Tories brought in and carried a third Occasional Conformity Bill, this time without the Tack, which received its usual treatment in the Lords, although there was a lively exchange between Archbishop Sharp, the Queen's favourite, and Hooper, the newcomer to the bench of bishops:

The Bishop [Hooper] spoke very largely and very fully upon it, which made Archbishop Sharp merrily tell him, that had those that brought him into that house, thought he would behave in that manner, he believed they never would have given him a seat there, to which Bishop H. told his Grace, they should have their seat again, if they would reimburse him the charge they had put him to, to come there.

In spite of Hooper's staunch loyalty to High Church principles, the Whig vote in the Lords was up on the previous year. Altogether, the Tories had suffered a setback, and Harley's contribution to their defeat was recognized by a great many people, including Marlborough, who wrote: 'I hope everybody will do you the justice to attribute the greatest share of it to your prudent management and zeal for the public.'

Enmity between Lords and Commons now reached its climax; the Commons felt bitter and thwarted, the Lords delighted by their growing power, and looking for new opportunities to assert their supremacy over the lower House. A quarrel easily blew up over the right of the Lords to interfere in election petitions; Wharton, a great election manager, and of all the Junto lords the one the Tories found most odious—he was profligate, corrupt and much given to bragging—had for four years been supporting the case of Ashby, a cobbler of Aylesbury, who alleged that White, the Mayor of the town, had deprived him of his vote. After a number of lawsuits, the Lords finally reversed the Commons decision, and this success encouraged Wharton to put forward five more litigants who had also been deprived of their votes, and who in their turn now tried to by-pass the Commons by suing White in the Law Courts.

The Commons, in a frenzy of offended dignity, declared the five guilty of breach of privilege, and Harley, who disliked the whole unsavoury business, was compelled to sign warrants for their arrest. They were imprisoned in Newgate, where they were kept well supplied with provisions by their supporters, and were allowed a stream of sympathetic visitors. Meanwhile the conflict in Parliament mounted, the Commons making declarations about their rights and the Lords replying with heavy pronouncements about the Commons. The Queen, deeply distressed by the ill humour and animosity which she saw all around her, was only too relieved to dissolve Parliament in March, an election being anyway due under the Triennial Act.

It was not a cheerful spring for the court. The Queen was distressed about politics, which made her gout worse than usual. 'There is never any balls at court now,' wrote one of the Verney ladies mournfully. Although some of the beauties blossomed hopefully into their best dresses for her birthday, the Queen refused to have any jollification, and a week later discouraged them further by going into mourning for the Queen of Prussia.

'The Queen must be put upon other thoughts,' noted Harley, seeing the vexation that her former Tory friends had caused. By this he did not mean that she should turn to the Whigs for comfort, but to the moderates who would listen to her wishes and try to govern according to the true interest of the nation. Marlborough was pushing her in the same direction. 'I think at this time it is for . . . the good of England that the choice might be such as that neither party might have a majority.' The Parliament which the triumvirate hoped for was one in which the two parties would be equally matched, giving the court a chance to hold the balance with the help of the moderates. This was difficult to achieve with any certainty. Although it was well known that the Queen could influence the course of an election by conferring favour on one party or the other, it was difficult for her to communicate to the electors her desire for a moderate government. Her friends hoped that if she appointed a few lukewarm Whigs this might have the desired effect; she was persuaded to part with her old flame, the Jacobite Duke of Buckingham, and to bring in, as Lord Privy Seal, the moderate Whig Newcastle, whom Harley had been caressing, to use the contemporary technical term. But they reckoned without the powerful Whig election machinery.

The Whigs had resigned themselves to a long period in the political wilderness when William died. Now, it seemed, Tory folly had put power back in their grasp, and they had no intention of missing any opportunities.

All over the country the powerful electioneering lords briefed their candidates to harry Tory gentlemen who in many cases were used to being elected without opposition after consultations among the leading gentry. In Warwickshire, for example, Sir Charles Shuckburgh and Sir John Mordaunt were shocked to learn that George Lucy, of Charlecote, backed by the Halifax interest, was 'hunting in the country to get votes' and was stirring up opposition among the dissenters in the county. Sir John was branded as a 'tacker', which was enough to make him hated by all non-conformists; not content with that, his political enemies spread a malicious story that he had cheated one of his relations over the sale of some land. Sir John's local vicar, a staunch High Churchman, was very indignant. 'These are practices upon New Moderation Principles which men of such eminent integrity must expect to meet with,' he stated. Fortunately for Sir John, the gentlemen and freeholders of Warwickshire stood together, but in many other areas the Whigs gained ground. It was a straight fight between the Church and the rest of the world; the Tories went into battle chanting their slogan 'The Church in Danger', and carrying banners decorated with toppling steeples. This motif so frightened a Whig bishop's horses at Worcester, that they turned and fled, very much bruising the coachman's 'outer man'. In Coventry the worshipful Mayor himself lost a tooth during an encounter in which the Church party, armed with little clubs, completely routed the 'phana-tick' party or presbyterians, who, it was claimed, were brandishing halberds. When sixty clergy at Chester headed by the Dean came in a body to the poll, some said that hell was broke loose and these were the devil's black guard. The rift between Whig bishops and Tory clergy was only too apparent at this election time, and country vicars harangued their superiors from the pulpit as enemies to the Church. In some places, cathedral windows were broken, all, of course, in the cause of righteous-ness. A neat piece of versification was circulating about the Queen:

> Now she's mother to the church
> She leaves her daughter in the lurch.

This was patently unfair to the woman who had renounced, in favour of the clergy, her right to the traditional dues of the first-fruits and tenths, and it was enough to make her turn against the Church which, at heart, she loved.

The Queen and her triumvirs studied the lists of new Members with considerable uneasiness. As the results came slowly in it was revealed that Whig gold and Tory folly had made their mark. Defoe reported that

Seymour's Western Empire was quite broken. Perhaps more disturbing still was the fact that many of the 'tackers' on the fanatical wing of the Tory party had come back just as before, and where the Whigs were victorious, it was usually at the expense of those who believed in 'the New Moderation Principles'. Godolphin was worried by the number of Junto Whigs, Marlborough was anxious about the tackers. Only Harley seemed unperturbed; he pointed out that the swing to the Whigs, although very marked, did not place them numerically far above the Tories even now, in fact the parties were almost evenly poised, with about seventy court supporters to hold the balance. This was the kind of situation he had hoped for. 'The Queen will be courted and not a party,' he wrote.

All the summer Harley worked hard to gain support for his ideas and to gather a nucleus of sympathetic men before the autumn session. The vote on the Tack had given a rough guide to Members who could be counted as Tory moderates, but the Whigs were less easy to gauge. Defoe advised a direct attempt on the Junto itself and thought that Harley could well work on Somers, who by nature was clear-headed and restrained. Such a frontal attack was, for the moment, too ambitious, but Harley played on Cowper, a Whig lawyer of integrity and good sense, as well as on a host of minor personalities. He kept in touch with Newcastle, assuring him that he would be the foundation-stone of a new Ministry which would include reasonable men of both parties. The Duke tended to be elusive in the summer time, for he was a keen sportsman and forgot all about politics when there was good stag-hunting to be had in Sherwood Forest. The Junto lords were distracted at the thought of his drifting out of their sphere of influence. 'Let me conjure your Grace to leave the diversions and the business of the country for this one year,' Somers wrote hopefully. 'I will not pretend to enter into the detail of particular reasons, for you know more and see a great deal further than I pretend to.' But the Duke was deaf to blandishments; he hunted until he had such a bile that he was easy 'in no posture but in bed'.

The Whigs were no less busy than Harley. They played on Godolphin's known timidity, reminding him that it was they who had thwarted the Occasional Conformity Bill, and who had come to his rescue the previous autumn when he was censured by the Tories for his Scottish policy. They knew that he wanted to effect a union with Scotland; they knew also that the Tories were against it, and that without Whig support he would never achieve his aim. They began to put pressure on him, demanding reward for their support in the past, and refusing to promise help in the future unless he complied with their wishes. This was the kind of pressure

Godolphin found almost impossible to withstand. Where Harley revelled in the subtleties of the central position and was content to play his tune by ear, dealing with each situation as it arose by using his own brand of political instinct, Godolphin needed to be certain, to see the future in clear-cut terms and to know that he had the weight of one or other of the big parties behind him. He did not see how he could rule in the face of criticism from both parties. The uncertainty of the future affected his health; in October, when he should have felt rested and ready for the new session, he was almost in a state of nervous collapse. When Archbishop Sharp asked him how he did, he answered coldly 'as well as a poor man could be, that was run down by them whom he had endeavoured to oblige'. He turned away, and the archbishop noticed that he seemed concerned and 'very near weeping'.

The summer of 1705 was hot and dry; Englishmen sweated in the unusual heatwave, and grumbled about the drought and the taxes. Blenheim seemed a long time ago; both landlords and tenants were feeling the squeeze and needed to have news of another victory. 'Money is a scarce commodity, except where good places help out,' noted Lady Pye, always a good barometer. Nothing was easy for Marlborough that summer; the allies were more uncooperative than ever, and the Dutch, refusing to let him advance, robbed him of certain victory. He complained about everything, even that he could not find any tea that was fit to drink, and by the end of the campaign his spirit was so broken that he had to go off to take the Spa waters. In July his spirits were temporarily raised when the French lines were forced at Brabant, but although Harley and others wrote to him full of extravagant praise, his old enemies, the High Tories, with their 'vile, enormous faction', seemed glad when he met with setbacks. He begged the Queen to protect Godolphin from the onslaughts of party men:

He is the only man in England capable of giving such advice as may keep you out of the hands of both parties, which may at last make you happy, if quietness can be had in a country where there is so much faction.

Marlborough's unhappiness was increased by the fact that his wife was interceding with the Queen on behalf of the Whigs. The Duchess subjected her friend to a war of attrition, but the more she railed, the more the Queen stubbornly adhered to her determination to be ruled by neither party. As for the poor Duke, he was, as Coxe put it, in 'a perpetual struggle between his irritability and conjugal tenderness'.

The Queen did not listen when people complained that the country was being ruled by a cabal of three. She stood firm when Godolphin told her that the Whigs were clamouring for admission. 'Whoever of the Whigs thinks I am to be hectored or frightened into compliance, though I am a woman, is mightily mistaken in me' was her forthright answer. Harley was equally uncompromising. 'I took up my principles not to lay them down because they please not the factious and humoursome,' he wrote to his friend Dr Stratford.

Marlborough was disappointed because the Queen did not root out all tackers and Jacobites in her administration. Godolphin was fearful because she would not come to terms with the Whigs. Already a doubt was lodged in Godolphin's mind; Harley, the faithful right-hand man, the efficient yes-man, was developing ideas of his own. Both Godolphin and Marlborough had always imagined that the Secretary would follow their directions and do as he was told. Instead he appeared to be taking his ideal of moderation so seriously that he was ready to sacrifice loyalty, friends, even the war, to achieve it. Harley denied all this, in the tone of righteous indignation which he had adopted years before when his father accused him of frequenting public houses:

And as to yourself, my Lord, I cannot allow a thought disagreeable to you. I have no other views, no other passions, than to be subservient to your Lordship; if I go astray it shall be only for want of your direction.

Godolphin took this at its face-value; but the Duchess began to look on the Secretary with deepening suspicion. There was something in his manner, his air of subservient, oily charm which to her suggested nothing but duplicity, and she was impatient with Godolphin and the Queen for failing to recognize it.

The Duchess was not the only one who viewed Harley with distrust. He was already learning the difficulties that beset a man of the centre. 'Both sides are against him,' Defoe heard people say, 'he has trimmed so long on both sides, and caressed both parties, till both begin to see themselves ill-treated, and now as he loves neither side, neither side will stand by him.' He himself admitted to Sir Robert Davers, a High Tory Suffolk M.P., that it had been his misfortune for twelve years running to 'get the ill word' from both parties on occasion. Davers evidently accused Harley of deserting his Tory principles, to which he replied that he had only parted company with the party when it ran into 'extraordinary things', and as for his principles, they were exactly the same as those he had held when he first entered the House of Commons. 'I never have willingly nor never will change them,' he asserted, and went on:

I can retire with ease every hour in the day to the same plenty and more peace than I now enjoy, and I shall think myself as great a man in my own bowling green at home, as now in a toilsome office at Whitehall.

The success of the Whigs in the election gave him an excuse, at any rate, to shed the Speaker's load:

I ran the hazard of my life last time, and having once escaped with a few scratches I don't desire to go again into the bear garden.

He would have liked to pass on the chairman's mantle to his old school friend, Simon Harcourt, who had been talked of a year ago as his successor, and who was ready and groomed for the part. But the House was not in a mood to accept another moderate. Each party wanted its own man, a biased zealot who would have no scruples about steering the business of the House along frankly partisan lines. The Tories chose Bromley, the archetypal country Tory, respected and liked both for his ability and his integrity. The Whigs supported John Smith who was favoured by the court and approved of by Godolphin. The contest caused a great deal of interest, both Tory and Whig Members receiving urgent letters pleading with them to come to town in time for the election. The House was split over the issue on clear-cut party lines, and Whig discipline only just prevailed. Smith was elected by a narrow margin, to the great elation of his party. Harley was uneasy about the Whigs and their triumphant attitude; he did not think that they could dominate the situation: 'His party ought not to think they have imposed him [Smith] upon the court, but take it as a grace that they have from the Queen's influence.' Having been Speaker himself for so long, he did not find it easy in the session of 1705-6 to sit back and listen to debates that to his practised eye appeared to be thoroughly mishandled. He complained to Marlborough about the 'Billingsgate language', the blustering and the malice of Members, and the long sittings that made him feel so weary he hardly had the energy left to put pen to paper.

In the autumn of 1705, relieved of his duties as Speaker, he moved into his larger office at the Cockpit which gave him a better chance of dealing efficiently with business. St John, less fortunate, viewed his master's move with a jealous eye. Certainly Harley had achieved enough to arouse the envy of others. All men could see that he was favoured; he held one of the most important offices under the crown; he was trusted and liked by the great. More important still, he had worked his way into the counsels of the Queen. Already, though few knew this, she was signing herself 'your very affectionett freind, Anne R'. He had exerted his magnetic charm, and she had fallen a victim. She listened to his theories, and decided that she liked them. And once Queen Anne made up her mind that she liked something, it took a great deal to change her.

Harley's family probably knew little as yet of the power he wielded over the monarch. Fame had done nothing to alter his friendly unassuming manner. Lady Pye, in London on a visit in the autumn of 1705, reported to his sister Abigail that he was still 'the same cousin Robin Harley; he was so kind soon to find me out and invited me to dinner'. He, for his part, set great store by what he called 'the intrepid virtue and constancy of so many relations'. In the difficult, even dangerous, times that lay ahead, the knowledge that his family would stand by him, the certainty that God watched over him, and the belief that the Queen would support him in every ordeal, was enough to lend him a phenomenal courage and calm.

CHAPTER 7

'THE QUEEN IS THE HEAD'

'MODERATION WAS THE WORD, the passepartout, that opened all the place-doors between the Lizard-Point in Cornwall and the town of Berwick-upon-Tweed,' wrote Roger Coke in the summer of 1705. The Queen, well-tutored by Godolphin, Marlborough and, above all, by Harley, made it clear that the pathway to her favour was the middle course. Harley, having taught her to appreciate men of the centre, would have liked to put the management of her affairs into the hands of moderates like himself. The Tories had lost so many seats at the election that the Queen was justified in replacing some of the Tory Ministers; in particular it was agreed that the time had come to part with Sir Nathan Wright. In the summer the unpopular Lord Keeper had been observed sprucing up his house and whitening the sashes of his windows; it was thought that he had a mind to be 'a sparkish widower', and as soon as the autumn came he had plenty of time on his hands for amorous activities. On October 11 the Great Seal was taken from him. Harley wanted Thomas Trevor, the Lord Chief Justice, to succeed him. Like Simon Harcourt, Trevor was a member of the old-boy network of Birch's Academy at Burford; he was an able lawyer and had been well schooled in the moderate line. As Lord Keeper he would have held a key position for the men of the centre, using his power to make appointments— including many Church ones—for the cause of good sense and forbearance. But he declined the post, and the Whigs were soon clamouring to fill the vacancy with their candidate. They had after all stood by Godolphin in times of crisis, and helped him to steer the money Bills through Parliament.

Reluctantly, Harley felt bound to tell the Queen that the Whigs must be placated. This did not mean opening the door to the Lords of the Junto—far from it. All through the summer he and others urged her to consider William Cowper, a man of good sense, whose appointment would act as a peace offering to the Whigs, and who might in time be wooed away from the main body of his party. The Queen had learned her lesson too well, as she showed in a letter to Godolphin:

I wish very much that there may be a moderate Tory found for this employment. I must own to you I dread the falling into the hands of either party, and the Whigs have had so many favours showed them of late, that I fear a very few more will put me insensibly into their power, . . . I do put an entire confidence in you, not doubting but you will do all you can to keep me out of the power of the merciless men of both parties.

Marlborough was in agreement with the Queen. 'All the care imaginable must be taken that the Queen be not in the hands of any party, for party is always unreasonable and unjust,' he wrote to Godolphin in July, and in September Harley was echoing the refrain:

If the gentlemen of England are made sensible that the Queen is the Head, and not a party, everything will be easy, and the Queen will be courted and not a party; but if otherwise . . .

On the one hand, Godolphin had to listen to the Queen and his two fellow triumvirs urging the non-party line. On the other he was nagged by Sarah Marlborough and the Whigs, who announced unkindly that they had the Lord Treasurer's head in a bag—not a position that he relished. He was grateful to Harley for supporting him in his campaign for Cowper's appointment, caring little that Harley urged the Queen to give only a little ground. All that mattered to Godolphin now was that he should succeed in placating the Whigs; if, later, they demanded more concessions, he would deal with that problem when he came to it. So, on October 11, Cowper went in Godolphin's coach to Kensington, where he received the Seal with a salary of £4,000 and the promise of a peerage.

The Tories, stung by their election losses, had no intention of playing a docile rôle in Parliament. Their October meetings at the Fountain Tavern were ominously well attended, and plans were laid to harry the Queen and her managers. The Grumbletonians, as Coke quaintly called them, were just as venomous in opposition as they had been in power. Rochester, realizing that he had irrevocably offended his niece, decided that he would ensure a better future for himself by befriending the next in succession. The Electress Sophia was said to favour him, and he had no scruples about increasing his popularity in Hanover by inviting her to visit England. Rochester and his cronies took a fiendish delight in observing both the annoyance of the Queen and the discomfiture of her Ministers who were faced with the dilemma of offending the present monarch, or of alienating the future one and appearing to be against the Protestant Succession.

Hearing about the Tory plot in the nick of time, Godolphin sent urgent messages to the Whig Lords to prepare their defences against the 'great guns' of the Tory attack. Admitting the dangers that might arise on the Queen's death when it was remembered that the Pretender could reach England in no more than three days, whereas the Hanoverian heir might take up to three weeks, the Whigs decided to press for a Regency Bill, to appoint regents empowered to carry on the administration until the arrival of the new sovereign. This move was calculated to spare the Queen's feelings and to reassure the Hanoverians. The Tories, in the end, did themselves more harm than good, for the Queen disconcertingly decided to listen to the debate. She was hurt by Haversham's tactless mention of the painful subject of the Duke of Gloucester and of how different everything would be if the child were still alive. Worse still, Anne's old admirer, the Duke of Buckingham, went so far as to prophesy that the Queen might survive her faculties and become a child in the hands of others, an idea she understandably found distasteful.

The old lady of Hanover never completely forgave the Whigs for depriving her of a pleasant trip to England. As she had once told King William, she was 'neither so philosophical nor so foolish as to dislike hearing a Crown talked of', and as she walked along the gravelled walks outside the Palace at Herrenhausen, and listened to the nightingales, and fed the ducks and swans, she often thought of England and the English. Englishmen who had visited her mother's court had often flattered her with their admiration, valuing her shrewdness and wit above her sisters' more obvious charms. So she held herself in readiness, nursing her ambition to have the words 'Queen of England' graven on her tomb. But Anne gave her no encouragement; the mere thought of the successor being invited over made her agitated and upset, and as she sat under the gallery in the Lords and listened to the Tories deliberately mortifying her with the suggestion, she turned with finality from those men who had, at the start of the reign, been so high in her favour. The final indignity came when Rochester brought up the controversy about the Church in danger, and a heated argument developed between him and Lord Halifax —'Hothead and Testimony,' Dartmouth christened them. It was left to the Whig Lord Somers to move that the Church had never been in danger since the time that King William set foot on England's shores, and was still safe under the Queen.

The complete failure of their tactics served to silence the Tories for the time being. Early in 1706, for a few brief months, the political atmosphere was calm. Godolphin persuaded Marlborough to 'live friendly'

DANIEL DEFOE

JONATHAN SWIFT

MATTHEW PRIOR

with the Whigs, and the Queen was in a grateful mood. For a while she and Sarah could feel at ease with each other:

I believe, dear Mrs. Freeman, we shall not disagree as formerly we have done; for I am sensible of the services those people have done me, that you have a good opinion of. . . . I am thoroughly convinced of the malice and insolence of others that you have been always speaking against.

The Whigs, appreciating the part that Harley had played in persuading the Queen to accept Cowper, looked on him with favour and learned to value his balanced judgment. In January Harley gave a public demonstration of his good relationship with the Whigs by giving a dinner party to which he invited Godolphin, Marlborough and any Whigs who were prepared to publish their friendly feelings towards the triumvirate. Somers went away to the country, somewhat pointedly, just before the party, but in spite of his gesture there was a cheerful gathering; political conviction had to be very strong before a man resisted the offer of an evening's entertainment with wine from Harley's excellent cellar. The host proposed a toast to 'Love and Friendship and Everlasting Union'. Cowper, under the influence of Harley's sweet, thick, Hungarian tokay, replied with a quip about the Secretary's love of dissimulation and tricks. 'His White Lisbon was best to drink it in, being very *clear*,' he said. Cowper was one of the people who could never bring himself to trust Harley. 'If any man was ever born under a necessity of being a knave, he was,' he wrote.

For the moment, however, the general atmosphere was friendly and good-humoured, and the early months of 1706 were relatively serene. On March 19 the Queen celebrated with a speech from the throne and Members went off to the country with her delight in the concord between herself and Parliament ringing in their ears. The Marlboroughs were quiescent, the Duchess satisfied by the progress of the Whigs, the Duke in such good health and spirits that some said they had never seen him look so well. His campaign on the continent began with the victory of Ramillies, and the Duchess was pleased when Harley wrote that her husband had united the characters of Scipio and Hannibal. Harley's brother Edward, now joint Auditor of the Imprest, scrutinized the Duchess's accounts, and the Harleys congratulated her fulsomely on her frugal housekeeping. When she complained that a spy had been detected among her personal servants, Harley pledged himself to chase the offender 'with all imaginable cheerfulness and diligence'.

In that summer of truce in the English political world, the Union

D

between England and Scotland was born. The situation between the two countries had grown almost intolerable; ever since the outbreak of war, the French had been sending agents over to stir up trouble north of the Tweed and to keep the English in a constant state of anxiety about their northern border. The Scots, proud by nature, resented any interference in their affairs, and their hatred of their English neighbours had been increased by the failure of the Darien scheme. Such a wild and ill-planned bid to escape from the endless toil and famine of life in Scotland's barren hills was probably doomed to failure from the start, and the humid swamps of Panama were hardly the best setting for Utopia; nevertheless the jealous English merchants had done all they could to bar the Scots from the Indies trade both in the West and the East. Scotsmen who had gambled their meagre savings in the hopes of helping their country capture trade in the rich markets of the world vented their hatred and disappointment on the English, and began to demand a King of their own, to guard their interests and to defend them against English selfishness. More far-sighted men realized that the best solution to the problem would be the union of the two countries under one Parliament, but attempts to effect this in the early months of Anne's reign failed because of the reluctance of English merchants to give concessions and the High Tories' unwillingness to accept the establishment of the Scottish Presbyterian Church.

After the breakdown of these negotiations the situation deteriorated rapidly. Feeling in Scotland ran high against Ministers who had treated with the English. The Scottish general election produced a Parliament dominated by the 'Country Party' which was primarily determined to defend the Presbyterian Establishment. Many Scotsmen hoped for the establishment of a Stuart King in preference to the Hanoverian heir favoured by the English, especially if James, the Pretender, could be prevailed upon to turn Protestant. The new Parliament brought in and passed the Act of Security, and in so doing gave itself the power to choose a successor on the death of Queen Anne; the Scottish monarch would be of the royal line and a Protestant but not the same as the English successor unless England pledged herself, among other things, to grant free trade between the two nations. In this Act the Country Party had the backing of the Jacobites, who hoped to influence the Pretender, and of the Duke of Hamilton who, being closely related to the royal Stuarts, saw himself as a possible candidate if James refused to turn Protestant.

Queensberry, who had done much good work as King William's and Queen Anne's Commissioner, was, at this crucial time, unable to

give the English any assistance. A moderate-minded Whig, and a Presbyterian who was devoid of bitter feelings towards the Episcopalians, he
had so far managed to carve a safe course for himself in all the conflicts
between Jacobite and Presbyterian, Country Party and New Party—this
last a group of independent Whigs known as the *squadrone volante*. But
he made himself so unpopular that the Queen felt bound to dismiss him
and call on the *squadrone* for help. The peers she turned to—Tweed-
dale, Rothes and Roxburgh—were no match for the experienced Queensberry. Although they promised to make the Scottish Parliament accept
the Hanoverian Succession, they found that they were quite unable to do
so, for they were faced by an unholy alliance headed by Queensberry,
who had temporarily joined the Jacobites. Hamilton, Queensberry and
Atholl used their combined strength to demand the Queen's consent
for the Act of Security. They threatened that if the Queen withheld the
touch of the sceptre they would refuse supplies and disband the Scottish
army. The time was August 1704, just before the news came through of
Marlborough's victory at Blenheim. The future looked dark, with little
hope of success on the continent and the prospect of insurrection and
anarchy in Scotland in the autumn. Godolphin felt he had no choice
but to advise the Queen to give her consent to the Act. If he had been able
to wait a few days longer and the news of Blenheim had come through,
he would have been able to withstand Scottish pressure, secure in the
knowledge that the French forces had been lacerated. As it was, the
deed was done, and in that session of Parliament he faced a vicious attack
from the High Tories. In December, Godolphin, hesitant and unsure of
himself in spite of the sympathetic presence of the Queen at the debate,
made a poor attempt at defending himself. He was attacked first of all
by Lord Haversham, the renegade Whig turned Tory who fancied himself as a speech-maker, and the Whigs then entered the fray in the person
of Halifax who unexpectedly echoed Tory criticism. But while Halifax
was still speaking, and Godolphin became progressively more nervous,
Lord Wharton ostentatiously crossed the House and engaged the
Treasurer in earnest conversation. 'Honest Tom', as he was called, was
obviously bargaining with Godolphin for Whig support. Certainly, when
the whispered colloquy was over, the whole tenor of the Whigs' approach
was altered. They supported Godolphin, saved him from his enemies, and
suggested that if the Scottish Parliament was not prepared to negotiate, it
must expect reprisal in the form of an Alien Act which would treat all
Scotsmen as foreigners and rob them of their principal exports, including
cattle. This measure was enough to ruin Scotland's economy but, although

it almost led to war between the two nations, it proved to both in the end that the time had come for an Act of Union.

The success of the Whigs in the 1705 election helped to create a sympathetic atmosphere for the introduction of negotiations, and in Scotland the nation vented much of its bitterness on the avengeful and unjust hanging of Captain Green, the twenty-six-year-old commander of the English trading vessel, the *Worcester*, who was accused on false evidence of seizing a Scottish ship and murdering her crew. The hanging of Green acted as a ritual murder; blood was let and national honour was saved. The weak lords of the *squadrone volante*, who lacked sufficient courage to announce Green's reprieve to the Edinburgh mob, were removed from office, and the moderate Seafield joined with Argyll and Queensberry to form a new Ministry. After a great deal of wrangling in Scotland throughout the summer of 1705 it was agreed to appoint Commissioners. The Scottish delegation was chosen in February 1706 and included, on Queensberry's recommendation, only those who had proved themselves good Unionists, and with no more than a single Jacobite. Archbishop Sharp was the only High Tory on the English Commission, which consisted of Whigs and ministerial Tories, including Harley.

In 1704, Harley declared in the House that he knew no more about Scotland than he did about Japan, but by 1706 he had become one of the most knowledgeable men in the government about Scottish affairs. His agents had been sending him reports of Scotsmen openly drinking the Pretender's health, and 'hugging an airy phantom', as one of the agents put it, in the shape of the Stuart succession. William Greg, who went on a fact-finding mission in 1705, put his finger on the deeper cause of discontent, the pitiful poverty of the Scottish nation, born of bad agriculture, barren soil and feudal conditions, and heightened by the failure of the Darien project and a succession of bad harvests. Greg told Harley that any remedy for this 'epidemical distemper' would be readily welcomed. When Greg was recalled, Harley sent Defoe to Scotland, charged with the task of spreading the news that the Queen and her servants were sincerely in favour of the Union. He was also expected to write once a week describing the true state of affairs across the border. Defoe's letters were shown to Godolphin who agreed that they contained valuable information which should be used as a guide by the Commissioners. Harley's agents gave an independent view, stressing the need to win the Scots by the offer of generous financial terms. With this advice in mind, the English Commissioners began their meetings at the Cockpit, only communicating with their Scottish counterparts, who met in a separate room, through the exchange of minutes. It was important that the Scots at home should not be led to believe that their delegates were being over-influenced by the English, and for eight weeks Commissioners on both sides showed great restraint, spending all day at the committee table and in the evenings keeping themselves to themselves. It was not hard for the Scottish Commission to accept the terms offered; although the 'bonny blewcaps', as Harley dubbed them, were to lose their separate Parliament, and all affairs were to be regulated by the united Parliament of Great Britain sited in London under the rule of a single monarch, Scotland was to keep her church and her native law. Since the Scottish taxpayer was to assume some of the burden of the national debt which had been contracted before the Union, a sum of £398,085. 10s. was paid over as an 'equivalent' and proved an invaluable aid in setting the frugal Scots on a more stable economic foundation. Part of the money was earmarked for the shareholders of the Darien company, who had certainly never expected to see again the money sunk in that pestilence-ridden scheme.

The only point which caused any considerable controversy was the number of Scottish representatives there should be in the English Parliament; but even this was settled after a joint meeting held under the surveillance of the Queen. Harley reported on the outcome to Newcastle who, though a member of the Commission, had drifted away to the country, unable to stand the heat of midsummer London, or to resist the temptation of a season's hunting:

We have stretched our consciences to forty-five *and no more* for the House of Commons, and sixteen for the Lords, and expect the Scots' answer on Tuesday, who are certainly in the right to take *an they can.*

On July 22 the articles were sealed and signed by the Commissioners and afterwards presented to the Queen at St James's Palace. Cowper, heading the Commissioners who filed into the presence in twos, forgot his lines, and had to search for the script of his speech in his pocket—a piece of English inefficiency which the Scots viewed with dour disapproval.

To the Queen it seemed a moment of great satisfaction. For once she was at the centre of a group of glittering court ladies, and she saw the eminent men of her day file past her, their feuds and jealousies forgotten. The signing of the Union Treaty was a proof that party differences could be laid aside in the interest of peace and unity.

As usual the Queen's satisfaction was short-lived. Once the negotiations were safely completed, the Whig lords turned to their own plans.

They had given Queen and court their full support and now expected a due reward. They did not relish the idea of serving with moderate Tories, a concept which, according to Halifax, was like 'mixing oyl and vinegar (very truly)'. Cowper's appointment was, to the Whigs, nothing more than the prelude to a large-scale take-over bid. The plan was to force the Junto members, one by one, into the Cabinet. Sunderland was to be the first; he was 'pitched upon', in eighteenth-century parlance, in the mistaken belief that the Queen would look kindly on him because he was the Marlboroughs' son-in-law. The Duchess was primed to press Sunderland's suit, which she carried through energetically, assuring the Queen that she did so, not for family reasons, but for noble political considerations. The Queen did not appreciate this approach; she disliked court ladies who meddled in politics, and would have been far more sympathetic if the Duchess had pleaded as a mother rather than as a high-powered female Whig. Subjected to endless teasing—the Duchess's word—the Queen became more stubbornly determined every day to resist Sunderland's intrusion. She did not like the man; he was hot-tempered and dictatorial, just like his mother-in-law:

I am afraid he and I should not agree long together, finding by experience my humour and those that are of a warmer will often have misunderstandings between one another.

As summer turned to autumn her resistance stiffened. Every letter was a political *credo*, a statement of her determination to be a Queen and not a slave:

All I desire is, my liberty in encouraging and employing those that concur faithfully in my service, whether they are called Whigs or Tories, not to be tied to one, nor to the other.

She vented all her disappointment, her irritation and humiliation in a famous *cri du cœur*:

Why for God's sake, must I, who have no interest, no end, no thought, but for the good of my country, be made so miserable, as to be brought into the power of one set of men?

Godolphin found the Queen's attitude exasperating. He knew that the Whigs would have to be placated. He had sold his soul to Honest Tom Wharton during the debate on the Act of Security. In those crucial few minutes, the Junto lords, not for the first time, had saved his skin, and he was now convinced that he was in their debt and must grant them their requests. He tried to explain his dilemma to the Queen, but she refused to see his point of view even though he pressed it upon her almost daily, with dogged persistence. At last the strain became too much and he began, once again, to talk of resignation. 'I cannot struggle against the difficulties of your majesty's business, and yourself at the same time,' he wrote, with brutal frankness. His tone became injured and pathetic:

I have no house in the world to go to but my house at Newmarket, which I must own is not at this time like to be a place of much retirement; but I have no other. I have worn out my health, and almost my life, in the service of the crown.

The Queen found this emotional blackmail upsetting, but still she would not give way, and for weeks Mr Montgomery and Mrs Morley, as she liked to refer to herself, continued to torment each other.

It is easy to understand the Whig point of view. The Junto lords knew themselves to be capable of administering the government, and naturally it made them impatient to stand by and watch the Queen cling to a few pallid moderates. They felt that instead of being grateful to them for their support of the war and their hard work in framing the Union, she was spitefully keeping them out of office and thus wrongfully exploiting the power and prerogative that still remained in her royal hands. But Harley's creed, too, had a rational foundation. In his eyes, the Queen was the only bridge between the parties. If she once allowed herself to be governed by one party or the other, the nation would be split into two angry camps, with the inevitable danger of the outbreak of civil war. So long as men of all parties had one common focal point of loyalty, the country would be safe. 'The foundation of the church is in the Queen,' Harley wrote in September, 'the foundation of liberty is in her! Let her therefore be arbitress between them.'

Harley had two other valid points which he tried to express to Godolphin. He was convinced that if the Queen capitulated completely to the Whigs, the opposition party might well become desperate. Banned from office, the Tories could metamorphose themselves into the great peace party, encouraging war-weariness and refusing to vote supplies. Harley's second point was that the Whigs, even when united, were still an 'inferior number', besides which he believed that there were many moderate Whigs who disapproved of the Junto's dictatorial methods: 'they will not follow those who make themselves their leaders.'

Marlborough, still on the continent, was distressed to hear of the uneasiness of his friends. It was well known now that his wife was on very bad terms with her royal mistress, and although he never ceased to warn her against meddling, the Duchess continued to force on the Queen a succession of unfortunate interviews and letters. When Queen Anne tried to be tender and heal the breach, Sarah Marlborough expressed herself 'uncapable' of changing her opinion, and continued to remind her, maddeningly, of distant days when things had been so different. Marlborough himself, somewhat against his better judgment, for he had no great opinion of his son-in-law's tact and temper, urged the Queen to admit Sunderland, for Godolphin's sake. But the political squabbling and the angry threats of the Whigs made him feel weary and that autumn his hair started to go grey.

Further worry was caused by rumours that Harley and St John were plotting trouble in the forthcoming session. The Duchess and her Whigs were suspicious of Harley's motives, and began to think that he was responsible for the Queen's intransigence. Cowper had never trusted Harley; earlier he had suspected him of failing to prosecute satirists who had vilified the Marlboroughs, in order to protect Tory friends. Now he complained to Newcastle that the Secretary had become 'less kind' than before. Harley, when approached, denied that he had any sinister motives, but his secretive, sly manner and his involved style of writing made people doubt his sincerity. His letters were said to be full of 'professions' or 'expressions' which the Duchess and her friends refused to take at their face value, and which made Godolphin feel uneasy. 'I doubt so much smoke could not come without some fire,' he commented.

At least Harley had the support of his disciple St John; the Whigs, St John believed, would not be satisfied until all the scum of their party had taken its share of employments. When Harley was in Herefordshire in November, a month of torrential rain, St John wrote:

Nothing, dear Master, will continue long which exceeds its due bounds, but a short-lived inundation may prove a lasting evil. The torrent may make such havoc and leave such scars in a little time as years will not repair. If you will give me leave to bring the allegory more close, no husbandman in his right senses ever let that flood violently in to spoil his ground and destroy his fruits which with care he might have guided in gentle streams to the improvement of both.

But St John's encouragement was not enough. The Queen soon realized that the Whigs were in an ugly mood, and she was afraid that if she provoked them further they would turn on Harley. Unenthusiastically and with a bad grace, she removed Hedges and reluctantly handed the Secretary's Seal to Sunderland.

CHAPTER 8

THE MALICE OF THE WHIGS

HARLEY PROMISED GODOLPHIN that he would remain faithful and continue to work for the good of the nation even though he disapproved of Sunderland's appointment. He kept his dislike of his new colleague to himself, and it was not for some months that the antipathy between the two men became common knowledge. His relationship with Hedges had been a happy one; both Secretaries had been hard-working and conscientious and ready to co-operate. Sunderland, too proud to attend to everyday routine, and determined from the start to treat his fellow Secretary as a junior partner, was a far less easy proposition, and it was not long before the strain of working with an uncongenial companion began to tell on Harley. He had been over-straining himself for years; like so many other politicians, he pushed himself too hard. On January 25 he collapsed at his office desk.

His brother Edward hastened to his side, and stayed with him until the doctors arrived and administered a bleeding. In the evening he was reported to be much better, but extravagant rumours about his illness began to spread through the coffee houses. The debate on the money Bill had reached a crucial point and Godolphin was once again in difficulties. The Tory opposition, still a strong force, had reserved its attack until the final clauses; criticism was concentrated on government spending of nearly a million pounds beyond the original estimate drawn up the previous year. The money had been used, wisely enough, to pay the forces used by Prince Eugene of Savoy, Marlborough's most trusted colleague in his successful campaign in Italy. Eugene, who had spent most of his life mastering the military art and fighting Austria's battles, was one of the few allied commanders who could be relied upon to put money to good use. But the Tories were out to make trouble, while the Whigs refused to come to Godolphin's rescue, determined as they were to teach him how dependent he was on their support.

Always careless of his own health and safety, Harley insisted on going to the House the next day to defend Godolphin. He appeared unexpectedly

D*

when everyone believed him to be fatally ill. He was a master of the showman's art, and he played on his condition, assuring everybody that it might well prove mortal. If he should die, he said, let them carve on his tomb that he had advised the Queen to spend the offending million in the national interest. Many Members were overcome with emotion. The Whigs rallied round and the proposition vindicating the expenditure was voted by a majority of 252 to 105.

Harley's well-timed effort helped the Ministry out of its difficulty, but Godolphin did not express any great gratitude, and the Secretary's friends were afraid that he had done himself a great deal of harm with the Whigs who were now less likely to trust him than ever. Many moderates were alarmed by the thought that illness or political misfortune might remove Harley from the scene. Defoe wrote from Edinburgh:

The body is not made for wonders and when I hint that denying yourself needful and regular hours of rest will disorder the best constitution in the world, I speak my own immediate experiences. . . . I beseech you, pity your country in the sparing yourself for a work so few but you are able to go through.

St John wrote expressing his unreserved affection, wishing Harley health not only as a friend, but as a good Englishman. Even more heart-warming was St John's report of an interview he had had with the Queen, in which she expressed her concern in deep-felt terms, said a great deal about Harley having prejudiced his health in her service, and in general seemed genuinely troubled.

Harley took a long period of convalescence, and was absent from the House in the final debates about the Treaty of Union, when Tory opposition to the establishment of a separate church in Scotland was overcome. In March the Act of Union was passed. When Defoe wrote from Edinburgh on March 10, guns were firing from the castle; his man brought him the Queen's speech and *Nunc Dimittis* came into his head—'Now let me depart from hence for my eyes have seen the conclusion.' The Union was proclaimed at the Cross, the Scottish Parliament adjourned in perpetuity, and Defoe's task was finished, except for a last tour of western Scotland to preach peace and good manners.

In England there was great rejoicing and on May 1 St Paul's was the setting for a magnificent thanksgiving service. The Queen travelled in a procession of four hundred coaches and the solemnity of the occasion was rounded off with a fine piece of music. Sir John Clerk noted with satisfaction that at no time were Scotsmen more acceptable to the English than on that day. But in Scotland there was less music and more discord.

Defoe began to think he would have to leave the country since the feeling against Englishmen was running so high. Many Scotsmen had foreseen a chance of quick profits and, before the Union came into force, imported many goods at the old low Scottish rates, hoping to flood the English market with cheap goods under the new free-trade clause. Even Defoe himself jokingly suggested that he should buy his master a tun of rich claret, which he said, might prove cheaper than a hogshead at present prices. The English merchants were disgusted by such tactics, and after an outcry in Parliament, customs officials impounded many Scottish goods. The Scots, in their turn, were outraged, and Defoe was reproached with all he had said about the honour and justice of the English Parliament:

'Aye, aye,' says one of them, 'Now you see how we are to be served! and what we are to expect from a British Parliament! How early they begin with us, and what usage we are to have whenever our advantage clashes with their interest.'

Defoe begged Harley to use his influence on behalf of the Scottish merchants, for bitter feelings were always near the surface. The Jacobites were only too ready to take advantage of the difficulties, and several of Harley's agents reported activity at Saint-Germain and plans under way for a great gathering at the Duke of Atholl's hunting lodge. There were even reports that the Pretender was due to arrive shortly 'incog', and that he would find 30,000 men ready at a word. But James missed his opportunity; nothing was ready, and while he ponderously made plans which took nearly a year to complete, the Scots had time to taste the advantages of Union. Harley helped to smooth over the difficulties caused by the initial influx of cheap goods, and before long economic interdependence began to bring the prospect of new prosperity to the Scottish lowlands and hills.

Godolphin found himself gloomily unable to rejoice about the Union. In the spring he was fretting about the future and predicting a thousand difficulties and inconveniences in the summer that lay ahead. He no longer trusted Harley, and although he continued his declarations of humble servitude—particularly when he wanted something done—the easy confidence of their earlier relationship had vanished. In the counsels of state Harley's influence was diminishing; once, when there had been difficulties about parliamentary procedure, he had been consulted as the expert, but now, when a quarrel blew up as to whether the first Parliament after the Union would be proclaimed as 'new', Harley's view (he considered that it should be termed the 'old Parliament' until the next election) was thought to be mere hair-splitting. Marlborough, who would once have bowed to his opinion, opposed him, and it seemed as if the General's trust, too, was wavering. Godolphin's depression increased when the news came through in April that the allied armies in Spain had been roundly defeated at Almanza; he knew that his political enemies would make all the trouble they could out of this military fiasco, and he knew too that he would be forced to turn to the Whigs for support. And the Junto continually made it clear that it would expect more rewards for its help.

In the spring of 1707 Sarah Marlborough's intermittent quarrel with the Queen boiled up to one of its crises. Abigail Hill, innocent-looking and discreet, became secretly betrothed to Prince George's Groom of the Bedchamber, Samuel Masham, the son of an impoverished baronet. The Queen approved of the match, since it meant that her favourite dresser would still be able to live in the Palace and attend to her needs as before. With almost indecent secrecy and haste, the marriage was celebrated at Dr Arbuthnot's lodgings in the presence of the Queen. Lack of tact, or fear of the gorgon's anger, or even plain defiance, made the Queen and Abigail neglect to inform the Duchess of their plan. At first she was prepared to be magnanimous, attributing the lapse to 'bashfulness and want of breeding'. She was generous-minded enough to embrace her cousin tenderly and wish her joy. But it was the last time Abigail was to be locked in those particular arms, for as the Duchess began to 'search to the bottom', she found out that whereas the Queen had been invited to the wedding, she, the girl's guardian and benefactress, had not even been asked to give it her blessing. For a long time now, she suddenly realized, she had been feeling uneasy about Abigail. Little incidents, disregarded at the time, came back to her. She remembered especially one evening when she had decided to visit the Queen, using a secret passage from her own apartments. As they sat chatting, the door burst open and Abigail came in with 'the boldest and gayest air possible'. As soon as she saw the Duchess, Abigail stopped dead, assumed an air of subservience, gave an exaggerated curtsey and asked, in the humble voice of a menial, 'Did your majesty ring?' With this she left the room.

The Duchess was alarmed. She had to face the fact that she had been supplanted, and she accused Abigail of ill designs. Abigail responded icily that she was sure the Queen, who had always loved the Duchess extremely, would continue to be very kind to her. Such condescension was more than the Duchess could stand. She tried to wrest an apology from the Queen, who simply said that Abigail was 'mightily in the right' to keep away from the Duchess, considering she was so angry. Sarah, of course, was sure that the situation was full of sinister undertones. She, more than anybody, knew just how the Palace staff was organized, and particularly how the Bedchamber Woman lurked within hearing-distance when Ministers visited the Queen, officially on hand to pour out another dish of tea if required. An unscrupulous politician could easily use one of the Queen's attendants as a spy, instructing her to listen to conversations and to report back in detail. Sarah Marlborough knew that the artful Harley was accustomed to placing spies in key positions; it was part of his job. He was a man 'who knew perfectly well the management of such an affair'. She leapt to the conclusion now that he was Abigail's 'great director', and convinced herself that the two of them were plotting a *coup* to undermine the authority of Godolphin and the Whigs. Marlborough tried to soothe her down, suggesting that she should do nothing until he returned and could, with Godolphin's help, tell the Queen what was 'good for herself'. If that did not work, the only solution was to remain quiet and let Mr Harley and Mrs Masham do what they pleased. The General owned that he felt quite tired; he could not stand much more of such female bickering. The Duchess, of course, refused to listen to her husband's advice. She continued to accuse and nag and make herself unpleasant both to the Queen and Abigail. 'As for her looks, indeed they are not to be described by any mortal but her own self,' Abigail told Harley. By the autumn even the Duchess herself had to admit that she had lost her influence at court. As she put it to a friend:

'Tis plain you live in the country by your writing to me to ask a favour of the Queen, to whom I never have the honour to speak of anything but what concerns my own offices, and in that I can't prevail.

The Duchess and her cronies, now alerted, watched closely for any signs of plotting between Harley and the Queen. The Whigs believed that Anne should show her favour by appointing only men of Whiggish persuasion in the key church positions. For them one of the most pleasant perquisites of power was the ability to distribute ecclesiastical plums to their friends and relations, and, most important of all, to ensure that the House of Lords was well packed with Whig prelates. Even such an upright character as Cowper was shocked to find himself recommending a prebend, against his better judgement on the advice of his mother, of all people. But the Queen closely guarded her own prerogative in the field of church appointments, and she tended to take the advice of her friend Archbishop Sharp, who was himself a Tory, although he refused to be used as a political tool. In 1706, when the Queen asked him to vote against his Tory friends, he gallantly replied that he always voted according to the best sense he had, and would always show himself a loyal subject— 'nay, and if she would give him leave to say it, *I loved her*, for which she thanked me.' Sharp certainly urged the Queen to choose men for their merit rather than for their political views, but most of those he recommended to her were, in fact, Tories. And in the summer of 1707, when the sees of Exeter and Chester were vacant, she and the archbishop resolved to choose two High Churchmen, Blackhall and Dawes. Dawes, in particular, was notorious for his Tory affiliations, since during William III's Whig era he had preached against the ministry. 'You have lost a see by a sermon,' his friends had told him then, to which he cynically replied, 'I never thought of *getting* one by preaching.' Without telling Godolphin, the Queen made promises to the men concerned. The Treasurer received a shock when he visited the Queen to suggest the candidates favoured by himself and Somers—one of whom was his own brother—and was calmly told that the vacancies had already been filled. The Whigs exploded with fury; now they knew for certain that somebody was working behind their backs. Nobody thought of blaming the archbishop; the obvious conclusion was that Harley had brought pressure to bear. 'The Queen has been speaking too freely with Mr. Harley and Mrs. Masham,' Godolphin wrote to Marlborough, and Sunderland echoed the sentiment: 'One would be astonished at the blindness of the Queen.'

The Queen was indignant, and strongly denied that Harley was in any way to blame. She sounded genuinely upset at the trouble she had made for her favourite. Her defence of Harley was strongly expressed in a letter to Marlborough:

I cannot think my having nominated Sir William Dawes and Dr. Blackhall to be bishops is any breach, they being worthy men; and all the clamour that is raised against them proceeds only from the malice of the Whigs, which you would see very plainly, if you were here. . . . I believe you have been told, as I have, that these two persons were recommended to me by Mr. Harley, which is so far from being true, that he knew nothing of it, till it was the talk of the town: I do assure you these men were my own choice. . . . I find Lady Marlborough has said, that I had an entire confidence in Mr. Harley. I know so much of my own inclination, that I am sure I have a very good opinion of Mr. Harley, and will never change it without I see cause; but I wonder how Lady Marlborough could say such a thing.

Harley was just as indignant as the Queen. He was under no illusions; the Whigs were after his blood. For two years he had seen the storm coming and now it had broken. He had served Marlborough and Godolphin with 'the nicest honour, and by the strictest rules of friendship', and yet he was to be sacrificed to 'sly insinuations and groundless jealousies'. As for the two bishops, he wrote, 'I never spoke of them nor ever thought of them or directly or indirectly ever recommended them to the Queen'. 'And, my lord,' he added, 'I must do myself this justice, that I am above telling a solemn lie; that I scorn the baseness of it; and that if I had known or recommended those persons, I would not have been so mean as to deny it, but would have owned it, and given my reasons for it.' But nobody would listen to his protestations. Soon it was being spread about that he was plotting to supplant Godolphin and head the government himself. The Whigs were convinced that his smooth exterior hid deep, corrupt designs, and in September the smear campaign reached its height. On the 10th, Harley wrote to Godolphin:

I am too well acquainted with the practices of a sort of people who wound those they do not like in the dark, and by whispers and secret misrepresentations would ruin the reputation of any one they do not fancy. I know your lordship is too just to admit any insinuations of that kind.

Two days later he communicated with Cowper on the same theme:

If anyone could really imagine that I intended to disturb public affairs, since it is well known I have not been unsuccessful in my endeavours last winter to keep them quiet and I should be fallen very low if the Dean or anyone else could influence me in these cases.

He reminded Cowper that the Queen's ecclesiastical power was 'immediately concerned'; was the aim of the Whigs to take 'the dependency of the clergy from the crown'?

'I did foretell all this a year ago,' Harley told Marlborough. He had warned everybody then that the Whigs were determined to subject the nation to the dictatorship of party. 'I see there are a sort of people will give no quarter,' he wrote to Cowper. 'They will not suffer themselves to be served . . . by indifferent persons, nor by their own friends unless they will pull out their own eyes and submit with blind obedience,' he had said a year before, and now he was more convinced than ever of the dangers of Whig infiltration. He was just as sure now as he had been the previous September, that domination by one party or the other could only lead to ruin:

I dread the thought of running from the extreme of one faction to another, which is the natural consequence of party tyranny, and renders the Government like a door which turns both ways to let in each party as it grows triumphant.

Other people might change their views, but this was the 'honest principle' to which he clung. And because he was the one man who had the courage to stand out for such a principle, he had to bear the burden of malicious attacks. 'As soon as I am gone depend upon it, my Lord,' he wrote to Marlborough, 'the stream will run too high to be stemmed, and there are not (whatever may be pretended) heads of either party who will be able to govern them.' He continued to expatiate on the old theme *ad nauseam*. 'Embracing some persons close and making others desperate,' he wrote in the draft of a letter to Marlborough, might turn out to be like holding a handful of sand—'The harder it is squeezed, the less it is, and slips through your fingers.'

Harley knew as well as everybody else that a crisis was coming. 'I am prepared for the worst,' he told Cowper on September 12. And to Newcastle he wrote, 'When I kiss your hands in town, I shall tell you such a narrative of ingratitude, treachery, folly and madness, as is scarce to be matched.' He had been what Sarah Marlborough called 'strangling' all the summer, whipping up his moderate Tory supporters, and trying to detach lukewarm Whigs from the fringes of the party. His friends and agents wrote to him with the welcome news that many even among the more violent Tories had learnt wisdom in defeat. In July, the thirty-year-old Earl Poulett, unassuming middle-of-the-road Tory and a kinsman of Harley's, wrote encouragingly that Whig folly and their own past mistakes had converted many churchmen to the ideal of moderation. This helped to strengthen Harley's conviction that the Queen's friends and 'managers' could continue to rule, with the help of court Tories and moderates, inviting the Whigs to join with them, but without submitting to the domination of party. This was the plan that gradually became known as Harley's 'alternative scheme'.

His enemies tried to make out that it was part of this scheme to dispense with the services of Godolphin, but he told the Treasurer that in reality he was just as happy to follow as to lead, provided the conditions were right and he knew that he was serving the Queen and not a party:

It had been always my temper to go along with the company and not give them uneasiness; if they should say Harrow on the Hill or by Maidenhead were the nearest way to Windsor, I would go with them and never dispute it if that would give content, and that I might not be forced to swear it was so.

Sometimes Godolphin seemed convinced by these protestations. On September 25 he wrote from St James's:

Yesterday at my return from Windsor, I found the favour of your letter, for which I give you a great many thanks, and have not the least doubt but that you sincerely intend all you say to me in it.

The Queen believed that there was room in her Cabinet for both Godolphin and Harley, so long as they would stand by her in her resistance to the Whigs. 'You say, that I must put my business into Mr. Harley's hands, or follow the Lord Treasurer's measures,' she told Marlborough. 'I should be glad you would explain yourself a little more on that.'

Marlborough believed that Godolphin would be wise to resign and let Harley try to stand on his own. Once out of service, Godolphin would find himself courted instead of criticized, and the Queen and others would soon be clamouring for his return. Threats of resignation had been Marlborough's perennial stratagem and this year he seemed in earnest when he advised his friend to quit and avoid further mortification. 'I am satisfied,' he wrote, 'it will be impossible for you and me to influence the Queen to anything that is right, till she has tried this scheme of Mr. Harley and his friends.'

But graceful withdrawal was not in Godolphin's repertoire. He had been in office for so long that he was almost a permanent fixture. And although the Queen was often stubborn and difficult he was still her servant and he could not abandon her, especially at this precise moment, when Marlborough was still out of the country. Nor was he particularly anxious to part with the hard-working, well-informed and experienced Harley. 'I never had, nor ever can have, a thought of your being out of the Queen's service while I am in it,' he said. And yet there was no denying that there was a rift between them. The Treasurer still could not throw off the memory of those times when the Whigs had come to his rescue in the Lords. They had boasted then that they had his head in a bag; at any time they could pull the strings tight round his neck. Harley, however, tried to point out that in spite of Whig support, the war had been less successful that summer than ever before. First there had been the resounding defeat of the allies at Almanza, then Marlborough's campaign had been frustrated by Dutch stubbornness, and in August a bold plan to march on Toulon had miscarried. But Godolphin refused to accept the implications of this long string of catastrophes. The Whig policy of endless war had its drawbacks; there was a limit to the endurance of the English people, while the allies might be tempted to make a separate peace if they became discouraged. 'I have been obliged to tell *the great man* the true state of things,' Harley told Newcastle on September 11.

Marlborough seemed to be the key to the situation. Godolphin refused to take any steps until he returned, and Harley hoped that he would be able to heal the breach. 'To see those persons uneasy,' he wrote, 'to whose quiet I would sacrifice all I have, and for whose service I would do the utmost in my power, and yet to be misrepresented to them is very hard for flesh and blood to bear.' It was a great disappointment to both Treasurer and Secretary when the General was held up on the continent and was unable to arrive in time for consultations before the opening of Parliament. Marlborough himself was tired out by the fruitless campaign and had little energy left for decisive political decisions. He complained of headaches, and Harley's agents wrote that he was much out of humour and peevish. Morale in the army was low, worsened by the known fact that only the previous spring the French had been tottering on the verge of collapse with an almost empty treasury. Now the summer campaign had given the enemy new heart.

Harley went down to Brampton at the end of September. The weather was as bad as usual. ' 'Tis always your lot,' Godolphin wrote, 'you forbear to go into the country as long as ever you can, and then go so late that the rain forces you to stay longer than you would.' He spent all October at the castle, writing self-justifying letters to Marlborough and Godolphin, and coming up to London at the beginning of November just before the opening of Parliament. Marlborough arrived a few days later, and Harley explained the scheme, which Sunderland had already dismissed as amounting to nothing, for carrying on the government with milder Whigs such as Newcastle and a group of able younger Tories like St John and Harcourt. The Queen was fully in favour; although she was threatened with a bad attack of gout, she struggled up from Windsor and made it heavily clear to everyone that she was not going to bow to the Whigs.

The Junto lords could hardly contain their desire for vengeance and their malice. They denigrated everyone who showed any resistance; they even accused Marlborough and Godolphin of plotting to bring in the Tories—'very obliging', said Marlborough, in one of his more sarcastic moments. Many people found the Junto men hard and unfeeling, locked as they were in a kind of mutual admiration society. They were expert parliamentarians, up to all the tricks, who decided, soon after the session began, to link the debate on supply with a vicious attack on the navy and its convoy system, thereby striking out not only at Prince George but also at Admiral Churchill, Marlborough's High Tory brother. An inquiry into naval affairs was overdue, for the convoy system was inefficient and wasteful, and French privateers had been known to seize ships almost in sight of their home ports. But at this moment it was a tactless move; Marlborough was offended and the Queen even more so. Her husband might be asthmatic and lethargic, but she liked to think of him as he appears in the mural at Hampton Court—an upstanding and healthy-looking Lord High Admiral with the navy spread out in an orderly fashion at his feet.

The Queen had been warned that, if her uneasy alliance with Harley continued, nothing would go well that winter, and there was certainly incipient madness in the air. In September Harley had prophesied in a letter to Cowper that the Whigs would 'join with their violentest enemies to be revenged on their friends'. His clairvoyance was justified when Whigs and Tories joined together to harry the government, and even such extremists as Nottingham and Rochester were heard supporting the Whig attack in the debate on Admiralty affairs. The Queen was apprehensive and confided in Sharp that she was afraid some of her Ministers were going to be called to account. The situation was complicated by the arrival of Scottish Members. Like the Junto, the *squadrone volante* expected rewards for its support of the Union. Joining with the Whigs, the *squadrone* was able to inflict a defeat on the Ministry by voting against a motion to continue the Scottish Privy Council. The parliamentary scene grew more and more stormy in the weeks before Christmas.

Harley kept in the background. He had done his caballing in the summer, and now sat back waiting for his direst prophesies to be fulfilled. He soon had the satisfaction of knowing that the Whigs were doing themselves a great deal of harm by their ruthless tactics. More moderate Members of their own party, like Newcastle, Cowper and Boyle, refused to support them. Marlborough was out of patience with them and was seen quarrelling openly in the House with Wharton, his particular *bête noire*. He was always riled when politicians made capital out of military matters, and although the holocausts in Spain were a fit subject for debate, both parties contrived to twist the evidence for their own ends.

The erratic Earl of Peterborough was due to face some searching questions about his conduct in Spain. He had retired from that country just in time to let others bear the brunt of inevitable defeat, and had recently arrived in England after an enjoyable tour of all the main courts of Europe. Marlborough had a poor opinion of his merits, but although he had always been a Whig grandee, Peterborough calmly claimed Tory support, and his erstwhile political enemies rallied to his cause, defending him on the grounds that supplies had been withheld from Spain and sent to the Netherlands instead. At this, for once in a lifetime, Marlborough shed his habitual calm, and lost his temper in the House.

Whig behaviour confirmed Harley's warnings that the Junto urge for power was a threat to the country's liberty. With Marlborough and the moderate Whigs preparing to line up against the Junto, his alternative scheme was beginning to seem less of a dream and more of a practical possibility. The Queen's favour could be taken for granted, and there was, besides, an unexpected bonus, for the High Church party now looked on Harley with some approval, believing the rumours that he had been instrumental in pressing for the appointment of the Tory bishops. Only Godolphin remained vacillating and uncertain, mesmerized by Whig power. Harley advised him to dissolve Parliament, and start afresh, for it was always possible that the electorate, tired of Junto dominance and the prospect of apparently endless war, would swing away from the Whigs and remove at a blow their chance to bully and bargain for greater power in the Cabinet Council. The Union, Harley thought, gave ample justification for such a move. But Godolphin was far too frightened of the Whigs to suggest sending them to the polls.

Harley did not press the point; a general election was due anyway in 1708 and he could wait. All he had to do for the present was to let the Whigs dig their own grave, just as the violent Tories had done before them, and meanwhile keep quiet and do nothing that might provide them with the means to bring about his own downfall. He knew that they were on the watch for some way of discrediting him, but it was unlikely they would be able to unearth any helpful scandals. His private life was impeccable; unlike his disciple St John, he had never fallen a prey to 'pretty charmers'. St John's friends complained that whoring flagged when he was out of town, and they selected handsome housemaids against his return, but Harley was immune to doubtful women who could be persuaded to barter their virtue for state secrets. In money matters he was equally incorruptible.

But, in the new year, fate dealt the Whigs a trump card. On December 31, 1707, it was discovered that William Greg, now a clerk in the Secretary's office, had been trading secrets to the French. He was arrested on New Year's Eve, and made a full confession of his guilt. Nobody was to blame but himself, he told the examining committee, hastily summoned to hear his story. Marlborough and Godolphin, who had been resting their battered souls at Woodstock and Newmarket, respectively, over the Christmas recess, were summoned to the Cockpit to hear Greg's story, which they and others were prepared to accept as the truth. Harley was calm, knowing that he was in no way responsible for Greg's crime. Sunderland, however, had different views. This was the opportunity the Whigs had been waiting for, and they had no intention of letting it pass.

CHAPTER 9

THE ALTERNATIVE SCHEME

IN A LONELY ROOM at the Cockpit, William Greg had often worked late into the night on his special task of censoring letters written by important French prisoners-of-war. He had been recalled from his roving commission because his knowledge of French fitted him for the job. He was an able and intelligent young man, and Erasmus Lewis gave him further responsibilities which he undertook with very little supervision. After a hard life as a special agent in poverty-stricken Scotland, Greg found his new work at the hub of the universe a very pleasant change. He was attracted by the glitter of London life and all its temptations, but his salary of two hundred pounds was a pittance to a young man bent on pleasure, and before long he was in debt.

The French espionage system was efficient and had its eye on government clerks who laid themselves open to blackmail. When Greg succumbed to the paltry bribe of two hundred guineas from an English merchant who wanted a French guarantee of protection from privateers, he had no difficulty in contacting French agents at the Crosskeys Tavern in Henrietta Street. The next stage was all too simple. In the room where he worked, the Secretary's foreign letters were brought up for sorting before being put into the appropriate mailbags. Defoe had pointed out the inadvisability of leaving secret mail open and unguarded, but the Secretary, overburdened with routine work and the time-consuming task of building up his middle party, had been unable to re-organize the system. He trusted his staff, who were mostly hand-picked; many of his clerks were men who had been tried out on dangerous assignments, and he had no qualms about Greg working unsupervised late at night in the very room where the mailbags were assembled. As it was, Greg found no difficulty in enclosing a letter requesting a pass for the *Mary of London*, with one written by Marshal Tallard, Marlborough's most important prisoner. Having slipped thus far, Greg fell further; he spotted a memorial written by Harley about the Dutch quota tucked temptingly into the letter book where it was due to be entered the following day. Greg copied it out and sent it, under the cover of a French prisoner's letter, addressed to Chamillart, the enemy War Minister. For several weeks he included detailed accounts of proceedings in Parliament. Finally he put in, for good measure, a letter the Queen had recently drafted to the Emperor with the proposal that Prince Eugene should be sent to Spain. He carefully marked the parts drawn up by the Secretary and pointed out Godolphin's amendments and additions.

It so happened that at the time there was a suspicion that secret information about shipping routes was being leaked to the enemy. Some-one—it may even have been Harley—had ordered that the mailbags should be searched. The French prisoners' correspondence was opened in Holland and Greg's secret activities came to an abrupt finish. His confession was clear and detailed. He swore that he himself was entirely to blame, that the letters were in his own handwriting and that the Secretary had no knowledge of what he was doing.

Greg's loyalty was reassuring, but Harley could have done without the discovery of his clerk's treachery, which had opened the door to criticisms of his method and system. It was true that he was only carrying on the routine used by his predecessors, but the Whigs were quick to take up the charge of inefficiency. The employment of Greg in a position of trust was in itself questionable, for he had a criminal record, and had been tried in 1697 for clipping and coining. His wife, who was pregnant at the time of the trial, had taken the guilt on herself, and the inexorable law had punished her, after her delivery, by burning her hand—the standard treatment for forgers and counterfeiters. The bitter month of January 1708 was full of ominous signs. The discovery of Greg's treason was followed by the nasty revelation that some of Harley's lesser instruments, two smugglers employed to go over regularly to Calais and bring back information, were really double agents doing intelligence work for the French about trade and convoys. Harley's protection shielded them for some time but they were brought to book at this very inconvenient moment. There was a danger that Harley's whole intelligence system might be subject to close scrutiny, and he knew that the Whigs were capable of garbling the evidence and accepting false testimony.

Harley realized he was in a perilous position now that the Whigs had received fortuitous help from a minor clerk and two smugglers. He there-fore decided to make an intensive effort to put his alternative scheme into practice before anyone had time to engineer his downfall. He could not wait any longer for Marlborough and Godolphin to make up their minds; they would have to follow or not as they wished. Godolphin, in particular, was not indispensable. Worthy, efficient, and experienced though he was, he had become something of a plodder, unable to take incisive action. Marlborough was different; his military genius set him above party men and his support could prove an adornment to any Ministry. As he had never dismissed Harley's theories outright, and obviously hated the Whigs, there was always a chance that he would go in with the alternative scheme. He genuinely admired the capable younger Tories who followed Harley's lead—St John, eloquent and energetic, Simon Harcourt, 'dearest Sym', the brilliant lawyer, and Mansell, the thirty-year-old Welshman who was witty, wealthy, good natured and an excellent companion. Marlborough's sympathy for the scheme came into the open when, in early January, he asked Harley to call a meeting of all those interested, so that he could have a chance to outline his plans.

The meeting was held at eight o'clock on the evening of January 14. It took place, significantly enough, at the house of Henry Boyle, Chancellor of the Exchequer, a ministerial Whig who had rebelled against the Junto dictatorship in the weeks before Christmas. The Duke of Devonshire, another rebellious Whig, summoned the clan and attended the meeting himself. He was Lord Steward, a spritely septuagenarian much in the public eye, who kept a noble house and equipage and paid great attention to the ladies. He was, according to Macky, 'of nice honour in everything but the paying of his tradesmen'. His presence lent considerable importance to the proceedings. Marlborough listened attentively, and Godolphin, who for so many years had taken the chair at every important council, had to be content with a back seat.

Harley's first point was that the Ministry he envisaged would be grounded on friendship. Boyle, St John, Mansell, Harcourt and Harley were all friends of long standing, joined by ties of common experience and background, and Marlborough and Godolphin had worked happily with Harley for most of the reign. 'We may not break friendship though either or any of us should happen upon particular points to differ from each other,' he scribbled on his agenda. The ministerial group he envisaged was to be bound by personal loyalty, but not subjected to a rigid discipline in every detail such as the Junto exercised over its followers. At the same time, the nucleus of friends could not run the country on its own, but would have to lean on one or other of the big parties, and it was understood from the first that the meeting had not been called to find out ways of making love to the Whigs. The more loosely organized Tory party, now chastened by experience in opposition, and rejuvenated by the blood of younger members, was the one to woo, and Harley had noted down for discussion the 'proper heads in which we may join and begin to found a confidence which it is reasonable to hope may increase by degrees'. At the same time it was important to treat the Whigs with care in case they in their turn should become 'desperate', and 'to prevent them from taking alarm, and to show them that nothing is designed but public good'.

Most of Harley's friends responded favourably to his plan to rally the moderates, turn to the Tories and resist the Junto. Even Marlborough seemed half-fascinated by the scheme. But at the shadow cabinet meeting, Godolphin, who was not used to being a fringe performer, looked more glum than usual. He apparently made up his mind then and there that the scheme would not work and, moreover, that Harley would have to be 'dropped singly' from his administration. Harley's open attempt to win the Treasurer over had failed, but this did not deter him; he was resolved to carry on with his plan alone and underground, and there was no time to be lost. Greg's trial was imminent, and the Whigs were sniffing round the evidence, hoping to scent something unclean.

In mid-January Members came crowding back to London, anxious to miss none of the excitement. Harley was now free to play his favourite game, lobbying Tories, flattering them, beginning to 'found a confidence' by hinting at schemes which would benefit them if they joined in. He was noticed whispering furtively, in the shadows behind the Speaker's Chair, to the startled Member for Liverpool to whom he offered, in return for support, a cosy little niche as Collector of the Customs. Buckingham was among those he worked on, a most unstable politician, notorious for his ability to flit from one party to the other. He approached individuals who succumbed singly to his charm, without realizing that his approaches were part of a comprehensive scheme.

While Harley waylaid his prey, loitering in the Court of Requests, chatting, wooing and charming, the debate on the conduct of the war in Spain began to loom. The management of the affair was entrusted to St John as Secretary-at-War, and he was advised to call for papers going back to 1706 or even 1705 so that the defeat at Almanza could be put into perspective and if necessary blamed on Peterborough who had dallied instead of marching on Madrid, and who had let his love-life cloud his reason. Members had to sit patiently listening while strings of documents were read out, but finally St John came to the account of troops present at the battle of Almanza. Having apparently failed to do his homework on the documents looked out by his staff, he blithely read out facts which were extremely damaging to the Ministry. It did not require a mathematical genius to realize that there was a discrepancy of 20,000 between the original estimate and number of men on the Paymaster's roll and the actual force of 9,000 which had been outnumbered two to one at Almanza. Nor was it long before the watchful opposition did its arithmetic and Godolphin found himself really under fire. He was extremely angry with Harley and St John for presenting the bald facts so carelessly without making any attempt to cover up; he thought them guilty either of inefficiency or treachery, and inclined to the latter view.

Harley was in touch with the Queen, letting her know the progress of his plans; she approved of his approaches to the Tory party and welcomed the thought of being released from Whig domination. She was becoming conditioned to the thought of parting with Godolphin. On January 22 or 23, Harley paid her one of his routine backstairs visits and probably told her the facts about the Almanza scandal, which were enough to convince her that the government was ripe for reorganization.

By the end of January the court gossips were chattering like monkeys; there was tension in the air and everybody knew that something was up, though they were in the dark as to what was really happening. A version of Harley's interview with the Queen, probably garbled, filtered through to Godolphin and convinced him that the Secretary was playing a double game, tattling about the Almanza numbers, persuading her to jettison her faithful servants and to bring in the Tories. This was enough. On January 29, the day that the stormy Almanza debate lasted until 3 a.m., Godolphin sent Harley a message by Harcourt, expressing his displeasure. No details were given.

The next day, January 30, Harley had an appointment with Marlborough at the Cockpit, but the General wrote a note to say that he was unwell and asked the Secretary to call at his house. Harley asked Marlborough to explain Godolphin's message and was told the current theory, which was that he had behaved treacherously over the Almanza debate and, worse still, had accused Marlborough and Godolphin of criminal neglect in an interview with the Queen. He went straight home and tried a letter of self-justification in his usual style of injured innocence:

I know it is impossible to ward against misrepresentations. . . . I do solemnly protest I never entertained the least thought derogating from your Lordship. . . . Let me by my actions demonstrate the uprightness of my intentions.

But Godolphin had been uneasy about the Secretary for too long. Now he felt he knew too much. This time he refused to accept Harley's defence as anything more than 'professions' and 'expressions'. He did not give the Secretary a chance to explain his actions and his answer was like the slamming of a door:

I have received your letter, and am very sorry for what has happened to lose the good opinion I had so much inclination to have of you, but I cannot help seeing and hearing, nor believing my senses. I am very far from having deserved it from you. God forgive you!

Harley had no time for regrets. The Whig attack was mounting: rumours were circulating, in spite of Greg's denials, that Harley had been an accomplice in his clerk's treason and was closely involved in a large network for selling secrets. Greg had already been tried and committed, but the Whigs had granted a stay of execution, in the hope that, to escape the stench and filth of Newgate, he would buy his release by giving evidence against his master. A man who could trade his country's secrets for a few hundred guineas might easily be tempted by a far higher sum and the promise of freedom. A letter from the prisoner, dated January 31, was reassuring. Greg begged Harley to release him from the irons which he had dragged along for a month now. 'A person in my circumstances,' he wrote, 'can never be too often on his knees, to which duty my irons prove a great uneasiness and interruption.' Greg was genuinely penitent, but he was also human; he had a devoted wife, he was young and he loved life. At any time he might succumb to Whig bribes. So Harley worked on in the first days of February, urgently but secretly, testing out individual Tories and plotting every move in the game with brilliant strategy.

On February 3 the Almanza debate was resumed. This was the testing time. The Tories who were still undecided watched him for a sign that he was in good earnest. Marlborough and Godolphin waited to see whether he would support them. Had he spoken up for his fellow triumvirs, the Tories would have condemned him as a double-crossing knave. So he remained silent and let Godolphin face the fury of Whig and Tory alike. Marlborough was disgusted.

The Queen now took a bold step. On February 6 she wrote a letter telling Marlborough that she was prepared to part with Godolphin. According to Swift, she entrusted the letter to St John and gave him leave to 'tell it about the town', which he did without reserve and with plenty of embellishments. He did not prove the most tactful of messengers, and it was thought that an indiscreet remark may have tipped the scales in Marlborough's mind. For a few days the General had been on the point of giving Harley his support; his old friendship with Godolphin had trembled for a moment under pressure, but finally held.

In spite of this, Harley and the Queen went ahead with their plans. The Queen told Marlborough that if he resigned 'he might as well draw his dagger and stab her', but at the same time made it clear that nobody came before Harley in her esteem. She had chosen him; she would have him. Harley, strong in the Queen's favour and seeing many Tories ready to come in behind him, told a friend that he had never felt safer.

On February 9 the Marlboroughs went with Godolphin to the Palace, the Duke with a draft of his resignation speech in his pocket, and his lady assuming an unnatural air of duty and submission. A Cabinet Council had been summoned for that day, but the two men could not bring themselves to sit at the same table as Harley, and resolved to waylay the Queen before she took her place at the board. Godolphin went in to her chamber first and was greeted with coolness. He told her flatly that he could no longer serve alongside the perfidious Mr Harley. The Queen made no attempt to dissuade him, but she gave him, in view of his long service, a day's grace to reconsider his decision. She added that he could do as he pleased since there were plenty of other people ready to take his staff of office. The Duchess was similarly given a day's grace to change her mind, and was coldly advised to retire to her small house at St Albans until Blenheim was fit for occupation. In later years the Duchess allowed herself the little illusion that the Queen had actually said that she could not bear to part with her. The Duke was received rather more cordially. To him she used 'soft expressions'. He was given the chance to make a pretty speech about past service and fidelity and the vileness of Mr Harley, and he expressed his intention of putting his much-used sword into other hands. 'If you do, my lord, resign your sword, let me tell you, you run it through my head,' the Queen replied. But his firmness prevailing over her feminine resolution, she left him and went through to the council room. Duke, Duchess and Treasurer, to the great wonder of the watching courtiers, stalked out to their coach, and Marlborough, visibly in a pet, carried his lady off to their lodge at Windsor.

Meanwhile in the cabinet room the Dukes of Devonshire and Somerset, the Earl of Pembroke, Lord Cowper, the two Secretaries and Prince George, were already assembled. The Queen took her place in the chair of state at the head of the table. The Prince's Council was called in to discuss Admiralty business and, when that was done, Harley rose and read an estimate for a hundred millions destined for the Emperor. When he had finished there was a long and very uncomfortable silence broken at last by the Duke of Somerset who rose to his feet and said that 'if her Majesty suffered that fellow (pointing to Harley) to treat affairs of the war without the advice of the General, he could not serve her; and so left the Council'. Pembroke echoed his sentiments, though less vehemently, and most of the other Lords did the same. The meeting then continued, and closed quietly with Pembroke expressing the hope that 'all fair means possible might be used to compose these dissensions, before they should come to the ears of the people'.

But it was impossible to stop rumours of the crisis from spreading. The Court had seen the Queen leave the meeting looking angry and upset; the departure of the Marlboroughs and Godolphin before the meeting and of Somerset while it was in progress was reported by gossiping tongues, and the backstairs were crowded with curious people anxious for news. Reports that the General had resigned caused a great deal of dismay; beyond the walls of the Palace people trusted him, and wondered what madness in high places could have caused his departure. City men were apprehensive about the effect of Marlborough's action on foreign nations, to whom the General was a symbol of all that was best in the British people. Both Houses of Parliament were aghast. The Lords did no business. The Commons passed a resolution to let the vital Bill of Supply lie on the table. Many Members resolved not to go into the Committee of Ways and Means. Harley, calm as ever, went into the House for a while and delivered some messages from the Queen. In his observations he said pointedly that it sometimes happened that those who served the public best were least considered, and having unburdened himself to this extent, he went away.

The Queen was full of resolution and made it clear that she was not going to be intimidated by a handful of Whigs. Among her visitors on the morning after the Council meeting was Newcastle, who tried to explain to her that the government of moderates they had all longed for was now an impossibility. Too many people had decided that they could not serve without Marlborough. But the Queen refused to listen to his measured advice, nor would she take any notice when her husband, roused from his lethargy by dire warnings from Admiral Churchill, tried to impress on her that everyone feared a convulsion in the state. She 'slighted' anyone who tried to reason with her and would not believe that Harley's plan was doomed.

In the afternoon Harley himself went to see the Queen. He told her that their scheme had failed. The dramatic departure of the Marlboroughs, he explained, had upset even the moderate Whigs, and this was calamitous. The break had come too soon, before there had really been time to rally Tory support, and now even those who had promised to come in were wavering. A well-meaning attempt to save the country from the dictatorship of party had been painted as a wicked plot to seize personal power at the expense of friends. Events had moved rapidly, and the slander campaign of the Whigs had done its work too well. There was bad news also from Parliament, where there had been a ballot to choose the seven men for the select committee to re-examine Greg. Their names struck a chill—Somerset, Devonshire, Bolton, Townshend, Wharton, Somers and Halifax, Whigs to a man. Everyone knew that they were bent on implicating Harley and would not be content until they could carry the matter as far as an impeachment. The Queen saw, at last, that she must acquiesce, just as she had capitulated over Sunderland's appointment. It had all been so nearly within their grasp.

The Queen wept, but agreed. Marlborough, Godolphin, Whigs, Tories, her husband, all these had failed to move her. Harley, the one man she wanted, the one man she was not allowed, he alone was able to persuade her to part with him. He left a few disjointed notes as a record of the sad interview: 'Concur for your sake . . . ready to serve you . . . leave for Controller, Attorney, Mr. St. John . . . stay a day or two . . . the Prince.'

On February 11 Harley left his office at the Cockpit for the last time. Two days later, with his friend Mansell, he went to the Palace to surrender his Seals. Afterwards both men went on to the House, where it was observed that Mansell was without his staff. The same evening, the Queen handed the Secretary's Seals to Henry Boyle.

Marlborough and Godolphin had hoped to drop Harley 'singly', but they were disappointed. 'We may not break friendship,' Harley had said at the meeting of moderates, and his followers took him seriously, demonstrating a personal loyalty which was quite unprecedented at that time. St John, against the advice of many friends, interrupted his career and resigned his post as Secretary-at-War. When he went to the Palace he was accompanied by Sir Simon Harcourt, wearing his Attorney-General's gown for the last time. 'In short, all the whole gang goes out,' wrote Vernon. 'The great shake' was over. Harley knew that he had missed his victory by the narrowest margin. He alone understood all the moves of the game. The world could only guess at the intricate events leading up to his resignation. 'Mr. Secretary Harley has been the public theme,' reported Vernon to the Duke of Shrewsbury, but, he added, 'these are depths I don't enter into.' Although nobody could piece together the whole story, it was generally agreed, as Swift told Archbishop King, that Harley had carried out 'the greatest piece of court skill that has been acted these many years'.

Many people admired Harley's cunning, others criticized what they believed to be his personal treachery, and his failure to 'manage' the Commons and to support Godolphin in the Almanza debate. As usual he himself had no qualms of conscience. He had done his best, under God's guidance, to stem the ambition of powerful men, to protect the Queen and the constitution and to give the country the kind of government it needed. It was Godolphin, if anyone, who was a traitor to the cause. Nor did he see himself as anything but open and honest:

Therefore my honest countrymen do as I do speak plain English in your markets,

he wrote much later in a long *apologia*, adding,

I have been for many years no negligent or incurious observer of what has passed upon the stage of the world . . . the mischiefs which I have seen perpetrated for at least fifty years are now united in one stream and come rolling down with fury upon us. I see the same hands, who acted what we with so much reason clamoured against in former reigns.

He had fought to save the Queen from those who wanted the court to appear 'their sworn vassals'. For the time being he was forced to leave the battlefield, but he was patient and might well find another chance. He believed that the Whigs were past their zenith. Other men might have given way to bitterness, but his great sense of mission made him start to prepare for the future even at this moment of defeat. 'I wish you as successful as I believe you unshaken by this storm' was Defoe's final comment on the affair.

CHAPTER 10

GREG

AS THE BITTER WINTER of 1708 turned to spring, the Committee of Lords examined Greg almost daily. The inquiry was the talk of the town, and it was the general belief that before long the prisoner would break his obstinate silence and reveal the ex-Secretary as a traitorous villain who had sold secrets to the French, and helped to bring on all the military and naval disasters of the previous summer. Greg, in his dank quarters at Newgate, received visitors who offered him his life and a pension of £200 for ever after if only he would implicate his master. But he still insisted that only 'the devil and his necessities were his prompters'.

Harley's friends and relations were distracted. His son Neddy's tutors at Oxford noticed that the young man was so worried that he could not concentrate on his studies. He was a sweet-natured youth with a handsome face unmarked by smallpox, too young to have come into contact with the wickedness of the world. His father, more experienced and buoyed up by a deep faith in God's mercy and a firm sense of his own innocence, faced the danger he was in with a quiet courage which amazed even those who knew him best. Auditor Harley, visiting his brother at his house, met the Bishop of Rochester, Dr Atterbury, on the stairs. 'Your brother's head is upon the block,' said the bishop, 'and yet he seems to have no concern about it, you should therefore persuade him to do something that may prevent the impending danger.' When the Auditor passed on this message, Robin Harley calmly replied, 'I know nothing I can do, but entirely be resigned to, and confide in the Providence of God.'

Harley knew as well as anyone the temptations to which Greg was exposed. He was bound to his master by gratitude, for the Secretary had taken him on in spite of his shady past and given him a position of trust. 'May the Queen never want such a servant, the Commons such a Speaker, nor I, such a patron,' Greg had once written, but that was years ago now, and loyalty could ebb. Besides, there was Mrs Greg, who bore the terrible scars on her palm; how long could a husband resist the pleadings of his wife?

To add to Harley's discomfiture, the 'Lords Inquisitors' arrested the two smugglers, Alexander Valière and John Bara, the other Harley agents who stood accused of counter-espionage. Valière was kept in solitary confinement at Newgate and 'many artifices were used to prevail with him to accuse Mr Harley . . . but after many examinations, Valière told the Lord Treasurer that he knew very well for what he was confined, but that he would sooner be torn in pieces by horses than do so vile a thing.' The two smugglers were in a different category from Greg; they were frank adventurers, denizens of the Sussex marshes, 'owlers' who prowled along the coast at night signalling to smugglers who came over from France. If challenged, they claimed that they carried lanterns only to attract and capture owls; the imitated hoot of an owl was a warning sign that they were in the presence of the law. Harley's two rogues had gone over to Calais with boats full of wool, and had come back laden with brandy. The information they gleaned in the process proved to be little more than common news; according to Burnet, Harley never passed on to the navy the one really useful piece of information they provided, which concerned the French Admiral Forbin's attack on the Russian fleet. It was said that the smugglers had sheltered behind the Secretary's pass for a long time; they were papists and insolent into the bargain, not the kind of men who should have been employed in government service. The committee of inquiry engaged a man whom the Auditor described as 'a most abandoned villain' to keep watch on the Kent and Sussex coasts, and this character, Captain Harry Baker, was given to declaring openly, over a bottle of wine, that Mr Harley knew too much to live, and that his head must fall, cost what it would. Baker later had the audacity to present a bill for his activities at the Auditor's office—an account which Edward Harley would have preferred to settle in a different currency.

For three painstaking weeks the Lords examined witnesses, promising rewards and threatening punishment. They proved that Valière had played 'Jack on both sides', which everyone knew already, but hopes of a great revelation gradually vanished. It was believed that a cipher used by Greg and Harley might provide useful evidence, but this, too, proved a disappointment:

Mr Lewis with the Secretary's consent carried it to them which was only one page with one letter for a name as H. for Hamilton &c., which Greg before he was in the office was sent with to Scotland. . . . This happened to be of a contrary nature to what they desired and was returned, being of no service to their design.

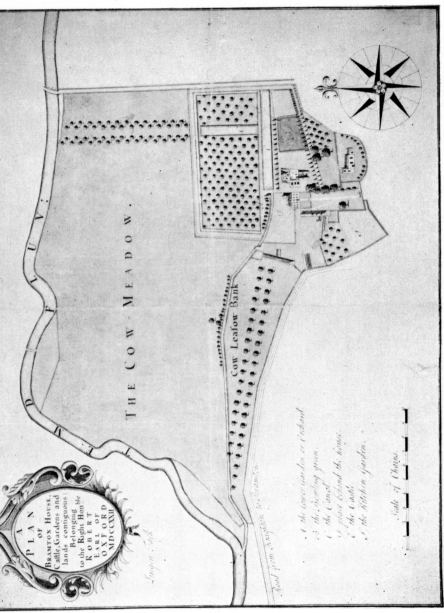

PLAN OF THE EARL OF OXFORD'S ESTATE AT BRAMPTON BRYAN

HENRY ST. JOHN

The proceedings soon began to verge on the farcical, and the committee members were so openly biased that sympathy for their cause began to dwindle. And, in the middle of March, the Greg affair, for so long the main topic of conversation, quite suddenly went out of the news. 'You hear no more of it than if it had happened in Queen Elizabeth's day,' wrote one of the Harley retainers at Westminster to Neddy, 'and now one had as good hold one's tongue or tell a story of Tom Thumb.' Greg vanished from the headlines and made way for James Edward Stuart.

The Pretender had at last completed his plans for an expedition to Scotland. He made his way to Dunkirk to join a fleet of French frigates, six thousand French infantry, a strange collection of English and Scottish Jacobites and a cargo of gold plate, royal liveries and insignia. 'He may soon be hear,' wrote Lady Wentworth to her son. Panic and pleasurable expectation were mingled in the bosoms of many London ladies, for James was a pleasant young man and only twenty years of age. But the belief that the Pretender might soon land on this side of the channel was not shared by Forbin; he was sceptical about the whole 'chimerical expedition', and was not keen to risk good warships in such a madcap scheme. If the plan could have been carried out the previous summer, when the weather was fair and Scotland still in a state of turmoil after the signing of the Union Treaty, there might have been some hope of success, but the opportunity had passed; Highland ire was beginning to die and Lowland earls were never keen to commit themselves to anything but talk. As for the element of surprise, that particular weapon had long ago been lost. For months British agents had been reporting the mysterious comings and goings of Jacobite messengers; in Holland the ringleaders had been drawing up settlements to prevent the forfeiture of their estates, and in Scotland there had been many secret meetings at noble-men's houses. The preparations at Dunkirk had also been well covered, although in January and February English Ministers had been too busy supplanting each other to take notice of what was going on.

Nothing ever went quite right for James Edward, and no sooner had he arrived on ship-board than he succumbed to a virulent attack of measles. This was hardly calculated to help the image of a conquering hero. Nevertheless, as soon as the rash subsided, and Admiral Byng's blockad-ing force was driven back into the Downs by stormy weather, Forbin was persuaded, much against his better judgment, to set out into the wind, ice, and snow. He gained a certain cynical pleasure from the sea-sickness of the despised Jacobites. 'It pleased me to see them so unwell,' he wrote.

The English, roused by a threat to their shores, went boldly into

E

action. Ships were manned and equipped with 'unusual expedition', and Byng's squadron was daily reinforced. Although many believed that there was an element of knight-errantry about the invasion attempt, nobody was prepared to take any chances, and the new Ministry earned itself great praise by its prompt action. All the same, it was well known that the Scottish army, such as it was, was thoroughly debauched and probably disloyal; Edinburgh castle was virtually unprotected, Forbin was speeding north driven by a gale-force wind, while Byng, in hot pursuit, was many leagues behind. After a week of suspense, British seamanship triumphed and Byng crept up so quickly that he almost trapped the French in the Firth of Forth. Some of the clans grew very excited, and the odd lord went to the hills, but all the Scottish people saw of the expedition was a force of eight men who landed at Spey to pick up provisions and, very sensibly in view of the weather, a batch of spare stockings. Forbin, with skill and courage, brought his fleet back more or less intact by way of Ireland, though sickness and hardship claimed the lives of many of his men. The convalescent James returned to Dunkirk bedraggled but unbowed, having achieved little save for a great deal of sisterly disapproval. In a public pronouncement, Queen Anne called her brother, for the first time, 'the Pretender'—and a popish one at that.

The repulse of the invader had a good effect on British morale. Previously there had been a great deal of grumbling, caused by cold weather, rising prices and war-weariness. 'Coals are above fifty shilling a chaldren to my grief,' complained Lady Wentworth, 'and coffy ten shilling a pound. I will leev it off if possible.' But the common danger made such sacrifices seem worth while. The Whigs began to regain their waning popularity, and the Tories, advocates of disarmament, were discredited. 'Well, man proposes but God disposes,' Godolphin remarked when he heard about Byng's success. It seemed, at the moment, as if he and the Whigs had the Almighty on their side.

The Committee's rather negative findings on the Greg affair were published when the Pretender still lurked off Scottish shores, and they made little impact. The most that could be proved against Harley was that there had been some negligence in leaving important letters on the table for any clerk to read, and the wisdom of using smugglers as agents was questioned. The printers worked overtime on the report all one Sunday late in March to hasten its appearance. It was a ponderous document, too cumbersome to be sent down by post to Neddy at Oxford. William Thomas, Harley's domestic clerk, described it in scathing terms

The part that relates to Greg is very frivolous, and a great part of it downright falsehoods, but they are such, as if true, would not generally affect either my Master's diligence or integrity. The other part concerning Valière &c. is scraps confusedly put together, and invidious turns and insinuations through the whole.

Greg was given further chances to supply some 'pertinent' answers, even after the report was published, but he continued to say steadily that he knew no more than what he had already confessed. He went to the scaffold with a clear conscience.

The people of London flocked to the execution, attracted by the prospect of a last-minute revelation. As the prisoner stood in the cart, one of the Sheriffs whispered in the executioner's ear, and told him to offer the traitor one final chance. Greg spoke his answer loud and clear in a voice that carried even in the great noise of the crowd, and Harley's name was heard 'a pretty distance' from the gallows:

Mr Harley is perfectly innocent as to any knowledge of the correspondence I was engaged in, neither he nor anybody had any hand in it, and I call God to witness that I die with a conscience clear from having concealed any thing I know relating to the Queen and the government.

Having spoken, Greg fell on his knees and for a man on the verge of death seemed calm and extraordinarily devout. Yet the Sheriff still tormented him. 'What would they have me say?' he cried, 'I have told all I know.' He handed papers to the Sheriff with orders that they should be opened after his death, which he now met with a bravery that cancelled out his crime in the minds of the onlookers.

At last the danger was over. The Harley family saw Robin's deliverance as a plain instance of divine providence. It seemed to them truly miraculous that a man like Greg, who had lived much of his life on the criminal fringe, should have resisted temptation right up to the moment of death. Harley's calmness won him many admirers. The Queen expressed great compassion and sympathy for him in his ordeal, and was disgusted at the treatment he had received, which, she said, was as bad as 'hanging him over and over'. The Whigs were infuriated by her mild comments on their precious report. They would have liked 'fire and faggot', but she deliberately damped everything down in deference to her fallen favourite.

Harley granted Greg's widow a pension of fifty pounds for life out of gratitude. He could afford to sit back and enjoy the discomfiture of his enemies. He himself had no responsibilities, while his successor Henry Boyle was so intent on the affairs of the nation that he hardly took time to eat, and Sunderland was forced to sit up all night to keep abreast of business. 'What may we not expect of such great men of such assiduity,' the Harley servant at Westminster wrote to Neddy. Now that he had gone, many people missed Harley and began to realize the volume of work he had tackled. Godolphin, in particular, knew the difference now that he himself had to handle many tasks that the ex-Secretary had, quietly and without fuss, taken off his shoulders. Bereft of Harley's expert advice and his valuable support in the House, Godolphin grumbled worthily on, his health deteriorating, work piling up and his happy days at Newmarket becoming less and less frequent. He had alienated the Queen and did not find his new colleagues congenial. He was still the butt of criticism; already people were laying the blame for the Pretender's escape from Dunkirk harbour at his door. The Junto continued to bully him, and the Duchess convinced him that Harley, the man he had jettisoned, was still plotting against him and caballing with the Queen. One evening, as Godolphin left the Palace with Marlborough, he met Harley leaving town by way of Kensington Gate. He went immediately to the Queen 'in a high fit of jealousy', according to Swift, reproached her for seeing Harley privately 'and was hardly so civil to be convinced with her Majesty's frequent protestations to the contrary'.

The high parliamentary tension which characterized the opening months of the year died down after Harley's fall. The question of the war in Spain ended tamely with a loyal address thanking the Queen for the measures she had entered into for the recovery of that unhappy country. The Earl of Peterborough turned an uncomfortable situation into a personal triumph, amusing the Lords with his 'large comments' and lacing his speeches with so much wit that people went to hear him for entertainment value that was second only to the opera. So 'a nice trouble-some business' ended and Members were free to retire to the country and make preparations for the forthcoming elections.

The fall of Harley did not bring immediate victory to the Junto. The vacancies left by the Secretary and his 'gang' were filled by moderates like Henry Boyle and Speaker John Smith—Lord Treasurer's Whigs they were called. Halifax's brother, Montagu, who had confidently expected to walk into Harcourt's place as Attorney-General, was kept waiting for months, doing the work without actually being appointed. Harley was accused of standing behind the Queen and urging her to resist any Junto appointments. Godolphin himself was not anxious to have his Ministry swamped by high-powered Whigs; all the same he knew that concessions would have to be made. The Junto was deter-mined to force at least one more of its members into the Cabinet Council and Swift was told in April by friends in the know that the Whig lords had applied to the Queen in a body for Lord Somers to be made Lord President of the Council. It seemed, however, that the Ministry would not agree, and that the Queen was adamantly opposed to the suggestion. It was the Sunderland story all over again.

Somers was the most balanced and brilliant member of the Junto, but the Queen entertained a strong prejudice against him, based on his behaviour as far back as the last reign, and, more recently, for the leading part he had played in attacks on the Admiralty before Christmas. Apart from her own ill opinion of him, she was sure that his appointment would give great pain to her consort. It was rumoured that the Duke of Devonshire had been asked to intercede with the Queen on Somers's behalf, an idea that was viewed with approval by Marlborough, who believed the Duke to be a very honest man who governed himself by reason. 'I wish I could say so of all our acquaintance,' wrote Marlborough. But in spite of his good character, Devonshire, so it was thought, would make no headway with the Queen, for the simple reason that 'the power and inclinations of Mrs Masham would be opposite'. Godolphin felt helpless; he had lost his influence with the Queen and he described her attitude in such strong terms as 'perverseness and imbecility'. She yielded nothing without a battle and often pointedly ignored his advice. One particular altercation, on the subject of Halifax's brother, lasted for hours, until the clock struck three and Prince George came in looking as if he thought it was dinner time.

The general election, held in May, proved very favourable for the Whigs; never, Sunderland declared, had there been such a Whig Parliament. The Junto was so determined to beat Queen and Court that it threw its weight into the Scottish elections, entering into an alliance with anybody who would guarantee support—Jacobites not excepted. This was the process that Swift described as 'driving in unison for want of moderation'. Inflated by success, the Whigs launched attacks on anyone who showed them the slightest resistance. Godolphin was blamed for failing to purge Tories from all minor offices. While Prince George lay desperately ill at Windsor, stricken with 'a spitting of blood, a lethargy, a hydropsy and something of a palsy', the Whigs went ahead with their nagging demands that Admiral Churchill, his only friend, should be removed. They even accused Marlborough of Jacobite tendencies, although his activities in this direction were limited at the time to talking 'polatiques' with his Jacobite sister-in-law, the Duchess of Tyrconnel, now old and hoarse, at her home in Holland. The Queen was also made to suffer when the Junto started negotiations for bringing over the Hanoverian heir. This bold and tactless step, taken without her 'privity', made the Queen so angry that she fell ill towards the end of May and those around her were in great concern for her health.

Harley watched the Whig machinations with growing apprehension. He still believed that, in spite of Whig gains, the Tories really expressed the will of the majority, and at any rate spoke with the voice of the country gentlemen. This made it all the more distressing to see 'how those who are the smaller part of the nation have made themselves formidable and terrible to the greater', as he put it to Bromley. He spent the summer months impressing on the Tories the need to stand together and cultivate the discipline and cohesion which was the Whig secret weapon—'though they hate one another yet they unite together to carry on their designs,' he explained to Bromley, whereas the Tories revealed a chronic tendency to splinter.

In May Harley left London to attend to his election at New Radnor. 'I hope nothing will interrupt your quiet enjoyment at Brampton,' Erasmus Lewis wrote. London was no place for Harley and his friends in the hot season of 1708. Erasmus Lewis for months avoided going into public places for fear of insults. Released from the cares of office, Harley could afford to relax, attend to his estate and enjoy his bowling-green. On July 17 he told Newcastle that he took no more pleasure in learning about the schemes and projects of the politicians 'than in hearing the dreams of a sick man'. This statement was a trifle disingenuous, but all the same, as Simon Harcourt put it, it was pleasant to know that 'nothing of the miscarriages of others, or their misfortunes, will call for any apology from us'. St John, who had lost his seat in the election, revelled in the prospect of 'three years time to live by myself, which is a blessing I never yet enjoyed'. When affairs on the continent were going badly and in particular when it looked as if the siege of Lille might fail, Harley rejoiced to think that he would take no share of the blame. He could afford to linger at Brampton, enjoying a leisured autumn, while Ministers hurried back to town. 'As for myself,' he wrote to Sir Robert Monckton on October 22, 'I have too much concern and pleasure to think of removing until the last minute, for as I am hors de jeu, it is requisite I should keep myself hors de blame et de soupçon.'

Nevertheless he did not spend a completely idle summer. His work on Tories and moderate Whigs began to bear fruit, so much so that in September the Tory Bromley wrote encouragingly, 'I am determined, notwithstanding anything past, to join with you . . . in affection as well as zeal', while the Whig Cowper, alarmed by the threatened break-away of moderates from his own party, urged Newcastle to prevent 'a division among honest men'.

One of Harley's tasks was to forge an alliance with Charles Talbot, Duke of Shrewsbury, who had returned from Italy in 1706, complete with an eccentric Italian wife. Handsome, charming and civilized, tolerant in outlook and in every way a kindred spirit, he was a talented man, lacking the pomposity of a public figure and renowned for his easy conversation and success with the ladies. The fact that he had lost an eye only added to his fascination. They called him 'the King of Hearts', with their craze for nicknames. But for all this he lacked ambition, and some had accused him of dallying in Italy far longer than his lung trouble justified, content to play the dilettante and dabble in the treasure-house of art. As soon as he returned, the Whigs, his old political allies, remembering the service he had given in William's reign before his diseased frame sent him south in search of sunshine, paid him great attention and it looked as if he would return to the Junto fold. At first the Shrewsburys left their names twice a week at the Duchess of Marlborough's door. After a while these attentions ceased, and Sarah, putting this down to their realization that she had lost her power at court, took against them with customary vehemence. She accused the Duke of sophistry and convinced herself that his charm was only a veneer.

Harley's temperate ideals appealed to Shrewsbury far more than the stern principles of the Whigs. The two men had kept in touch when Shrewsbury was abroad and the Duke averred that from first acquaintance he had felt a sincere esteem for Harley. They were linked by a common interest in old papers, and on one occasion Shrewsbury had shown one of Harley's rare manuscripts to the library keeper at the Vatican. In the summer of 1708 the friendship grew and flourished; the Duke urged Harley to break his journey at Heythrop, his country seat, for a bed, or a dinner, or both, whenever he went to Herefordshire. Harley intensified his efforts to lure Shrewsbury away from his Whig friends and met with some success, although the Duke was cautious. 'It would look too much like mystery if we were to meet at any third place,' he wrote, 'and think the most natural and unexceptionable way would be that you would either dine here or lie here one night.'

But apart from a brief visit to London in July, Harley spent the summer quietly at Brampton. The Duchess of Marlborough continued to believe that he was hanging about the court, creeping in through secret doors at midnight. He knew that she blamed him for influencing the Queen. 'The difficulties (I am well informed) they complain of,' he wrote to

Abigail on October 16, 'are not to be imputed to me; and therefore they should consider that it arises from the unreasonableness of their own demands, and my Aunt's [the Queen's] true judgment and right understanding.' He had no opportunity of influencing the Queen in the summer of 1708, but he had done his work well in the past, and Anne continued to cling to the principles he had taught her.

CHAPTER 11

COUSIN ROBIN AND COUSIN KATE

'MRS MASHAM is forbid the court,' wrote Swift when news of the great shake spread through London circles. But to the chagrin of Lady Marlborough and her Whig friends, the Bedchamber Woman remained, even though Harley and his supporters were discarded. 'The Heifer wherewith he had ploughed,' as Coke put it, 'either was so inconsiderable at that time that she was overlooked, or so firmly rooted in the Queen's favour, that there was no shocking of her.'

The Duchess was rueful when she discovered that her rival was to stay and a new series of recriminations and attempted reconciliations broke out between her and the Queen. 'Female jars,' as Coxe called them, were followed by embraces that lacked satisfaction. By the end of March relations were more strained than ever, and the Queen expressed her exasperation in a letter which reached Marlborough just before he left for Flanders:

You know I have often had the misfortune of falling under the Duchess of Marlborough's displeasure, and now, after several reconciliations, she is again relapsed into her cold unkind way, and . . . she has taken a resolution not to come to me when I am alone, and fancies nobody will take notice of the change. . . . Can she think that the Duchess of Somerset and my Lady Fitzharding, who are two of the most observing prying ladies in England, won't find out that she never comes near me nor looks on me as she used to do, that the tatling voice will not in a little time make us the jest of the town?

There was little that Marlborough could do. The Duchess was half mad with jealousy, and even her husband was moved to complain of her 'indifferency', in a dismal letter written on the eve of the battle of Oudenarde. The General was uneasy about the Queen and about the Whigs' anger which, he said, must make 'the Lord Treasurer and I not only uneasy, but unsafe'. However, he added, all these anxieties would be bearable, if only he could be so happy as to gain his wife's love and esteem. But the Duchess was so obsessed by her hatred of Harley and Abigail that she had no time even for her husband.

E*

Aided and also certainly abetted by her secretary and admirer Arthur Maynwaring, the Duchess wrote anonymous letters to Abigail by penny post, full of dark threats and reminders of her low station:

You cannot but have heard your master Harley often talk of the Greeks and Romans because he is always showing his small learning out of season and [he will] tell you how those great and wise nations proceeded against persons that they thought endangered their state. Death was always the reward of such people . . . and if you and your oracle H are not traitors to this state 'tis certain there never were any.

The Duchess went on to suggest that Abigail should emulate her namesake in the Bible, go out on an ass to meet the Duke—'our David and deliverer'—and fall down upon her 'frightfull face', but even Maynwaring blenched at this and the missive was never sent.

Marlborough, too, was plagued with letters about Squire H. and Mrs Abigail, as the Duchess called them. Her dislike of the pair was positively pathological. When she was not mercifully occupied buying thousands of yards of brocade and velvet for Blenheim, the Duchess bombarded the Queen with letters written in a head-magisterial tone. She delivered lectures on the subject of chambermaids and their unsuitability as royal confidantes. A 'handy' servant was one thing, but to put an uneducated menial on the 'foot of a friend' was quite another.

The quarrel exploded just when Marlborough had won his third major victory. The Duchess laid out most of the crown jewels for the Queen to wear at the thanksgiving service for Oudenarde in August, spending hours on the task. She was cut to the heart when Anne failed to put a single one of them on. At previous services the Duchess had made an impact with simplicity of dress while the Queen, in contrast, flashed exhorbitantly at her side. The whole effect was spoilt when both women appeared unadorned. The Duchess voiced a suspicion that Abigail was responsible for persuading the Queen to leave off the jewels, the Queen denied it, and they quarrelled gracelessly all the way to St Paul's, and even in the cathedral itself, until the Duchess hissed at the Queen to be quiet. It did not stop there; a further instalment took place behind closed doors at the Palace, in voices so high-pitched that the pages could hear what was going on from the foot of the stairs. The Duchess departed, weeping, and leaving the Queen also in tears.

Not content with such scenes, the Duchess raked up an old promise the Queen had made, giving her permission to build on a site at St James's, previously used for the keeping of pheasants, guinea-hens, partridges and other fowl. The Duchess planned to dislodge the birds and spend a large sum of money on a house built to Wren's design. Caged birds were less disturbing neighbours than the neurotic Duchess, and if the Queen was apprehensive, the General was horrified by the thought of more money being poured into bricks and mortar. The bills for Blenheim, even if the nation was expected to pay, were enough to turn a frugal man still greyer than he was already. However, both the Queen and the Duke would have welcomed any distraction if only it could have kept the Duchess's mind off Harley and Abigail, but even her monumental quarrels with Vanbrugh about the building at Blenheim were not enough to do that.

It was not a happy summer for the Queen. All she wanted was to escape from the world and devote all her attention to the Prince, who was very ill indeed. A small house at Windsor had been bought for royal use some time before, and the Queen decided to go into residence there in hopes of finding some peace and quiet. Abigail went with her and she also was none too happy. She was pregnant, for one thing, and had to keep working, even in the hot summer sick-room atmosphere. She was cut off from the world, and the Queen clung to her, refusing to let her take even a few days' leave in London. She was receiving poison pen letters from the Duchess and she knew the Whigs were out to make trouble. 'I am very ready to believe they will try all ways to ruin me,' she complained to Harley. Her enemies over-estimated her influence with the Queen, and she often found her mistress stubborn, overbearing and moody, and none too keen to discuss public affairs with a mere dresser. 'I would fain . . . have talked of the main point in hand,' Abigail wrote, describing an interview, 'but whenever I said anything relating to business she answered, "pray go, for if you begin to talk I shall not get to bed in any time," though I think she is in good humour and has not a desponding countenance as sometimes she has.' All the same it was generally believed that Abigail Masham wielded great power:

> Bright Masham's the whirlwind that turns us about,
> One whiff of whose breath can bring in or put out . . .

ran a contemporary ballad which the Duchess took care to send to the Queen. The Duchess was convinced that the Queen spent the summer in the small house at Windsor expressly so that Harley could come and see her without being observed. To satisfy the Queen's whims, she claimed, the Prince, though gasping for breath, had to live in a place that was 'hot as an oven . . . [so that] those Mrs Masham had a mind to bring to Her Majesty, could be let in privately by the garden'. But whenever anyone accused the Queen of seeing Harley and being guided by his 'insinuation', she stolidly denied that this was the case, and in spite of Sarah Marlborough's perpetual charges, there is no evidence at all that Harley continued to visit her when he was out of office.

All the same, Harley was not a man to miss a good opportunity, and he took the precaution of working out a cipher to make communication by letter with Abigail possible. She was his cousin, after all, and there was nothing to prevent him writing to her about family affairs. The code he invented was based on the names of relations and places connected with the Harleys, and any letter using the full code appeared to be ostensibly about domestic affairs. It was unlikely that letters would fall into enemy hands, since they were conveyed by Abigail's brother, Jack Hill, when he went down from London to Windsor. But there was always a danger that the watchful Whigs would find some way of intercepting the mail, and so, if any letters had fallen into their hands, they would have conveyed nothing except gossip about jointures, lawsuits and estate matters concerning the Foleys, Stephenses and other cousins and their property at Chavenage and Essington. It was a simple screen and an effective one, so effective that copies of important letters written by Harley to Abigail lay undetected at Longleat, filed under the name of 'Catherine Stephens' until Geoffrey Holmes recently deciphered them:

CODE		
1. Queen	Aunt Stephens	1.
2. D. Marlborough	Cosen Nat	2.
3. Duchess Marlborough	Lady Pye	3.
4. Lord Treasurer	Sir Charles Pye	4.
5. Junto	Estate at Essington	5.
6. Tories	Cosen Palmer	6.
7. Clergy	Estate at Fairfield	7.
8. Hanover Family	Mrs. Packer	8.
9. Mrs. Masham	Cosen Kate Stephens	9.
10. Robert Harley	Cosen Robin Packer	10.
11. Duke Shrewsbury	Cosen Dick Pye	11.
12. Courage	Ready Money	12.
13. Victory	Lawsuit	13.
14. Peace	E. M. Barnett	14.
15. Parliament viz. House of Commons	Cosen Robin Stephens	15.
16. Queen's favour	joynture at Chavenage	16.
17. Whigs	Cosen Hadley	17.
18. London	Walton-in-Surrey	18.
19. Windsor	Brampton	19.
20. Dutch	Aunt Foley	20.

Using the cipher, Abigail reported on the heavy pressure that the Whigs were exerting on the Queen. On July 21 she wrote:

Oh my poor Aunt Stephens is to be pitied very much for they press her harder than ever, since what happened lately she is altered more than is to be imagined, no ready money at all to supply her with common necessaries.

When Abigail told the Queen about the court that was being paid to the Hanover family, Anne looked very melancholy, but said little. Abigail feared that her resistance was weakening. 'I am very much afraid of my Aunt's conduct in her affairs, and all will come from her want of a little ready money,' Abigail reiterated on July 27.

At the end of September, Abigail was brought to bed at Kensington and a messenger was sent express to Windsor, by the Queen's positive order, with the good news. The child was hastily christened the following week, with ladies of the court standing proxy for the Queen and the Prince who had agreed to be godparents. In less than a month Abigail was back at her post, and on October 10 Harley wrote her a letter which was destined for the Queen's ears, and calculated to bolster her courage at this difficult time:

I heard last week that Sir Charles Pye says, it is impossible to comply with the Estate at Essington and yet my Aunt's business cannot be done without it . . . he will let her have no other friends, and I do not know what he means by my Aunt's business, but indeed his own projects . . . though he enjoys the whole jointure at Chavenage that does not content him.

On October 16 Harley wrote even more urgently, warning Abigail that the complete subservience of Godolphin to the Junto was imminent:

Some things which were come to my knowledge . . . I think it would be very necessary should be communicated to my Aunt, if you think it proper . . . if I had not preferred her interest to my own advantage, I need not have run those hazards which I have undergone.

To overcome the Queen's 'true judgement and understanding' had become the Marlboroughs' main aim. Pride, ambition and covetousness prompted the Duke and the Whigs to reject any offers of peace on the continent, largely on account of their own vested interests:

They would not agree to the terms my Aunt Foley thought reasonable for herself, and now it is come to pass that my Cousin Nathaniel Stephens has lost his reputation. His sordid avarice is the root of all evil.

Their first priority in the new session would be to force Somers—'chief tenant of the Estate at Essington'—into the Cabinet Council. At the same time, Harley reassuringly added that the Tories were ready to make a great appearance at the opening of Parliament.

At the end of October, when Harley was still at Brampton, events took a serious turn. News came to him on October 28 from Erasmus Lewis that the Prince was dead. It was sudden, at the end, for that very morning Dr Sloane and other physicians had given him a good report. 'Thus has the Queen lost her companion,' Erasmus Lewis ended. Harley wrote to Abigail at once:

I write most earnestly to my Cousin Kath. Stephens that she will redouble her care . . . for there is nothing in the world so mischievous to body and mind as for persons to be too much alone.

There was a great danger that those who had already so 'notoriously abused' the Queen's favour would seize their opportunity now; the widow, prostrate with grief, all defences down, could all too easily, in this moment of sorrow, squander all the remnants of her power and favour.

Abigail did her best to follow Harley's instructions and stay close by the Queen's side, protecting her from the Duchess who in her turn leeched on to the bereaved woman, intent on keeping away 'that jade my cousin Kate'. The Queen, to escape them both, went into the Prince's closet and bolted the door. Her grief was real. Although the Prince's health had been precarious for a long time, this did not make the loss any easier to bear. The Queen refused to see anybody, although on November 14 Archbishop Sharp was admitted. 'We both wept at my first coming in. She is in a very disconsolate condition,' he reported.

All the Queen's thoughts were bound up with her own grief. She told Godolphin to arrange for a great many Yeomen of the Guard to carry 'the prince's dear body that it may not be let fall, the great stairs being very steep and slippery'. She sat, mourning, in the dim little closet where her husband had passed his waking hours. All her 'ready money' was spent, her courage to stand against party had ebbed away. The great barrier which the Whigs had battered at for so long fell without a struggle, and Somers, Wharton and Halifax were soon admitted into the courts of power.

When Sarah Marlborough heard that the Prince was dying, she decided that it was her duty to be at the Queen's side, although she had not entered the royal presence since the jewel dispute. The Queen received her coldly, but she was not a woman to be put off by a simple snub. Deciding that the widow must be taken away from scenes that might remind her of her husband's memory, the Duchess carried her off to Kensington. The Queen went unwillingly, casting backward glances at Abigail, and leaving last-minute messages about the care of her dogs. She could think of nothing but her own sorrow, and found it impossible to concentrate on affairs of state, thus adding to Godolphin's troubles. The Duchess thought that she was being morbid, and when she insisted on returning to St James's, began to remove objects of sentimental value. Even the Prince's portrait was taken down off the bedroom wall. 'For God's sake,' wrote the Queen, 'let the dear picture you have of mine be put into my bedchamber for I cannot be without it any longer.' Worn out with the long vigil at her husband's sick-bed and overcome with grief, the Queen soon succumbed to 'flying pains' followed by a sharp attack of gout. She spent most of January 1709 lapped in a purple nightgown and quilt in an enormous bed hung with purple and black. The court ladies had to cast aside their silks, only matt materials were allowed, coats of arms were erased from coaches and even coloured handkerchiefs were forbidden. The Palace was draped for years with sombre hangings. The Duchess deprecated both the spirit and the expense of all this mourning and showed her disapproval by being the only lady to appear with powder in her hair and a patch on her face, on the first night that the Queen felt able to see company after her bereavement.

The late Consort's closet was a dreary room that looked out on to a dark courtyard where Abigail hung out washing, and the Duchess was convinced that the only reason the Queen stayed close to it was because it was sited at the head of the backstairs and was therefore convenient for late-night meetings with Harley. There was no doubt in the Duchess's mind that Harley came to the back door when the pages were asleep and there was nobody but Abigail to lead him upstairs with a candle. This the Queen denied, and Swift bears out that Harley made no attempt to have any private interviews until the beginning of 1710.

The Queen might deny that she saw Harley, but the Duchess no longer trusted her; she certainly lied at times to save herself from the Duchess's wrath. There was one notorious occasion when Sarah detected that her own lodgings at Kensington were being used by Abigail:

The Queen said it was a lie. Then I told her Majesty that I could bring several people that had seen her goods and her servants in my rooms. To which she answered in the same breath almost that she had given the lie—How could she help using them? Meaning I suppose that her lodgings were too little for her great occasions.

Abigail moved hastily out of the lodgings she had annexed as soon as she was discovered, and found somewhere else to prepare the invalid Queen's plasters and bandages, but the incident was typical of the atmosphere of suspicion and mistrust that surrounded the Queen and her most intimate attendants.

Whether he visited the Palace or not that winter, Harley kept very quiet on the political front. But the Whigs feared him even when he was silent, and would have been very glad if he had lost his seat like St John and Harcourt. In the new year they continued to persecute him, raking up papers and reminding the owler Valière, who was still in Newgate, that any help in removing Harley would not go unrewarded. St John remarked that Harley seemed 'singled out for destruction', and his friends and relations were alarmed by the new threats to his safety. Tabby trembled when she thought of the 'implacable rage and malice' of her father's enemies, and Neddy expressed his fear in a letter to Aunt Abigail:

I hope God, who had so wonderfully preserved our dear friend from their hellish malice . . . will still continue his mercy to us.

At the end of January it was moved that all the papers relating to Greg's trial should be put before the House. On the day the titles were read out Harley stood up and called for the confession which Greg had handed to the executioner and which nobody had yet seen. He knew well enough that if the confession had contained anything useful to the Whigs, they would have made good use of it long ago. He himself rose to give an account of Greg's discovery, apprehension and conviction, and added that, if any Member wanted further information, he was quite ready to answer their questions. He turned the tables on his opponents so expertly that he once again earned many admirers.

The Whigs had to learn that, although apparently subdued, he was by no means a spent force, and to persecute him was to drive him underground, where he could carry out dangerous work. He had, for example, promised the Queen, in one of the code letters, that he would have all his friends ready to meet 'cousin Robin Stephens'—the House of Commons—at the opening of Parliament, and he had achieved an enthusiastic response, even among Tories who were discouraged by the party landslide at the polls. With Mansell organizing the Welsh borderers, and many other key agents whipping up the landed gentlemen in different parts of the country, it was proved possible to muster Tory strength almost as efficiently as the Whig party machine could rally its forces. The reason for the summoning of the Tories had been an outside chance that a split in the Whig ranks might have made it possible to smuggle

Bromley in as Speaker, and although this attempt was not made, the experiment in Tory discipline proved very valuable.

In the spring, Harley chose to prove his power once again. The Whigs had brought in a Treason Bill which had a clause stating that in Scotland estates would be forfeit in cases of treason. This did not apply in England, and Harley, always an enemy of repressive legislation, tabled an amendment which would give the Scots the same treatment as the English. The Whigs countered his move by proposing that the amendment should not take effect until after the death of the Pretender, but experienced unexpected difficulty, in passing their version. 'It vexed them dreadfully,' Tabby wrote, 'and yesterday they assembled all their forces, the lame and blind and all, and yet it was carried by but six.' The 'honest interest', as the Whigs called themselves, had to face the fact that in Harley they had met their match as a parliamentary tactician; this they had always known and it was one of the reasons why they disliked and feared him. When he persuaded Tories and moderates to back him, he could command a disconcerting number of followers. Harley was their natural enemy; where they were straightforward, blunt to the point of tactlessness and direct in their approach, and so lacking in hypocrisy that they were sometimes accused of atheism, Harley was tactful, secretive, indirect, full of honeyed words and pious sentiments. They had planned to remove him not only from the political world but from this planet as well; Coningsby, the old enemy, had declared, with true Whig honesty, that he was after Harley's head. He proved maddeningly elusive, and the more the Whigs attacked him the more shadowy and tortuous he became—a target that vanished away into mist.

1709 should have been the Whigs' year of triumph, but they suffered a succession of disappointments. The war-party *par excellence*, they had come to power just when everyone was clamouring for peace. Bitter weather and rising prices made the longing for an end to hostilities more pronounced with every week. And the harder the honest interest tried to gain favour with the Queen, the more they repulsed her. They reached new heights of tactlessness in introducing an address encouraging the Queen to re-marry. The possibility of an English heir, they thought, might make the Electress Sophia less eager to visit the country she hoped to rule. It was a delicate proposition, requiring that sympathy of touch which the Whigs particularly lacked. As the Queen was forty-five, very recently widowed, notoriously unsuccessful in breeding live children, and hardly seductive in looks, the motion had its ludicrous side. The House found it hard to take the matter seriously, all the more so since it was introduced by three young sparks, including little Lord Lumley and Mr Watson—commonly known as the fillet of veal. Aunt Abigail, who wrote to Neddy on February 7, thought the address was more like the work of superannuated women than reasonable senators:

How glad some of their wives would be to have it in their power thus to revenge themselves when they were hardly cold in their graves. Methinks the next step shall be to make it penal for anyone to live a month a widow, which I hope would not want the Royal Assent.

In the streets the vendors were selling a paper entitled *The Hasty Widdow or the Sooner the Better*. The Queen was humiliated.

The Whigs controlled Cabinet and Commons, but not the Crown. They found it difficult even to gain admittance to the royal presence. Somers, the least arrogant of all the Junto lords, was the only one to swallow his pride and pay his court to Abigail. Once he had bent the knee to the Bedchamber Woman he gained access to the Queen whom he charmed with his good manners and sensible advice. The Duchess was annoyed. She exaggerated Abigail's part, and accused Somers of hideous ingratitude. Had he forgotten that she had canvassed ceaselessly for his inclusion in the Cabinet, that she had pleaded, pestered and teased, making herself unpopular in the process? Once Somers had respected her so much that he had stood up in his coach when he saw her go by, but he had merely done so, the Duchess now concluded, because he hoped to get something out of her. 'After he was in possession of his employ-ment,' she wrote in her usual furious way, 'he never made me but one visit but employed himself wholly to worship Abigail.' Marlborough, as ever, tried to soothe her. How could Somers hope to influence the Queen unless he used the only practical way of gaining access? The Duchess herself had become useless as a go-between, on account of her ceaseless quarrelling. 'Do not endeavour to injure anybody making their interest with Mrs Masham,' Marlborough advised.

Unwillingly the Whigs had to turn their thoughts to peace-making. War-weariness ignored can lead to mutiny and there was a current feeling that Whigs and moneyed men, dining together at Pontack's, one of their favourite haunts, took decisions about paying for and running the war without consulting the rest of the country. 'Is there any need of Parlia-ment meeting? Put it! Put it!' Harley wrote to Simon Harcourt. But even the war party found it difficult to ignore the outcry against growing hardship and waste of life. Fuel grew more and more expensive in a winter so bitter that the post boys were sometimes found dead, frozen to their horses, and so prolonged that Londoners were still lighting fires at the end of April. The Queen's famous remark, made spontaneously when she heard about the victory at Oudenarde—'Oh Lord when will all this dreadful bloodshed cease?'—was ungrateful to Marlborough, but expressed succinctly the widespread hatred of wasted life and squandered manhood. And if England was suffering from the icy winter, in France conditions were even worse. Starving peasants stormed into the towns foraging for food, and rioting when they found there was none to be had. Rumours reached England that Madame de Maintenon had decided to enter a convent, that the King was ready to go on his knees to beg for peace, and that the whole nation was on the verge of revolution. Louis was so genuinely cowed that he sent his foreign minister, Torcy, to confer with allied delegates at the Hague. By the end of May 1709, forty preliminary articles had been agreed by Austria, Great Britain and the Dutch, and it looked as if peace was really in sight.

But wars are easier to start than to stop. Easy promises made at the outset often prove impossible to fulfil without endless expense of life and energy. What begins as a pitched battle between well-trained armies ends in a sordid massacre of conscripts, a death-struggle in which innocent children starve and whole countries are laid waste. So it was in this war which William had planned with the simple aims of making the Dutch safe, of securing England's trade routes and of sapping Louis XIV's power. All this had now been achieved. The task of establishing Charles of Austria on the throne of Spain was a secondary consideration, and one which many believed to be impossible. Yet the Whigs now dedicated themselves to its achievement. 'No peace without Spain' was a slogan to which they clung relentlessly and without wisdom. In the Thirty-Seventh Preliminary Article drawn up at the Hague it was stated not only that Charles should be granted the whole of Spain, but also that he should have it handed to him within two months. Louis was prepared to accept all the other articles, stiff and humiliating though they were, but he knew that however much he himself might wish it, he could not possibly dislodge his grandson Philip of Anjou, who was now contentedly occupying the throne of Spain in Madrid. The Spaniards liked him and wanted him to stay, and it was asking too much to expect a young man to quit a kingdom at the whim of some distant diplomats.

The Tories would certainly have waived this clause and reached some kind of a compromise. But the Whigs, ignoring the fact that Spanish public opinion was solidly behind Philip and bitterly opposed to Charles, clung stubbornly to the terms demanded in the Thirty-Seventh Article.

On May 31 the news came by the Ostend mail that the French had refused to sign. It was an unhappy omen for Marlborough. Had the war ended after Oudenarde, or better still, after Ramillies, he could have retired at the height of success and fame. As it was an ungrateful nation was beginning to turn against him; his successes, the Duchess noticed, seemed to lower rather than raise his credit with the Queen, and Erasmus Lewis had remarked on the lack of enthusiasm at the Oudenarde victory celebrations; few people bothered to watch from their windows and balconies. By 1709 there were rumours that Marlborough intended to set up a military dictatorship, and unpleasant whispers of 'Cromwell' and 'John II' were coupled with his name. Many people alleged that the General did not even understand the *métier de la guerre*. He had struck one or two lucky chances, but had a genius 'of a size adapted to getting money by all sordid and dishonourable ways'. Although to all appearances a happy man with many successes to his credit, he was often 'vexed to the soul' by the ingratitude of his colleagues.

Godolphin was equally unhappy. The experiment of managing the country in partnership with the five tyrannizing Lords of the Junto, as the Queen called them, was proving just as difficult as Harley had prophesied. Rumours were current about 'great heats' between Godolphin and his new partners. Sometimes they even 'roasted' him with unkind speeches in the House. He became more querulous than ever and went back to his old moan about public service being worse than rowing in the galleys. Neither he nor Marlborough felt at ease with the Whigs; they often complained about Sunderland's arrogance and Halifax's pride. The only comfort was that Wharton, whose honesty and frankness they quite failed to appreciate, was destined to go to Ireland as Lord-Lieutenant—a prospect that was not relished by his lady, who went into convulsion fits at the very thought. Even the Duchess began to grow disillusioned with the party she had championed for so long, and she quarrelled with the Junto lords, accusing them in turn of ingratitude.

Harley was a useful scapegoat and they blamed him for everything. They accused him of visiting and influencing the Queen all through the summer of 1708, an imputation he himself disproves in one of the code letters when he states categorically, 'It is now eight months since I have had no sort of communication with her, and several months that I have been at this great distance.' The Queen's lack of enthusiasm over Ouden-arde was attributed by the Duchess to 'the pure effect of art, the product of that wonderful talent Mr Harley possessed, in the supreme degree, of confounding the common sense of mankind'. Marlborough blamed him for all the rumours proliferating on the continent, which said that the Queen had no further use for her General and Treasurer. He covered his tracks so well, he was so bland, so convincing, so priggishly certain that he enjoyed the special protection of the Almighty. It was easy to imagine him guilty of all kinds of deep designs.

In the months after Oudenarde there had been definite moves in the Dutch camp to obtain a separate peace with France, and it is certain that Harley made contact with the Dutch peace party. We know that in one of the code letters he warned the Queen that Marlborough's 'sordid avarice' might make him stand in the way of peace talks. Love of money had always been Marlborough's Achilles heel; it was a fact accepted by Louis who two years before had offered the General a *douceur* of two million livres if he would negotiate a peace. Marlborough turned down the offer because he considered the terms unfavourable, but in the autumn of 1708 he smuggled a note to his nephew Berwick who was commanding the enemy forces at Lille, expressing his readiness to initiate peace proceedings if the *douceur* was still available. Louis, suspecting a trick, refused to follow up the offer, but the fact that it was made at least absolves Marlborough of the charge of selfish war-mongering. He had given the best years of his life to the fight, and now that the Sun King had lost his lustre, he could see no justification for causing further bloodshed. He was as anxious as anybody to obtain a settlement before the summer of 1709 and thus avoid the rigours of yet another campaign. He disagreed with the Whigs over their stubborn adherence to Article Thirty-Seven, but was too unsure of his position to press his opinion with the Queen or the Junto. It was the inflexible Whigs, not Marlborough, with their arid motto of 'no peace without Spain', who drove the nations on to the horror of Malplaquet.

After the breakdown of negotiations in May 1709 both the French and English took on a new mood of belligerence. No topic but the war was talked of in the London coffee houses, and this time it seemed that nothing less than the dethroning of the Old Monarch would be considered satisfactory. The French managed to draw on unexpected reserves of strength, and on a wave of hatred for the merciless enemy that had refused to make peace, Louis pawned his jewels, the nobility melted down gold and silver plate, and the peasants, following the promptings of starvation, surged along in the wake of the army bread waggons. For most of the summer the armies manœuvred idly, neither side anxious for an engagement until, suddenly, on September 11, at Malplaquet, they fell on each other almost savagely. Marlborough snatched victory from the verge of defeat, but the casualties sustained appeared terrible even to hardened campaigners. The experience shattered Marlborough's health; for days he lay fevered, haunted by the memory of the dead and the dying. What made it all the worse was the thought that the carnage could have been avoided if peace terms had been agreed in May. 'It is melancholy,' Marlborough wrote, 'to see so many brave men killed, with whom I have lived these last eight years, when we thought ourselves sure of a peace.' Nor was Malplaquet the kind of battle to end all battles, for the French army, far from being annihilated, had gained confidence from its phoenix-like recovery. Harley explained the implications of 'the late bloody battle', as he called it, to Newcastle in a letter written on September 15, 1709:

The Dutch murmur that their troops are ruined; and what is worst, the French have recovered their reputation, not only amongst themselves but also with the allies, and it is a dangerous thing to have a good opinion of the courage of an enemy.

Many people feared that the alliance was breaking up, and disconcerting reports that the Hanoverian troops had refused to attack during the battle seemed to bear this out. There was bound to be much heart-searching and laying of blame when Parliament reassembled, but at least Harley had the comfort of knowing that the tragedy of Malplaquet could not in any way be laid at his door.

Another leisured summer without the cares of office gave Harley a chance to attend to family affairs, and he succeeded in arranging a desirable match for his daughter Abigail. Unlike many of his contemporaries he was incorruptible in money matters and did not take advantage of his position to amass a fortune, but he did see to it that his children benefited from his political success. If their father had remained a solid backbencher, Edward, Abigail and Elizabeth would probably have married into the Shropshire or Herefordshire gentry, but as it was they could set their sights far higher. Tabby's hand was offered to Lord Dupplin, son and heir of the Scottish Earl of Kinnoull. As a by-product, Harley gained two useful political allies north of the border. Socially and politically the match was one of Harley's *coups*; his enemies did their best to sabotage the matrimonial plan with their usual 'groundless malice'—the more groundless the charges, the fiercer the attack, in Harley's opinion. 'I thought indeed that I had suffered enough in my own person,' he wrote to Newcastle on September 15 '. . . but because I bore my own persecution so patiently, they have thought fit to persecute my family, and this match was thought too good for me . . . I cannot but say it is very hard a man cannot be suffered to be at ease in his private family affairs.'

When all the excitement was over, Harley made 'a little excursion into the country to avoid the noise which often attends weddings'. Apart from this domestic excitement, the summer followed much the same pattern as the year before. Harley kept away from the court, but maintained some contact with the Queen through the Mashams. Abigail's husband was such a nonentity that nobody could suspect him of meddling in important affairs, so the technique used was for Harley to meet him in town and give him messages for Abigail which were then conveyed to the Queen, who listened to them 'over and over'. Abigail was pregnant again—it was becoming an annual event. The baby was expected in mid-September, and the Queen refused to let her travel up to London from Windsor. 'She says I am so near my time the journey may disorder me so much that I may not be able to come hither again,' Abigail wrote. She regretted being unable to congratulate her young cousin in person, and on September 4 she wrote:

I might have had an opportunity of waiting upon my Lady Dupplin to wish her an uninterrupted life of happiness and contentment. I know you are so just as to believe you have not a friend in the world more heartily rejoices at her being so well disposed of than myself . . . my enemies are so very angry at it.

Abigail was in a state of nerves, and felt herself hedged about with enemies. It riled her that she could not enjoy the normal pleasures of family life, and had to work for such a hard taskmaster as the Queen, who was just as difficult as ever and often highly uncommunicative. Mr Safe, as they called Masham, refused to carry messages when his wife was out of order, and this added to Abigail's worries, since she did not trust any other messengers.

In October, a whole month later than expected, Abigail was brought to bed of a girl. She took the risk of moving back into the Duchess of Marlborough's lodgings to have her child in a modicum of comfort. But it was no time to relax, for there were rivals at court. All through the summer the Duke and Duchess of Somerset had been visiting the Queen. Harley noticed that the Duke was a most 'sedulous attender at Windsor'; more important, it seemed as if he was courting the Queen, not as a Junto spokesman, but as an independent, and one who could 'stand on his own legs'. With the persistence of dedicated ambition he stayed close to Windsor all the summer. 'It is certain,' Harley reported to Newcastle, 'he is not now any favourite of the Junto.' The Duchess quickly gained ground with the Queen. Red-headed Elizabeth Somerset knew how to be charming without appearing to domineer, and she had the nobility of birth which Abigail lacked. She also realized that if Sarah Marlborough continued to vex and tease, the office of Groom of the Stole would soon be vacant and she fancied herself in the part. The Duke of Somerset, self-important and proud, saw himself as a national leader, above faction, above party, above almost everything. Not for nothing was he nicknamed the Sovereign. Sarah Marlborough had her own cutting comments to make:

She [the Duchess] was never quite so kind as after she had taken the resolution to supplant me, for then she not only came to dinner and made meetings for play oftener than before, but I remember she took it into her head still to kiss me at parting, which was quite new.

Unfortunately, the Queen did not in any way share Swift's aversion to women with red hair, and soon the new Duchess had all the look of a new favourite. Abigail wisely took the minimum time off after her lying-in and went back to look after her own interests and Harley's.

Unable to go to court himself, Harley spent his time flattering Dukes and Earls by letter. He continued to woo Shrewsbury, following up his success of the previous summer. 'The hermit of the Cotswolds', as he was called, needed continual bolstering. He frankly preferred the peace of Heythrop to the bustle of London. Had it not been for his ambitious wife, he would have been content to stay out of politics altogether. He had no natural taste for responsibility, and his delicate health was a liability; his 'crazy corpse' as he himself called it, put a limit on his activities. 'I am sorry you are pained in so many places at once,' one of his friends had occasion to say. He preferred to remain uncommitted, an insignificant cipher rather than a bad public figure. But the 'Etalyon'— Lady Wentworth's spelling—drove him on. She wished to take her place among the peeresses of the realm and to rub shoulders with Queens. For a while, London society was buzzing with stories about this Duchess's exotic behaviour; among other things she was given to chucking her husband under the chin in public. Lady Cowper paid tribute to her ability to entertain and divert people, though she added rather primly that the Italian would 'sometimes excel the bounds of decency'. It was rumoured that the Duchess was the one person who could make the Queen laugh, and had none of the native reserve of English ladies, who were scandalized when she boldly approached the mourning Queen with the words 'Oh, my Queen you must not think always of the poor

Prince'. With such a social climber behind him there was a hope that Shrewsbury might be driven to play his part, and Harley wanted him to come in on the right side. So he worked hard to gain the Duke and to keep him in the correct frame of mind.

Renegade Whigs, doubtful Tories—Harley worked on them all. He even approached Haversham, the fanatical Whig turned fanatical Tory, who preferred to sit on the fence until he could meet all his friends in town and see what they intended to do. Patriotism, he cynically assured Harley, was a sentiment altogether too noble and generous for our northern clime; most English people, he believed, bereft of 'the warm and ripening sun', were inclined to nonchalance, and were quite incapable of adopting a cause.

Harley's followers were also hard at work. George Granville, a moderate Tory with strong electoral interest in the West Country, a man of culture and good sense, had, as he termed it himself, formed an 'inseparable attache' to Harley. He proved this by visiting key people, seeing if he could make 'alterations', confirming some in the right notions, and putting others in touch with 'proper acquaintance'.

St John, by contrast, was critical of his master's methods. He disapproved of drawing in members of the fringe groups—the Court party and moderate Whigs—and believed that any promises made to such people would prove 'clogs and fetters' at a later date. St John was not interested in mild magnificoes like Shrewsbury and Newcastle. As far as he was concerned, all faith must now be put in the Tory party, a Tory party strengthened and renewed, with the moderates, whom Harley had worked so hard to detach, reunited with the main High Church body. 'You broke the party, unite it again,' he urged. Harley did not agree. He was still chary of the High Church element. Although many of the zealots had learnt wisdom, as St John put it, 'in the fiery trial of affliction', there was always the danger that High Tories, once back in power, would return to their old bullying ways. So, although he went so far as to make Abigail ask favours of the Queen on behalf of Rochester, and briefed Granville to woo the Duke of Beaufort, a rather comic old Jacobite of great electoral power, he refused to lend his support openly. Vague promises, nebulous good-will and policies couched in general terms, all these were Harley's stock-in-trade, but they did not satisfy St John. 'Why do you not gain Bromley entirely?' he had asked in 1708. Bromley, influential and widely respected for his honest views, ex-Tacker and leader of the younger generation of Tories, was puzzled by Harley's approach. 'I wish you had pleased to have been something more particular,' he complained,

'I hope you will be more free and open.' St John felt frustrated; he believed that Harley was the one man who could persuade the country gentlemen to shed their desire to be independent of party, their impractical yearning to act according to the promptings of their own good sense rather than the dictates of party leaders. 'No one living is able to do so much as you towards removing our present evils,' St John wrote. He urged his master to teach the Tories to forget their factions, their jealousy and pique, and to inspire 'the vile generation' with patriotism. But still Harley refused to treat with the party as a whole. Openness and precision were not in his line. He was never one to put all his cards on the table. He preferred to write equivocal letters about peace, couched in his muddy style, to noblemen in country mansions—to weaker Whigs and Tories who might be persuaded to waver towards the moderate cause. By the autumn of 1709 he felt confident, in spite of Shrewsbury's warning him, that although some might profess themselves heartily in favour of a peace policy when discoursed with 'singly' in the country, they could all too easily change their minds when subject to other pressures in the convivial atmosphere of club or coffee house.

All the same, many letters did find their mark, and soon a further batch brought friends and relations hurrying up to the opening of Parliament. Mansell, on the coast of Wales, received his summons in a letter which 'the fish man brought to the captain'. He promised to come at once, and many other squires arrived to help oppose the Whig plan to raise six millions for the war by means which included the levying of taxes on household goods such as coal, beer, candles and malt.

Parliament reassembled on November 15, 1709. The Queen, for the first time as a widow, opened proceedings with due ceremony, though she faltered a little as she read her very Whiggish speech. It was plain from what she said that the war would be continued, whatever the cost.

The superb confidence of the Whig managers was not echoed by men and women who sat huddled over the expensive glow of a fire in the hearth, and who were more interested in warming their own skins than placing Charles of Austria on the Spanish throne. It had been a bad harvest, and hardship was already hitting many homes. Many families were in mourning for relations killed at Malplaquet. The Dutch people also had had more than enough, and there were signs that they would not scruple to make a separate peace. In order to stiffen their resolve, the Whigs persuaded them to sign the Barrier Treaty in October 1709. It was a tempting bargain for the Dutch, and a bad one for the English, who had to promise equal trading rights in Spanish America; worse still,

Minorca, one of England's most precious prizes, had to be conceded to Charles of Austria. The Dutch were offered everything their hearts could desire in the Spanish Netherlands. The Whigs apparently thought nothing of sacrificing national pride; as Swift wrote in his *Remarks on the Barrier Treaty*, 'a reasonable person in China . . . would conceive their High Mightinesses the States-General, to be some vast powerful Commonwealth, like that of Rome, and her Majesty to be a petty prince.' Marlborough was disgusted with the treaty, and refused to have anything to do with it. He had led the English armies to glory, and all that had been achieved was a grovelling parley with the Dutch.

In the face of such ineptitude, the peace party gained ground, Harley's patience had been rewarded, and the prophesied swing had come. The Queen, public opinion, a group of friends and allies becoming known as the Juntilla, and the main body of the Tories—all these were now behind him. His stock was far higher now than it had been in the days of the alternative scheme. Many people saw him as the only man who could lead the nation into peace. And he himself was beginning to see this task as a sacred mission which he intended, with God's help, to achieve.

CHAPTER 12

A NONSENSICAL HARANGUE

IN THE 'GREAT SHAKE' of 1708 everything had hinged on Marlborough. Harley's *coup* had failed because the General's reputation was legendary, and when it came to the point, few people dared to join a regime he had abandoned. Now, with peace moves in the air, the situation had changed; the General's usefulness was almost finished and his stock was low. In the autumn of 1709 he made a false move. Worried about his present position and fearful of the future, anxious also to stand above the impermanence of party, he asked the Queen to make him Captain-General for life. Anne was disturbed, remembering that people had called her faithful Freeman a second Cromwell. His friends had warned him against making such a request, and his enemies soon made capital out of the blunder. In the new year he realized how much his standing was impaired, for when he went to the Queen and suggested a suitable candidate for the office of Lieutenant of the Tower of London, she told him that he had come too late since she had already appointed Lord Rivers, a renegade Whig who had recently fallen under Harley's spell. She went on to demand that the colonelcy left vacant by Rivers should be given to Abigail Masham's brother, Jack Hill, an undistinguished individual who shared Abigail's gift for mimicry and was somewhat addicted to the bottle. Marlborough knew that the appointment of a court favourite above the heads of experienced officers could only cause discontent in the army, and his expression as he left the royal presence convinced the watching courtiers that there was trouble in the air. A second interview with the Queen was no more successful than the first. He was unable to draw a single kind expression from her and she remained cold and unyielding. To appoint bishops without consulting anybody had been bad enough, and now this stubborn stupid woman thought she could dispense regiments as if they were vacant sees. It was the finish. The Queen must learn that she meddled with his precious army at her peril.

Marlborough swept off to Windsor Lodge as he had done at previous crises, and there he penned a firm note stating that the Queen must choose between himself and Abigail. Godolphin was instructed to show the letter to the Queen. But the Treasurer wavered; his timidity spoiled the scheme and other Ministers took fright at the thought of an open breach. Sunderland alone was determined to carry it further and planned an address in Parliament praying the Queen to dismiss her favourite. This hurly-burly at court caused a great stir. The House of Commons was crowded with Members hoping for a grave sensation. None came; instead Marlborough wrote a watered-down letter to the Queen, begging for protection from the malice of a Bedchamber Woman. The Queen, after she had brooded a little over advice given her by Somers, decided not to insist on Hill's appointment though she stood her ground over Rivers.

If the Ministers had all supported Marlborough, the Queen would have found it hard to insist on the appointment of Rivers, and she might have been forced to part with Abigail. Maynwaring thought that it should be child's play for any man 'to hold the first post in a government and not have it in their power to remove such a slut as that'. It was an alarming development for Abigail and for Harley too, but in the end they were encouraged by the lack of cohesion among the Whigs, and by the appearance of a rift between them and Marlborough. And the more the Duchess harried the Queen, the more firmly Anne stuck to Abigail. Maynwaring incited Sarah to write letter after letter on the subject of Mrs Masham who was called by a variety of uncomplimentary names including 'Carbunculata'. The Duchess did not flinch from conveying to the Queen the information that the nefarious Rivella Manley, a female denizen of Grub Street of the most malicious kind, had hinted in her pamphlet, *The New Atlantis*, at unnatural passions between the royal Olympia and Hilaria—the Queen and Abigail. In this scurrilous document Sarah herself was accused of being Godolphin's mistress, a libel she ignored. The Queen, however, was asked to take note of what gossip said, and on the strength of it to dispense with Madame Masham.

Naturally such endless attacks upset the Queen and affected her health. Her physician, Sir David Hamilton, a psychologist before his time, noted how frequently her attacks followed mental disturbance. Gout rose from the feet and knee to grip the whole nervous system, upsetting the circulation and giving rise to vapours. Sir David advised his patient to avoid emotional scenes. Following this prescription, the Queen refused to see the Duchess whenever possible, and if she did see either of the Marlboroughs remained distant and unsympathetic, refusing to become embroiled. The Duchess interpreted her attitude as one of complete inhumanity, indulged in at the instigation of Harley, or Abigail, or both.

If Marlborough was sensitive about his lack of influence with the Queen, the Whigs too were exasperated, realizing now that she could checkmate them over and over again. They tried a desperate throw to gain her favour and one that proved to be inept. On November 5, 1709, Henry Sacheverell, that firebrand preacher who had hung out the bloody flag of defiance early in the reign, and had been railing against Whigs and Dissenters ever since, preached an inflammatory sermon in St Paul's before a large congregation, which included the Lord Mayor of London, Sir Samuel Garrard. Oozing unction, and with a 'gogling wildness of his eyes', Sacheverell loosed some seasonable fireworks on the subject of non-resistance to the monarch. This delighted the Mayor, a zealous High Tory, who took the preacher home in triumph in his coach and afterwards encouraged him to print the sermon. The Queen was less pleased, for November 5, besides commemorating gunpowder, treason and plot, was also the anniversary of William's landing at Torbay. Sacheverell could be accused of questioning the legality of the bloodless revolution, not to mention the Queen's right to the throne. This gave the Whigs their chance. They decided to ingratiate themselves with the Queen by prosecuting Sacheverell and making a public example of him. Sunderland was set on pushing matters as far as an impeachment and Godolphin was in a vindictive mood. Sacheverell had arraigned those 'wily Volpones' who had deserted their own party, and Godolphin took this personally, since his own nickname was 'the Fox'. 40,000 copies of the published sermon were being avidly read throughout the country, and the Whigs were determined to punish the culprit for circulating such treasonable innuendoes.

The excitement caused was out of all proportion. 'I cannot think one firebrand could cause such a flame unless the fuel were very dry and prepared for it,' wrote Nathaniel Harley from Aleppo. It seemed as if one spark was enough to set the country aflame, rousing all the dormant hatred between Whig and Tory, churchman and dissenter. And to make quite sure that the case really made a stir, it was decided to try Sacheverell in Westminster Hall, where special scaffolds for spectators were designed by Sir Christopher Wren. It was impossible to accommodate all the people who wanted to come and there was an ugly scramble for tickets; peers were rationed to eight apiece, ladies had to make love to lords to ensure a place and Wren was criticized for not making the most of all available space:

Then he told them plainly that the Q— was positive she would have nobody over her head, which made the house laugh coming so pat to what had been so lately the discourse of the town.

Ladies of fashion had to endure the torture of rising in the small hours to secure their seats, and while Whig beauties applauded, fair Tories wept. Tabby Harley, now Lady Dupplin, told her aunt how one party adored Sacheverell and the other would hang him. 'They think me very stupid that have so little concern about the matter,' wrote Tabby, who was expecting a child and had more important things to think about.

The trial opened in February; at its height Harley came up to town and at once caught a bad cold. His sister Abigail reported that he was much out of order; as usual he dosed himself with gruel and refused to stay indoors. As the trial progressed the excitement mounted. Sacheverell's mob went about wrecking meeting-houses and burning the pews. Aunt Abigail told Neddy that in one place 'they did not so much as spare the poor woman's clothes that lived in the house, but burnt all she had but a feather bed'—it was a wonder they managed to resist such an inflammable item. The weavers rose in the city, the trained bands were called out, and, as so often happens, the peace party soon excelled itself in acts of violence. 'This is methinks an odd way of defending passive obedience and non-resistance,' Aunt Abigail reflected. Up from the country, Abigail enjoyed a ringside seat at the trial; she was shocked to the depths of her Puritan heart by 'the horridest blasphemy that ever was vented among those called Christians' and by one passage which said that the Queen had no more title to the crown than 'my Lord Mayor's horse'. Like many other female observers, she began to grow weary of the proceedings. 'What is mankind that a nonsensical harangue from a pragmatical insignificant man should make such a terrible work?' she inquired.

Although 'Robin the Trickster', as his enemies called him, was well in the background, many blamed him for stirring up the mob with the express purpose of making the trial rebound unfavourably on the Whigs. He marshalled his force of writers, and pamphlets soon began to fly about like hail, as Coxe put it, and the Tories managed things so skilfully that the hawkers refused to cry the Whig pamphlets. One particularly cunning and insinuating paper was thought to be written in Harley's style, but of course nothing could be proved against him. Obliquely, the Trickster moulded Sacheverell's public image, and although many believed at heart that the play-acting parson was a charlatan, a wave of admiration swept through the country. The fair sex, in particular, was carried away; many children baptized that year were graced with the name of Sacheverell.

The Lords, it was said, having set out to roast a parson, made the fire so high, in their zeal, that they scorched themselves in the process. Sacheverell could hardly fail; he had public opinion behind him, the clever Simon Harcourt to conduct his defence and the equally able Atterbury to write his speeches for him. And when the Lords retired to consider their verdict, they found themselves in an awkward dilemma. Were they to stand out against public opinion, or to give in to mob violence, thus appearing to approve of Sacheverell's doctrine of non-resistance? And were they to pander to the Queen, who had begun by favouring their cause, and had now become alarmed by the violence of feeling aroused? The Queen told Sir David Hamilton that she thought the riots must have been pre-planned because they flared up so suddenly, and she was all for playing down Sacheverell's punishment to avoid further trouble. At the trial, Abigail Harley noticed that at times the Queen appeared pensive; she did not give any clear indication of where her sympathies lay, and no handkerchief came out to catch the hoped-for Tory tear. The mobs who surrounded her chair as she travelled from St James's each day shouted amidst all the hurraying and huzzaing, 'We hope your Majesty is for the High Church and Sacheverell', but she gave them no answer. When Abigail suggested that she should let people know her mind, she said stiffly that it was her friends' advice not to meddle. All the same, as the trial went on, the Whigs began to realize that they had done themselves no good. Many Court Tories went with the Queen rather than the Ministry—another blow for Godolphin.

The Lords found Sacheverell guilty by only seventeen votes and inflicted a faint-hearted punishment. He was ordered to abstain from preaching for three years, and one copy of his sermon was publicly burnt by the hangman. Three years of silence was a hellish torment for such a loquacious man, but many martyrs have fared worse. Due, perhaps, to Harley's influence, a comfortable living was found for him in the border country of Shropshire and his journey there turned into a triumphal procession. Thomas Foley reported to Harley that at Worcester there was bell-ringing and much merriment at the expense of pompous officials out to prevent demonstrations. When a woman defending her celebration bonfire was kicked by an officious gentleman, she unceremoniously threw his periwig into the flames. Other women dressed up Charles I's statue with flowers, and when the beadle climbed up to remove them, the women pulled the ladder from under his feet.

The Rivers dispute followed by the Sacheverell fracas had finally unbalanced the Duchess. Her fixation was out of control; the Blenheim muniment room boasts boxes of endless self-vindication written at this time. The Queen found her insufferable, and at the trial she upset everybody in the royal box with a petty squabble over whose privilege it was to sit down in the Queen's presence. At last, hearing that somebody had told the Queen that she spoke about her disrespectfully, she demanded an interview to clear herself. It was typical of her to imagine all kinds of small causes for the Queen's disfavour when the real reason was to be found in her own character. Pathetically anxious to make everything right before the Easter Communion, she went to the Palace at Kensington on Maundy Thursday and so frightened the Page of the Backstairs with her expression that he went in to confer with the Queen. The Duchess waited impatiently on the window sill in the long gallery, like a Scottish peeress with a petition, as she herself described it. After what seemed to her an unnecessary and humiliating delay, the Duchess was admitted. She had rashly said in recent letters that she would simply state her case and not require an answer, so the Queen parried all her raging with the stolid refrain—'You said you desire no answer and I shall give you none. Whatever you have to say you may put it in writing.' Convinced that the offending words had been put into the Queen's mouth by Harley and Mrs Masham, the Duchess began to weep hysterically, overcome by what she termed the Queen's barbarous behaviour. The only flicker of emotion she managed to evoke was a slight start when the Somersets were mentioned; the Queen also blushed and turned away from the candle when the Duchess tried to bring up the supposed calumnies which were the real reason for her visit. There were things which always remained unsaid between them; every time, as they came to the point, the Queen turned away and terminated the interview. Nobody will ever know what Sarah was supposed to have said, but we do know that she made many accusations including those which concerned Harley's supposed late-night visits to the Palace, and these were enough to anger the Queen.

Sir David Hamilton noticed a marked deterioration in the Queen's health at the time of the Sacheverell trial. He was sure this was due to the stresses she had been subjected to since the beginning of the year—letters from the Duchess, threats to Abigail and 'outside pressure', as the doctor put it, from Harley and his friends. Hamilton craved Godolphin's help when he met the Treasurer coming out of the Queen's closet one day with his usual gloomy expression. The doctor had cut out all the potions prescribed by other physicians and substituted common sense and spirit of millipedes. He noticed that the Queen was liable to be

F

particularly upset when she was 'troubled inwardly', and so he asked the Treasurer to avoid all business at certain seasons. The Treasurer complied, but by the beginning of 1710 the Queen was so distressed that she was quite beyond the help of millipedes or of the considerate behaviour of her Treasurer. 'Between teazings of two different sorts,' the doctor said, the Queen was being torn apart.

By 1710 the Queen's friendship with Sarah Marlborough had reached its *dénouement*. Furthermore, though this her doctor did not realize, she had made the decision to assert her authority and govern with the one man she really liked. One evening she sent Robert Harley a letter which, according to Swift, was delivered to him, all dirty, by one of the under-gardeners at Hampton Court or Kensington. Thus encouraged, Harley went up the privy stairs once again and together he and the Queen worked out a plan to liberate the Crown from its enslavement to party. The Queen gladly agreed to his moderating scheme with its emphasis on peace. For the time being this was all he required. It was enough that she wanted to be freed from Junto tyranny. Later he could explain to her the need to put her trust in the Tories.

The moment for a change had come. In the mounting turmoil of the Sacheverell trial, Harley worked out where the first blow was to fall. Few people guessed what he was about to do. His family had no inkling of his deep designs. The Whigs were sublimely unaware. They still thought they could ruin him, and it was rumoured that they intended to impeach him for secretly corresponding with the Dutch peace party. Such threats, and the risks he was about to run, left him undisturbed. Had he lacked courage, he would have retired long ago to his books, his bowls, his ruined castle and his rather dull wife. Whatever the dangers involved, he was bent on satisfying his ambition to give the Queen the government she needed—a government managed, of course, by himself.

CHAPTER 13

THE SHAKING SEASON

THE FIRST TREMOR of the approaching 'shake' was felt on April 14, 1710. The Marquis of Kent, that uninspiring creature of the Whigs, received an unexpected call to the Palace. 'The Bug', or 'his Stinkingness', as Arthur Maynwaring even more unkindly called him, was one of the least valuable members of the Household; his tenure of office had been undistinguished and it seemed understandable that the Queen might feel tempted to exchange him for someone less malodorous. He proved pathetically ready to barter his Staff and Key for a dukedom, even though some said he had paid the Duchess of Marlborough £10,000 to obtain them. Kent's departure caused the Junto little dismay; he could hardly be described as a pillar of the party. But when the Queen called Shrewsbury to the Palace they were less pleased, for only a few weeks before the Duke had voted against them on the Sacheverell impeachment. More serious still was the fact that Godolphin knew nothing about the change until he received a stiff letter from the Queen as he snatched a few days' rest at Newmarket. It was humiliating for him to realize that she had not even bothered to consult him before appointing a man in a post of great social and ceremonial importance at Court. Had he served her all these years to meet with such treatment? He replied to her letter at once, decrying her action. Shrewsbury might well be pleasant and amenable, a useful addition to the government in troublous times, but as he had been caballing with Harley everyone would fly from him as if he had the plague.

Godolphin posted to London, to find the Queen icy and distant, his colleagues uncertain and suspicious. Nobody really knew who was behind the move, and ironically enough Godolphin and Marlborough were blamed for engineering Shrewsbury's appointment. It was like fighting a battle in a thick fog. For a few days everyone waited for further changes, but none occurred and the excitement died down. It was always possible, after all, that the Queen had appointed Shrewsbury because she liked him, and not for any ulterior political motive. She was nervous of taking such a step without the blessing of her most experienced counsellor, but she told Sir David Hamilton that the whole operation had passed off with far less trouble than she had expected.

The rest of April went by without further changes and May too was uneventful. All the same a mounting propaganda campaign directed at Sunderland seemed to suggest that he was next on the list. There were constant rumours of revolutions at court and alterations in the Ministry. The Marlboroughs were in trouble again over the army appointments. The Queen was annoyed because the Duke had failed to appoint Abigail's two nearest and dearest—the Colonels Masham and Hill. Marlborough gave in over Masham, but held firm over Hill. He was sure that the appointment of this worthless man would make a mockery of all army promotions. The Whigs failed to back him up, and his daughter Lady Sunderland told the Duchess that she thought dear papa might just as well humour the Queen in so small a matter. The Harleyites watched the quarrel with satisfaction; the more disagreements in the enemy camp the better they were pleased. It was essential to break the Junto. 'If the Whigs stand fast they will be on as sure a bottom as that foundation of your house at Woodstock,' Maynwaring told the Duchess.

While the Whigs waited and wondered, Harley and his friends were preparing the wedge to split them in pieces. The Juntilla had already decided that Sunderland must go but was held up for a successor. Harley wanted Lord Anglesey, a friend of Nottingham's who knew how to act independently. His inclusion would have reassured the Tory zealots without giving them too much power, and it would also have provided a useful counterbalance to Shrewsbury and other Whiggish lords. But at this point the Queen intervened, ironically enough using the power that Harley had taught her to value. She wanted Dartmouth, a more moderate Tory, for she was still very chary of anyone connected with Nottingham. Harley stood out for a while but before long decided to bow to the Stuart stubbornness. Dartmouth had much to recommend him. He had been working at the Board of Trade for eight years, quietly and without fuss, and was reliable and discreet, if uninspired. Count Gallas, the Emperor's envoy, found that to converse with him was like talking to a brick wall. Sarah Marlborough described him as 'a jester himself and a jest to all others' which was hardly fair, although Macky confirmed that he made jests and loved to laugh at them. On the day the Queen came to the throne he was tactful enough to tell her that he was 'all joy without the least alloy', or so he said, and he was undoubtedly one of the men she was able to view with esteem. He was painstaking and nobody could find any particular fault with him. It would have been foolish to waste time arguing with the Queen about Sunderland's successor while the chance to overthrow the Junto slipped away.

At last, on June 14, Secretary Boyle was assigned the unenviable task of collecting the Seals from Sunderland's house. The cantankerous peer had been expecting this move for so long that he met it with unaccustomed dignity and a cold rejection of the proferred pension of three thousand a year. 'If I cannot have the honour of serving my country,' he said, 'I will not plunder it.'

For a few days repercussions were awaited. It was thought that Sunderland's cronies might resign in sympathy, as Harcourt and St John had done after Harley's fall in 1708. But nothing happened. Godolphin pleaded for him, rather feebly, on the grounds that he was Marlborough's son-in-law. 'Must the fate of Europe depend on that?' the Queen tartly inquired. Nobody liked Sunderland enough to make great sacrifices for him. Godolphin, for the last time, threatened to resign, and for the last time, he did not carry out his threat. The Queen had a right to remove someone she found increasingly odious, all the more so since he had been forced on her in the first place.

So far all that had happened was that the Queen had taken into her counsels a man she liked, and removed one she abhorred. If it stopped there, nobody could object. All the same there was an uneasy feeling about that a large-scale *coup* was planned; and there were grave dangers attending a change of government. A mass departure of the Whigs could cause alarm on the continent and panic in the City. Many Whigs genuinely believed that the French would feel they could dictate peace on any terms they chose from a Tory government.

Harley allowed for these fears and used them as counters in his game. Like a military commander he could only outline his general objective, mount his attack and trust his own judgement in parrying the enemy counter-move. It was just the kind of delicate, intrigue-ridden operation at which he excelled. He had long ago mastered the art of dealing with people singly so that they failed to realize they were pawns in a larger game. He had a talent for playing on their ambition and pride, and 'luring their cupidity', as Coxe put it. There was no score for such a work; as usual he played it by ear with a sure touch. He foresaw many of the difficulties that were likely to crop up in such an audacious political manœuvre but in one thing his intuition failed him—he underestimated the reviving strength of the High Tories. From the first they harried him, urging him to push on quickly with his plan, and they soon grew impatient with his caution and delaying tactics. 'I might have lost the summer if I had stayed to see the fruits of the secret consultations which were to change the world,' Sir Thomas Hanmer, an influential Tory, wrote to Matthew Prior. 'Methinks they ripen very slowly, and I wish they be not overtaken and nipped by the winter.' Lord Dupplin, Harley's son-in-law, who was trying to build up Scottish support for the plan, was frustrated by 'the slowness at London'.

But Harley knew what he was doing. An open and impetuous attack on the Whigs could cause a crop of resignations, perhaps a counter-attack, with consequent dismay among the moneyed men and European allies. Above all the Whigs feared a dissolution. It was certain that they would have to face many losses at the polls. They were determined to stay on at Westminster, praying that circumstances would swing public opinion back in their favour, as the Old Pretender had so obligingly arranged with his invasion attempt in 1708. Harley understood that if he could flatter some of the Whigs with the belief that only a minor 'shake' was intended, and that the present Parliament would in all probability be allowed to continue, there was a good chance that he would be able to buy their support. Some of his more bigoted Tory friends reacted badly to the idea of a compromise with the Whigs, but he ignored them; it was still part of his creed to avoid making the enemy 'desperate'. He continued to play on Somers and Cowper, knowing that if he could win them it would be possible to found a new Ministry on that broad bottom which eighteenth-century moderates sought as the ultimate perfection. Somers, with his perfect manners and obvious ability, had by now won his way into the Queen's good grace, and in June, on the eve of Sunderland's dismissal, he was paid £1,000 from the secret service accounts—a neatly timed gratuity.

In the main, Harley did not resort to bribery; he had neither the means nor the inclination to depend on financial incentives. To caress and make promises was in most cases just as effective. He was so successful in working on Somerset's inflated ego that the Duke was expelled from the Whig Kit-Cat Club for suspicious dealings with Robin the Trickster. Elaborate security precautions surrounded Somerset's secret consultations with Harley. In July, when there were evening meetings at his house, a servant had to wait about under the clock at his gate. He was instructed to admit straight into the hall the clandestine visitors who came with the curtains of their chairs securely drawn. Harley's coach was also seen at the door of the Whig Secretary, Henry Boyle, while Somers and Halifax were observed paying Mrs Masham a great deal of attention.

With the Dukes of Shrewsbury and Somerset at his side, the Duke of Newcastle in his pocket, two Junto lords making advances and the Tory party looking to him for a lead, Harley was in a promising position.

Godolphin still refused to respond to any advances. He was the one man who had enough experience to play Harley at his own game and to outmanœuvre him. The Queen, although she was bored with the Lord Treasurer, who had served her faithfully if gloomily for so many years, found it difficult to dismiss him. In May she told Sir David Hamilton that she believed the City would soon be in an uproar if she turned him out. Besides, she added rather pathetically, he studied her 'ease'. Sir David, who was already beginning to overstep the mark as a purely medical adviser, was commissioned to ask Godolphin whether he would break off with Sarah Marlborough. The Treasurer, in his loyal way, refused to entertain the suggestion, which gave Harley just the handle he wanted. He made the Queen believe that Godolphin was a helpless puppet, over-ruled and guided by the passion of a mad woman. He told Newcastle that Godolphin was growing more sour and rude with every day that passed. 'The Queen grows every day more and more uneasy at Lord Godolphin and the Duchess of Marlborough,' he wrote on July 1, 'and both of them continue to give daily more and fresh occasion of distaste.' The Duchess had just announced that she intended to publish the Queen's private letters in order to prove how badly she had been treated. This mad threat did little to further Godolphin's cause, and at the beginning of July the Queen wrote him a letter of dismissal, not sent at once because there were matters to be decided before the Treasurer could be removed.

Since the departure of Godolphin was likely to cause concern, it was important to reassure the allies in advance and also to soothe the City men. Harley had his own friends in the City and all through the month of July he spread the news among the merchants and bankers of his acquaintance that a new administration would not lead to an irresponsible financial policy—rather the contrary. The moneyed interest must learn that Godolphin was not the only person who could deal with Treasury affairs. To encourage the allies, the Juntilla chose an emissary, James Cresset, to put its case to the foreign courts. There were maddening delays as the Whig-controlled Admiralty put every obstacle in the way of Cresset's departure. And then, just as he was at last about to leave, he was suddenly taken ill and died, some said from a dose of Whig poison. It was observed that Harley lost his customary composure and looked distinctly worried until he had Cresset's papers and instructions safely back; this was hardly surprising if the gossips were right in assuming that Cresset carried a message promising the Elector of Hanover Marlborough's place as Commander-in-Chief of the allied forces. The day after Cresset's death, Somerset summoned Shrewsbury and Harley to a meeting in the Queen's presence, and urgent discussions were held to choose a second emissary, who would be able to leave at once and counter Whig propaganda. It was not easy, for most of Harley's supporters wanted to stay in London in the hope of landing a profitable place in the new Ministry. Rivers, the man whose promotion Marlborough had once opposed, and one of his wife's pet aversions, was sent off in September. He too fell violently ill just before leaving, which could have made him wonder whether his cook had Whiggish tendencies.

Rivers did his best to be polite to the Electress Sophia, but she was not a woman to be taken in by compliments as she frankly let him know at his first audience. 'My Lord,' she said, 'Your person is welcome. You tell me you have given me great instances of your esteem, I thank you for it. You tell me you are ready to give me greater, I don't believe you can, nor do I desire it.' Rivers had anyway lost a great deal of time, and Marlborough had the opportunity to work on the monarchs of Europe long before he appeared on the scene. As a result, the Emperor of Austria wrote the Queen a letter in his own hand, expostulating with her for contemplating changes in the Ministry. 'The Emperor cannot be snubbed for meddling in our domestic affairs that concern the alliance,' Halifax wrote to Newcastle on August 1, the day the letter was delivered. But the Queen did not agree. No foreigner was allowed to dictate to her or tell her how to rule. She gave the Emperor a stern rebuff and dealt summarily with other envoys.

A delegation of bankers, headed by Sir Gilbert Heathcote, received similar treatment. Even a barrage of Bank of England directors failed to cow her. She listened to the grim tale of falling stocks and vanishing credit but refused to be moved. Ignoring what Harley called 'their tragical expressions,' she primly assured them that no further changes were expected. Heathcote, rich financial wizard, the great power in the Bank and the New East India Company, exclaimed when he heard this news, 'God be thanked.' Her denial had a soothing effect, though the Tories still seemed to be in a state of elation, hugging themselves at the prospect of all the political plums which they were sure were coming their way, whatever the Queen chose to say about it.

With the Tories becoming impatient, the dismissal of Godolphin could not be long delayed. But the choice of a successor was again proving difficult. Harley was too wise to claim the post for himself, and he made approaches to Shrewsbury as a potential temporary figure-head. But the Duke automatically shrank from responsibility. On July 22 he wrote:

I have ten reasons, every one strong enough to hinder my doing it, but that of engaging in an employment I do not in the least understand. . . . In my mind you should be at the head, because you then come naturally into the Cabinet Council, where you are so much wanted.

In the circumstances it was decided to put the Treasury in Commission after Godolphin's dismissal. So the last days of July were spent in sounding out friends and allies who might be willing to serve as Commissioners. Harley's faithful follower, 'Swallow' Poulett, Henry Paget, an anaemic Tory linked by marriage to the Foley family, Mansell, and Benson, another sound moderate, were all asked to join. Such men were acceptable to the Queen and gave no offence to tepid Whigs like Newcastle and Somerset. On August 5 Harley felt that his preparations were complete. 'I am to go this night to the Queen,' he told Newcastle, 'and I hope the whole chimerical matter will be at an end.'

The Queen knew about Harley's intentions; she had already written a letter of dismissal and yet when Godolphin treated her, on August 7, to a lecture on the subject of governing by secret cabals, and finished by asking 'Is it the will of your Majesty that I should go on?', she replied, without hesitation, a simple 'yes'. The next day the dismissal letter was sent. Some said it was delivered by Somerset's liveried coachman, who left it with the porter. Others said that it was conveyed to him by his friend, Mr Smith. It was in any case not the kind of letter a statesman likes to receive at the end of a long conscientious career. Not a glimmer of gratitude lit the dry, carefully selected words of its single paragraph:

The uneasiness which you have showed for some time has given me very much trouble, though I have borne it; and had your behaviour continued the same it was for a few years after my coming to the crown, I could have no dispute with myself what to do. But the many unkind returns I have received since, especially what you said to me personally before the Lords, makes it impossible for me to continue you any longer in my service; but I desire that, instead of bringing the staff to me, you will break it, which I believe will be easier to us both.

The Queen was determined to avoid an emotional scene; the ordeal of actually taking back the White Staff from her faithful servant was more than she could stand. And although Godolphin had often been morose and had frequently nagged her to accept measures of which she did not approve, he had 'managed' for her for eight years and raised the money for her glorious war. Neither she, nor Harley, nor anyone else involved in

F*

the plot, felt easy about the dismissal. Shrewsbury, Somerset and Harley all blamed each other, and the Queen said she thought 'how ungenerous it was to my Lord G— who had been an old nurse to her, and whom for so many years she had consulted as a father, to be sent a message of dismission by the Duke of Somerset's coachman'.

The letter was delivered at about nine o'clock in the morning, and by twelve the news that Godolphin had been turned out was flying about the town. He attended to a few routine matters and in the evening he broke his staff and threw the pieces into the empty grate. There was no outcry. The Whigs did not stand by him. Nobody resigned in sympathy, and Godolphin himself entreated Marlborough to carry on for the good of the nation. The Whigs met at Boyle's house on the evening of the dismissal to decide what they should do, but instead of making a plan of action, they decided to stand back and watch the new Treasury Commissioners ruin the economy and bring about their own downfall. Like most people, including Marlborough, they believed that Godolphin was the only man who could control the nation's finances. All the same, under his management the national debt had grown to grave proportions, and there was hardly enough money in hand to pay the current expenses of the army. The civil list was nearly £700,000 in debt and, worst of all, the Bank, the stockbrokers and many City men were resolved to strangle any new Ministry at birth by withdrawing their support and sinking credit.

Harley had foreseen these difficulties. Knowing that every community has its malcontents, he soon sought out City Tories and those shut out of the magic circle of Bank or East India Company directors. Tory aldermen and councillors, anyone who nursed a grudge or who disliked the Bank's stranglehold—all these might be asked to back a new Ministry by raising a loan if it should run into trouble. Harley had his own tame tycoons. He also had the help of his brother, the Auditor, who understood the inner workings of the nation's finances, and Defoe, who came back ecstatically into his master's service. Finance had always been Defoe's particular interest, a subject that he had studied and thought about deeply. On July 28, sensing that Harley needed help, he asked for an interview so that he could offer advice about ways and means of preventing the ruin of public credit. He also offered his services as an unofficial government spokesman on financial affairs. In August he wrote his *Essay upon Credit*, and this, with later pamphlets, helped to expose the people who thought they could bring down a government by refusing to advance money. He pointed out that by withdrawing their loans, the moneyed men could ruin themselves, for in doing so they would lose their interest and thus their income:

I would attempt to bring those men of paper to know themselves a little by showing how well the government can do without the Bank, and how ill the Bank can do without the government.

One thing was certain—there was no time to waste. The day after Godolphin's fall, the Whig John Smith was asked to surrender the Chancellor of the Exchequer's Seal, which was handed forthwith to Harley. He had at last come out from his favourite position behind the curtain, and it was now a case of open warfare between himself and the financiers—such ruthless self-made men as Sir Henry Furness, son of a bankrupt grocer, and other speculators. Harley told Newcastle on August 13 that there had been 'great labouring with the Bank and Sir H. Furness not to deal'. This situation, coupled with the fact that the army was completely without subsistence, called for immediate measures, and he set to at once to raise a loan large enough to maintain the army for the time being. He astonished both his friends and his enemies by procuring a vast sum in under a month, and on August 26 he was able to report to his sister Abigail that the first hurdle of the Commissioners had been surmounted. They had managed to provide for the army, an event everyone had thought to be impossible. By the same post he explained his action to Newcastle in greater detail:

I have had no rest night or day, but notwithstanding all the arts and malice which have been used, we have found ways to remit yesterday subsistence for the whole army in Flanders till Christmas. Since the new Commission, we have remitted thither £430,000, and we found the army with but one week's subsistence. This is the greatest remittance made at once since the war [began], and at a much easier rate than Sir H. Furness; and now the next care will be to provide for other pressing services.

Modestly, to his family, Harley attributed his success to the good care of the Almighty, but the Whigs were forced to acknowledge that he possessed some quality which they ignored at their peril. Here was a man who could outwit Croesus himself. He had given the lie to all the prophets of doom. Stock was no lower than it had been all the year. The Bank had learnt that it must humour and not try to govern those in power.

Arriving back in London on August 26 after a short absence, Harley was greeted by bonfires and signs of public rejoicing. The news had come through of Stanhope's victories in Spain. At Almenara and Saragossa, Stanhope had avenged the ignominy of Almanza. The road to Madrid was open. Fortune smiled on Harley, for this news told him that in all probability his new Ministry would be able to negotiate with France from a position of strength. No wonder he told his family that he felt 'the comfort which springs from divine love'. He experienced further pleasure when at the end of July his daughter, Lady Dupplin, made her contribution to the general weal by giving birth to a son. The child arrived at the height of the political crisis, but Lord Dupplin's letters, full of news about Scottish politics, contained some fatherly references to the son and heir who, like his grandfather's *coup*, was progressing well. 'Little Tommy is as fine a child as ever you saw,' he wrote, 'and sends his duty to his grandpapa in the best manner he can.' Lord Kinnoull proudly described the little boy as 'the bravest fellow in Britain'.

There were many who rejoiced at the prospect of a new government and a release from Whig rule. Reassuring letters came through from the provinces:

I humbly beg leave to acquaint you with the great joy the county received the news of your being at the head of the new Ministry and that they will pay their taxes very cheerfully, since they now think their Church out of danger.

wrote Sir Henry Belasyse, M.P. for Durham. All the same, even though a good start had been made, there were still delicate problems to overcome. The Tories looked to Harley as a new champion and expected him to create a thoroughly Tory government. But he himself wanted a balanced administration and still longed to have the best of both worlds. So he spent the month of September placating hot Tories and wooing lukewarm Whigs. Halifax, Somers and Cowper had been flirting with him for several months, and Halifax had committed himself openly by going off to the Hague in July to help Townshend with the peace negotiations which had been started there. He had made up his mind that the welfare of the nation was more important than party feuds and he told Newcastle on August 17 that he thought 'all heats and resentments should be laid aside'. Sure that a dissolution would be catastrophic, he wanted to find out how far he would have to go to meet Harley with the purpose of avoiding an election and a new High Tory, Sacheverell-inspired House of Commons. He preached to his friends that public credit must be supported, and backed Harley as the one man who was capable of governing with prudence and moderation amidst the folly, rage and villainy of the two parties.

Somers, now well ensconced in the Queen's favour, seemed for a while prepared to treat, but Harley doubted his sincerity. On August 5 he complained to Newcastle that he was finding it impossible to bring

Somers and Cowper 'out of general terms to particulars'—a complaint that the Tories, at the same time, were making about him. At the beginning of August, Cowper was looking amenable; on the 4th he wrote a letter expressing a desire to acquit himself as an 'honest and impartial man', and saying that he wished Harley 'all imaginable good':

I think so very well of you as to believe, though you have had great provocation, and have so much in your power, yet you will forego the opportunity of retaliating . . . I would not say this to flatter you, if I had not these hopes firmly rooted in me.

Such hopeful overtures could not be ignored, and Harley, too busy battling with the Bank to have much time for winning a wavering Whig, delegated the task to Robert Monckton, one of Newcastle's henchmen, a moderate Court Whig who was more ready to obey the Queen than the Junto.

On August 27 Cowper received a letter in which Monckton offered to act as a go-between. But it was hard work trying to break down Cowper's 'natural reserve'. Hearing that he was beginning to say things had gone too far towards the Tories for his liking, Harley visited him on September 18, offering to let him continue in his place and promising to treat him better than the Junto had ever done. The interview was sticky, and Cowper never reacted well to Harley's blandishments. In his *Diary* he wrote:

Harley gave me the history of the 3 months past, short and broken so that hard to be remembered. . . . Used all arguments possible to persuade me to stay in place. All should be easy. The danger of going out. A Whig game intended at bottom; enumerated what Whigs in; declined (shuffling) to tell me all the removes intended . . . and much broken and unintelligible matter.

Cowper considered it infamous to stay in place when all his friends were going out; he said that if power were put in Tory hands, the zealots would soon be clamouring for his fall. He had already suffered mortifications from Dartmouth. Unsuccessful though this interview was, the persistent Monckton followed it up, pursuing Cowper into the country. Lady Cowper had chosen this moment of tension for her lying-in, but such small matters did not deter Monckton who played his persuasive part all over again and without a thought for the lady in labour. Moreover he continued the dialogue in the coach when Cowper finally went back to London.

The political atmosphere was unhealthy that September. The long faces of declining courtiers contrasted with the fulsome joy of Tories who thronged the court. Men were motivated by ambition, fear, and uncertainty. Old friendships and allegiances crumbled, treachery was everywhere. The whispering and the wooing went on, the professions of sincerity and candour. Many men were waiting to jump until they could tell which side would bring them the greatest advantage. The Whigs sensed their danger but were almost hypnotized by Harley's 'trick, contradiction and shuffle', as Hamilton put it. Reports did come through to Harley of 'mighty intriguing' amongst the Whigs, with great meetings at the houses of Sunderland and Orford and open-air gatherings at Putney bowling-green. But in general the Whigs were strangely dispirited. They seemed incapable of concerted action; for once their discipline flagged, each man was out to save his own skin. The prospect of Halifax going over to Harley, and others giving every appearance of being ready to jump, took all heart out of the rank and file. In Swift's words, 'The Whigs, like an army beat three quarters out of the field, begin to skirmish but faintly; and deserters daily come over.' There were deep groans from the Whig clients of the St James's coffee house when the news of the victories in Spain came through, for success there appeared to give the Tories a certain chance of making a good peace. All the luck had gone over to the opposition and it seemed useless to fight.

The Tories, on the other hand, were altogether too uppish. The moderates were growing uneasy at the attitude of the zealots. Whigs like Newcastle were happy enough to join a Ministry dedicated to peace, liberty and the Protestant Succession, but they had no desire to associate with a rabble of near-Jacobites. Lovers of the middle way were appalled as they sensed that they were to be driven yet again into the thraldom of party rule. 'I cannot be persuaded,' wrote Robert Molesworth, one of the Harley border clan, 'that you, the Duke of Shrewsbury, my Lord Poulett, with several others of my acquaintance, after having rescued the nation from the tyranny of one set of men, can be for subjecting it to another of priests.' Harley's friends warned him that the Tories were already talking about jettisoning him as soon as they came into power. Monckton, listening in at Tory dinner parties, when the squires opened their hearts as well as their bottles, and were 'mellow and talking of the times', reported that he had heard Harley described categorically as a necessary ladder which would be discarded as soon as possible as part of the scaffolding.

Harley began to wonder now whether the Tories had in fact learnt wisdom from their past folly. He did his best to correct the impression that a new ministry would support intolerance and commissioned Defoe to organize a press campaign assuring people that they were not all going to be 'devoured and eaten up . . . that moderate counsels are at the bottom of all these things; that the old mad party are not coming in'. Swift, arriving in London in September—'this shaking season for places,' as he described it—was immediately set upon by both parties, who were anxious to engage his biting wit in the service of their cause by contributing to the pamphlets and half-sheets now pouring from the presses. Harley won Swift over with flattery and friendship, his warm, familiar manner being a great contrast to Godolphin's; Swift found the ex-Treasurer 'altogether short, dry and morose'. But even Swift's pen could not calm the Tories now. The old, dreaded party was rising again. A new generation of country squires had now come of age; hot-headed young men, who had no desire to listen to their elders, were scaring off the marginal Whigs and mellow Tories.

On September 19, Somers, sensing a coldness in the Queen's behaviour, and feeling that his hour of favour had passed, resigned his post as Lord President. He was followed by the Duke of Devonshire, openly peevish for some time, and by Henry Boyle, who had always been ready to meet the moderates but who was now alarmed by the Tory resurgence. Boyle supped with Harley a few days after his resignation and told him that all along the Whigs had laughed at Halifax behind his back for treating with the Tories. If that was true, they had missed their opportunity. Had they come into the open weeks earlier they could have brought Harley's plan to a halt. A mass resignation in July would have caused confusion; now, in September, it was a gesture that lacked dramatic impact. The Whigs did not normally want for either political acumen or loyalty to each other; their strange lack of cohesion in the summer of 1710 was a proof of the demoralizing power of Harley's underground working.

The Earl of Rochester, a High Tory chastened, it was hoped, by experience, was appointed Lord President. The Duke of Buckingham, as sour-looking, haughty and unpopular as ever and now over sixty, was called in to take Devonshire's place as Lord Steward. St John became Secretary of State. On September 20, these three Tories went to be sworn in at a Council meeting. The Whigs who remained in the Cabinet scarcely felt inclined to give the newcomers an enthusiastic welcome. Rochester's High Church excesses were too recent to be forgiven, Buckingham had always been known as a Jacobite, and St John had for months been preaching the doctrine of complete subservience to the Tory party. Such appointments confirmed Cowper's fear that matters had gone too far towards the Tories for any Whig to remain happily in office. And further offence was caused when the Queen announced peremptorily that there was to be a dissolution and asked for a draft proclamation to be ready. This was duly drawn up and the clerk 'rattled it off in a minute'. Cowper, Orford and Wharton were stunned; it had always been one of the conditions of their continued support that Parliament should not be dissolved, and they thought Harley guilty of a breach of trust. Besides, it was most unconstitutional to draft the proclamation before the Council had been given a chance to discuss the matter. But before they could protest, the Queen left the room as rapidly as her gout would allow and there was no further chance for discussion.

Wharton and Orford tendered their resignations that very afternoon. The Queen accepted the departure of these two dislikeable lords without demur. She was glad to banish their angry faces from her Council table. But when Cowper went to the Palace it was a different story, for he was a man she liked. On the legal side he was well qualified for his job, and he also possessed more integrity than most. At heart he was a moderate. But rather than set his Seal to a proclamation which declared that the Council had agreed to the dissolution, he handed the insignia of his office to the Queen. At first she refused to accept it and thrust it back into his hand:

She strongly opposed my doing it, giving it me again at least 5 times after I had laid it down, and at last would not take it, but commanded me to hold it, adding 'I beg it as a Favour of you, if I may use that expression', on which I took it again . . . so, much to my dissatisfaction, I returned home with the Seal. But the next day I gave up the Seal, on my knee; which the Q. accepted.

Cowper thought that he owed his overnight reprieve to the fact that 'the Mrs', as he called Abigail, had not had time to clamour for his removal. Like most Whigs he overestimated her power, and in this he under-estimated both the Queen's judgement of character and his own obvious claim to stand above party on personal merit. He was more accurate when he guessed that Harley would have liked him to counterbalance the Tories. He would have been even nearer the truth if he had realized that Harley was finding it very hard to find a substitute Chancellor.

A new leader who has spent some time in opposition often finds it hard to draw on younger men with any experience in government. Harley's friends, Harcourt, Granville, Poulett, Paget, Mansell, were mostly middle-aged like himself. He could call on elder statesmen, past their prime and tarred with the High Tory brush, but St John alone was both young and experienced. He was also the only man of outstanding talent in the Harley stable. The rest were mostly worthy, reliable and mediocre. The moderate ideal tended to attract men of moderate ability and there were not enough able men to go round. Harley had been driven to offending more people than he had intended. After the Council meeting when the dissolution was announced, the Duke of Somerset flew into a passion and left the room abruptly. He went home, shouted and swore at all his servants, refused to eat the meal that was laid out ready for him and went off in a 'pet to Petworth'. It was thought that Somerset was particularly angry about the dissolution because 'he had the vanity to think he could manage that House of Commons as he pleased'. He also felt that he had been duped by Harley.

One key figure remained. The Duke of Newcastle had once again, and in spite of the crisis, spent almost all the summer at his seat in the north, courted by letter and wooed by the written word, deaf to all the prayers of his friends who implored him to come and make his influence felt at the scene of action. Harley and the Whig lords vied with each other to flatter and cajole, or to commiserate with him after his frequent falls while enjoying the pleasures of the chase. In September, Godolphin, who, as Viscount Weymouth remarked to Matthew Prior, was fallen but not buried, had joined with others in attempting to make trouble between Harley and the Duke. Accusations were made, which Harley hurriedly denied in a letter written on September 23:

I assure you there was never any intention of offering anything to you that could be liable to any misinterpretation. The thought was purely my own, that the Lord Steward had a great many valuable places in the family below stairs in his gift, and that as they fell void you would bestow them freely on deserving persons; but then the thought that it was lower in post made me check myself.

Newcastle accepted Harley's assurances and stood firm, keeping Halifax friendly too. This was comforting, but as Halifax put it to Newcastle on September 26:

Our friends have quite gone off the stage, and those who were most reasonable and most disposed to set things right on the other side are not so much the masters of the field that they were.

Shrewsbury, Newcastle, Halifax—these three were the only Whig survivors and their foothold was precarious.

Harley was disappointed, of course. He would have liked to make Cowper 'practicable' and to keep his old friend Boyle. He did not show his feelings, however. At a time when tempers were running high, and every other political figure seemed to be in a pet or 'flying out' for one reason or another, Harley remained calm and sphinx-like. He had shouldered responsibility and courted danger, but he apparently took no notice of the risks he ran. His family was far more aware than he was of the hazards to which he had exposed himself. His brother Nathaniel, while he admitted that the *arcana imperii* were somewhat beyond a merchant's understanding, wrote from Aleppo in some concern when the news of Robin's manœuvres came through to him:

When I consider how many enemies he had before, and how many more this last revolution at Court must have made him, how slippery the ground is on which he stands, and inconstant the favour of princes, I protest it strikes me with fear and concern for him, and makes me think that as in war a good retreat is esteemed equal to a victory, so in the scuffles at Court it is much to be preferred before it.

But Robin had no intention of retreating now. The ground might be slippery, but he knew how to balance. He had broken up the close ranks of the Junto Whigs and had virtually seized power without a mandate from anybody except the Queen. She had shown him great esteem, and he had accomplished his mission of freeing her from the war-mongering men she so disliked.

In October he left London for Hereford. His relations had been attending to his election at New Radnor under his instructions. Many less busy men had been in the shires, canvassing, for weeks. But Harley's visit was brief, and before long he returned to London, to the world of 'grimace and cringes', to the intrigue and the gossip, the jostling place-hunters and the waiting Queen.

CHAPTER 14

CHECKS AND HINDRANCES

THE TORY REVIVAL GREW, with increasing momentum. Harley preached moderation at every opportunity, and paid his hired writers—Harley's hacks they called them—to do the same. In the summer of 1710 he launched the *Examiner*, which was to be the official organ of the milder Tory viewpoint. But nothing he could do would make the electorate pause at that vital point of equilibrium between the extremes. Sacheverell's tour to his border parish had stimulated all good Tories along the route. In the elections the old reactionary cries rang out. 'The Church in Danger', that hackneyed slogan, was heard again. The response of the country Tories was overwhelming. The Duke of Beaufort reported rapturously that at Gloucester he met with 'so handsome an appearance of gentlemen &c as never yet was seen together in the memory of the old men'; he was almost deaf after hearing 'huzzas for the Queen, Church, prosperity and success to the new faithful Ministry, a good Parliament and a speedy and lasting peace'. Sir John Verney, now Lord Fermanagh, who had repeatedly tried to find a seat in Parliament, was successful for the first time in his life, having come out openly for Church and Queen. 'I am glad my fellow bumkings has been so wis at last,' wrote one of his female relations. The Queen was fêted throughout the country as the guardian of the one established Church, and loyal addresses were drawn up at meetings of country gentlemen in which she was honoured as the divine authority, bound to her subjects by a mutual adherence to 'Apostolical Principles of unconditional loyalty' as the Warwickshire address rather heavily put it. The Whigs, often unfairly, were accused of encouraging atheism, which, Abigail Harley told her brother, was spreading through the country like leprosy.

It was useless for Harley to curb Tory zeal by appointing moderate Ministers and promising toleration to the dissenters. Most of the Tories were past listening. George Granville's success in the western empire that had once been Seymour's stamping-ground was typical of the general landslide:

Trevanion and Granville, sound as a bell
For the Queen and the Church and Sacheverell

was the election cry. Sarah Marlborough accused the Tories of gaining
their votes by bribes, debauchery and intimidation, and maintained that
they hired mobs to drive would-be Whigs away from the polls. The truth
was that there was little need to resort to such methods, so great was
the surge of High Church feeling. Apart from the usual goodwill
payments to blind beggars, and the occasional tip to 'roarers of the word
Church', results could be obtained without great expense. It was the
Whigs who needed to dip their hands into their pockets.

When the results came out the worst prognostications of the wilting
Whigs were fulfilled, and the figures appearing in the *Gazette* proved
depressing also for the moderates. The final count showed sweeping
gains for the High Tories who achieved a clear majority. All the summer
Harley had been preparing the Queen for a Tory victory, but he had not
paved the way for such a shock as this. And his enemies were soon accusing him of Jacobite leanings. The Scottish Tories were always suspect,
and Sarah Marlborough believed that everything was prepared for the
Pretender's coming, with men regimented and ready at a call. She also
taxed Harley with 'deluding a great many unthinking men'.

Even when the election results were out, Harley continued to appoint
tepid Tories such as Lord Berkeley, who became Chancellor of the
Duchy of Lancaster. In spite of Tory clamour no move was made to
turn out Whig Lords-Lieutenant, High Sheriffs and Justices. There
were rumours that Harley was favouring the retention of the Whig John
Smith as Speaker, which made Granville write anxiously from Menabilly
in Cornwall:

We have had a report very industriously spread amongst us that Jack Smith
was to be proposed by the Court for Speaker. 'Tis not to be imagined what an
alarm it gave for some time. I hope we shall never split twice upon the same
rock.

In spite of all warnings, Harley persisted with his own policy. To oppose
the Tory tide seemed 'as vain as to attempt to stop the stream at London
Bridge with one's thumb', in Haversham's image, but although Tories
outnumbered Whigs by two to one, and there were half as many court
Members as before, although credit had fallen apparently beyond hope
and Jacobites were everywhere exultant, he refused to be deflected.
'I hear myself called a rogue almost every day and take no notice,' he
told one of Maynwaring's friends. Instead of going down to Brampton

he stayed in London working out his plan of action, based on his pre-election manifestos.

The need for peace had been a prime motive in Harley's bid for power and he intended to achieve it, believing as he did that prolonged hostilities could only ruin the nation's economy. He had inherited financial difficulties which the Whigs confidently pronounced him incapable of solving, but he himself was less defeatist and worked hard in October on a proposition to restore credit. His family had strong links with the dissenters and by promising tolerance in the religious sphere he found many allies among affluent non-conformists. To show that he was in earnest he substituted for 'tolerance to dissenters', the phrase which had always been used in the Queen's speech, the far stronger epithet 'indulgence'. This caused a stir in the House; the dissenters were pleased and the High Churchmen furious.

Harley's motto might be peace, financial stability and toleration, but the Tories who thronged the meetings in the Fountain Tavern had no inclination towards leniency. The young hot-heads, returned in droves by the electorate, had little patience with 'old fashioned out of the way gentlemen'—they were attracted by youth and vigour and vitality. The experience of middle age did not appeal to them and they cared little for Harley's caution and good sense. St John was their natural leader. He was the right generation, and they admired his wit, his good looks and his wicked ways. The young bloods asked him to join the revivified October Club, to drink their heady ale and listen to the more passionate among them toast James Stuart in their cups. St John enjoyed their admiration, and understood their impatience. He himself was beginning to tire of the pedestrian Harley. His 'dear master' had failed to take his advice and put himself at the head of the High Tories, and now St John had no scruples about taking on the task himself. He was sure that Harley had tried to keep him out of the inner Cabinet and as a result felt that he had every justification in returning to the party which had been his first love.

The Duchess of Marlborough complained that the star of ingratitude was in the ascendant that winter of 1710–11 and Harley could have agreed with her on that point if on no other. Without him the Tories would have lacked the impetus to throw out the Whigs; it was his skill and his cunning that had achieved the revolution. Thanks to him they dominated the parliamentary scene, but in spite of this they were happy to cast him off in the moment of victory. The Queen, too, showed signs of being dazzled by St John's brilliance, and was not immune to the 'insinuating' charms of the Duchess of Somerset. The Duchess was trying her hand, all too successfully, at Harley's backstairs game. Although the hot Percy blood which flowed in her veins made her ambitious, she was tactful enough to learn how to humour the Queen, and seldom upset her. Unlike her husband, she did not indulge in childish tantrums. Sir David Hamilton advised the Queen to see more of this friend whose presence was so soothing, and therefore good for the royal health. On every side Harley was hedged about with rivals. Dr Arbuthnot, originally Prince George's doctor, was a powerful solicitor for Tory friends and Scottish compatriots, but Sir David Hamilton was also ready to go beyond his brief as a mere doctor and intercede with the Queen on behalf of Harley's Whig enemies. Mixing clinical advice with political expedience, Hamilton had strongly advised the Queen to decamp to Windsor at the height of Harley's summer activities. He knew well enough that once she was away from London it would have been far more difficult to remove Whig Ministers or announce a dissolution. Such treatment might have improved her gout but would hardly have proved a tonic for Harley. The practitioners who attended to the Queen's aches and pains threatened to become as powerful as Abigail Masham, who was herself being visited by crowds of place-hunters many of whom, Peter Wentworth said, he had heard in times past 'wish her damn'. A host of hangers-on always stood hopefully at the door, waiting, in court parlance, to 'nick' the opportune moment and to make capital out of the current confusion of parties and people.

In spite of these difficulties, Harley entered the new era with all the exuberance of a man who has at last been entrusted with the task he has longed for years to do. No shadow of guilt about the methods he had used to displace his enemies clouded his conscience. He was completely self-assured, secure in the certainty that God looked benignly on his machinations. He had proved himself proficient when it came to toppling a government; now he had to show that he could shine in the positive task of building an administration. With the careless energy of a man who believes implicitly in his own resources of strength and his fitness for the job, he carried his responsibility lightly. Swift was amazed to see him as merry, as careless and as disengaged as a schoolboy on holiday or a young heir at twenty-one. He had never been afraid of hard work and now he did not spare himself. Besides attending to affairs of state personally and writing endless letters in long-hand, or visiting the Queen at Windsor from Saturday to Monday, he indulged in a whirl of social engagements which would have exhausted other men, and indeed proved far too much for Swift's poor head. His talent for friendship stood him in good stead, and he turned the sporadic unofficial Cabinet meetings of earlier administrations into a weekly dinner engagement at which policy problems could be discussed in a relaxed atmosphere over a bottle of best tokay. Harley had won Swift's affection rapidly, flattering him by using his Christian name on first acquaintance; thanks to Harley's efforts the Queen consented to remit the Irish first fruits and twentieths, and Swift thus achieved in three weeks what previous emissaries had craved for years. Before long he was appointed editor of the *Examiner* and admitted into the circle of friends who dined together every Saturday except when the Queen was at Windsor. There he met Granville, ex-playwright and practising poet, learned, extravagant and charming, a man who had started his career by writing lines on beauty and heroic love and who, by contrast, had now been appointed Secretary-at-War. Prior, like Granville primarily a poet and only second a politician, was another regular diner, and his pen, too, had been conscripted in the government cause. Harcourt was often there, as well as Poulett, Shrewsbury and Ormonde, the newly appointed Lord-Lieutenant of Ireland. Peterborough, who had been driven into the Harley camp by his deep hatred of Marlborough and Godolphin, lent his amusing company to the gatherings. The social nature of these meetings built up a camaraderie which produced a group of men as close as the Junto, though far less formidable. Members of the Saturday circle, many of them painted at this time by Kneller in unbecoming velvet turbans, had the uniformly double-chinned, self-satisfied look of the establishment. They were in power, and enjoying the sensation. Maynwaring told Sarah Marlborough that the old philosopher Heraclitus, who always wept when he saw an ill man, would certainly have broken his heart to see this new 'Junctilio'.

In spite of his self-confidence. Harley began to meet with more and more difficulties in the last months of the year. The Queen was noticeably cool; she held back and refused to hand him the White Staff of the Lord Treasurer's office. Her reluctance to choose a prime minister gave rise to fears that the nation would soon be subjected to a petticoat government consisting of the Queen, the Duchess of Somerset and Abigail Masham. The October Club was glorying in its new-found supremacy and growing every day in discipline and power. And although Harley was far less vindictive than most in his attitude to Marlborough, army officers suspected him of planning their general's downfall. In December 1710 some of them were ordered to sell their commands at half value 'for drinking destruction to the present ministry, and dressing up a hat on a stick and calling it Harley'.

When Marlborough returned to England in the new year, Harley made a bold attempt to win him over. The Duchess, as always, suspected his motives:

All the ministers came to see him, and made professions to him, except Mr Harley, but that gentleman only sent him compliments, desiring to have some opportunity of speaking to him in the council room or the court or treasury, as by accident, after which he would do him the honour to come to his lodgings.

The Duke, going by back ways to avoid the admiring mob that pursued him with cries of 'no popery, no wooden shoes'—the Whig equivalent of the Church-in-Danger slogan—went to Harley's house as requested. It did seem as if both men wished for a *rapprochement* which, if achieved, would have been of great benefit to themselves and to Europe as a whole. St John enjoyed making life difficult for Marlborough, but Harley was wise enough to see that the General's credit with the allies was too valuable an asset to throw lightly away. The interview between the two men was, however, marred by Marlborough's attempt to intercede for his wife. 'That was the rock which all would break upon,' Harley said, whenever the Duchess was mentioned, for he knew that the Queen could not bear to hear her name. Marlborough found this out for himself a few days later. He tried to mention the Duchess, but whenever he did so, the Queen fell silent and looked guilty, like someone convicted of a crime. And that January, in spite of all the Duke's pathetic attempts to save her, the Duchess was dismissed from her posts of Groom of the Stole, Mistress of the Robes and Keeper of the Privy Purse. When Marlborough told his wife that she must surrender her keys, she unceremoniously threw them at him.

Harley's failure to make peace with Marlborough was typical of many setbacks. The new year dawned darkly for the men of the Juntilla. Their ebullient spirits could only be dampened by the course of affairs. They now had to admit that they had failed to gain name after name that would have added strength to their cause. In the summer they had been unable to win over Sir Thomas Hanmer, the rich young Tory who had great influence in the Commons. In September Cowper had slipped from their grasp. And now, in January 1711, Robert Walpole, who had been kept on in the Treasurership of the Navy in the hope that he would co-operate, finally dissociated himself from the Tories and was dismissed. Hopes of reappointing John Smith as Speaker had been dashed by the Tories' election victory, and William Bromley, occupying the Chair at last, was too good a Tory to help Harley curb the October Club. The House soon embarked on a series of measures that ran contrary to the restrained policies outlined in the Queen's speech, and Harley, the great Commons manager, was forced to sit back and let others call the tune. As part of a general campaign to protest against Harley's moderation, St John and his followers brought in the Landed Property Qualification Bill, which was designed to make sure that only a country squire could qualify for membership of the House, and aimed at removing all those moneyed men who had tried to ruin credit the previous summer. It was true that the Bill might have encouraged speculators to invest their money in land, but had it had the effect intended by its promoters, it would certainly have secured Tory supremacy for ever. As it was the lawyers soon found ways and means of legally evading the qualification.

It was galling for Harley, the mild leader, to be associated with the excesses of the rank and file. If things had continued in that way, his conscience would have told him that he must resign. The Court, it seemed, was to be overwhelmed by Tory power. In January Swift summed the situation up succinctly:

The ministry is upon a very narrow bottom, and stands like an isthmus between the Whigs on one side and the violent Tories on the other. They are able seamen, but the tempest is too great, the ship too rotten, and the crew all against them.

Now that St John had joined the October Club zealots, Harley was without a man of outstanding ability in his Cabinet. He was propping up the Ministry almost alone, overworking, drinking, eating well and keeping late hours. His health, of which he took little care, began to alarm his friends. He suffered frequently from sore throats and gravel. 'Pray God preserve his strength, everything depends on it', wrote Swift.

The Queen continued to tease Harley by looking on St John with favour. Harley, overburdened with cares of state, found it difficult to see the Queen as often as he had done before. She was a hard taskmistress, expecting her servants to wait on her frequently and at such 'unseasonable hours' as Harley himself described it. Inclined to be sensitive about such matters, the Queen punished Harley by smiling on St John's lunatic scheme to send an expedition to Quebec. St John had decided to employ Abigail's worthless brother, Jack Hill, as commander of the forces, which pleased the Bedchamber Woman greatly. As a result Harley was obliged to offend both the Queen and Abigail by opposing this quixotic scheme. His brother, Auditor Harley, had warned him that St John was making requests to the Treasury for large sums of money which he suspected were being used for illicit purposes—probably to finance his expensive private life. St John, incautious and unbalanced, was revelling in the whole situation, and he took every opportunity to humiliate his old master in the House. He headed vindictive attacks on the Whigs, including a peculation charge levelled at Walpole, which he knew Harley would dislike. Harley's disapproval made the sport all the more enjoyable. And encouraged by the Queen's favour and by the young Tories' idolatry, St John decided to set up as a serious rival for the Lord Treasurer's White Staff, which the Queen so tantalizingly refused to hand to anybody. Let Harley and his moderates do as they please; the younger element was not to be denied. In early February, Harley and his friends dined with St John in the hope of bringing the Secretary to see reason. They were unsuccessful. St John was obviously bent on governing the House. After this, Harley never crossed the threshold of St John's house again.

Although 'the most fearless man alive, and the least apt to despond', Harley confessed to Swift late in February that all seemed lost. He had risked all in an attempt to set up a government in which Court moderates would manage the government, helping the Queen to rule in a partnership with the predominant party. And he had fallen a victim to what Harold Wilson has described in a tribute to Ramsay Macdonald, as 'the most ruthless law of politics'—the law of coalitions:

When a leader, wielding power, becomes dependent on men who unaided could not achieve power . . . he then becomes the prisoner of those men, who, once they have achieved power, no longer need him.

If the Tories were proving difficult, the Whigs were by no means quiescent. Swift thought them 'the most malicious toads in the world'. They were busy 'bawling' criticism in pamphlets, satires and lampoons. With the help of Halifax, Defoe and the Auditor, Harley had worked out the scheme for a lottery, which the Whigs now set out to wreck. According to the Auditor, every kind of 'wicked artifice' was used to prevent people taking out tickets. Such a bold effort to save the nation's economy ought to have been allowed a safe passage, exempt from party sniping, but this was too much to hope for in the present atmosphere. Financial ruin seemed unavoidable, unless peace could be achieved quickly, but all hopes of a settlement in Europe appeared to be receding. In the constantly changing pattern of world affairs, Louis was tempted to hang on, waiting for a better chance to negotiate from strength. In the autumn, a couple of allied victories in Spain, followed by a triumphant march on

Madrid, had made the peace-makers pause. Spain would have proved a valuable counter in the peace talks, but by Christmas the allied cause had met with a complete reversal; British forces were trapped at Brihuega and Charles of Austria retired to Barcelona with a remnant of his forces, leaving the rest of Spain to Philip of Anjou. Peace *without* Spain now seemed to be the only possibility, and Harley was anxious to show Louis that he was prepared to proceed on the assumption that Philip would be allowed to stay in Spain. Contact had to be made with France through a secret channel, and Jersey, the Jacobite, who stood well with Harley although he had not asked for office under the new regime, suggested a means. Lady Jersey was a Catholic who regularly attended Mass at the private chapel of Count Gallas, the Emperor's envoy, and she had met there a French priest named Gaultier who had once been chaplain to Marshal Tallard. Gaultier had been in London for many years, mixing a little discreet espionage with his priestly duties. Harley and Shrewsbury decided that such a man was a suitable instrument for their secret designs, and early in the new year they despatched him with a message for Torcy. The French were understandably hesitant of trusting such an unlikely envoy, but after a good month's delay they sent Gaultier back with a guarded statement that they, too, were ready to discuss the subject of peace. It was a disappointingly lukewarm response, in keeping with all the other checks and hindrances. An eager demand from Louis for immediate peace-talks would have caused Harley's stock to rise at once. But at this point nothing was going in his favour.

In the last weeks of February it seemed inevitable that Harley would have to abdicate in favour of St John. The swinging pendulum of party had passed the point of equilibrium, and he had become a victim of the two-party system. He knew that if he stayed in office he would have to lend his name to intolerant measures running counter to all he believed in. This he could not do, and his fall was imminent, when, on March 8, 1711, the Guiscard assassination attempt restored his fortunes as surely as the Greg affair had temporarily ruined them.

CHAPTER 15

GUISCARD

By the end of February, Harley was facing a crisis of confidence. According to Swift the nation resembled a bankrupt merchant, with all the Ministry's efforts to save the economy being sabotaged by hostile bankers. On the continent the alliance seemed to be breaking up, peace was as remote as ever, and there were constant rumours that the High Tories planned to bring over the Pretender at the first convenient moment. The difference of opinion between old Tories and young Tories, between moderates and zealots, between Harley and St John had grown into an open rift. And in February Harley intercepted treacherous letters bound for France which suggested that St John might prove a more dangerous enemy than anyone realized.

Harley's brother Edward, a shrewd and loyal ally, was making good use of his position at the Treasury, for money can be the clue to men's motives. He had already given advance information of St John's intended Quebec expedition, and the previous October he had warned his brother that somebody was passing information to the French about the Camisards, the Huguenot resistance movement. A French minister, who came to collect money for Protestants rowing in the galleys in France, reported that two rebels had been betrayed and broken on the wheel. It was thought that the information had been passed by the so-called Marquis de Guiscard, a Frenchman living in England. This sinister individual, who went about with a dagger and a bottle of poison in his pocket, had a plausible manner and a fiery dissolute temperament which made him gravitate naturally into St John's debauched circles. An ex-priest who had been expelled from France for misconduct, he was thought by some to be a brother of Marshal Guiscard, Governor of Namur. Others said his real name was de la Bourlie, and that he had no claim to any kind of title. In 1705 he had come forward with a plan to land Huguenot refugees, backed by British troops, on the coast near Bordeaux and to start an uprising among the persecuted Protestants in southern France. There was every chance of stirring up trouble among the Camisards, and Marlborough liked the idea of drawing French troops away from Flanders. Guiscard was given the rank of colonel and entrusted with much of the planning; not surprisingly he was in and out of the office occupied by St John, then Secretary-at-War, almost every day. Although five Huguenot regiments were raised during the winter of 1705–6 and twelve British battalions kept near Portsmouth in readiness, Guiscard's merits as a commander were not put to the test, since the plan was finally shelved after the victory of Ramillies. He served with a foreign regiment at Almanza, after which he retired on a modest pension of five hundred pounds granted to him by a grateful British government. Such a sum soon proved inadequate for a man of his tastes, and he applied to have the pension increased. Harley, who had failed to learn from Greg the lesson that an underpaid profligate can prove a danger to the nation, listened to the promptings of the Puritan within, and showed his disapproval of wine and women by actually reducing the pension to four hundred pounds. This did nothing to cure Guiscard of wenching, and he continued to live extravagantly on a modest income—always a bad sign, and in this case particularly so, in the light of Auditor Harley's information.

Guiscard decided that if the British government would not pay for his pleasures, he would offer his services to the country that had once dismissed him in disgrace. He chose as his go-between the Countess of Dorchester, that tall thin lady who had once been James II's mistress. 'Who would have thought that we three whores should have met here?' she was to remark at a later date when she encountered, at the court of George I, the Duchess of Portsmouth and the Countess of Orkney, the mistresses of Charles II and William III respectively. Now, in 1711, she was as lean and unlovely as ever and respectably married to the Earl of Portmore, British envoy in Portugal. Guiscard, thoroughly at home with whores, high-ranking or otherwise, asked the Countess to convey his letters under cover to her husband in the diplomatic bag. Lord Portmore soon grew suspicious of these surprise packages, opened one of them, and the treachery was revealed.

Rochester and Shrewsbury, who were allowed to share the secret, were anxious to have Guiscard arrested immediately; for one thing he was inclined to hang about the court and might prove a danger to the Queen; for another he was so closely associated with St John that the two of them at one time shared a mistress. There was always a fear that St John, who was inclined to be indiscreet, might give away secrets in the meanwhile. Harley, however, preferred to wait and have Guiscard watched, in the hope of intercepting more letters, and of finding out the name of an officer in Marlborough's army whom Guiscard was apparently using as a channel. Harley wrote to Marlborough asking him to try and warn French Protestants of the danger they were in, and begging his co-operation in tracking down the traitorous officer.

Harley's patience was rewarded, and in February two very choice packages came into his hands; they contained letters addressed to British officers in Flanders and revealed secrets known only to members of the Cabinet Council. Significantly, Harley had not told St John of his discoveries, but now he went to the House and called the Secretary across to his favourite clandestine corner behind the Speaker's chair. Without any preamble he drew the packages from his pocket and confronted the startled St John with the handwriting he knew all too well. St John's reaction was to let forth a stream of oaths most offensive to his prudish master's ear.

That same evening Harley was stricken with a fever, and for a day or two was only able to attend to the minimum of business. The Almighty, with the help of Dr Radcliffe, who administered a cupping, watched over him as usual, and on March 7, though by no means well, he was able to struggle out to put before Parliament schemes for lessening the national debt. The Whigs, convinced that Harley's days of power were numbered, treated his projects with ridicule, and Godolphin, with gloomy relish, remarked that the Chancellor had hung a millstone about his own neck.

March 8 marked the anniversary of the Queen's inauguration. Because of the 'solemnity' of the day, Harley donned a thick embroidered waistcoat, richly decorated with gold brocade flowers on a background of silver and blue. This colourful garment had originally been designed to grace the Chancellor's person on the Queen's birthday a month before, but Mrs Harley frugally made it serve again with the addition of a silver fringe. Harley's sister, who saw him that morning in his closet, agreed that it looked very smart, and later the family was to overcome its disapproval of extravagant taste in dress, and to bless Robin's love of adornment. Since he was still feeling the effects of his cold, he put on a flannel waistcoat under the finery, and wore on top a new coat in heavy buff cloth, very well stiffened across the chest. This was a style the tailors had only recently adopted. Thus fortified against the elements, Harley called his chairmen and was carried to the Palace across the park, where he caught sight of Guiscard walking alone in the Mall.

The traitor, it was later known, had already been to court, in fact he had been to St James's twice already that morning. The first time he had been stopped by the Yeomen of the Guard, who considered his dress 'indecent', the court being still in mourning. He went back to his lodgings, changed into a more subdued suit and, in the process, forgot to transfer from one pocket to another his supply of poison and his dagger. He was just returning from the second visit when Harley saw him.

Harley offered the Queen the necessary compliments and then told her that he had seen Guiscard. She knew by now that this treacherous rake was under suspicion and would be safer in custody. Harley advised her to have him arrested at once, preferably before he had time to reach his lodgings. The Queen agreed, Harley sought out St John, who fortunately was still at court, and took him down to Mrs Masham's lodgings where they found pen, ink and paper. Harley wanted to make sure that St John did not try to warn his old associate, and stood over him while he wrote out the warrant for arrest on a charge of high treason. Two trusty messengers were sent to effect the capture. St John undertook to have Guiscard's two lodgings searched, including the rooms where he kept a whore. The Secretary had no difficulty in explaining where these were to be found.

Guiscard, taken by surprise as he strolled in the park, flew into a rage when he saw the warrant, and asked the messengers to kill him at once. It was said that St John's signature was what particularly incensed him. There had been a coolness between them ever since their mutual mistress had produced a child, and each had done his best to fix the paternal honours on the other. Guiscard was naturally angered to find that the very person with whom he had shared so much could have had the audacity to issue the warrant.

At the Palace, Harley, helped by 'Swallow' Poulett, wrote hasty notes summoning members of the Cabinet Council to a meeting at the Cockpit in the afternoon. He attended the Queen at dinner and was then carried in his chair to the Cockpit. When he arrived, he found that none of the other Council members was present. He glanced into a small room adjoining the Secretary's office to make sure that Guiscard had been secured and saw the traitor walking up and down, alone.

The Secretary's room was, of course, extremely familiar to Harley, being part of the office accommodation granted to him by the Queen in 1705. Two doors led into the room, one from the Secretary's private apartments and the other from the main entrance. There was a chimney-piece at the end nearest Westminster and big windows looked out over the garden. It was here that Greg had been first examined after his arrest on the last day of 1707, and Simon Harcourt who was next to arrive, could not resist remarking, 'Last time I was in this room was about Greg's business, I wish we may have better luck now.' The others, as they came hurrying in, were curious to know the reason for their unexpected summons. The whole Council was soon present, with the exception of Shrewsbury, who was entertaining foreign diplomats, and the Archbishop. Rochester, as Lord President, was in the chair, and the other members took their places on either side of him at the large oval table covered with a green cloth. On his right he had Buckingham, Harcourt and Dartmouth, on his left, Newcastle, Queensberry and St John. Poulett suggested that Harley and St John should sit next to each other, as Harley was best acquainted with the business in hand. Harley produced the packets, and Rochester, well known for his 'exactness and regularity', asked the members to put in writing any questions they wanted to ask. He realized that they were dealing with a clever rogue and must be careful; he knew Guiscard well by sight and had never liked the look of his face.

Harley called for two clerks to take the minutes, and stipulated that they should understand French, as the examination was to take place in that language. At the same time he warned the Council not to make remarks in English to each other, as Guiscard would understand them. The two clerks were found and set at a small table which was brought in for the purpose. According to custom, members had placed their hats on the table in front of them, and when Harley handed St John the two packages of letters the Secretary hid them under his hat. Somebody then pulled the crimson silk bell-cord which dangled above the table, and the messengers were told to bring the prisoner in.

Meanwhile Guiscard, who had had nothing to eat since breakfast, persuaded the Chamber Keeper to send down to the nearest coffee house for food and drink. Bread, butter and some sack were brought up by the coffee house boy, who wisely refused to let Guiscard keep the breadknife. Determined to have a weapon of some kind, Guiscard helped himself to a penknife which he found in a 'standish', and which was standard equipment in all rooms at the office. He had already been searched and his sword had been taken away, so he now hid the penknife in his pocket without fear of discovery.

When Guiscard was brought in, he stood behind Harley and St John, so that he was facing the light and they could observe his facial expression. His handsome but dissipated appearance was not improved by a large bruise on the left side of his face; St John told Harley in a whisper that this had been caused in a quarrel with one of his associates.

Various questions were asked, to all of which Guiscard answered a simple 'non'. This technique worked well, and he began to assume an

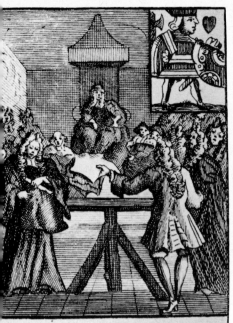

re an *Archbishop's son* ye *Church impeaches,*
hose Sire if living would abhor such Speeches.

The Queen's Address'd, and by new Senate told,
They'll Act with more Obedience than Her old.

s would Swell with Pride, if thus cares'd,
he bears humble Thoughts within his Breast

See London Citizens with Heart and Voice,
chuse Loyal Members that deserve their Choice.

EPISODES FROM THE SACHEVERELL IMPEACHMENT
As portrayed in contemporary playing cards

ANTOINE · MARÇ
GVISCARD · COM
DE · LA · BOVRLIE ·
NEWI · SVR · LOIRE
LIEVTEN^T · GENE^L ·
ARMEES' · DE · LEVR · M
IMP^E · ET · BRITA^E · CO
DVN · REGIM^T · DES' DR
ENGLOIS' DES'12 COMI
TIRE · A LA HAYE LA
1705 PAR LE SIEVR BR.
BEINS' UNDER EXAMI
BEFORE THE COUNCIL AT
COCKPIT MAR^{ch} 8 1710 S'
WITH A PENKNIFE M^r HA
THEN CHANCELLOUR OF
EXCHEQUER NOW EAR
OXFORD WHO HAD DIS'C
HIS' TREASONABLE CORRE

Photo: B

THE MARQUIS DE GUISCARD

"[Erasmus] Lewis had Guiscard's picture; he bought it and offered it to Lord Treasurer, who promised to send for it, but never did; so I made Lewis give it me, and I have it in my room; and now Lord Treasurer says he will take it from me. Is that fair? He designs to have it in length in the clothes he wore when he did the action; and a penknife in his hand; and Kneller is to copy it from this that I have."

(February 18, 1712)

arrogant expression, believing that the Lords would be unable to prove anything against him. It was at this point that Harley noticed him fiddling with something in his pocket. St John then asked permission to show the packages and drew them out from under his hat. Guiscard leant forward to examine the handwriting, but when asked if he knew it, he again replied '*non*'. This was too much for St John, who broke out in English, with the inevitable oath, 'I know it to be his.' Guiscard was by now growing thoroughly over-confident and he began to answer questions triflingly, with a scornful smile. Harley told him sharply to be serious and take care what he said. He then denied corresponding with officers in the army, and since he was obviously determined to be unco-operative, Rochester decided to ask no more questions and to adjourn the proceedings. St John pulled the bell-cord to summon the messengers. Harley, possibly feeling unwell since he had not fully recovered from his illness, took his eyes off Guiscard and rested his head in his hand. Guiscard appeared to hesitate and then moved towards the table. One of the Lords said '*Passez par là*', pointing to the door leading to the Secretary's department.

Suddenly Guiscard sprang at Harley with all his force and stabbed him with the penknife which he had taken from his pocket. This unheroic implement went right through the cuff of the sleeve, the buckram lining, the embroidered waistcoat and all the flannel swathing until it came to rest against the Chancellor's breastbone, the *cartilago ensiformis*. Harley was pushed backwards in his chair by the force of the blow and, as he recovered, he saw the assassin's hand raised up to strike again. After this, he could remember nothing until he regained consciousness and beheld a scene of pandemonium. Cabinet Lords were panicking about with drawn swords, St John was crying 'the villain has killed Mr Harley', the two French-speaking clerks had fled from the room, and the messengers were rushing in. As Guiscard was chased into the corner by the fireplace, Harley stood up, felt the wound, 'smelt whether his guts were pierced' and then, as Guiscard was chased back towards him, picked up a chair and defended himself, to the amazement of his colleagues, who thought he was dead. He then sank down into the Duke of Newcastle's chair while the messengers chased Guiscard along the wall by the windows and the Lords between them managed to inflict three wounds, all in the back. St John attacked his old friend so viciously that he broke his sword. Guiscard implored Ormonde to finish him off, but the Duke replied that it was no task for honest men, ' 'tis for the hangman'. Seeing Harley alive had brought most of the Lords to their senses and they realized that Guiscard would be no use to them unless his life were preserved. Harley was well

G

aware of this fact. 'Pray let nobody hurt him,' he said. But the messengers and footmen who had been called in by Queensberry showed no mercy and had no intention of being deprived of their sport. They battered and bruised their victim, tied him up by the neck and heels and had him carried off to Newgate.

St John lost his head completely. He ran out bareheaded and, according to Harley's sister, 'without a sword in the utmost confusion ran away to St James's, went to Mrs Masham's lodging in a fright, and haply that day she dined with her sister'. One of the Dukes fled up the Privy Garden and was not seen again that afternoon. Poulett, the most practical of them all, went for medical aid, and soon an apothecary from King Street brought smelling salts, followed by a doctor named Monsieur Bousier. 'I have brought you the best surgeon in England,' said Poulett reassuringly.

The blade of the knife was found stuck into the flannel stomacher. Harley insisted on removing it himself, and with his usual *sang-froid* took the handle, which had been found under Newcastle's chair, and the blade, and wrapped them in Poulett's handkerchief. The collector's instinct did not desert him even at this moment of crisis. His calmness was altogether phenomenal. He asked Rochester to break the news gently to the Queen, without causing her unnecessary alarm. He gave orders that Guiscard should be given the best medical attention. He then asked whether his own wound was mortal, and said that he was not afraid to die.

The knife had only made a small incision, but the surgeon, for some reason best known to medical practitioners of the time, felt it necessary to cut him six or seven times more. He then put in twelve dressings, known as 'docils', and allowed the patient to go home. A hackney chair was called and Harley was carried back to York Buildings with the faithful Poulett walking at his side; Swallow showed great care and tenderness throughout the whole episode. The news that the Chancellor had been stabbed by a Frenchman spread rapidly, and a great crowd converged on Westminster. So Harley made his slow painful way home with a cheering mob in attendance. Other men might well have been overcome with pain and emotion, but he kept calm and even remembered to give five shillings to the chairmen.

Swift and Dr Radcliffe were among those who hurried to York Buildings that evening. The doctor could not resist letting blood—as if enough had not been spilt already—and that evening Harley was reported to be lying quietly 'in a breathing sweat'. Although the wound itself was not too serious, there was considerable risk of gangrene, especially as Harley had been in poor health at the time of the stabbing. Dr Radcliffe showed some signs of professional jealousy; he criticized Bousier's efforts roundly and called in another surgeon, Dr Green, whom Harley also sent to attend to Guiscard in prison. For two days the patient was allowed nothing but gruel to drink, but on March 10 the doctor let him have some chicken rice with hartshorn boiled in it, and a little sack whey. He had several restless nights and a rising temperature; the wound was slow to heal and at one time threatened to become a fistula. Harley bore all this with courage, but he was not above turning the situation to advantage. Whether or not he himself really believed he was going to die, he made quite sure that the country as a whole should think that he was hovering on the verge of extinction. From his bed he sent dying requests to his friends, including an urgent appeal that the Quebec expedition should be cancelled. Letters of sympathy came in by every post, expressing shock and astonishment. 'Nothing is too barbarous to be committed by a French subject when nothing is too villainous to be commanded by the French King,' wrote Sir Constantine Phipps, Lord Chancellor of Ireland. Ralph Thoresby, a scholar of Leeds, said that all learned men were solicitous to hear of the recovery of so great a patron who was also the greatest of statesmen and the best of Privy Councillors. Prior was moved to write 'a handsome paper of verses' to commemorate the occasion and capture the spirit of the moment:

> The guilty stroke and torture of the steel
> Infix'd, our dauntless Briton scarce perceives;
> The wounds his country from his death must feel,
> The patriot views; for those alone he grieves.
>
> The barbarous rage that durst attempt thy life,
> Harley, great counsellor, extends thy fame;
> And the sharp point of cruel Guiscard's knife,
> In brass and marble carves thy deathless name . . .
>
> Meantime, thy pain is gracious Anna's care;
> Our Queen, our saint, with sacrificing breath,
> Softens thy anguish; in her powerful prayer
> She pleads thy service, and forbids thy death.

Gracious Anna was so shocked when the news was first brought to her by St John and Arbuthnot that for a while she refused to believe that Harley was still alive. Her coolness towards him had been nothing more than a veneer. She was so upset that she 'wept uncontrollably for two hours, passed a sleepless night, and was so distraught with anxiety for the next two days that she worked herself into a high fever, and four of her doctors had to be specially summoned to her bedside at 5 o'clock on the Saturday morning to administer emergency treatment'. Harley's danger made her value him more than ever, and the whole affair revealed where her true affection lay.

All Harley had done was to suffer an unprovoked attack with courage and calm, but anyone would have thought he had repulsed a French invasion single-handed from the way people worshipped him. A year before, a crop of babies had been christened Sacheverell; now, Harley became the popular Christian name. The general opinion was that Guiscard's attempt had been the first move in a Jacobite bid for power. It was now known that Guiscard had been writing to Irish officers and telling them that England was on the verge of a great revolution. Harley was the saviour who had discovered the treachery in time, saving both the nation and the Queen. The horrid truth came out that Guiscard had often been seen at court, and had even enjoyed the freedom of the backstairs. At any time he could have entered the Queen's chamber, stabbed her to the heart, and then offered her vacant throne to the Pretender. Even more revealing was the fact that Guiscard had made up to a member of the Queen's Ewry and asked to see the Queen's bread. Since he had also tried to gain an entrance into the bakery where the royal bread was made, it seemed probable that he had in mind a foul plot to poison the Queen. Her sworn servants had not let him see the Queen's loaf, which it was thought he intended to copy, and the baker's wife, having seen the stranger alight from his chair at the end of the street, had barred his way to the bakery door. When all this came to light, there was a surge of loyalty for the Queen; the Commons declared that they would effectually stand by and defend her person, and prayed that she would 'please to take care of herself, and issue a proclamation to banish all papists 10 miles from London'.

The Lords examined Guiscard on several occasions but failed to extract anything except the vaguest generalities. The traitor was determined to die and take his secrets with him to the grave. He refused to have his wounds dressed and tried to conceal the dangerous injuries caused by the battering he had received at the hands of the messengers. He tantalized his inquisitors by hinting at dark plots and refusing to give any details. One day, however, the Lords promised him that the Queen would show mercy if he made a full confession. According to the Auditor, he changed his mind completely after this and made up his mind to live. He took food and allowed his wounds to be dressed. All went well until, a few days later, a note was delivered to him, written by his old crony St John. The story was that St John told him the Queen would not keep her merciful promise after all, because he had 'trifled' with her. As soon as he had read the note, Guiscard flew into a fury, pulled off the bandages and opened up the wounds. After this there was no further hope for him. His sordid career was almost at an end. 'A poor wench that Guiscard kept sent him a bottle of sack, but the keeper would not let him touch it, for fear it was poison,' wrote Swift. Guiscard's other visitors were less kind-hearted. As he lay on his bed, with only a few hours to live, the Dukes of Ormonde, Shrewsbury and Dover stood over him, with the Lords Rochester, Poulett and Dartmouth, and Mr Secretary St John. As ruthlessly as the Whig Lords had plagued the condemned Greg, these Tories now waited for Guiscard's final confession.

Many people believed that Guiscard's death, when it came, was a great relief to St John. If the villain had been brought to trial, he might well have made public their shared *amours* or, even worse, accused the Secretary of plotting for the Pretender or of passing secrets to the French. It had been observed how clumsily eager St John had been to make Guiscard a corpse immediately after the assassination attempt, with the pretence of avenging Harley. True to his word, St John had seen to it that Guiscard's lodgings were searched; he had seen to it also that nothing had been found. Nor did Harley ever see again those vital intercepted packages which made their last appearance on the green tablecloth in the vicinity of Mr Secretary St John's hat.

However distressed St John had appeared to be when he saw the Chancellor of the Exchequer inert in his chair, his disappointment was manifest when he saw Harley rise, distinctly bloody but equally unbowed. St John tried to counter Harley's sudden popularity by sedulously spreading a story that Guiscard's knife had really been aimed at himself. In his version it was claimed that Guiscard had asked to have a word with St John privately, and when this favour was refused, he tried to knife St John but was foiled by a table which stood between him and the intended target. He then attacked Harley, as a second-best choice, with a cry of 'Have at *you*, then'. Auditor Harley dismissed this account as a 'groundless fiction'; he was, of course, a biased witness, but his own careful and detailed account carries conviction and tallies with the spontaneous stories told by agitated aunts in letters written on the day of the crime. Harley's friends were sure that he had been singled out by the Jacobites as the man who stood in the way of their plans, and some recalled seeing verses which had been circulating several days before, and a copy of which is to be found among the Harley papers at Longleat:

> Harley beware, thy certain doom's decreed,
> October swears they'll make thy carcass bleed.

The Harley relations, too, were sure that St John was suspect and that their adored Robin had once again become the victim of malicious enemies. The incident at any rate did little to improve the relationship. Harley found it more difficult than ever to trust St John, especially as he took advantage of the situation to press on with his Quebec expedition, and to gain favour with Abigail Masham. As for St John, he became more jealous of Harley than ever, and the last drop of loyalty for his old master evaporated as he watched his rival climb to martyr status.

St John continued to work at his scheme, and Harley, although feverish and still bleeding from the wound, was not a man to sit back and do nothing. He used his enforced rest to take a detached look at all the problems which had crowded in upon him during the last few months. In particular he turned over in his mind possible solutions to the financial crisis which he had inherited from the previous Ministry. Protected from insignificant petitioners and everyday worries by the sick-room aura, Harley was free to concentrate on his plans, which were designed to release the country from the grip of speculators and army contractors who had fared so well in the war. Defoe had taught him to by-pass the worn-out theories and try new ways that might in time lead into realms of unimaginable prosperity. For nine years now the war had dragged on, nine monotonous years of winter truce and summer activity, of march and counter-march, of siege and skirmish. There had been victories, brilliant but inconclusive, and still the promised march on Paris had never taken place, little indeed had been gained, save for some Barrier towns of value only to the Dutch. England, for all her efforts, had achieved nothing except a chronic national debt and a waste of manpower. Was this all the soldiers had fought for on the fields of Flanders?

Defoe had other ideas; his advice was for the British to let the Dutch haggle over their own fortresses and allow the Bourbon Philip to keep his Spanish throne, but to claim a trade monopoly in the South Seas as a reward for all the money spent and the battles fought. The grounding that both Defoe and Harley had gained at school in trade, economics and geography now stood them both in good stead. While their Church of England contemporaries had been tied to Greek and Latin texts, they had looked to wider horizons. They understood each other when they talked of the natural wealth of the Americas, and planned to establish settlements and exploit the resources of underdeveloped territories in the southern hemisphere. They did not echo the mistakes made by the planners of Darien. Defoe was not interested in the mosquito-ridden swamps of central America; he turned his thoughts towards the western seaboard, to Chile, where cool breezes off the Pacific provide a temperate climate suitable for exiled Europeans. Given an unlimited supply of slaves from the forests of Africa, Britain could build up her trade and gain a supremacy which years of military endeavour had failed to achieve. The key to the problem was to gain the *asiento*, the monopoly of the slave-trade. Happily the highly developed consciences of these two dissenting men did not prick them at the idea of selling human beings for money and depriving them of their freedom. Anything that was conducive to industry was, to the Puritan mind, right and just. And so Harley planned to found a South Sea Company which would help to consolidate the national debt, and with the help of the Auditor, he worked out the details during his convalescence in March and April. Using the established East India Company as their model, they outlined a new business concern which was to shoulder from the start the whole floating debt of ten millions. Creditors of the state would be asked to transfer their debts to the new fund at an agreed interest rate of six per cent, while the revenue from certain taxes was to be paid into the company in perpetuity. Working hard with no interruptions save for the occasional haemorrhage from the stab-wound, the two brothers brought the visionary scheme down to practical reality. The plan was drawn up, ready for the time when the Chancellor should feel well enough to return to the world of politics.

That day came on April 26. News that the Chancellor was to reappear spread rapidly and there was a large crowd to greet him at the House. During his absence, Members had forgotten his faults and discovered his virtues. In the six weeks he had been away there had been confusion and chaos. The October Club was quite out of hand and would not even listen to St John. Trouble-makers of all party hues joined to harry the leaderless Ministry. The leather tax was thrown out, debates grew bitter and unbalanced and Members longed for Harley's mitigating and controlling influence. 'Several politicians that could not endure Mr Harley,' observed Peter Wentworth, 'say they can see now there's no man the Court employs has enough to manage the House of Commons but him.' He was treated to a speech of congratulation from the Speaker, and received a general ovation. On April 28 his daughter gave an account of the occasion to her aunt:

My dear father is pretty well. His looks are very much mended within these few days.

I hear the Speaker made a very fine speech, my father was received in a very extraordinary manner, there was not one in the House but what took occasion to make their compliments to him and crowded about him. The House was very full. I hear the speech is to be printed.

Once again the family had cause to give thanks to God for the especial protection He had extended to His faithful servant. It has to be admitted that at times the Almighty relaxed his watch and allowed the great Robin to run into the most alarming dangers, but always, in the end, the bountiful mercy was extended and he emerged unharmed. So Harley's friends and relations gave thanks for the embroidered waistcoat, the flannel stomacher, the breastbone and the frailness of the knife. The coat and waistcoat were carefully preserved and can be seen at Brampton, the coat torn where the knife entered the sleeve and above the breastbone. The inch tip of the blade, which Harley picked up off the floor, was re-attached to the knife by the goldsmith with a small silver link for the benefit of 'those who may be desirous to see it', as Harley wrote in a note attached to the knife which is also preserved at Brampton. Had the little weapon not broken, the second blow administered by Guiscard would certainly have been fatal, for the bruise it left was directly above the heart. And if Harley's family blessed all these happy chances, Harley himself, in his wry way, showed some gratitude to the villain for restoring his declining popularity; he obtained Guiscard's portrait and hung it on his wall as a reminder of the strange workings of Providence.

CHAPTER 16

THE WHITE STAFF

ON MAY 17, 1711, Harley presented his scheme for trade in the South Seas to an attentive House of Commons. That evening there were bonfires and bell-ringing in the city. Even the Tories were enthusiastic, for they realized that this much-maligned man was doing his best to give them the financial power they had always so envied in the Whigs. The scheme appealed to the older men, in whose minds it aroused nostalgic memories of the legendary Spanish Main, while the younger men liked its spirit of adventure, and Tories of every age welcomed the emphasis on Britain's seapower. The Whigs were impressed by the commercial insight of the whole conception. In spite of themselves they had to admit that Harley was something of a financial wizard. Only the creditors reserved judgement, suspicious of a scheme that pre-supposed Spanish readiness to surrender supremacy in the South Seas. They were reluctant, too, to lose the comfortable feeling that because the government was indebted to the tune of ten million pounds, they could hold the entire nation to ransom.

The lottery, which once had seemed doomed to failure, was now proving even more successful than the one which the Godolphin Ministry had organized the year before. With the help of Halifax, Harley had ironed out the weakness of the earlier lottery. Better odds and rewards were offered because in Halifax's opinion 'the hope of good fortune is the chief allurement, [and] the more scope and swing is given to people's expectations and fancies the more certain you are to draw them in'. The double chance was particularly well contrived, and at Halifax's suggestion the tickets were made larger, more valuable and less easy to lose or mislay. Auditor Harley took over from the Bank the task of collecting in the subscriptions and this method had worked so well that within seven days the whole sum was over-subscribed.

Although the balance of parties had not changed in Harley's absence, the Guiscard affair and the papist scare had done the High Tories little good. At last, the prudent Poulett wrote, the Ministry could free itself

G*

from 'the taint of old courtiers'. The only Jacobite of the old school remaining was the Duke of Buckingham who, as Poulett sagely remarked, could 'never be dangerous and will in many ways be useful'. Many High Tories who had refused to accept Harley as first minister were now prepared to acknowledge his lead. 'You are, and are to be very soon declared *le premier ministre*,' Somerset had to admit on May 18. It was now clear that the Queen intended to make him Lord Treasurer. She tantalized him a fraction longer, indulged her womanly whims a little further by keeping the staff in her cupboard for another week, but at the end of it he had the coveted rod in his hand. In the same week he was created Earl of Oxford and Mortimer and for the last time dined with his friends as Robert Harley Esq. On May 29 Swift wrote to Stella:

My Lord Oxford had the staff given him this morning, so now I must call him Lord Oxford no more, but Lord Treasurer; I hope he will stick there; this is twice he has changed his name this week; and I heard to-day in the City (where I dined) that he will very soon have the Garter.

The new Earl was 'at the height of power and favour'. Outside the Treasury vast crowds waited to hand him petitions as he passed by. The ladies of the family basked in the new glory, and Swift shared in the family celebration when he dined on May 27 with the new Countess and Lady Betty, Harley's daughter Elizabeth, 'these three days a lady born'. Lady Dupplin, Oxford's other daughter, was honoured by an invitation to dine with her kinswoman Mrs Masham at Kensington and strolled there in the garden in the cool of the evening. Harley bore his new honours with becoming modesty and it was several days before he allowed his friends to address him by his title. 'When I called him my Lord, he called me Dr Thomas Swift, which he always does when he has a mind to tease me,' Swift reported. Hating the forms of grandeur as he did, he remained as unassuming as ever, even though his self-satisfied expression in the Kneller portrait shows that he enjoyed wearing the robes and decorations that went with his new position. Though outwardly charming and civil to everyone, he was under no illusions about the general calibre of those who jostled for position in his presence. When Swift went to his levee, Harley swore that he had come out of spite 'to see him among a parcel of fools'.

Three months before, nobody would have guessed that by the end of May Harley would hold the magic wand in his hand and become 'Primere Minister', as his brother Edward called him. It seemed as if a turn of fortune's wheel had lifted him out of range of the jealous plots and schemes of his enemies. But popularity won by a fluke has to be maintained by skill, and good luck, in its turn, is often followed by bad. In this case death took away much of Oxford's hard-won equilibrium. In April, smallpox, the universal scourge, removed from the European arena the Emperor of Austria, leaving the throne vacant for his younger brother Charles, who was still trying ineffectually to establish himself in Spain. The news, confusing to the allied cause, upset afresh the balance of power in Europe. It had an invigorating effect on Louis and drove further away all hopes of a quick peace. Then, a more personal blow came. In recent months, Oxford had built up a firm friendship with the Earl of Rochester, who had mellowed with age and proved, with his integrity, experience and good sense, a valuable influence in the Cabinet Council. He was seventy-two and apparently in good health, but on the night of May 2 he died suddenly, having complained only that evening of a pain in his stomach and a shaking in his hand as he wrote a letter to the Queen. The bonfires lit to celebrate Harley's proposal, for the South Sea fund could not cancel out this loss, and triumph was mingled with sorrow. For a moment Harley seemed to despair, but Poulett, faithful as ever, urged him to continue:

It is the greatest encouragement imaginable for you to go on of yourself, and to hold the scales in your hand, which at this time is fairly offered you . . . to balance the fate of Europe. . . . Every friend Rochester had will be yours to a man. . . . The credit of Rochester's confidence and friendship remains alive in you.

In June fate dealt an even more bitter blow. The Duke of Newcastle had suffered yet another fall out hunting, when riding a favourite old nag grown too weak to carry him. The doctors hurried out to the hunting lodge and administered the usual remedies. After being bled, the Duke began a slow and painful journey in a chaise back to the house; his blood rapidly 'stagnated', and according to Oxford's report the medicine which the doctors forced down his throat had the effect of choking him; soon afterwards he died. Newcastle was a friend whom Harley had courted for years, and who had remained faithful in the summer of 1710 when so many others had faded. They had become so close that negotiations had begun to make a match between Newcastle's only child, Lady Henrietta Holles, and Oxford's son Edward. The Duke's death removed at a stroke an intimate friend, a political ally and adviser, a link with the Whigs, a name backed by the prestige of large estates and electoral power, and one of the few men of any ability left in the Ministry.

Such shocks were difficult to bear, and they shattered an already weak Cabinet. Marlborough's description of the feebleness of its members to Robethon, the Elector of Hanover's confidential secretary, bears this out:

He [Harley] never speaks except upon Treasury or Parliamentary business and then only with extreme timidity. Each fears to venture too far and thus lay himself open to others. The result is that no one takes the direction and all drifts at hazard. Lord Shrewsbury is even more timid. . . . The Duke of Buckinghamshire is bold enough, but he has neither the capacity to steer the ship nor enough reputation to make others follow him. The Duke of Queensberry is a nonentity. Only the Secretary of State, St. John, applies himself to business, and being a man of talent will soon learn how to deal with it. . . . He speaks more boldly to the Queen in Council than anyone else.

Oxford had already scraped the bottom of the barrel and was hard put to it to fill any vacancies. And to everyone's annoyance he prevaricated, keeping hopeful candidates in suspense. Procrastination was one of his less endearing characteristics, and it grew on him the busier he became. Hating to disappoint, he often promised more than he could achieve, and he began to make many enemies amongst those who watched and waited for favours.

The removal of Rochester's experience and wisdom, and of Newcastle's name and reputation, made those who were left a prey to St John. There was no counterpoise to the Secretary's masterful presence. Somerset, as ambitious as ever, still coveted his right to attend Cabinet meetings, but St John refused to sit at the same table with a man who, he said, had done nothing but betray his colleagues. The Duchess of Somerset was also a menace; as the summer wore on, she gained ground daily with the Queen, while Abigail, expecting yet another child in September, found court life almost unbearable in the hot humid weather.

Once the acclamation died down Oxford had to face the plain fact that his South Sea scheme could not succeed unless there was a quick and favourable peace. At the same time it was evident that no settlement could be reached before the start of the summer campaign. It was most desirable to have success in the military field to provide a good basis for subsequent negotiations. Since Marlborough was the man most likely to achieve a helpful victory, Oxford forgot that he had ever called the General a war-monger. Both men discovered suddenly that it would be to their mutual benefit to become friends. Great expressions of respect passed to and fro, and Marlborough wrote to the Duchess reproving her for writing too freely about Mr Harley and other Ministers. 'I am in their power,' he reminded her '. . . so I beg of you, as for the quiet of my life, that you will be careful never to write anything that may anger them.'

Now that the Duchess had been relieved of all her responsibilities, there was hope that she might settle down quietly and leave the Queen to her own devices. She had no contact with the court, for the Queen had seen to it that none of her daughters succeeded her. Of these Sir David Hamilton had said that the one was cunning and dangerous, the other silly and imprudent, and Lady Montagu was just like her mother. This last was enough to put anyone off. And in spite of her dismissal, the Duchess was unable to avoid one last row. It was all round the town in May that when leaving her lodgings for the last time, she had ripped out all the fittings and even torn the marble mantelpieces from the walls. 'Come come,' Harley admonished Maynwaring, who affected to know nothing about it, 'you must have heard what was done by the Duchess.' She alleged that Harley was exaggerating in order to paint her as greedy and grasping. 'Everybody knows that *cheating* is not the Duchess's fault,' the Queen had said the previous summer when someone tried to work up a peculation charge in connection with the building of Blenheim. The Queen knew, as Marlborough himself did, that the Duchess's unbalanced rages caused the harm. Marlborough begged her, in several letters, to keep her temper and be kind. He wrote to her from Flanders in May with the urgent plea that she would not remove any of the mantelpieces. Between Harley's propaganda and the Duchess's persecution mania it is hard to see where the truth lies. She swore that she took only what was hers, and this did include a portrait of the Duke of Gloucester, which was set in the marble of one of the chimney-pieces. But there is no doubt, from the inventory which she herself caused to be drawn up, that she took her last pound of flesh—even the brass door-handles, and other trivial fittings, which, in the circumstances, she would have been wise to leave behind. It is not surprising that the Queen was incensed. Maynwaring tried to intercede with Harley on the Duchess's behalf, but learnt that the Queen was inexorable:

The Queen is so angry, that she says she will build no house for the Duke of Marlborough, when the Duchess has pulled hers to pieces, taken away the very slabs out of the chimneys, thrown away the keys, and said they might buy more for ten shillings.

The Duchess, naturally, accused Oxford of influencing the Queen, and of persuading her to discontinue the building of Blenheim. Now, at any rate, since he was feeling magnanimous towards Marlborough, Oxford made it one of his first actions under his new title to prevail with the Queen to sign a warrant for £20,000 for the continuation of Blenheim, although Maynwaring reported that the Treasurer's 'airs and grimaces upon this occasion were hard to represent'. The Duchess had no difficulty in believing that it was Oxford's idea, and not the Queen's, to continue building. 'She never did a generous thing of herself,' wrote the Duchess, who had by now lost interest in Blenheim. She had alienated Vanbrugh with her endless disputes about extravagance, and thought the place had grown too big and unwieldy and was nothing but a 'heap of stones'. She was more interested at present in the house that Wren was building just down the road from St James's, in nice neighbourly proximity to the Queen. But Marlborough thought differently. For him, Blenheim was a symbol, a huge tangible mark of the nation's gratitude, and he wanted it to be finished. Oxford realized this, and it was just the kind of lever he knew how to use. The Duchess, tactless to the last, made the lever all the more effective by her waywardness over the brass locks. The story about the chimneypieces may well have been a 'dirty piece of malice' spread by Oxford's Grub Street friends, as the Duchess alleged, but it had some foundation in fact, and he knew all too well how to make capital out of it.

Marlborough, like Oxford, had accepted the necessity of another summer in the field. So, for a few months longer it was expedient for him to grovel before the men in power. The Earl of Stair, who acted as a go-between in the summer of 1711, assured the Treasurer that the General would never let personal pique affect the success of military affairs. Oxford, for his part, did what he could to re-establish Marlborough's position. He dissuaded the Queen from thinking that she had a right to make army appointments according to her own whims. He sent away officers who, in 1710, had been encouraged to preach disloyalty. Argyll, the most powerful and influential of them all, was despatched to Spain, and Orrery was given a diplomatic mission at the Hague. With these indications of good will and trust, Marlborough had to rest content. 'I am entirely sensible,' he wrote to Oxford in July, 'that without the Queen's favour, and your confidence, it will be impossible for me to carry on the service.' But it was only a partial truce. Marlborough was no longer in intimate touch with affairs of state. His close, everyday contact with the Queen had gone. On matters of policy he was no longer consulted. The army was his sphere, and he was made to see that he must stay in it. He accepted his diminished role, and set his mind to the task ahead, albeit with the usual complaints about tiredness and depression. In August he forced the French lines at Bouchain in a manœuvre which army experts considered to be one of the most brilliant in his career. But it did little to alter the balance of power, or to provide the allies with an extra counter in the peace game that lay ahead. Already Marlborough was turning over in his mind the possibility of keeping the British force in the field through the winter months, ready to attack, in the early spring, a French army unprepared and unassembled. It was a new conception of strategy, calculated to break the deadlock on the Franco-Dutch Border, and to finish the conflict once and for all. But while Marlborough pondered this idea, one of his countrymen was already locked in consultation with the French. Ministerial impatience could not wait until the spring for the fruition of Marlborough's plans. What was wanted was an early peace, and peace at any price.

It was well known, even among foreign diplomats, that Oxford's interests were geared to home affairs, to the niceties of politics and the complications of finance. The ins-and-outs of the European power-game had never been his particular study. This accounts for the fact that although he was among the first to agitate for peace, he never seemed eager to attend to the details of negotiation himself. Up to April 1711 he had let Jersey put out the preliminary feelers; but once he had shown that the British were earnest in their desire for peace, Jersey's usefulness was exhausted. With his Jacobite tendencies he would have been unacceptable to the English people as a serious negotiator. Already he had overstepped his brief and was talking of surrendering the deep natural harbour of Port Mahon in Minorca. The bizarre character of proceedings that involved a French priest and an acknowledged Jacobite was disconcerting for those few Ministers who were in the secret, and Shrewsbury, careful as ever and very anxious to share his responsibilities with others, urged the Queen to tell the whole Cabinet what was going on. This was done towards the end of April, and St John, who surprisingly enough had known nothing about the negotiations so far, immediately took the affair into his own competent hands. He became a kind of unofficial foreign secretary, and began to get down to business at once. Oxford, busy with his South Sea Scheme, had let the peace talks drift, but St John could see that this was putting the cart before the horse; a favourable settlement first, with trade concessions—then would be the time to make golden plans for conquering the wealth of South America.

Jersey having served his turn, a new negotiator had to be found, someone unobtrusive whose movements would not arouse interest or cause comment. Oxford and St John chose their friend Matthew Prior who was shrewd, intelligent, and experienced in diplomatic affairs at the court of

France. He could speak French fluently and was just the kind of well-mannered, witty individual likely to appeal to the French. In England, if he was known at all, it was for his poetry, and he had been without place and position since he had been removed from a pleasant niche in the Board of Trade in the purge of Tories in 1707. He left for France in July, in the greatest secrecy, furnished with a note from the Queen herself. 'Le sieur Prior est pleinement instruit et autorisé de communiquer à la France nos demandes préliminaires,' it ran, 'et de nous en rapporter la réponse. A.R.' Oxford was to bless that small piece of paper and the initials 'A.R.' at a later date; experience had taught him to be chary of writing anything that might later prove useful to his enemies, and the impeachment of Somers early in the century had been a warning to all politicians. It was certainly wise to shelter under the umbrella of the Queen's prerogative in this vital matter.

Travelling under the assumed name of Jeremy Matthews, Prior made his way to Paris in July and presented his 'memorial' which contained the Ministry's preliminary demands. In his diary he recorded three meetings with Torcy, one of which took place melodramatically under cover of darkness in the gardens of Fontainebleu. Torcy, the French Foreign Minister, who had been juggling with Jersey for the last few months, was expecting considerable concessions on the English side, and hoped to be able to indulge in some pleasurable barter. He therefore opened the proceedings by showing Prior some letters from the Pensionary's special envoy Petkum, that indefatigable worker for peace, in which it was made clear that the Dutch, like the English, were angling for a separate settlement. Torcy hinted that the French intended to treat with whoever offered France the best bargain, but St John had instructed Prior to be bold in his approach and to concede nothing. At the second meeting, which took place when Torcy and the King had run through the memorial, the French Minister expressed amazement at the English demands, as well he might. Besides the expected clauses about the Dutch Barrier and the recognition of Queen Anne, St John claimed Gibraltar and Port Mahon in the Mediterranean, Newfoundland and Nova Scotia in North America, with all the best fishing rights, not to mention the slave trade monopoly in the South Seas and, for good measure, the destruction of Dunkirk, that favourite haunt of the French privateers. It seemed to Torcy that the English demanded, as a reward for their glorious but inconclusive victories, the entire trade of the world. He found it necessary to point out that France was bowed but not beaten, and Prior's confidence was a little shaken at the first meeting when Torcy, running

his eye down the preliminaries, stopped short at the clause about concessions in South America and the West Indies and said that such things
would never be granted:

Here my heart ached extremely and I was ready to sink, but recollecting myself,
I thought it time to say that . . . I was very sorry that my coming hither was
of no effect, and that I looked upon myself as very unhappy, while I told him
with the same plainness, *ouverture de cœur*, that he used to me, that it was
impossible the peace should be made upon any other condition.

It was a case of the irresistible object and the immovable force; Prior
had been told to yield nothing, while Louis, who had recovered much of
his self-assurance since the dark days of winter 1709, and was just as
astute as ever, saw great possibilities for himself. He liked the look of the
rift between the allies and took a saturnine pleasure in promoting it. He
also appreciated the fact that if the South Sea Company was to succeed,
the monopoly of the slave trade must be secured. Since the English needed
this concession so badly, he would make them work for it. The English
were prepared to let Philip keep Spain, and Louis could not resist pointing
out that they really had not got Spain to give, with their candidate cower-
ing in one corner of it. 'You ask in America all that which [with] our
sweat and our blood we have been endeavouring for a hundred years
past to acquire,' said Torcy. On July 19 Prior was told that the King's
Council found it impossible to agree to some of the 'terrible articles', but
had decided to send a new agent, Nicolas Mesnager, Comte de St Jean,
a diplomat well versed in commercial matters, to accompany Prior back
to England. As a reward for his pains, Prior was granted an interview
with the King, and after much bowing and many pretty compliments
in French, Prior wished the monarch long life and prosperity, expressed
veneration for his person and took his leave.

Great secrecy surrounded the return journey. The boat landed at
Deal and the travellers showed St John's pass. All might have been well
had not John Macky, who had taken such a good look at English court
characters before describing them to the Electress, been a customs
official there, and recognized the man he had written about in his *Characters* as 'thin and hollow-looked'. Prior was arrested, and the secret came
out, to the astonishment of his cronies, who knew he had been out of town
for some weeks but had no idea that he had been abroad. 'People confidently affirm he has been in France, and I half believe it,' Swift wrote to
Stella. 'It is said he was sent by the Ministry, and for some overtures
towards a peace. The Secretary pretends he knows nothing of it.' Swift

amused himself by writing a twopenny pamphlet entitled *A New Journey to Paris* which purported to be the diary of one Sieur Baudrier who had acted as valet to Prior in France, and which, conveniently for the Ministers, gave a very vivid picture of a forceful Prior dictating terms to the humble French. Oxford was delighted with the piece and teased Prior by calling him Monsieur Baudrier from then onwards.

The Whig pamphleteers used less complimentary epithets. Matthew Pint-Pot they called him, harking back to his humble boyhood when he had helped his uncle at the Rhenish Wine House in Cannon Row, or Matchiavel P - - - r. Not unnaturally, there was a great deal of talk and criticism when it became known that the government had embarked on secret negotiations, but by then it was too late to renege. The overture was over; the main work had begun. The need for peace was as great as ever; each campaign rendered the country more impoverished, complaints about hardship emanated from all sections of society and particularly from the overtaxed landed gentry. Lady Pye offered up a typical lament when she told Abigail Harley that although all her daughters were now of a marriageable age, there was not the slightest chance of getting them off. 'Country gentlemen's daughters must be content to stay,' she wrote, 'few go off except fortunes, which these twenty years' taxes makes most families want'. It was the popular demand for peace which had swept the Tories into power and they were bound to honour their election promises if they wanted to avoid an outcry. So St John spent the greater part of August and September closeted with Mesnager, two men of brilliant debating skill arguing the toss, each reluctant to give ground and equally unready to break off negotiations. The Asiento monopoly was granted, but towns in the Spanish Indies were refused, nor could Mesnager give any guarantee that Britain would be granted territories in South America. He demanded Lille and Tournai in exchange for the destruction of the fortifications at Dunkirk. On the question of Newfoundland a bitter compromise was reached which was to cause difficulty between French and English fishermen for many years to come.

Oxford left the haggling to St John. He had more than enough on his hands. Although he appeared to be in surprisingly good health and spirits, always ready to jest with his intimate friends, the pressure of business began to mount and his family complained that he was always rushed. In August, a close season for the majority of people, he was particularly busy. Long leisurely interviews were a thing of the past, and even people with appointments were kept waiting. 'I was with him this morning at his levee, for one cannot see him otherwise here, he is so hurried,' Swift wrote on August 6. The petitioners were endless, Swift counted at least fifty who had asked him to solicit the Treasurer for them, and there were scores of others. He was always kind and polite and promised to do what he could. On one occasion he said to Swift, '*Laissez faire à don Antoine*; which is a French proverb, expressing, Leave that to me.' Unfortunately it was all too soon to become simply a case of *laissez faire*. Oxford's porter, Read, was well known throughout the town for his extreme gravity of mien and his ability to admit only those who were prepared to oil his palm, and he was trained to keep the importunate away. 'I did myself the honour to wait on you the other day, between your levee and couchee,' wrote one unfortunate, 'and I hope that person of wonderful gravity at your gate did me the right to acquaint you with it.' In August 1711 Read fell ill, and Swift had some caustic comments to make:

His famous lying porter is fallen sick, and they think he will die: I wish I had all my half-crowns again. I believe I have told you he is an old Scotch fanatic, and the damndest liar in his office alive.

In spite of all that Read could do to protect his master and fleece the visitors, life was still busy for a man who had so recently been near to death and whose wound had never healed properly. As late as July, Green, the surgeon, was paying professional calls and changing the plaster dressings which were still necessary.

The removal of the Queen to Windsor made the programme even more complicated. The Treasurer went down to visit her on Saturdays, having dealt with urgent business in the morning, and came back either on the Monday or the Tuesday. While St John battled with Mesnager, Oxford dealt with home affairs and gave his mind to the reconstruction of the Cabinet Council. He had hedged for long enough, and in June he moved the ineffective Duke of Buckingham into Rochester's place as Lord President, a sad substitute, but one that was acceptable to the Queen. John of Bucks had become the very soul of moderation, thanks to his rather negative temperament. Robert Benson, one of the members of the Treasury Commission, was appointed Chancellor of the Exchequer. He was an anaemic moderate, who had found it convenient to become a convert to the moderate Toryism of his brother-in-law Dartmouth. He had no outstanding talents, but gave good dinners, an asset in convivial Tory circles. Newcastle's place was far more difficult to fill. The High Tories were unlikely to accept another Whig, and were clamouring for someone of their own hue almost as loudly as the Whigs had pressed for Sunderland. Oxford realized, reluctantly, that they would have to be placated, and advised the Queen to make a gesture by inviting in the Jacobite Jersey. The Queen did not approve. She did not share Oxford's belief that he must 'manage' with the help of one party or the other. And her reluctance delayed the announcement. Oxford had to summon all his influence and power to move her. Nor did he wish to persuade her against her will, as that was exactly what he had blamed Godolphin and the Junto for doing. No decision, he reminded her, is ever simple. 'Balance the good and the evil of taking him in or keeping him out,' was his advice on this and on other occasions, 'weigh everything and compare the convenience and inconvenience.' In more favourable circumstances it might have been possible to reject a man whose name conjured up memories of the bad days of High Tory misrule. But reality had to be faced, and the sad truth was that Jersey was the only man of any stature who could satisfy High Tory demands and help hold the Ministry together at this vital time when peace was 'upon the anvil'. 'Your Ministry will crumble all to pieces,' Oxford warned the Queen, promising her that if she made this one concession, he would not trouble her again with a candidate she disliked. At last she agreed. It was rumoured that 'the stubborn business', as Swift called it, was finished and that Jersey's appointment was imminent. Then, on August 26, he died suddenly of gout, or apoplexy, or both. The decimation of his thinning ranks was a blow for Oxford, especially as he had not had time to please the High Tories by publishing his intention of appointing Jersey, and he had upset the Queen for nothing.

All the same, Oxford, to everyone's surprise, was not at a loss. He maintained a tantalizing silence for a day or two and in the evening of August 29, as he dined with his friends, he proposed a toast to 'my Lord Privy Seal'. 'So privy,' punned Prior, 'that we know not who it is.' The next day it was announced that John Robinson, Bishop of Bristol, was to be given the Seal. After the first surprise it was agreed that Oxford had made a clever move. Robinson was a Churchman who had been chaplain to the British Embassy in Stockholm and done valuable diplomatic work at a time when relations with Charles XII of Sweden had been particularly difficult. He was knowledgeable about European affairs, had the merit of being little known, and his politics were unexceptionable. The Queen liked him, and the Churchmen were placated by the inclusion of a practising clergyman. Only the Whigs were angered by the idea of a clergyman occupying a ministerial post; they felt it was a retrogressive step, since no Bishop had sat in the Council since the days of Archbishop Laud. But there was nothing they could do; not until they came to power were they able to take practical steps to ensure that no cleric could be given secular power.

So another crisis was surmounted, and Oxford looked forward to the autumn, knowing that he enjoyed the whole-hearted favour of the Queen and a better relationship with the Tories.

CHAPTER 17

THE QUEEN'S FRIEND

IN THE SUMMER OF 1711 the difference of opinion over Jersey was the only slight cloud in the easy relationship between Oxford and the Queen. Her Lord Treasurer brought her the calm and comfort which her life so often lacked. Mesnager, the French envoy, recorded in his Minutes:

Let her chagrin be never so great, the new Lord Treasurer, Harley, always had it in his power to cheer her by his representations, and generally left her composed and happy.

With others she might be silent and uncommunicative, but to Oxford she opened her heart, telling him her worries, her fears and her aches and pains. Her letters to him are a remarkable and touching record of a monarch's affection and trust. 'I beg you would never make any more excuses for long letters, for I do assure you it is always a great satisfaction to me to hear from you.' . . . 'I pray God send you your health and preserve your life for the good of your country and all your faithful friends; none I am sure is more so than your very affectionate friend Anne R.' . . . 'I cannot determine anything in my own thoughts, and therefore I shall give no orders to the Secretary till I can know your opinion.' . . . 'I have been in so much pain all the last night and this day that it is not easy to me now to write.' . . . 'Please God send me a tolerable good night.' . . . 'I hope you will excuse the blots of this letter, for I am in haste and can not write it over again.'

The Queen had been forced to spend the previous summer mainly in London, because of the ministerial shake, but this year she compensated by enjoying a long stay at Windsor, with plenty of hunting. She drove her own chaise, furiously, like Jehu, in Swift's famous description. Although her letters reveal her as an emotional woman, to the rest of the world she was stolid and uninspiring. Swift described the embarrassed silences that greeted those who were brave enough to venture into her official 'drawing-room', which was actually held in the bedchamber, since so few people appeared:

We made our bows, and stood about twenty of us round the room, while she looked at us round with her fan in her mouth, and once a minute said about three words to some that were nearest her, and then she was told dinner was ready and went out.

Food was always an important factor in the Queen's life and one of the few real pleasures left to her, but it seems that for a few months in the summer and autumn of 1711 Oxford, with his magnetic charm, was able to give her the kind of friendship she seldom had the chance to sample.

In August the Queen suffered a severe attack of gout and there was some alarm about her condition; rumours of her illness sent bank stock tumbling by three or four per cent. Oxford wanted her to see Dr Radcliffe, but nothing would persuade her to consult the practitioner with whom she had quarrelled in earlier years, even though her friend had such faith in his powers. She assured Sir David Hamilton, much to his relief, that 'Dr Radcliffe was the last man she would take in, and gave me leave to say so'. Fortunately she rallied at the end of the month, and on August 30 she wrote to Oxford:

I give you many thanks for your kind enquiry after my health, which I thank God is so much mended within these two days that I hope, with the help of a stick, to be able to walk to Council a Monday.

Mesnager noticed that the Queen was 'a passionate lover of the common people, as they generally were of her'. It was her affection for her people that made her a determined supporter of the peace negotiations. She greeted the news of Marlborough's success at Bouchain ungraciously, and was not impressed when she heard that her General had opened up the way for an invasion of France. 'I think the D. of Marlborough shows plainer than ever by this new project his unwillingness for a peace, but I hope our negotiations will succeed and then it will not be in his power to prevent it,' she wrote. She grew alarmed every time there was a deadlock, and sent a message to St John telling him not to insist on any proposition if Mesnager seemed very averse to it. 'I think there is nothing so much to be feared as the letting the Treaty go out of our hands,' she told Oxford. Shrewsbury, the one member of the Cabinet who had any scruples about the shabby way in which the allies were being treated, tried to express his doubts, but she brushed them aside. 'He seems a little fearfull,' she told Oxford, with a touch of scorn.

On August 22 Abigail Masham gave birth to a boy. He was christened on September 7 at Kensington in his mother's bedchamber. It was something of a family affair; Oxford was a godfather and Abigail's sister a godmother, and Oxford's son and son-in-law, Lords Harley and Dupplin, were guests. Lord Rivers, the other godfather, and Swift, were the only outsiders. Since both Masham and Swift were members of St John's Brothers' Society, the boy was jestingly referred to as Swift's 'nephew'. Abigail, although she had had an easy time at the birth, being only an hour in labour, had been unwell ever since, but she sat up in bed while the infant, unimpressed by the fact that he had a Lord Treasurer for a godfather, 'roared like a bull' throughout. St John was not present, which was perhaps significant; his stock with Abigail was high, but relationships with the Treasurer were strained. Their mutual friends were doing all they could to prevent an open breach. Oxford was not a member of the Brothers' Society, but most of its members were his friends or relations. The difficulty was that most of them were also attracted by St John's 'wit, capacity, beauty, quickness of apprehension, good learning and excellent taste'. It was not an easy situation. And for all his good qualities, St John had a jealous nature. He was envious of his master's peerage; like many other people, he felt that the Harley claim to the Earldom of Oxford was extremely tenuous. He was sure that he himself should have received similar honours.

St John had openly defied his old friend by pressing on with the Quebec expedition, and in spite of his growing prestige he was behaving as irresponsibly as ever. Gallas reported to his masters in Vienna that St John's arrogance and 'excessive fiery temper' increased every day:

Beside this, he is given to the bottle and debauchery to the point of making a virtue out of his open affectation that public affairs are a bagatelle to him, and that his capacity is on so high a level that he has no need to give up his pleasures in the slightest degree for any cause.

Swift and Lord Radnor, strolling in the Mall one evening in August, encountered St John who quickly left them and hurried away to other business; they took it for granted that he was off to find a wench. This was the man who was engaged in secret negotiations, and who was discussing the future of the whole of Europe.

St John's affairs met with a check early in October when the news came through that the Quebec expedition had failed. The Admiral in charge had omitted to obtain a skilled pilot for the treacherous waters of the St Lawrence, many ships and men had been lost and the survivors so disheartened that the whole force had been withdrawn just when it should have pressed on to Quebec. St John was mortified. The failure was really due to the incompetence of the commanders he had chosen, but he blamed it on the storm which had driven ships on to the rocks. Mrs Masham and Mrs Hill put a bold face on it, and went out to a concert, just to show the world that they were not cast down, but St John was disappointed. A success story would have placed him high above Oxford in everyone's estimation. It was hardly surprising that, in spite of the news, the Lord Treasurer appeared to be 'just as merry as usual'.

On October 13, soon after the Quebec sensation, the *Daily Courant*, one of the more reliable newspapers, published details of 'The Preliminary Articles of October' which had been signed the previous week by St John and Dartmouth, the two Secretaries of State, and by Mesnager. The *Courant* alleged that these terms had been 'offered' by France. There was an immediate outcry, with most of the criticism being directed at St John. English indignation was aroused by the feeling that France, who was supposed to be the defeated nation, had dictated the terms, and the rage of the allies knew no bounds. Although Shrewsbury had persuaded St John to promise that certain points, in particular the Barriers for Holland and Austria, should be discussed at a future conference, the general duplicity of the proceedings inflamed the countries who had fought at England's side for ten costly years. They knew now that St John had been lying; both he and Oxford had been talking blandly about plans for future campaigns and denying all the many rumours that they were in the middle of peace talks. Hoffmann, the Imperial Minister in London, had met Oxford at court on October 5, and the Treasurer had asked him to hasten plans for a campaign in Spain. Hoffmann replied that he thought there was little need, since Spain and the Indies were to be given to the Duke of Anjou. 'There is no question of that,' said Oxford. He was right, of course, since, as Torcy had pointed out to Prior, the allies had not Spain to give. The Dutch were angry because only so recently they had reluctantly abandoned the very favourable peace terms they had been offered by France, when the Whigs had bribed them with all the promises of the Barrier Treaty to continue fighting until Spain was won for Charles. Now all this had been thrown over, and Britain, moreover, was helping herself to the entire Asiento, which she had once promised to share with the Dutch. As for the unfortunate Charles of Austria, who had spent so much time campaigning in the Peninsula with inadequate forces, he was to be abandoned as if he had never existed.

St John provided a specious answer to all these complaints. He cared little for the allies. Marlborough had complained often enough of the pig-headedness of the Dutch, who after all had themselves gone very far in separate negotiations a year before. As for Charles, St John suggested that he should go back to his crumbling Austrian Empire and his imperial crown; he could fend for himself, together with all those 'indolent, droning Princes' as St John called the minor German potentates.

Marlborough was in the middle of making his plans for keeping the army in forward positions all winter, but the Dutch were being uncooperative. But despite all the slights and difficulties he had met with, he still remained faithful to the alliance and the common cause. At home Marlborough had been accused of avarice; his own people had called him 'Oliver' and accused him of setting up as a dictator. On the continent they still thought of him as the great milord. He was on good terms with the Elector, and the Electress, shrewd as ever, was disgusted by the way the British Ministry had bargained with France without a word to the man who had won all the victories. 'If the Queen had made an ape her general, and this ape had gained so many battles and towns, I would be equally for him,' she said.

'I hope you will go on in winning of battles, taking of towns and beating and routing the French in all manner of ways', wrote Marlborough's little grandson, but the Ministers thought differently. They wanted him to retire gracefully, and if he refused, he risked a barrage from the lampoonists and pamphleteers whom he so disliked and feared. Oxford could shrug off the assaults of his enemies, but Marlborough, brave though he was in the field of battle, was frightened of the printed word. When he read villainous reports of his victory at Bouchain, he wrote almost pathetically to Oxford, begging for protection:

The authors of these papers . . . are not only my enemies, they are yours too, my Lord; they are enemies to the Queen, and poison to her subjects.

Oxford replied:

I know I am every week, if not every day, in some libel or other, so I would willingly compound that all the ill-natured scribblers should have licence to write ten times more against me, upon condition they would write against nobody else.

The press war was at its height. The Ministry knew how to use what Coxe called 'this engine of policy'. The *Examiner* and the *Review* continued to express the moderate approach. In the *Post Boy*, St John encouraged the virulent expression of High Tory and Jacobite sentiments, and in particular libelled his enemy Gallas, whom he had caught sending very uncomplimentary reports home about himself. Oxford was under fire from Maynwaring in the *Tatler*, where he was pictured hugging himself in his closet and avoiding frequent appearances in public in order to be 'as mysterious as possible'. He was ridiculed in ballads about the South Sea project, and he received a stream of anonymous letters, sometimes signed 'Your humble servant the devil' or with slanderous rhymes:

Though G------d's knife did not succeed,
A Frenchman's yet may do the deed.

St John was none too philosophical under attack and was soon despatching state messengers with warrants to arrest a score of booksellers and publishers, after the first outbreak of lampoons criticizing his peace preliminaries. But Oxford maintained an Olympian indifference. He continued to laugh and joke with his friends, punning and inventing new nicknames for them all the time. 'He is a pure trifler,' wrote Swift affectionately, remembering a happy occasion in September 1711 when he had driven up from Windsor with his friend and they had joked and laughed all the way about the inn signs along the route, and the Treasurer at Swift's instigation had written two bad lines in verse on the subject of The Bell and Dragon. Thereafter his friends were to call Oxford 'the Dragon', 'by contraries' because, according to Swift, 'he was the mildest, wisest, and best minister that ever served a prince'. His enemies were very happy to adopt the nickname, giving it the more obvious connotation.

In spite of his high spirits and good humour, the Treasurer was not in good health. As the autumn drew on, he suffered from sore throats and gravel. His friends were worried, expostulating with him about his late nights and good dinners. They knew that everything depended on his being fit with the great debates on the peace due in the new session. By the middle of October he was really ill, and on the 19th the Queen wrote anxiously from Windsor:

I intend, an it please God, to be at Hampton Court Tuesday or Wednesday next, which will be near to you; however, I desire you would not come thither till you are easy, which I hope will be soon.

She offered up prayers for his health—'I pray God send you your health and preserve your life for the good of your country and all your faithful friends. . . . I shall continue my prayers for the perfect recovery and confirmation of your [health] being truly sensible how much the welfare of our poor country depends on you.' In spite of this royal intercession, the Treasurer's health mended very slowly. On October 21 he took physic and voided a great deal of gravel, but although he was in considerable pain, he continued to attend to business in his room. Swift, calling on him at noon on the 24th, found him 'eating some broth in his bedchamber, undressed, with a thousand papers around him. He has a little fever upon him, and his eye terribly bloodshot'. To add to all this, he still felt pain in the stab wound, but he insisted on dressing and going out to the Treasury. Swift was growing tired of chiding him.

By November, Oxford was on the mend, though by no means fit. Early in the month, the Queen, still at Hampton Court, suffered a severe attack of gout, and several lords, including the Duke of Shrewsbury, coming back to London and indulging in a round of reunion dinners, were similarly afflicted. Both Queen and Ministry felt unfit for the opening of Parliament and decided to postpone it for at least a fortnight.

The Whigs were planning to oppose the Preliminaries with all the weapons at their command. Seventeen of their most influential party Members, including Robert Walpole, met in late October and discussed policy. Sir Robert Davers, the Suffolk Tory M.P., gave Oxford a timely warning that many lords from his part of the country intended to be up on the first day. 'Be on your guard,' he wrote. Trying to play Oxford at his own game, the Whigs attempted to frighten the Ministry with a few riots on November 17, the anniversary of Queen Elizabeth's birthday. They organized a procession at midnight to incite the rabble and add a little colour to the normally harmless celebrations of the London apprentices. Sparing no expense, they ordered the manufacture of figures to grace the procession, including the Pope, the devil—who bore a marked resemblance to the Treasurer—and Sacheverell. The burning of these effigies was calculated to stir up a mob protest against the Ministry, but it was too sudden and did not spring from a deeper feeling as the Sacheverell troubles had done. The mob, advancing on Oxford's house, was headed off by the trained bands, which had been called out in good time, and although the papers were soon full of the news, the trouble died down at once.

Having failed to rouse much popular feeling, the Whigs concentrated on the House of Lords, where their real strength lay. They knew that a preponderance of Whiggish peers, gathering some malcontents from the other party, might well be able to foil the peace plan in the upper House. So they worked hard on the haverers who were weary of the unrestrained conduct of the October Club. The rift between Oxford and St John had not gone unobserved, and in late November Somerset was sent to sound out Oxford himself, and Halifax tried to engineer a meeting at his house. They tempted him with a promise that the Occasional Conformity Bill, so dear to Tory hearts, would be allowed a free passage in the Lords, provided he agreed to a motion for 'no peace without Spain'. They were angling to pull the Treasurer out of deep Tory waters, and to interest him in plans for a coalition. But Oxford was too wise to succumb to easy bribes. He knew that the country was not as yet tired of Tory rule; even if the Whigs forced another election, there was no guarantee that the High Tories would not be just as successful at the polls. Besides, his own love of peace was deeply built into his own character and policy; how could he barter a profound belief for a Bill of Occasional Conformity which he anyway disliked? So he wrote to Somerset on December 1, politely but firmly, confirming his opinion that it was in the interest of all the Protestant states 'to get out of this ruinous war as soon as we can with safety and honour'.

Oxford worked hard to put his case to his own people and to the allies. Protestations of good faith emanated from his pen, he began his long and fitful flirtation with Hanover and sent the Dutch envoy, Buys, with a message of good will. Swift was commissioned to write an *apologia*; working under pressure he produced in only a few days a pamphlet entitled *The Conduct of the Allies and of the Late Ministry in the Beginning and Carrying on the Present War*, a brilliant exposition of the theory that England had engaged in a long war with remarkably little gain to herself, and which prophesied that unless somebody took a firm step towards making peace, there was nothing to stop the Flanders war dragging on for another twenty years. 'The French may yet hold out a dozen years more, and afford a town every campaign at the same price,' ran one passage. He criticized the short-sighted policy makers, who could think only of fortress towns on the continent, when all the time, for far less cost, the British could have been disporting themselves on their natural element, the sea, and harrying the Spanish navy so that no money came out of America 'except in our own bottoms'. He pointed out how badly the English had been treated by their allies, so much so that they had become the dupes and bubbles of Europe.

The Conduct of the Allies was published on November 27; the evening before, all the great men of the Ministry had been sent their copies. The very day after its publication it began to cause a stir. It was published anonymously and Swift was gratified to be told by several people that he must buy it at once as it was 'something very extraordinary'. On the 29th the second edition was announced and the printers worked day and night to produce it. A thousand copies were sold in two days and *The Conduct* became, by the standards of the day, a best-seller. This was all the more remarkable since it was an expensive book for those times, selling at a shilling a copy. Nor was its success due to the fact that the party bought up a great many copies to give away, as the opulent Whigs were apt to do. It sold on its merits, and ran into four editions.

St John was not satisfied. He wanted to launch a more specifically personal attack on members of the last administration; it was one of the pleasures of power to be able to make life unpleasant for your enemies. All summer the Commissioners of Public Accounts had been probing into the finances of the previous government, and it was certain that in the new session the Commons would call for their report. Fraud, extortion and embezzlement were all hinted at, rumours were rife of a missing £60,000 and Marlborough himself was under suspicion. It was all too easy to accuse a man of peculation; only those, like Godolphin or Oxford who patently made nothing over and above their official salary, were safe from attack. Legitimate perquisites and percentages were claimed by almost everybody, but these could look bad on paper. Sir Solomon Medina, one of the principle contractors for food supplies to the army, revealed dark secrets to the Commissioners about payments for bread that never reached the bread waggons. Marlborough, arriving quietly on November 17, the day of the riots, learnt that he was to face an attack from a grateful country and a Secretary of State who had himself made a very fat sum out of supplies destined for the Quebec expedition.

Members were soon hurrying up to London to make sure that they missed none of the excitement of the peace debate, the peculation charges and that old friend the Occasional Conformity Bill. All the same, there were many Lords and Commoners who did not appear, some on account of genuine illness, others through sheer apathy. The vote in the Lords was likely to be marginal, and it was vital to make sure that every possible Tory was rounded up. The highly organized Whigs had mastered the art of whipping in their supporters and had a well developed system of organizing proxies for those who could not attend, but the Tory party machine was primitive by comparison. Oxford, the busy first minister, with all the responsibilities of state on his shoulders and his health at breaking point, was expected to write personal letters to many peers, beseeching them to send their proxies if unable to come themselves. Shrewsbury wrote to Oxford on November 23:

As I apprehend our House to be the place our enemies have most hopes to prevail in, so I recommend you to take the requisite care that our friends come to town in time.

Swift, sensing that the Whig lords intended to be peevish and to attack the peace preliminaries, was worried about Tory casualness:

Our ministers are too negligent of such things: I have never slipped giving them warning: some of them are sensible of it; but Lord Treasurer stands too much upon his own legs. I fancy his good fortune will bear him out in everything; but in reason I should think this ministry to stand very unsteady; if they can carry a peace, they may hold; I believe not else.

In the future, Oxford was to give over the organization of proxies to his faithful henchmen, Dartmouth, Poulett and Masham. For the present he could only do as much as time allowed. The Bishop of Exeter wrote to say that bad roads, the difficulty of preparing in haste for a long journey, his own old age and infirmity which only enabled him to make the distance in very short stages, not to mention an outbreak of smallpox in his family which had caused the death of his elder son, made it unlikely that he would arrive in town until after Christmas. 'I can't be secure that I have not taken the infection,' he wrote pathetically, 'and if so should choose to be sick, or (if it should please God) to die, at home rather than on the road or in strange lodgings.' But at least the Bishop of Exeter had the good sense to give his proxy to the Bishop of Chester, proving that the Queen's appointment of the Tories Blackhall and Dawes, which had so shocked the Whigs in 1707, was now paying off from Oxford's point of view. Archbishop Sharp, according to Swift, was in great danger of being 'seduced' by the High Tory Nottingham, and Oxford wrote to him, paying elaborate compliments to his 'great mind and primitive piety' and asking him to come up to town in time for the opening of Parliament: 'There is reason to believe something very extraordinary will be attempted the first day of meeting and if you cannot be present, at least you will send up your proxy in time.'

Oxford asked his son-in-law, Lord Dupplin, to look after the Scottish lords. Dupplin, who had recently become a father again, received some sharp raps from Scotsmen who considered that they had not received nearly enough notice, and who were none too keen to come posting south in the winter to support a government that showed little sign of making it worth their while financially. Kinnoull was particularly sour; as father-in-law to the Lord Treasurer's daughter, he had expected to benefit from nepotism, and when Oxford failed to show him the expected favour, he sulked and said he would rather go home and plant trees and live in the country. And on December 3 he wrote peevishly from Edinburgh:

George, you sit in London and prescribe impossibilities to we poor worms in Scotland, you order me to . . . be at London against the seventh of this month. It is your own fault otherwise I should have been at London a fortnight ago.

Lord Mar also complained at the lack of reasonable notice. Most of the lords, he said, were at their country houses, and it would be days before they could even reach Edinburgh. The expense of the journey and a prolonged stay in London had to be considered. The Earl of Home, who was in such parlous circumstances that he found it difficult to get credit for even a couple of hundred pounds, and had spent so much on his last visit that he was reduced to living on credit, remarked gallantly, 'the devil take him if it were not his circumstances that he has an old family to preserve . . . he would serve the Queen without asking a farthing;' all the same Kinnoull asked his son to make sure that Home could 'be supplied and that timely'. As many proxies as possible were sent up from Edinburgh by the flying packet, but the truth was that the summoning of the Scottish peers had been mishandled.

The first days of December were frenzied, with the educational élite arguing over *The Conduct of the Allies*, lords and commoners struggling up from the country, and the Whigs intensifying their efforts to win over anyone who might care to join them. At last, to their great satisfaction, they gained a strange ally in the devout Nottingham, the black-browed earl whose High Tory politics had so distressed the Queen in the first years of her reign. More dismal than ever after his years in the wilderness—Poulett said he was 'as sour and fiercely wild as you can imagine anything to be that has lived long in the desert'—he succumbed to the bribe which had been previously offered to Oxford. Lured by the prospect of bringing occasional conformists to book, he agreed to give his support to the motion for 'no peace without Spain', taking over on to the Whig side no one knew how many attendant High Church cronies. It was a bad outlook for the Ministry. Swift visited Oxford on the 5th, and found him 'a little touched by the present posture of affairs' though as pleasant as ever. Mrs Masham seemed uneasy. The Queen talked to Cowper for half an hour and tried to persuade him to vote for the Ministers. The Secretaries put the last touches to the Queen's speech, refusing to modify its sentiments in deference to the stormy situation. From the throne, the Queen uttered the galvanizing words 'notwithstanding the arts of those who delight in war, both place and time are appointed for opening the treaty of general peace'. Having said her incendiary lines, the Queen descended from the throne, divested herself of her robes and re-entered the House *incognita*, in the vain hope that her presence might calm the heats of debate. Oxford went to join her, and was with her when the gaunt Nottingham rose to his feet and expressed sentiments that fell so strangely from a Tory tongue.

AUDITOR HARLEY
Photo : Dean

LORD EDWARD HARLEY
IN 1715
Photo : Dean

THE HOUSE OF COMMONS IN THE FIRST HALF OF THE
EIGHTEENTH CENTURY

'No peace,' Nottingham declared, 'could be safe or honourable to Great Britain or Europe if Spain and the West Indies were allotted to any branch of the House of Bourbon.' Marlborough acquiesced, and the amendment to the speech, though rejected in the Commons where the Tories were now well organized, was carried in the Lords by a small margin. Everybody recognized this as a great blow to the Treasurer. Worse still, the Queen, as she left the House, gave further encouragement to the exuberant Whigs. She may have meant nothing by it, but her every look and word was significant. The Duke of Shrewsbury asked her whether he or the Great Chamberlain should lead her out. 'Neither of you,' she replied, and offered her hand to the treacherous Duke of Somerset, who had been vocally on the side of 'no peace without Spain'. A murmur of fear went through Oxford's supporters. 'The Queen is false,' they said, now and in the days to come.

The Treasurer's friends met him later that day. 'He appeared in good-humour as usual,' Swift wrote, 'but I thought his countenance much cast down. I rallied him, and desired him to give me his staff, which he did; . . . Arbuthnot asked how he came not to secure a majority? he could answer nothing, but that he could not help it if people would lie and forswear. . . . There fell from him a Scripture expression, that "The hearts of kings are unsearchable".' He might have said the same of himself, for nobody could search his innermost heart. Everyone believed that his career was finished. For a day or two he looked grave, and then cast off his dejection and set to work. He was determined to find out some way of taming the House whose ways were so much less familiar to him than those of the Commons, where he had worked for so long and where he knew every move in the game. He would not repeat Godolphin's mistake of trying to work with two Houses at loggerheads with each other. And he decided to show his fangs to the placeman who had voted against the Court—the nurse that suckled them—and vowed that they should be turned out. His son Edward was told to make a list of the offenders.

Many people said that Parliament would be dissolved before the new year; the Queen, they thought, had been seduced by the Duchess of Somerset and was going to bring in a Whig government. But Oxford did not believe the Queen was false. Only a few weeks previously she had written to him, begging him to be careful and wishing him joy of his grandson. 'You have a budget full of miracles upon all occasions,' Poulett wrote admiringly. It seemed that even now the Dragon had something in hand. Swift went to the Mashams on December 15 and found Oxford

H

there, looking more cheerful than he had done for ten days. 'Poh, poh, all will be well,' he remarked, when anyone expressed pessimism.

The Whigs were sure that Oxford would be bound to come to some compromise. Halifax renewed his assurances that he was ready to help, still believing that Oxford should lead the country. 'Accept of my good wishes that you may have a happy Christmas, and many of them,' he wrote. The Treasurer was, in fact, having a far happier Christmas than anybody would have prophesied. He answered Halifax with the tantalizing assurance that there was 'one way left'. 'Pray let me know it,' Halifax riposted rather impatiently on New Year's Eve.

On the last day of the year, the Cabinet met in the Queen's presence and considered the report of the Commissioners. It was decided, in view of the peculation charges, that Marlborough should be dismissed from his employments. That evening the Queen informed him of the fact in a note which, in one of his few rages, he threw into the fire. He recovered himself at once and wrote a dignified reply, expressing sorrow that her advisers had prevailed with her to dismiss him on the grounds of a 'false and malicious insinuation contrived by themselves'. When Louis XIV heard the news, he exclaimed that 'the dismissal of Marlborough will do all that we can desire', and he ordered Te Deums to be sung 'in the Church of Notre Dame in our good city of Paris'.

The Treasurer, so often accused of being dilatory, had been very busy over Christmas. His enemies guessed uneasily that he was at his miracle-working, and his friends waited anxiously to see whether he could once again burrow his way out of his difficulties. Here and there people were flattered when they learned that they were to be offered peerages, but nobody suspected anything unusual in this. Then, on New Year's Day, everything was made clear. Among the lords and Ministers who went to pay their respects to the Queen, and to wish her joy of the New Year, was the Secretary, Lord Dartmouth. To his amazement she drew from her pocket a list of twelve peers, and asked him to write warrants for them straightaway. Never had there been such a new year's honours list. Almost too surprised to expostulate, since there had been no prior discussion or intimation of any kind that she was to take this extraordinary step, he asked her whether she really meant to make so many lords all at once. But the Queen asked him coldly whether he had any objection to the legality of such a device:

I said no, but very much doubted the expediency, for I feared it would have a very ill effect in the House of Lords and no good one in the Kingdom. I thought it my duty to tell her my apprehensions as well as execute her commands. She thanked me and said she liked it as little as I did, but did not find that anybody could propose a better expedient.

The news of this ruse, as it spread about the town, caused shock and even some hilarity. The dismissal of Marlborough was pushed into the background. Needless to say all the new peers were carefully chosen, and owed their promotion to the fact that they were likely to vote on Oxford's side. Four were members of the Brothers' Society and included the faithful Mansell and also George Granville, who had nursed hopes of being created Earl of Bath, but had to content himself with the title of Baron Lansdowne. The Queen had reluctantly agreed to let Masham become a peer; she was afraid of losing a useful menial and had always opposed the Mashams' promotion because she disliked the idea of a peeress having to do menial tasks. To Abigail it was most welcome, for the Duchess of Somerset's success with the Queen made her own future precarious and there was no guarantee that she would not be flung out at the new favourite's behest, without title, position, or means of subsistence. 'A peerage will be some sort of protection to her upon any turn of affairs,' Swift wrote.

The Whigs were indignant when they found that their doubtful trick of bribing Nottingham had been countered by an even more shady ruse. 'Lord Oxford packed juries to carry causes,' Sir David Hamilton indignantly told the Queen. But she had her answer ready. 'King William made more,' she said. 'Not at one time,' Sir David replied.

On the day the new peers went to Westminster to be introduced, there was a great crowd to watch them and the House was packed. The Whigs enquired whether the novices were going to vote according to their 'foreman'. One of the best jokes circulating in town concerned Lady Oxford and the Duchess of Shrewsbury, the one well known for her piety and the other for her bad English. 'I know no Lord but the Lord Jehovah,' the sanctimonious Countess was reputed to have said. The Duchess, who had been bred in Catholic circles and was unfamiliar with dissenting terminology, was puzzled. 'Oh dear! Madam, who is that?' she enquired. 'I believe 'tis one of the new titles for I never heard of him before.'

Even so, despite the anger and the amusement, Oxford's action was not universally decried. His friends were pleased that he had taken decisive action at last, and had shown that some steel still lay beneath the velvet of his obsequious manner. He knew the law well enough to ensure that he did not overstep its limits, and he had seen to it that there should be no more dangerous rifts between the two Houses. He displayed further firmness when he persuaded the Queen to follow the creation of the peers by the removal of Somerset. By mid-January all London knew that the Duke of Somerset was definitely out. The Treasurer's victory was mirrored in his cheerful countenance, while the Duchess of Somerset, Swift noted with relief, looked 'a little down'.

Somerset might have departed from the court, taking all his yellow liveries with him, but the Whigs were not going to surrender their Duchess without a struggle. Sir David told the Queen that she must keep Elizabeth Somerset at her side for the good of her health. 'She seems to converse with courteous calmness,' the doctor pointed out, 'which makes her the more suitable for your Majesty's temper.' For a few days the matter stood in the balance, and Oxford and his friends were uneasy. Swift was particularly anxious, and on January 10 he wrote:

I sat this evening at Lord Masham's with Lord Treasurer; I don't like his countenance, nor I don't like the posture of things well. We cannot be stout till Somerset's out: as the old saying is.

Fortunately the Duke decided that he did not relish having his wife at Court when he was languishing at Petworth, and he removed her, out of spite, to the great relief of the Ministry and of Lady Masham.

CHAPTER 18

ROBIN AND HARRY

ONE NAME was conspicuously absent from the list of new peers. Oxford omitted St John, and the Secretary became even more hostile after the slight. He was now the outstanding figure in the Commons, swaying the listening ranks with his brilliant oratory and scintillating wit. Now that Oxford himself had quitted the Commons scene, and had called to the upper House so many of his friends and relations, St John was able to domineer over the lower to his heart's content.

Some of the more level-headed Tories like Sir Thomas Hanmer had begun to grow tired of the antics of the October Club, but its membership was still over a hundred and fifty and St John had now been elected its president. At long tables set out at the Bell in King Street, Westminster, the zealots dined and vowed to harry Oxford and the moderates. They complained about Oxford's procrastination, his timidity, his failure to hound out the Whig placemen. Swift refused to join the October diners, because of their disloyalty to some of his ministerial friends, and in mid-January he produced a twopenny pamphlet entitled *Some Advice Humbly Offered to the Members of the October Club*. He reminded members of their debt to 'one great person' who had engineered the 'mighty change in the most important posts of the kingdom'. He also pointed out that 'cross intrigues' often made it impossible for a Minister to carry out all his promises, and told the Tories that they should be proud to think that their party was less vindictive than its rival, and therefore less able to find places and rewards for its friends. The essay was written out by an acquaintance so that even the printer did not know who its author was, and when it was published, on January 23, Swift dined with Masham:

Lord Dupplin took out my new little pamphlet, and the Secretary read a great deal of it to Lord Treasurer: they all commended it to the skies, and so did I; and they began a health to the author. But I doubt Lord Treasurer suspected, for he said, 'This is Dr Davenant's style', which is his cant when he suspects me. But I carried the matter very well. Lord Treasurer put the pamphlet in his pocket to read at home.

Swift himself was well pleased with his *Advice to the October Club*, but, in spite of its cheapness, it sold far less well than *The Conduct of the Allies* and did little to mitigate the zeal of the Club's members. Bromley was finding it a strain trying to keep his hot-headed friends within bounds. 'No one can tell,' he told Harley, 'how far their well-meant zeal may carry them.'

In their meetings at the Bell, the October Club members pressed for revenge on the past administration. They also clamoured for a series of reactionary measures. After Christmas Bromley had to let the fiercer members of his party off the leash and allow them to proceed on the report of the Commissioners for Public Accounts. Robert Walpole, as Swift put it, was to be 'swinged' for bribery. As Secretary-at-War, Walpole had authorized the payment to one of his friends, of two sums of £500 each in connection with an army contract. Many office-holders were guilty of similar, and far worse, crimes, but the Tories made the most of that £1,000, and they profited to the extent of removing an able opposition leader whose sallies in the Commons, and defence, in pamphlet form, of Whig finances, had been a major irritation. There were those, even among the Tories, who felt that a committal to the Tower was hardly justified, and it was only achieved by twelve votes, a narrow margin for a party with such a large majority. Walpole remained in the Tower for five months and returned to the House a martyr, having been re-elected by his faithful friends in Norfolk.

Marlborough was the next to be accused, although the charges against him were equally tenuous. The 2½ per cent which he had received on the pay of British troops had been spent mainly on secret service payments, and although the accusation that he had received a percentage on the army bread contract was more serious, many people felt that in view of the General's service to the nation, it would be far better forgotten. Oxford and the other 'managers' wanted to let Marlborough off lightly; they informed him that if he was prepared to accept the findings of the Commission and prevent his friends from speaking out, they would treat him magnanimously. But Marlborough declared that he would rather lose his head than submit to such a horse-deal. Bromley wrote to Oxford, urging him to organize his whips or 'orderly men', and to take care that supporters turned up in force — 'better care than last Thursday,' he added, with a rueful reference to the narrow majority on the Walpole vote. Oxford's attitude to the censure motion was hard to assess. Swift said that he was motivated by personal pique, but although Oxford often behaved towards Marlborough with apparent ingratitude, he was usually driven by expediency rather than by dislike. In this case he found it necessary to remove a General who seemed determined to side with the allies against the government, but he regretted that it had to be done on a party-inspired vote calculated to disgrace Marlborough in the eyes of the world.

Where the Treasurer faltered, St John went ahead, with more determination and less wisdom. He would not allow his Peace to hang fire. In January, Britain's two plenipotentiaries, Lord Strafford, Lady Wentworth's beloved son, and John Robinson, the Bishop of Bristol, were sent to the Congress at Utrecht in Holland. The atmosphere there was unhappy from the start. The allies were disgruntled because they considered that Britain had already helped herself to the spoils, and they were jealous of Savoy, St John's favourite and the only country which had received a favourable mention in the Preliminaries. The French arrived with proposals that included the surrender to Louis of a string of fortresses along the border. Some said that Lord Strafford was an agent of France; at any rate he consistently disagreed with Robinson. Neither of them were men of distinction, and Swift went so far as to affirm that Strafford was wholly illiterate.

In January Charles of Austria, now Emperor Charles VI, who had returned to claim his native throne, sent Prince Eugene over to England to persuade the Queen to continue the war in Spain. Since Gallas had quarrelled with St John and gone home, the Imperial Court had been without an Ambassador in England. The Prince, though yellow-complexioned and ugly, was a romantic hero in the eyes of the English, and cheering crowds greeted him as he sailed up the Thames. To St John, on the other hand, he was *persona non grata*, and he had told Strafford to try and intercept him in Holland and prevent him coming. The Prince openly visited Marlborough, and the two commanders were cheered when they sat together in a box at the opera. St John encouraged rumours that they planned to overthrow the Queen and set up a military dictatorship; it was said that Marlborough intended to kidnap her, gout and all.

Eugene's visit coincided with the Queen's birthday, and he had two suits made for the occasion. There was high excitement among the Tory women who had ordered extra-special finery; the Whig ladies had to conquer their disappointment and stay away in deference to their husbands as a mark of disapproval. The court was fuller than it had ever been before; Oxford, dining beforehand with Lord and Lady Masham, took his wife and two daughters, who, Swift reported, 'were monstrous fine'. In a quiet moment, away from the crowds, the Queen presented Eugene with a diamond-hilted sword worth four thousand pounds; he fared, in fact, rather better than Marlborough, his comrade in arms, whose only gift (Blenheim apart) had been a note of dismissal.

Oxford invited the Prince to dinner at his own house. 'I consider this day as the happiest of my life, since I have the honour to see in my house the greatest captain of the age,' said Oxford, raising his glass. The generous-minded Eugene could not sit back and accept the honours that were due to his friend. Nor could he forget that it was thanks to his host that Marlborough had been dismissed. He raised his glass in return, and gave a cutting reply. 'If it be so, I am obliged to your lordship for it,' he said. Never one to be put off by a snub, Oxford did his best to part the best of friends, and before the Prince went home he paid him a private visit, creeping up the backstairs at dead of night in his usual conspiratorial fashion. Eugene was persuaded to return the compliment. 'I entered his own house in the deepest secrecy,' he wrote, 'through a particular door which is usually kept locked.' On both occasions the Treasurer was charming and talked largely about nothing in particular.

Eugene failed to persuade the Queen to continue the war in Spain. The government was committed to peace without Spain, and peace whether the allies liked it or not. With the help of the twelve new peers, Parliamentary assent for the peace policy was received early in the new year. Royal assent had never been wanting.

In January the October Club began to press hard for measures which were alien to Oxford's whole way of life and thought. Its members turned their attention to the Naturalization Act which had been passed in 1709 and allowed the naturalization of foreigners provided they were prepared to accept the sacrament according to the rites of one of the Protestant Churches. Extremist Tories thought that they should not be allowed to take out papers unless they promised to become communicating members of the Church of England. Nottingham joined in the vote for the repeal of the Act, which was carried easily in both Lords and Commons. Because he relied on the Tory majority, Oxford was forced to associate himself with the repeal. As Defoe put it, 'Things were carried over his belly, which however he bears the reproach of.'

In February a new Place Bill was introduced, one of the Tories' stock favourites. Proud, independent Englishmen disliked the growing block of placemen in Parliament who tended to side with the government for fear of losing their livelihood. Cowper spoke contemptuously of those 'necessitous lords' who voted according to the promptings of their pockets rather than their consciences, and indeed there were still Whig placemen in office who supported Oxford and were grateful to him for resisting Tory attempts to remove every Whig in sight. The Tories, in their zeal, forgot that a Bill severely limiting the number of placemen in Parliament was also likely to eliminate at a stroke a large number of government supporters, and to upset a working majority. Oxford, alarmed at this one stable element being removed—an element which enabled him to 'manage' for the Queen without subjecting both himself and her to the domination of party—was instrumental in framing an amendment which stipulated that the Act should not come into force until after the death of the Queen. This was the ruse the Whigs had used when he opposed them over the Scottish Treason Bill. Now the Whigs were in a mood to support anything which might cause Oxford discomfort, and although the Lords had quickly dismissed a similar Place Bill a year ago, they now decided to shift their position. Some days before the Bill was introduced, the Whigs held one of their big party meetings, always an ominous sign, and all the more so since it was attended by the renegade Nottingham and some of the milder Whigs whom Oxford liked to see in his own camp. It was surprising to learn that Cholmondeley was present; this delightful moderate lord had been allowed to keep his place as Treasurer of the Household, and therefore should have been prepared to vote with the government. He was, however, detached enough in outlook to be careless about his place, and he had already voted independently in the 'no peace without Spain' motion. He had assured Prior in July 1710 that he was just as happy to sit and philosophize at home as to move in court circles, and he felt that his books, his garden, and his two little rooms over the greenhouse were his best tenure. 'The Bug' also went to the meeting, not surprisingly in view of the treatment he had received in 1710; and, more serious even than the defection of Whig placemen, was the revolt of Scottish peers and commoners who were holding indignation meetings of their own and threatening to abandon the government.

The previous December the Lords had refused to let the Duke of Hamilton take his seat on being created an English peer. As Duke of Brandon he had every right to sit in the Lords, but the Whigs, striking at the very Union they had once so industriously promoted, joined with Tories to declare his claim, and all future Scottish claims, invalid. This made the Scottish Members forget their differences. Squadrone and Jacobite lords joined together as they had never done before. The Earl of Mar told Swift that although he would have liked to vote for the

H*

government, he dare not, for fear of being cold-shouldered in Scotland ever afterwards. Oxford went to work indefatigably, canvassing and persuading and soothing Celtic ire; by the time he had finished, the Scottish lords had come to heel, and his vital amendment to the Place Bill was passed by a narrow margin of five.

It was a triumph for Oxford, but it had cost him time and energy which he could not spare. These tense battles were taking their toll in terms of health, and there were still the visits to the Queen, the petty petitioners and the levees. It was at this time that Swift peeped into the Treasurer's chamber and saw 'a hundred fools' waiting their chance, while the street outside was crowded with coaches. At the beginning of March he fell ill. For three years running he had been unwell at this time of year, but in 1712 he had more serious symptoms, due as much to fatigue as to the bad weather. On March 6 he went home early with 'a swimming in his head' and was cupped; he celebrated the anniversary of the assassination attempt by taking physic, and was unable to attend the Cabinet meeting. His friends noticed that he seemed depressed. The effort of working with such a small margin in the Lords was proving too much for him, and made him a prey to petty faction. He had so much to do that he was simply unable to attend to everything, which made some people accuse him of laziness. Sir Scipio Hill, who had been left in the air for months about a matter he considered important, wrote bluntly, 'If I had that sloth in my temper that you have, I would on purpose keep a man to pull me by the sleeve to remember me of things that I was to do,' and he added, in a postscript, that he had ordered his black slave to stay at Oxford's house until a reply was forthcoming. When Godolphin was in power, especially during the early years of the reign, he had been able to rely on Harley to attend to many matters for him and at least to keep the Commons friendly and under control, but Oxford had no such right-hand man. Erasmus Lewis, who had been appointed Under-Secretary of State in 1709, was still doing useful work. There was the faithful Poulett, always ready and willing, but one swallow does not make a summer. Oxford's son Edward, now serving his political apprenticeship, was able to take some of the load of canvassing and whipping-in off his father's shoulders; between them they put the fear of God into the placemen in April, when a Bill was brought in to resume William III's land grants. This question always aroused much interest as it reflected on the Crown's ability to bribe its servants with land and salaries, and stolid country Members were always sensitive about economy, or lack of it, in the sovereign's cofferers. The Bill was passed in the Lords by one vote, but such marginal victories were a strain on everybody's nerves, particularly the Lord Treasurer's.

To add to the political stress, a band of young bloods was terrorizing the town in the evenings. The Mohocks, as they called themselves, were said by the Tories to be all Whigs, and there were rumours that they had designs on the Ministry. Oxford was warned that the Mohocks intended to emulate Guiscard, should they happen to light on the Treasurer in one of their nightly forays. But on the whole they were impelled by high spirits rather than by politics; anyone in a rich-looking chair was fair game, and Oxford had graver matters to worry about.

In February, smallpox spread with terrifying swiftness through the French royal family. The King's son had died the previous year, and now his grandson, grand-daughter-in-law and great-grandson were all carried away within a few days of each other. Nothing now stood between Philip of Anjou and the French throne except one sickly baby of two years old, brother of the great-grandson who had just died. His nurse had so far managed to preserve the little prince's life by wrapping him in a blanket, keeping him warm and locking out the doctors, but nobody expected him to live through the epidemic. This rearrangement of the European scene was a serious blow to the Tory peacemakers. The whole basis of their talks had been that there should never be a union of the crowns of France and Spain, and now it looked as if Philip would become the possessor of both. Nothing would persuade Philip to give up Spain. He had won his throne and the love of the Spanish people. No plenipotentiaries round a conference table could rob him of that. Another factor was that Star-hemberg, the allied commander in Spain, last heard of retreating igno-miniously from Madrid, suddenly decided to win a surprise victory at Cardona, showing that all hopes of military success in the peninsula were not completely dead.

Another spring had nearly come, and still no peace treaty had been signed. The grass was growing; as soon as there was green forage the armies would be moving into position ready for the next campaign. Neither side dared to neglect military preparations, since a victory would give great advantages in the peace talks. The Duke of Ormonde, Marl-borough's successor, a handsome High Tory described by Sir John Clerk as 'a good natured, profuse, innocent man, of little or no experience in military affairs', arrived in Holland on April 9. Eugene had been appointed commander of all other allied forces, and the two generals, starting in a favourable position with superior forces, could have inflicted a defeat that would greatly have improved the allied position at the conference table. Eugene responded well to Ormonde, even though he had taken Marlborough's place, and described him as 'the finest cavalier and most complete gentleman that England bred, being the glory of that nation, of so noble spirit that he would sacrifice all for his Church and sovereign, very popular, his great affability winning the hearts and affections of all people'. But St John sowed the seeds of mistrust; he insisted that no British forces should be answerable to Eugene, and ordered Ormonde to proceed with caution and even to avoid action wherever possible. In May St John wrote a letter to Ormonde stating that it was 'the Queen's positive command' that he should avoid engaging in any siege, or hazarding any battle until further notice. These were the famous 'restraining orders', which had also been communicated to the French.

All the evidence points to the fact that the orders were despatched by St John on his own authority and that Oxford had no knowledge of them. The insistence of foreign observers that Oxford was immersed in home politics helps to exonerate him from direct responsibility for the shameful behaviour of his countrymen. Eugene saw him as a smooth-tongued Richelieu or Mazarin, dominating the Queen with his insinuating behaviour, and managing the caballing parties with such dexterity that he kept in with both. All the same, as the head of the government, the responsibility was his, and he himself was far more ready than other men of his time to accept the fact. His friends, at times, called him 'Prime Minister,' and although there was no post as such, the name was frequently applied; and he was prepared, as premier, to take the blame for his colleagues' actions. He made this clear by his attitude during the hot debates that began in Parliament that summer.

Rumours were soon rife that the British were playing their enemies false. Eugene, watchful and suspicious, noticed the strange behaviour of the English General and his reluctance to move. More significant still, he observed that the French confronting the English were taking no precautions and appeared to know that they would not be attacked in that sector. The belief that Ormonde had a commission to act only defensively soon spread to England, and Halifax, who opened the debate in the Lords on May 28, expressed a general feeling of uneasiness that the army 'so accustomed to conquer' was being ordered to desert its allies. The Whigs had called one of their large-scale meetings at Lord Orford's house that morning and decided to give the government what it deserved. 'Poultney could not forbear calling the Court a weak and treacherous Ministry,' wrote Sir Thomas Cave. Oxford, in reply, said that he could not reveal what orders had been given to Ormonde without the Queen's permission, and anyway he did not consider them 'fit to be divulged'. There was a grim truth in this. In justification of St John and Ormonde he went on:

He would adventure to say that, if the Duke of Ormonde had refused to act offensively, he did not doubt, but he had followed his instructions; and it was prudence not to hazard a battle upon the point of concluding a good peace, especially as they had to deal with an enemy so apt to break his word.

Under pressure from Wharton, Oxford said it might be acceptable for the English to help in a siege, but not engage in a battle, a most unmilitary concept, as Marlborough was not slow to point out. In his hair-splitting way, Oxford at least had the courage to defend restraint, whereas St John, the real author of the orders, did nothing but prevaricate when questions were asked in the Commons, and as a result was let off far more lightly. According to Swift, everything went 'swimmingly'.

It was as well that nobody knew as yet that the orders had been kept secret from the allies, and revealed to the French. St John had exposed Eugene to the most appalling danger; he said himself, unashamedly, that he expected the allied army to be cut to pieces. The Lords were not aware of this, but the debate was stormy enough in any case. Eventually, Oxford closed the proceedings with a vigorous denial that the government intended to sign a separate treaty.

Nothing of that nature was ever intended, for such a peace would be so foolish, villainous, and knavish that every servant of the Queen must answer for it with his head to the nation.

Wharton assured the Treasurer that he would keep him to that promise. 'The allies are acquainted with our proceedings, and satisfied with the terms,' Oxford concluded, cunningly leaving it uncertain whether he was referring to the Restraining Orders, or to the peace talks. He knew how to wriggle out of trouble, and thus reassured, the Lords rejected Halifax's original censure motion by a majority of sixty-eight to forty. The debates caused a great deal of interest in both Houses, the Whigs 'raved very violently' and according to Bromley there were at least four hundred Members present in the Commons—a record attendance for the time of year. The English people were so sick of war that they were ready to back St John's dishonourable peace, and the proposals put before both Houses were approved by a large majority.

Thus encouraged, the Secretary arranged an armistice with the French, and the British soldiers, suffering slights and agonies of shame, marched away across the Flanders countryside. The Dutch commanders of the towns along their route refused to open the gates, and there was a real fear that the French might break the truce and cut off their retreat. Such dangers had not been foreseen by St John, who hastily sent a force, under the command of Jack Hill—a sop for Lady Masham—to secure Dunkirk as a haven for the discredited army.

Louis, encouraged by these events, became more intransigent. The British plenipotentiaries felt that they were making little progress at Utrecht. In early August, when the 'high cherry time' as Swift called it, was just over, St John, at last raised to the peerage as Viscount Bolingbroke, set off for France, accompanied by Prior. At the court of Versailles, the handsome and talented Bolingbroke, fluent in French and practised in the art of fine words and good manners, achieved a great personal success, and was made much of by the French King. He persuaded Louis to agree to several disputed points, stayed for only a few days and returned the conquering hero, leaving Prior in charge of further negotiations.

When he arrived back in England, Oxford behaved coldly towards him, and attempted to transfer to Dartmouth the task of further negotiations. Swift tried to play peacemaker, and Lansdowne did his best to bring the two men together at the christening of his eldest daughter in October. He was unsuccessful. 'God direct your Lordship to heal the breaches made among us,' wrote Defoe.

The differences between Robin and Harry, or Castor and Pollux as they had once been called, were partly due to obvious differences of character. Temperamental incompatibility lay behind their political differences. Oxford, pious and a family man, was hesitant and cautious, Bolingbroke, fiery and impetuous, was contemptuous of churches in general and unfaithful to his wife who called herself a 'poor discarded mistress'. They had now reached the stage of real dislike and petty jealousy. When the Treasurer received the Garter in 1712 to add to all his other honours, St John was incensed, all the more so because, when the Queen finally conferred a title on him, she only made him a Viscount instead of an Earl. 'My promotion was a punishment, not a reward,' he wrote. The new Lord Bolingbroke, suspecting that his old master had arranged the title with the Queen with the careful design of humiliating him, turned all his rhetorical gifts to rending the 'idlers'. Gone were the days when he could write, 'I shall submit to your correction as becomes one who truly values and ever must be faithfully and entirely yours.' He had forgotten those 'millions of instances' in which the Treasurer had, in the past, shown kindness to him. He conveniently obliterated the

memory of the days when Oxford had helped him to power. As Defoe
put it:

[He] made all moderate measures appear criminal, and arraigned the clemency
of the administration, as a negligence of the staff, and an omission of duty,
and with an impetuosity natural to his temper, he was one of the first who fell
upon the staff, plowing with the heifer, founded a cabal in the administration,
which opposed all the measures of the Prime Minister and acted independent
of him, upon whom the general calumny of their action lay.

Oxford, for his part, was jealous of Bolingbroke's influence over the
Queen. He could not forget that the Restraining Orders had been framed
in secrecy by the Queen and the Secretary alone. It was a situation which
made everyday administration even more complicated than usual. On
October 6, Erasmus Lewis, writing from Windsor Castle, revealed the
small-mindedness of the two Ministers:

When I laid before my Lord the instruments you left with me on Wednesday
last, his Lordship made some difficulty to present them to the Queen because
my Lord Bolingbroke had not given him the least intimation that any papers
were to be recommended to him from your office. . . . Yesterday I put into my
Lord's hands the other parcel enclosed in yours of the fourth, which, by his
Lordship's order, I now send you back unsigned, his Lordship being persuaded
it is not my Lord Bolingbroke's desire that he should concern himself in the
business of his office, since he has taken other methods for laying his foreign
letters before her Majesty.

Bolingbroke's actions became more and more embarrassing to Oxford.
The more he tried to free his name from the Jacobite stigma, the more
Bolingbroke laid the Ministry open to the suspicion that it intended to
bring back the Pretender. In March 1712, Oxford made a special appointment with Cowper and did his best, in the dark and confused manner
which Cowper disliked so much, to free himself from the Jacobite association and to insinuate that the previous administration had been just
as deeply embroiled. There was such anxiety about the Pretender in the
autumn that the warming-pan theory had to be resurrected; rumours
that St John had been seen at the theatre with James Stuart during his
stay in Paris did not help matters. But when Sir David Hamilton told the
Queen that Cowper believed the Pretender was 'designed in all places',
she replied sharply, 'Oh fye, there is no such thing, what, do they think
I'm a child, and to be imposed upon?'

The complexion of the times seemed particularly unpleasant. Bolingbroke's attempts to kill opposition newspapers and pamphlets by imposing
a stamp tax of a penny a sheet had cleared the murk of Grub Street for

a short while, but Whig funds were soon made available for penniless journalists of the right hue and in the autumn they were busy 'mauling Lord Treasurer, Lord Bolingbroke and me', as Swift complained. The cleric was growing disenchanted with the London world; he felt that a 'devilish spirit' was abroad. He was weary of trying to keep his friends 'from breaking to pieces upon a hundred misunderstandings' and began to long for the gentle willows and river walks of home. 'When I reason with some friends,' he wrote, 'we cannot conceive how affairs can last as they are.' It was a melancholy outlook for the supporters of Oxford and Bolingbroke.

CHAPTER 19

THE LONGED-FOR PEACE

IN THE AUTUMN OF 1712 the Queen's health began to give cause for anxiety. She had been ill, on and off, all her reign, and it was sometimes suggested that she assumed illlness when it suited her. Some said that she had shut herself up at Hampton Court with her gout and her Treasurer to avoid seeing angry allied plenipotentiaries the year before, and in January she had succumbed to a 'psychological' attack of gout to help out her Ministers who wanted an excuse to prorogue Parliament for a few days longer. In the summer, in the cleaner air of Windsor and Kensington, her health had been comparatively good, but in the autumn it took a more serious turn and began to cause some speculation. In her letters to Oxford she continually complained of sharp gouty pains, and in September Dr Arbuthnot sat up with her all one night when she had a crisis. 'The doctor tells me she has passed the night as well as could be expected,' Abigail told Oxford, 'and is in great hopes it will go off without either ague or fever.' All possible political capital was made out of the Queen's illness, as Bromley reported to Oxford on October 27:

The faction are busy in reporting the Queen to be in a very ill state of health. I hope this is only their malice, and that she will many years enjoy the fruits of that blessing she is giving her people.

From now on, the Queen's delicate state of health became an important factor in the situation, and accounted for many of the vagaries of ministerial behaviour. The possibility of her death was no longer remote and Ministers began to feel that it was wise to keep in both with the Court of Hanover and with the Pretender, just to make sure.

In October Oxford was unwell himself; in fact the Queen, the Lord Treasurer and Lady Masham were all ill at the same time. Abigail, inevitably, was pregnant again, and in October she had some kind of fright when out in her chair at Windsor. The Queen was so worried that she sat up late at night by Abigail's bedside.

The controversy between Oxford and Bolingbroke was at its height, but in spite of this there were no parliamentary crises that autumn to match the 'no peace without Spain' motion of the previous year. The October Club was by no means a spent force, but it had been weakened by the defection of more balanced Members who wished to dissociate themselves from the Club's excesses and in particular its Jacobite leanings. In March there had been a break-away by a splinter group of members who wished to press for the Hanoverian succession, and when the extremists tried to 'tack' the Land Grants Bill to Oxford's vital Lottery Bill, the March men, as they were called, were able to rally enough support to foil the attempt.

For a while the tempo of life became a little slower, and Oxford even had time to attend to family affairs; in what Swift described as the 'snowy, slobbery weather' of mid-December, Oxford's favourite daughter Elizabeth was married to Lord Carmarthen, heir to the first Duke of Leeds, who as Lord Danby had played such an important part in political life at the end of the century. Lady Betty was in luck, for Carmarthen had an income of £7,000 a year and 'three houses furnished'. His seat at Wimbledon was particularly fine, and near enough for the 'Prime Minister' to drive out and dine with his daughter. Oxford missed a Cabinet meeting in order to attend the festivities.

Meanwhile the peace talks were progressing slowly. The Queen's objections to Prior as an envoy, based on her dislike of being represented by a man of humble origin, had been overcome, and he had been hard at work in Paris. Prior in fact had been working so diligently that his letters talked of nothing but business, to Bolingbroke's chagrin. The Secretary would have liked to hear something of the eloped nun, who, it was rumoured, had taken the place of the famous 'nut-brown maiden' in Prior's affections. The poet, with what Bolingbroke called his '*visage de bois*', was a success with the ladies, and spent some pleasant hours with Madame Torcy, wife of the Foreign Minister, teaching her to drink '*à Harré et à Robin*'. Bolingbroke would have liked to hear something of his own conquests too, one of whom rejoiced in the name of Claudine Alexandrine Guérine de Tercin.

In the autumn, Prior was joined by Shrewsbury, who had been hastily chosen to take the place of the Duke of Hamilton, killed in a duel on the verge of his departure for Paris. Hamilton's appointment had caused a great deal of controversy on account of his well-known Jacobite tendencies, and some said that the duel had all been the work of the Whigs. Shrewsbury was a far less controversial figure. He disapproved of Prior's intimacy with the French, and preserved an air of aloofness throughout his mission. Prior, indeed, was frequently under fire for his friendliness with French people, female or otherwise; Oxford's agent, Drummond, reported from the Hague that there was 'great railing against poor Matt Prior by his own countrymen . . . that he is a pensioner where he resides'. Prior was himself continually complaining about his lack of funds, which, he claimed, prevented him from doing his job properly, or from living with the dignity expected of a British envoy. 'It seems his patron has not opened his purse strings wide enough,' Drummond reported.

The negotiations were complicated in the extreme, and there were endless 'sticking-points'. As usual the Dutch Barrier caused difficulties, and agreement had to be reached with Holland before bargaining with France could continue. The Dutch were chastened by their lack of success in the campaign that followed the Restraining Orders, and, having themselves declared an armistice, they were as anxious as everyone else to conclude the peace as soon as possible. They accepted the principle that the Spanish Netherlands should be ceded to Austria and were given more or less the Barrier they asked for; but it was still a far less favourable treaty than the one worked out with the Whigs in 1709, and which the Tories had torn up without a qualm.

While the delegates at the conference table re-arranged the map of Europe, and the islands of the Mediterranean waited to learn which particular European powers were to be allocated their deep harbours and strategic shores, the English Ministers dined and caroused, whiling away the time until the peace terms were settled. Swift was bidden to the Lord Treasurer's almost every day of the week, and was chided and teased if he did not go. Politics were seldom discussed, and the Treasurer seemed to linger over the meal, putting off rousing himself to go to Court or to meetings. Sometimes there were family gatherings, with a dozen relations, including 'the Dupps', and with Swift as the only outsider. Saturday was the great day, which Oxford called his 'whipping day', when his friends rallied him about his faults, all of which he took in good part. He seemed in relatively good health and spirits.

Everyone hoped that the main treaty would be settled by Christmas, but they soon realized that this was over-optimistic. On March 13, 1713, when there was still no definite news of completion, Swift thought that Oxford seemed pensive; 'he was playing with an orange by fits, which, I told him, among common men looked like the spleen,' he wrote. Oxford aimed at making the session of Parliament as short as possible, in order to avoid trouble and to wait until the treaty was through as a basis for discussion. Various excuses were used, through the autumn and early spring, for proroguing Parliament, and when Passion Week was reached, that provided a further splendid reason for putting off the opening for another fortnight. There were disagreements between Oxford and Bolingbroke on this as on almost everything else. 'Delay is rooted in Eltee's heart,' wrote Swift on March 23, resorting to a cipher for the Lord Treasurer's name for fear, he told Stella, that his letters would be opened. Swift, who was expecting place and position in recognition of his good services, and even hoping that he might land a Bishopric before he returned to Ireland, was losing his customary detachment and becoming caught up in the atmosphere of tension.

Nobody particularly liked to be reminded that it was now nearly three years since the Ministry had come in, dedicated to the policy of an early peace. And now yet another spring had almost come, nothing was settled and Prior reported that Louis, in a remarkable state of health and spirits for his age, was still enjoying his delaying game. The Spanish were also stiffening their terms. The only good news was that the little Dauphin, as Shrewsbury reported to Bolingbroke in a letter on March 13, was growing stronger every day, and was a frail fortification against the possible unification of France and Spain under one crown.

The delay was almost intolerable. 'We wait with impatience,' Bolingbroke wrote to Oxford, 'for that happy hour when we shall go out of such a war as I heartily wish our children's children will never see.' Oxford, uncharacteristically, communicated very 'plainly' to the plenipotentiaries, urging them to sign at once. Bolingbroke despatched a strong letter to Louis threatening to break off negotiations. At last the French King knew that the game was up. He had no desire to rally his exhausted country and prepare for hostilities again, and finally, on April 3, the coach carrying Bolingbroke's half-brother George St John, who had been entrusted with the precious document, arrived in Whitehall and was met at the door of the Cockpit by the Secretary himself. As the dusty messenger handed over the treaty, the Secretary uttered words that were, for him, remarkably pious. 'It is the Lord's work and it is marvellous in our eyes,' he exclaimed.

The English people, overjoyed to learn that the great struggle was over, indulged in the usual bonfires and bell-ringing. But although the populace was weary enough to accept peace without caring too much about the terms, there were lords at Westminster who were more particular. When the treaties were discussed in the Great Council on April 8, Cholmondeley 'warmed himself without provocation', as Bolingbroke reported to Shrewsbury, 'to a degree of heat not becoming that place'. The next day,

Cholmondeley was removed from his place as Treasurer of the Household. At a dinner party held on the night the treaty arrived, Addison expressed some Whiggish objections to the terms, but Bolingbroke, who was present, 'answered them with great complaisance'. The Secretary was well pleased with his work, and although he admitted that he had been forced to give back to France too many frontier towns, he had won most of the concessions required by his own country, now so greedy for trade. Gibraltar and Minorca were retained by Britain, and other possible bases were given to nations who had no naval pretensions. Victor Amadeus of Savoy received Sicily as a reward for his consistent cultivation of British favour, and the landlocked Emperor Charles was granted Sardinia, which had been seized for him when he was still struggling to become Charles III of Spain. All this was admirable, but there were darker matters which men of loyalty could not ignore. In the Spanish Treaty, the Catalans, who had fought with such bravery for the allied cause, were deserted without any guarantees, and left to the mercy of the Spaniards against whom they had rebelled. Portugal also was disappointed. The Whigs noted these points carefully, and stored them up for a future time.

The first reactions to the treaty were on the whole encouraging:

> Thus shall fair Britain with a gracious smile
> Accept the work; and the instructed isle,
> For more than treaties made shall bless my toil,

wrote Prior. Oxford knew that the Tories would stand together and accept the treaties in the Commons. In the Lords, death and accidents among Whig peers had made the position less marginal. To be on the safe side, the proxies of absent lords were hastily collected, but there was none of the anxiety that had preceded vital debates of a year ago. 'Lord Treasurer is easy as a lamb,' wrote Swift on April 8. The arrival of the longed-for peace brought Members thronging up to London. In her speech, which Ministers had been working on for several weeks, the Queen made a plain statement of the excellence of the peace terms. The Address of Thanks congratulated the Queen on providing for the 'true interests and just pretensions' of the allies.

The war was over; now was the moment to look ahead and plan for the time when a new King would reign in England. The shadow of the Queen's poor health lay across the scene, perpetuating a feeling of uncertainty. Queen Anne, a woman who loved peace, had been destined to come to the throne at the start of a ten-year war, and now, when her subjects might have settled down to a period of calm, and her government could have devoted its energies to constructive legislation for the good of the people, her illness touched up all the old bickering differences, revealing the deadly rift between Hanoverians and Jacobites.

In this situation, Oxford extended to the continental scene the policies which had governed his political behaviour for over twenty years. He did his best to keep a foot in both camps, and ended by being trusted by neither. The French might take Bolingbroke to their hearts, but they were no more ready than Hanover to trust the cautious man who had all the time been a curb on the Secretary's extravagances during the peace negotiations. Torcy had said openly that if it had not been for Oxford's reluctance, they might have been able to conclude a separate treaty with the British, but Oxford had always made a distinction between 'separate treating' and a separate treaty. Marlborough had gone into exile in the autumn of 1712, followed by his Duchess who had raffled her diamonds among her grandchildren, and travelled with a vast amount of luggage, including a five-pint tea kettle. The Duke was capable of doing Oxford a great deal of harm at the Elector's court, and though Oxford swore, by all that was sacred, that he intended 'faithful service' to the Hanoverians, Marlborough and the Whigs cancelled out such assurances with their tales of the Treasurer's 'trickish temper'. And it was known that Oxford did not like the idea of a foreign ruler—he had learnt the dangers in King William's reign. So the Pretender's advisers kept a hopeful link and Gaultier told James to 'write to me often and always in English so that I can show Oxford all your letters; always put in something flattering and pleasing to the Queen for I am assured he will show her everything you send. Never mention Bolingbroke or any other in the letters I shall read to Oxford'.

The Frenchman understood the English political game too well, but nobody could really fathom Oxford's moves. 'You don't see all the wheels of this machine,' said Defoe. Hanmer told friends at the Pretender's court that everyone was tired of Oxford's 'dark, trimming methods'. He was 'disobliging' both parties and pleasing neither. 'Oxford keeps a balance on his own power,' wrote Hanmer. Even some of Oxford's friends grumbled about being treated like footmen, and Defoe thought he could have secured more supporters by a 'more open distribution' of Treasury funds at his disposal. To please the Tories, Oxford had removed a few Whigs from places of profit, but he did this so reluctantly that he did himself little good. The Tories had an uneasy feeling that whenever it suited him he would strike up an alliance with the Whigs, and this was accentuated when, in the spring of 1713, Oxford started approaching

Halifax and actually visited his house at the end of March. The whole town buzzed with the news, and Swift told Stella that Oxford would certainly declare for the Whig interest immediately after the peace: 'You must know this is what they endeavour to report of Lord Treasurer.' Halifax did not command a great following, and most of the Whigs invited to meet Oxford refused to come. A large-scale reconciliation was obviously out of the question, but the Treasurer was always ready to do some caballing here and there, just to confuse both his friends and his enemies.

Oxford remained on good terms with Bromley, and continued to keep in with as many High Tories as possible, including the scholarly Bishop Hooper:

The Earl of Oxford . . . frequently visited him, insomuch that it drew great inconveniences upon him, who loved study much beyond state, for as my Lord Treasurer would generally go to the Bishop as soon as he saw him in the House of Lords, and sit down by him on their bench, where he whispered him about wind and weather, and his coach waiting two or three times a week at the Bishop's door at Kensington, made every one conclude, that my Lord was a great church man, and the Bishop a great favourite, whereas he was never let into any of their secret measures, or consulted upon their designs. This seeming favour drew a crowd of mistaken people about the Bishop, for not only the great people visited him, but he had a perfect levee of all sorts especially those who were suitors for places, or any other favour from my Lord Treasurer, interceding for his recommendation, and only begging he would mention them to my Lord T.

Lord Parker, the Lord Chief Justice, who lived next door to the Bishop, was encouraged by all the coaches, to pay his court, and although he had been one of the most bitter Whig managers at the Sacheverell trial, he did not hesitate to curry favour with a High Churchman in order to assist his own advancement.

The session of Parliament which had begun so late did not prove to be an easy one for Oxford. In May there were meetings of Whig Lords, and one which was particularly well attended took place at Somerset's house. Even more alarming was the startling news that the Whigs were joining with the Scottish lords to bring in a motion repealing the Act of Union, on the grounds that the Act had done nothing but accentuate the differences between the two peoples. The very men who had been architects of the treaty were now prepared to destroy their own handiwork. But the threat produced in the Lord Treasurer a mood of unwonted determination. Here was an issue that raised him clear of the haze of compromise in which he usually moved. The Whigs, in supporting the dissolution of the Union, insisted that there should be a clause safe-guarding the succession, but the Scotsmen had gone rashly ahead without testing public opinion in their own country. The Whigs wished for a delay, so that assurance could be sent across the border, and Oxford's spies soon acquainted him with the difficulty. He seized on this omission and moved in the Lords that the motion should be discussed at once, before there had been any chance for consultations. It was then decided by a vast majority that the Bill should not be brought in at all, 'all the Whigs voting against it, because it was proposed out of concert before they had time to prepare it'.

The parliamentary manager had not lost his skill, but these were last-ditch tactics, hardly the work of a first Minister confidently at the helm. And when Bolingbroke's Commercial Treaty was brought before Parliament in June, Oxford was frankly defeated. The problems of commerce posed by the peace settlement had been dealt with separately, and although Britain gained many advantages, including the treasured Asiento contract, there were a number of clauses that angered the trading community. It was thought that the interests of British merchants were insufficiently safeguarded, and the allies felt that once again they had been sacrificed in favour of the common enemy, France. Portugal was treated particularly badly and not only Whig merchants, but also many country farmers, were likely to suffer from a diminution in the wool trade which was paid for mainly in port wine, the Whigs' favourite beverage, and also in Brazilian gold, so necessary for the nation's economy. Increased trade with France was bound to mean that England would be flooded with French luxury goods, such as claret and silk, for which she would expect payment, not in wool, but in hard gold which the country could not spare. Fear of free trade with France prompted the country landowners to rebel against the government, and there was a mass defection, rare in Tory annals. Sir Thomas Hanmer, the independently minded country landowner, led a revolt of eighty Tories who, joining with the Whigs, were able to defeat the Commerce Bill by a narrow margin.

For Bolingbroke this was a bitter blow. The Dutch laughed openly, which increased his chagrin. He blamed everybody but himself and, remembering Oxford's dinner party in March with Halifax, was ready to believe that the Treasurer had entered into a shady deal with the Whigs. Surely, if Oxford had wanted to, he could have exerted his in-fluence and averted defeat? 'You have retrieved many a bad game in your time; for God's sake make one push for government,' he raged. Oxford's actions were becoming increasingly muddled; for a while he seemed to support the Treaty, fearing a split in the party, and then he withdrew. Bolingbroke was tired of Oxford's lack of clear-cut policy; 'no principle of government established and avowed, nobody but my Lord Treasurer, and he cannot be in every place and speak to every man,' he wrote, impatient to reorganize his supporters on firmer lines. 'To play, like children, with it, till it slips between our fingers, this distracts a man of spirit,' he told Prior on July 25. And he even said to the Auditor, 'If your brother will not set himself at the head of the Church party, somebody must.' It was too easy to accuse the Treasurer of being a lukewarm Churchman, and Harcourt, attracted by Bolingbroke's more brilliant light, joined with Atterbury, who had recently been appointed Bishop of Rochester, to work on the inflammable denizens of the one established Church and prejudice them against the Treasurer. On July 27, Bolingbroke frankly told Oxford that the reason for government failure was weakness and lack of direction in its leader:

You are forced to execute more than you should, and cannot therefore supervise. You are pulling at the beam when you should be in the box whipping and reining in, as the journey you have to go or the ways you pass through require.

Bolingbroke harked back to the old grouse about the non-party men and Whigs who had been allowed to stay in their places. 'A great part of the honey is consumed by drones who clog the administration' he complained, and then issued what turned out to be nothing less than an ultimatum, couched in the usual breezy Bolingbroke style:

Separate, in the name of God, the chaff from the wheat, and consider who you have left to employ; assign them their parts, trust them as far as it is necessary for the execution each of his part; let the forms of business be regularly carried on in Cabinet, and the secret of it in your own closet.

Still the Treasurer refused to give in. He suggested that his ally Bromley, so popular with the High Tories and so well respected by all, should be given an important office to placate the zealots. Bolingbroke did not accept this ruse. 'Can Mr Bromley be in any post so useful as in the chair?' he enquired. It was not difficult to find a vacancy for Bromley to fill. Dartmouth, Bolingbroke's co-Secretary of State, had been uneasy for a long time; he was essentially a man of the centre and Tory excesses filled him with gloom. The desertion of the Catalans, too, had disturbed his humane conscience. Abigail told Oxford that the Queen had commanded her to say that 'she will endeavour to persuade Lord Dartmouth not to give up the Seals, but she has thought him out of humour a good while, by things he has let fall to her'. Typically, Oxford refused to let

Dartmouth go altogether; he was demoted to the post of Lord Privy Seal, which was vacant since Robinson had been bribed out of politics by the promise of the see of London. There was a further surprise; even as Bolingbroke was criticizing these half-measures, he found that he himself was to be transferred to the southern branch of the secretariat, thus losing direct control over affairs at the Hague, which now became the responsibility of the more reliable Bromley. There was fire in the Dragon after all. Sir Thomas Hanmer, wooed for so long, agreed to take the Speaker's Chair.

An election was due under the Triennial Act, and Oxford hoped that his pointed Cabinet re-shuffle might persuade the electors to vote for moderate candidates. But the gesture was too late and too half-hearted to work one of the Harley miracles. Bolingbroke, helped by Harcourt and other friends, was combing through the lists of placemen and marking off all those with Whiggish tendencies. For three years Oxford had stood out against a purge, and, looking back on it afterwards, he dated his real decline in power from the time when Bolingbroke went ahead and removed almost every Whig he could find. It was the negation of Oxford's principles.

For the moment, however, he had more pleasant matters to attend to. His friend Newcastle was dead, but in the months before his death the Duke had made definite approaches with a view to arranging a match between the personable Edward, and charming red-haired Lady Henrietta Cavendish-Holles. Many of the nobility had solicited for her hand, including the Duke of Somerset for his son, and Lady Wentworth for hers. 'If you gave out I was dead,' Lady Wentworth had advised Lord Raby, 'and I will goe and hide in some corner, then I am sure she would have you, for she has an avertion to a mother-in-law, as many has and not without reason.' There had even been talk at one time of a union with the Elector's son. The girl had, from the first, been given everything the heart could desire, including two parroquets, two land turtles and a diminutive lion 'not bigger and as tame as a rabbit', all shipped from the West Indies. All the same, she was well pleased at the thought of marrying the good-tempered and pleasant Lord Harley. The Duchess of Newcastle, soured by a contested will and the sequestration of her estate, and thinking regretfully of Harriet's more noble suitors, made herself unpleasant both to the Harleys and to her daughter. But, apart from this disadvantage, Edward Harley was blessed in his bride and in the fortune that went with her. The marriage took place in August at the handsome seat at Wimpole which was to be the young couple's home. Oxford, with his usual secrecy, went out of town at the height of the political crisis and neglected to tell anybody where he was going. On August 24, Bolingbroke wrote from Windsor, where he was comfortably ensconced in Oxford's absence:

I receive this moment your letter of yesterday's date, and though you do not mention your being at Wimpole, which place, by the way, all the town knew on Friday you were gone to, yet no man living is more sincerely rejoiced than I am at the occasion of your journey.

Anyone would think, Bolingbroke added in a subsequent letter, that Oxford had gone to get a mistress for himself, rather than a wife for his son, if a secretive air was anything to go by.

Bolingbroke's felicitations had a hollow ring. He certainly rejoiced, but one must believe it was rather on account of his rival's absence than on his successful match-making. The departure of Oxford into the depths of Cambridgeshire gave Bolingbroke a heaven-sent opportunity to work his way into Abigail's confidence and in general to plot for the Treasurer's downfall.

CHAPTER 20

HANOVER AND SAINT-GERMAIN

THE GENERAL ELECTION of 1713 dealt the last blow to Oxford's hopes of managing the state with a group of moderates, in partnership with the Tories and in accordance with the wishes of the Queen. The old cry of 'the Church in danger' rang out louder than ever, drowning the Whig shouts of 'no popery, no wooden shoes'. Bolingbroke's nicely timed weeding-out of Whig government officials ensured another victory for the Tories which thoroughly consolidated their position. 'The party are far from laying down the cudgels,' reported Lord Weymouth, with a great deal of truth. The Tories came back breathing abuse at Oxford for his failure to be vindictive towards the Whigs. The 'persecuted sneak', as Steele unkindly called him, could do little now to curb Bolingbroke and his followers.

Oxford spent a fortnight at Wimpole from August 21 to September 4. It was too long. In the interim Bolingbroke worked on the Queen, and 'ploughed with the heifer', bribing Abigail with a tempting allocation of shares in the South Sea Company. On September 5, Oxford went down to Windsor and stayed for ten days. On the 15th he was joined there by Lord and Lady Harley, and the bride and bridegroom were able to crave the Queen's blessing. She greeted them coldly, having sent a message by Bolingbroke to say that the bride must be called, not Lady Harley, but Lady 'Herriot' Harley, to remind everybody that she was a Duke's daughter. Oxford tried to obtain Newcastle's title for his son, but the Queen took umbrage at the request, and Oxford believed that she was never the same again after he had made this inept, and bitterly regretted, move. And if the Queen was cold, Abigail too was distant. She had not attended the wedding, and made a weak excuse for not visiting Lady Carmarthen at Wimbledon. 'I may desire Lord Harley to do me the honour to bring her [Lady Harriet] to my lodgings,' she wrote.

In the summer Oxford was ill again, adding sore eyes to his usual symptoms. In October, the Queen noted that his 'indispotion', as she called it, prevented him from visiting her at Windsor. She could not refrain from mentioning her own discomfort: 'I have felt the sharp weather in one of my feet.' Bad health, his waning influence with the Queen and Bolingbroke's ascendancy made Oxford feel that it was useless to struggle on any longer. On October 20 he made up his mind to visit the Queen and tender his resignation. 'This is the question,' he wrote in some notes scribbled down before the interview. 'Is it for the service either public or private that Mr H should continue to be employed yea or no? If no . . . he is not so blind as not to see . . . and will find a hole to creep out at . . . he was always indifferent but now is more earnest to get rid of a service.' The Queen, perversely, would not let him resign; it was always like this when it came to parting with one of her servants. And Oxford had been her friend for so long. She could not let him creep out like a trapped animal. Although Bolingbroke had taught her to notice Oxford's procrastinating ways and to doubt his sincerity, she was unable to make the break.

Oxford's friends implored him to continue. They knew that without him, nobody would be capable of hindering Bolingbroke's repressive measures. Dartmouth, in particular, feared and disliked the High Tory regime. He knew that he could do little unless he had Oxford's help. The Queen liked him and believed him to be an honest man, so he clung to whatever power and favour remained to him and urged Oxford to do the same. The Treasurer, thus encouraged, gathered his remaining reserves of health and strength and went on.

He was struggling out of a bad bout of illness at the beginning of November and was just starting to go out and about again, when he received one of the most bitter blows of his life. Lady Carmarthen, the beloved Betty, died giving birth to a son less than a year after her brilliant marriage.

No record remains of the statesman's reaction to this private loss. Defoe believed that Oxford, who had always put 'the public care' above his private interest, would be able to apply the sovereign remedy of resignation, which in his public life had led him to greatness. But although Oxford had been able to treat the dangers and difficulties of his career with calm detachment, the loss of his treasured child was more than he could bear, and his family believed that he never recovered from the shock.

The Queen sent a message by Abigail expressing her great concern. Bolingbroke, too, sent his condolences, and there were rumours that the two men were at least temporarily reconciled. But although Bolingbroke had to be resigned to Oxford's presence in the Cabinet, since the Queen would not let him go, he could not refrain from making remarks about Oxford's slowness and procrastination. 'I am sorry there is little show of government when the difficulties we have to struggle with require that all the powers of it should be exerted,' he complained on December 3 from Windsor. 'A little shove from your Lordship' was what he asked for on another occasion. 'Do not once entertain a thought that I give myself airs, or have the least lukewarmness,' he added, in his facile way.

Bolingbroke's dislike was now focused on Dartmouth, whose continued presence at court was a constant minor irritation. 'The pigmy stretches and struts, and fancies himself a giant,' he told Oxford. The Lord Privy Seal, he reported, was monopolizing the Queen for two hours every evening, entertaining her with his conversation, while his lady fancied herself as a second Duchess of Somerset. The truth probably was that Dartmouth was trying to keep Oxford's place open for him while he was away nursing his health and recovering from the death of his daughter.

Oxford was expected at Windsor early in December, and Bolingbroke awaited his arrival with impatience, not for the pleasure he was likely to find in his company, but for the many matters which required the Treasurer's approval. At last, towards the end of the first week in December, Oxford paid the Queen an uneasy visit which prompted her to write:

Now that I have a pen in my hand I cannot help desiring you again when you come next, to speak plainly, lay everything open and hide nothing from me, or else how is it possible I can judge of anything? I spoke very freely and sincerely to you yesterday, and I expect you should do the same to her that is sincerely your very affectionate friend.

He went away again almost immediately, leaving the Queen little clue to his thoughts or intentions.

It soon became evident to the little scheming circle of people at the Queen's side that the Treasurer was offended. His long absence from Windsor was beginning to cause comment, and explanations that it was due to grief and ill health were beginning to wear thin. Bolingbroke was anxious. He did not want an open breach just at this time. He had decided to throw in his lot with the Pretender and needed to keep the Treasurer in a position to reassure the Hanoverians and to act as a screen for his plots. A few more months with Oxford playing the part of an innocent dupe would give his plans time to mature, and it was trying to find the elder statesman absenting himself from the court in such an obvious manner. In mid-December he wrote Oxford an obsequious letter, trying to lure him back with tantalizing hints of a union between the two branches of the party:

Though my head aches with writing all day, I cannot however leave my office till I have sent you the enclosed. ... I see an opportunity of giving new strength, new spirit to your administration, and of cementing a firmer union between us, and between us and those who must support us. If you go to Windsor alone on Saturday, I'll talk to you on the subject. If I am wrong you will not lose much time in a coach on the road. Believe me for once, what I always am, and have been to you, sincere, however I may have been too warm and your Lordship, allow the expression, too jealous.

The letter failed to lure such a shrewd judge of character. Oxford was never gullible, and he was not taken in by this rather sudden change of heart. He had no wish to associate himself in the eyes of the world with Bolingbroke's Jacobite leanings, and if he could not control the Cabinet and the progress of affairs, he preferred to stay away, sphinx-like as ever.

Bolingbroke wished to lead the High Tories and head the government, but when it came to the point, he felt nervous at the thought of being on his own. There were signs, too, that Bromley was trying to keep the High Churchmen loyal to Oxford. The Queen's health worried Bolingbroke. He wanted her to live long enough to give him time to prepare for the Pretender's coming. She seemed to be on the mend at the beginning of December, when the weather turned unusually warm for the time of year. But on Christmas Eve, Bolingbroke arrived at Windsor to find her seriously ill. He wrote to Oxford immediately, asking him to come without delay. 'Her symptoms are the same as in her last ague but stronger and more severe. God in his mercy to these kingdoms preserve her.' It was a heartfelt prayer. Everyone knew he was for the Pretender, but he was caught with his preparations uncompleted. The Whigs on the other hand felt that Hanover's hour had come, and spent a merry Christmas hurrying to and fro to each other's houses in their chairs and coaches. Soon a report was spread that the Queen was dead, which increased Whig joy and Tory despair—it was possible to tell a man's party allegiance by the expression on his face. Bolingbroke's look of sheer panic proved how involved he was with the Pretender's court.

Meanwhile, the Treasurer, spending a quiet family Christmas in town, remained as calm as ever. 'You know she has every year an ague,' he told Prior. He refused to be drawn into the general undignified pandemonium, since he knew that if he went hurrying down to Windsor he could put the whole nation into a state of turmoil. To lower the temperature and kill the rumour that the Queen was dead, he went for a spin round the town in his chariot for all the gossiping world to see.

Everyone else of any consequence converged on the Castle. Lady Masham stayed by the Queen day and night, scared to death by rumours that the Duchess of Somerset had arrived in the town. Dr Arbuthnot was treating the Queen, but on Christmas Day Sir David Hamilton was hastily summoned, to make sure that Whig justice was done at the bedside. By lunch time on that festive day most of the Cabinet Council had arrived in answer to Bolingbroke's urgent summons. All day they waited for news of the Treasurer's arrival and still he did not come. By evening Bolingbroke was beside himself:

We expected your Lordship here this morning with the utmost impatience, for indeed the Queen has been, and still is, extremely ill, though some of her bad symptoms are abated. . . . Your Lordship is the best judge what measures to take, but surely in all events and in all respects you should be here.

The Treasurer was still a key figure. Nothing could be done and no momentous decisions taken without him. Whigs, Tories, Hanoverians, Jacobites, were all left in suspense without his lead. 'Besides the pain everybody suffers from the Queen's illness, we have the additional uneasiness of your not being here, which is the second topic of discourse,' wrote Erasmus Lewis, 'and I take the liberty to tell you everybody stands amazed at it.'

By evening the Queen's symptoms had abated a little, and she seemed inclined for sleep. The physicians were powerless either to diagnose or to treat, being unsure whether the illness was the prelude to a severe fit of the gout, an 'intermitting fever', or 'a continued one upon the spirits'. It was the last that they feared. Doctors being what they were, her best hope was that they would leave her alone and refrain from administering remedies, such as those which had choked the Duke of Newcastle.

The Treasurer believed that an alarmist visit might well have upset the Queen and convinced her that she was dying. So he came down when the danger was passed, 'but not the fright, which still sate on every bodies face,' as Swift put it. When his friends remonstrated with him about his seeming heartlessness, he replied, 'Whenever anything ails the Queen, these people are out of their wits, and yet they are so thoughtless, that as soon as she is well, they act as if she were immortal.'

By the new year the Queen's recovery, which some thought nothing short of miraculous, was almost complete. 'She recovers as fast and as well

CHARLES, DUKE OF SOMERSET

Photo : Courtauld Institute of Art

ELIZABETH, DUCHESS OF SOMERSET
WITH HER SON ALGERNON

Photo : Courtauld Institute of Art

JAMES STUART, THE OLD
PRETENDER

THE ELECTRESS SOPHIA

as an honest heart can wish,' wrote Bolingbroke to Oxford on New Year's Eve. The more he talked about his own honesty and sincerity, the more two-faced he became—a typical symptom of the scheming man. He talked to his old master with an air of respect, but his protestations were no more than a veneer. For the time being he concentrated his efforts on making trouble for the Whigs, telling the Queen how they had behaved during her illness—how triumphant they had looked, and how happy at the thought of her imminent death. 'The result was,' Swift reported, 'that the Queen immediately laid aside all her schemes and visions of reconciling the two opposite interests, and entered upon a firm resolution of adhering to the old English principles, from an opinion that the adverse party waited impatiently for her death.' The first signs of the Queen's change of heart came when she countenanced further changes among her civil servants and visited her displeasure on the Horse and Foot Guards who were her personal attendants at the Palace. Some of the officers were known to gossip about court affairs when they went off duty and repaired to the gaming-ordinaries or coffee houses, especially those haunted by Whigs in the vicinity of the Palace gates. It was uncomfortable to feel that such men, after decorously attending courts and levees, went straight out to spread exaggerated tales about the Ministry's bias towards the Pretender.

Oxford's theory was that gossip of this kind, if unchecked, always proved relatively harmless; suppress it and you rouse more dangerous passions of bitterness and revenge. But the Queen no longer listened to Oxford's theories. She had been taught to doubt his sincerity, to notice his procrastination and to forget his virtues. 'The Queen's countenance was wholly changed towards him, she complained of his silence and sullenness, and in return gave him every day fresh instances of neglect and displeasure,' Swift recalled, adding that there was nothing but murmuring, discontent, quarrel, misunderstanding, and animosity between him and his former friends. Had Swift been given the appointment in England which he longed for and well deserved in view of his excellent service to the Ministry, he might still have managed to reconcile his friends, for he remained loyal to them both. But he suffered the fate that too often overtakes men of mordant wit; his cleverness rebounded on himself. He had been fool enough to write a lampoon on the subject of the Duchess of Somerset, in which he twice called her 'Carrots'. Great Anna—'O Thou whose name Is backwards and forwards always the same'—was incapable of forgiving such pointed lines, and firmly made him Dean of St Patrick's. It was a case of 'Hibernian politics, O Swift,

I

thy fate', as Pope had it. Prior also might have helped, but he was still in Paris, waiting for somebody to remember him and reward him for his services. When Swift came back to London on a visit in the spring of 1714, matters had gone too far for anybody to provide the remedy.

Oxford might have refused to join in the general panic which greeted the Queen's Christmas illness, but the alarm shown by her doctors told him that from now on her days were quite definitely numbered. This knowledge made him more cautious and non-committal than ever, and wherever possible he avoided taking sides in any matter that might offend either the Pretender or the Electress. Such an attitude was bound to have a stultifying influence; it was the middle-of-the-road view of politics carried to the point of absurdity, and it lent strength to Bolingbroke's strictures about the lack of leadership or government of any kind. For weeks now, the Treasurer had done little except deal with routine matters, and even those he had neglected and put aside in his now customary manner. The High Tory Parliament elected the previous autumn had been given no chance to show its teeth; St Stephen's Chapel had been silent since the summer and now, in the new year, there were endless prorogations. The rejected Treaty of Commerce still hung fire, and could not be completed until Parliament had been given a chance to meet. Discussion about the commercial clauses grew more bitter with every month's delay. In the first enthusiasm for the peace, many people had been prepared to accept more or less anything, 'even like to a stale virgin that cries, Any, good Lord, any'. But mature reflection—and there was plenty of time for that—made them more fastidious. Defoe reported a mounting clamour against the French trade, although he thought this was raised not so much from 'zeal for our commerce but for a handle, and to raise a party against the Ministry . . . the dispute about trade is but a circumstance, an excrescence grown out of the general party broil, taken hold of . . . as men drowning take hold of one another and drown the faster'. The South Sea Company greeted the Asiento concessions with unexpected coolness. 'Instead of joyful accepting, there rose a great many warm debates,' it was reported. The demolition of Dunkirk was another focus of discontent and controversy; the destruction of the walls that gave safe anchorage for the French privateers was proceeding so slowly that some said Bolingbroke was conniving with the French to save the fortifications. Other voices were raised in protest because the task seemed negative and unnecessary.

In the new year the pamphlet war broke out again; 'paper darts' were landing on target and Steele expressed Whig views on Dunkirk in strong terms, also preparing supporters for the forthcoming session, with a twelve-penny treatise called *The Crisis* which, according to Swift, was a pamphlet against the Ministry; it talked of slavery, France, and the Pretender, and caused a rush of dukes, earls, viscounts, barons, knights, esquires, gentlemen and others to the office of the publisher. It made a clear enough statement of the fact that the Protestant Succession was not safe under the present regime, and for proclaiming such a theory openly Steele incurred the rage of the Ministry and was expelled from the House of Commons. The Queen was indignant about Whig attacks and told Hamilton that the *Flying Post* should be suppressed. The Whiggish doctor replied tartly that 'the only way to suppress the *Flying Post* was to suppress the *Examiner*'.

The Queen's illness had given a further stimulus to the battle for a place at her bedside. To be near her at the moment of death might make the difference between power and disgrace in the next reign. The over-eagerness of her doctors became so embarrassing that in the spring Dr Arbuthnot suggested that only one physician should attend her each day in rotation. In February Sir David pressed the Queen to take steel, but on the whole he dosed her with Whig propaganda rather than anything else. If he himself was unwell and unable to attend the royal patient, his main anxiety was that he could not indulge in his usual 'discourse'. During his professional visits he administered small draughts of information and gossip, for example that nobody spoke well of Harley but herself. The Queen refused to let him go on his knees to ask a favour, for fear that somebody might come in and 'make ill use' of his being in such a position. Members of the Harley family, including the Auditor, did their best to find out how far the Queen confided in Hamilton, and what his influence with her amounted to:

I told her [Sir David wrote] Mrs Harley asked me if the Q. knew [of a private affair of his own]. I asked her whether I should own it or be silent. She commanded the latter, as an argument of her secrecy in any access she admitted me.

The Harley clan probably suspected, rightly, that Sir David repeatedly pleaded the Duchess of Somerset's cause; he certainly lost no opportunity of denigrating Abigail Masham. After a fracas in August 1713, when there was loud argument among the women and a screaming of children, Mrs Smith having 'thrown down' one of the small Mashams in the Queen's presence, Abigail flew into a passion. This gave the doctor an opportunity to point out how unsuitable such a passionate woman was for the Queen's temper, and how bad for her gout such outbreaks and upsets were. But his efforts produced little result, for in spite of all warnings, the Queen remained loyal to the Keeper of the Privy Purse, as Abigail had become in the general share-out of the Duchess's offices.

Lady Masham's usefulness outweighed the disadvantages caused by an occasional fit of temper, but her presence was becoming far from an asset to Oxford. At the same time Oxford's bouts of sickness were coming more and more frequently, and while he was unable to attend the Queen, the more energetic Bolingbroke worked tirelessly to supersede him. But for years the prim monarch had been fed with stories about St John's excesses with women, and his bad reputation in this respect prevented her transferring her affections entirely. From Bolingbroke's point of view it was unfortunate that Oxford's personal life was so spotless; it would have been more convenient if he had indulged in a little wenching or embezzling. The only hope was to exaggerate his fondness for good wine, and to picture him as a dypsomaniac wedded to the bottle. An alcoholic aroma certainly offended the royal nostril at times, when the Treasurer came straight to the Queen from a convivial evening, and it was easy to accuse him of being drink-sodden and incapable of managing the nation's affairs. It is hard to say how far such rumours were based on the truth, for even the Queen, it must be remembered, had a reputation for liking her own little drop. Physicians often recommended some comforting doses of wine or port, especially for gout sufferers, the theory being that it dispelled the 'flying pains' and brought the poison to one particular point, which was then treated with other horrible remedies.

Ill health, addiction to drink, fear of the future, or despair about the present, all combined to make Oxford shun larger issues. He attended Cabinet meetings as before, but his notes became ever more confused, the paper covered in scrawls and blots. Secrecy was becoming a disease with him; as if his writing was not illegible enough already, he began putting some of the names in his lists in a Greek code of his own. He ignored the advice of his friends and continued to stay up late and to enjoy good dinners and witty conversation. He mixed more than ever with literary men, and in his last year of office became a member of the Scriblerus Club, an even more select group than the Brothers' Society to which the Treasurer had received only an occasional invitation. Some of the Brothers had grown tired of their crowded, expensive dinners and looked for a more intimate and intellectual atmosphere. A new generation of writers, including Alexander Pope, found a focus in the new club whose object was to ridicule false taste in learning. Its patron was an imaginary character, Martinus Scriblerus, and Dr Arbuthnot, who invented him, wrote most of the essays directed at false learning and pedantry, which were published in later years as the *Memoirs of Scriblerus*. John Gay, still in his twenties, and Parnell, only a few years older, were among the young *letterati* who congregated in the Doctor's pleasant lodgings at St. James's Palace. Oxford was invited to join the informal meetings in a verse penned 'by order of the Club', by Pope, Gay, Arbuthnot and Swift, who was on his last visit to London:

> Then come and take part in
> The Memoirs of Martin,
> Lay by your white staff and grey habit;
> For trust us, friend Mortimer,
> Should you live years forty more,
> Hoc olim meminisse juvabit.

'Greatness itself condescended to look in at the door to us,' wrote Parnell in later years. Pope noted that Oxford used to send trifling verses to the club almost every day, and talk idly with its members every night, even when his all was at stake. 'The Dragon', as they all affectionately called him, patronized the arts with real understanding, though his own verses were distinctly banal. Gay, in particular, had good cause to remember the Treasurer with gratitude, since it was thanks to Oxford that he was appointed secretary to the goodwill mission to Hanover, and he celebrated his luck in a poem that included a charming rhymed request for extra pocket-money:

> If when with the swains I did gambol,
> I arrayed me in silver and blue;
> When abroad and in Courts I shall ramble,
> Pray, my Lord, how much money will do?

The Treasurer's tendency to while away his evenings in such a frivolous manner alarmed the more mundane Auditor Harley. 'You should appropriate more time for the despatch of business,' he rebuked his brother, even advising him to get out and about earlier in the morning. Indulgence in 'little passions and habits' had often proved fatal to great men in the past—'the leak that is sprung cannot be stopped without pumping,' he pointed out. He knew that if his brother was to survive the new session of Parliament, he would have to give all his time and energy to rallying support in Lords and Commons, and in 'obtaining an entire confidence with the Queen by an insidious and punctual attendance'.

Oxford might appear to be idling away his time, but he was not altogether inactive. In January 1714 he made up to court placemen by paying arrears of pensions and salaries. Among those to benefit was the portrait painter, Sir Godfrey Kneller, whose claims had, in the past, been foiled by the 'stingy, penurious, griping' Duchess of Marlborough and who complained that he had not even been given his travelling expenses. More important was Oxford's attempt to sort out his own position on the succession issue. He knew that the forthcoming session, when it finally began, would turn on the whole problem of who was to succeed. In his own mind he never wavered from the principle of the Protestant Succession, but his dilemma was that he depended on Jacobite support and could not afford to alienate it. After the Queen's Christmas illness he wrote in his notes:

Electrice—the same principle which made me so active for the first act of Parl. will constrain me to act for the Prot. Succession . . . this alarm has shewn how steadfast everyone is for the Queen's interest.

On the other hand, he disliked the thought of Germanic rule, and, like many Englishmen, he reacted more favourably to the idea of an English-born King than a German-speaking one. If the Prince of Wales could be persuaded to turn Protestant he might prove a better candidate than the Electress's pig-headed heir. So, towards the end of February, the Treasurer wrote a letter which James read with amazement. 'The whole is filled with obscure expressions, some puerile,' he wrote to Torcy on February 26. 'Can it possibly be that Lord Oxford is the author?' James was a man of sincere piety; he could hardly believe that anyone would think him capable of putting a throne before his God and his religion. 'I shall always be ready to sacrifice my comfort and even my life for my country, but to sacrifice for it my honour and my conscience is too much . . . who ever could trust me if I changed my religion for so gross a motive of self interest and temporal advantage?' James possessed a dignity and moral fibre which set him above his father and uncle, and it is possible that if he had succeeded to the English throne, he would have reigned with tolerance and without corruption. But the only practical way of gaining the throne, Oxford told him, was to become a Protestant, and he vowed that, by the grace of God, he would remain a Catholic until his last breath. 'If I thought otherwise,' he wrote, 'I am sure that Lord Oxford himself would despise me, for after all, I think him a man of honour and not capable of inspiring sentiments so contrary to it.'

Early in March, the Queen, Oxford and Bolingbroke learnt that there was no hope of converting the Pretender. The Jacobites in France, for their part, realized that from now on there was little to hope for from 'My Lord D'Oxford', although they continued to keep in touch with Bolingbroke, himself too involved to draw back. And as far as Bolingbroke was concerned, the religious issue was unimportant; he wanted James because he knew that he personally would fare better under Stuart than under Hanoverian rule. Oxford realized that Bolingbroke had no scruples, and he knew that the rift between them was now wide open. As Defoe pointed out, this was no time for a slack rein; either the party he was supposed to be leading must prove itself faithful to the Protestant succession, or it must go on without him. His friends knew that he was in earnest when he said that he must resign his Staff if he could not hold it with honour. Bolingbroke and Harcourt were not pleased; infuriating though the Dragon was, they liked to shelter behind him. His resignation would prove to everybody that he was a Hanoverian and they were not; his departure would expose them to violent attack. 'The concern I am under is inexpressible,' wrote Harcourt. 'I most sincerely desire to see your Lordship, as long as I live, at the head of the Queen's affairs,' echoed Bolingbroke. And on March 22, Abigail refused to take to the Queen what was probably his message of resignation. 'I am surprised at your Lordship desiring me to name what I know will be so disagreeable to her Majesty,' she replied. 'I did not expect you ever would send me of such a message; you must excuse me, for I never will carry it, and I hope your Lordship will consider better of it both for the Queen's sake and your own.'

All through the short parliamentary recess at the end of March, Tories of every hue worked to avert the disaster which they all knew would come to them if Oxford resigned. The shadow of Whig revenge in the next reign lay across their minds, and they believed that Oxford could save them, firm as he was for the Protestant succession. Oxford himself, weary and uncertain, was hesitant, but his friends prevailed, as they had done the previous October. On March 29 Erasmus Lewis told Thomas Harley that Oxford and Bolingbroke were prepared to go on 'cheerfully and unanimously'. The Auditor was more guarded. 'So at present things seem to be made up,' he wrote.

The Queen's speech, drafted by Oxford and delivered at the beginning of the session in February, laid stress on the need for continued peace, non-involvement on the continent, and the importance of England's maritime power. This should have pleased even the High Tories, but the Jacobites were angered when the Hanoverian Hanmer was elected Speaker; a large group began to meet together as a club which, in its protest meetings, clamoured for plans to be made quickly for the Pretender's coming. Pressure was put on Bolingbroke to accelerate his preparations. The Whigs, greatly encouraged to see the Tories showing their chronic tendency to split, intensified their efforts to harry the government. Sir Thomas Cave reported that the Whigs were proving very 'troublesome'; continual close attendance at the House was demanded, so much so that Cave complained he was unable to dine before six more than two days in the week 'nor did I go out for my chocolate'. As a result of his efforts he was 'walking very lean' in the opinion of his friends. If the session was a strain for a backbencher, it was all the more so for a Minister who had been in the forefront of affairs for over a dozen years and was now on the verge of collapse. But Oxford summoned all his energies at the end of March and, in spite of the Tory split, managed to save the government from defeat.

The Ministry, so precariously patched up after Oxford's attempts to resign, was faced almost at once by a censure motion which suggested that the Protestant Succession was not safe under the present administration. Hanmer, free to express fears which Oxford shared but could not reveal, voted against the Ministry, taking his Hanoverian Tories with him. The Tories' comfortable majority dwindled alarmingly, with the Hanoverians and Whigs voting together, but the motion was defeated by a narrow majority. In the Lords the situation was even more tense. Ever since the 'no peace without Spain' troubles, Oxford had devoted much time and energy to building up an upper House that could be relied on for support; first there had been the creation of the twelve peers, then the gradual removal of recalcitrant Whig placemen, followed, in the summer of 1713, by the acceptance of the 'Queen's list' of Scottish peers, which had been compiled for her by Oxford, with help and advice from his son-in-law Dupplin. Thanks to generous grants of place and pension— the impoverished Earl of Home was liberally furnished with journey money—the delegates from the north were as docile as could be and voted all the way for the government. This was just as well in the difficult days of the Tory split. Knowing how doubtful the Lords' vote might prove, Oxford worked energetically beforehand to assure a majority, and at the time he made one of the best speeches of his career. The motion was defeated by twelve votes—exactly the number created by the Queen on New Year's Day, 1712. 'Saved by your dozen,' Oxford's old enemy, Wharton, told him laconically, when the result was known. Oxford, now thoroughly dependent on the Tories, split though they were, had just managed to scrape home. And a few days later, on April 13, he achieved an even more marginal victory, when a measure brought in by the Whigs concerning safety precautions in the event of the Pretender's arrival, was defeated by a majority of two. On this occasion even the High Tory bishops voted against the Ministry; after all, they themselves had no wish to be governed by a papist King.

Tory support had barely seen Oxford through the crisis; it was largely through his skilful management that a catastrophe had been averted. The party would have been wise to forget its differences, acknowledge Oxford's lead and declare by word and action that it was hearty for Hanover. Oxford himself despatched his cousin Thomas to the Elector's court, and refrained from further correspondence with the Stuart court in Lorraine. But Bolingbroke could not resist the underhand game, and the Jacobite splinter group was still holding its indignation meetings. Thomas Harley was continually alarmed by rumours that orders for his recall were going to be issued from the Secretary's office at the Cockpit, and Erasmus Lewis told him that, in spite of the apparent reconciliation between Oxford and Bolingbroke, things were still very 'disjointed', with the Whigs sitting by waiting for the Tories to tear each other to pieces. 'Happily they have made a push at us,' wrote Erasmus on April 9, 'and we were together yesterday, whether we shall ever be so again I know not.'

The Treasurer had scarcely drawn breath after a vicious attack by Argyll accusing him of bribing Jacobite highlanders, when he was forced to face an even more delicate situation. The Electress Sophia, feeling that old age was at last overtaking her, and fearful lest her ambition would never be fulfilled, wrote, on her own initiative, to Schütz, the Hanoverian agent in London, encouraging him to demand a writ of summons for her grandson, afterwards George II, whose promotion to the English peerage as Duke of Cambridge had already caused controversy. The Duke had every right to sit in the House, but the Queen's aversion to the presence of any of the Hanoverians in her country, and the inflammable situation in general, had made his arrival most undesirable. On the other hand, the English Hanoverians, and Sophia herself, believed that it would render the succession doubly sure if a member of the Elector's family were ensconced in England at the Queen's death. So Schütz delivered his mistress's tactless message to the Lord Chancellor. Harcourt was horrified. He summoned the Cabinet Council at once, and a tense midnight meeting ensued. The Queen was very angry. 'I never saw her Majesty so moved in my life,' Oxford reported. Bolingbroke, feeling that it was to his advantage, took her side and encouraged her to refuse the writ, but

I*

Oxford, always alive to legal arguments, knew that it would have to be issued. Failure to do so was to risk impeachment in the next reign. The Queen, who only a few days ago had herself faced a similar dilemma when forced to decide between setting a price on her brother's head or appearing to support him, now completely failed to appreciate Oxford's predicament. His choice was between the Queen and Hanover, with the law and safety in the next reign on Hanover's side. When he chose Hanover, he fell from favour with absolute finality. Bolingbroke, restored and confident, was delighted to see the Treasurer's discomfiture, and he destroyed in a moment the united front which had been achieved only a fortnight before.

The majority of the Cabinet supported Oxford. With the exception of Bolingbroke, the rash opportunist, members realized that it was a case of backs to the wall. They were saved by the Treasurer's foresight in planting his trustworthy cousin Thomas at Hanover. After the meeting, Oxford went home and wrote a clear and powerfully worded letter intended for the Elector's eyes. This was not the work of a dithering dypsomaniac, but of a wise statesman, used to working himself out of a difficult situation. He guessed, rightly, that the Electress had acted out of turn, without consulting her son, and that Schütz, innocent of the subtleties of English politics, was dabbling dangerously in matters he could not understand. Oxford said that he had tried hard to meet him and help him avoid 'running into mistakes'. There were alarmist rumours that Schütz was busily going from place to place making lists of pro- and anti-Hanoverians. Jacobites blenched at the thought of their names being entered on a black list which would have them booked for certain death if Hanover succeeded. Fear about their fate in the new reign might well force the Jacobites out into open revolt and into a move to bring over the Pretender at once to ensure their own safety. Oxford pointed out that, besides facing the Queen's dislike, the Duke, by coming over, would plunge himself straight in a maelstrom of party politics. The conflict between a popish Pretender and 'the Serene House of Hanover' could change into a more dangerous contest between 'the present possessor and the future successor', with the Tories going to one side and the Whigs to another in a situation that had all the ingredients of civil war. 'I could add many other reasons which make such an attempt stark madness,' Oxford wrote, adding that he personally would do all he could to calm things and show his zeal by voting arrears for the Hanover troops.

The contents of the letter were duly conveyed to the Elector, who took its clear warning and refrained from sending his son to England. Schütz was hastily recalled and, after the death of Sophia at the end of May, the Elector took English affairs into his own hands and saw to it that no further blunders were made. Much harm had already been done, and the Queen's anger was slow to cool. Her health was suffering as a result of her mental turmoil and in May she was reported to be very much indisposed. On May 19, unaware of Oxford's successful efforts to prevent the Duke of Cambridge's arrival, she wrote a very stiff letter to Sophia: 'Propose whatever you think may contribute to the security of the succession, I will come into it with zeal, provided that it does not derogate from my dignity.' The words chilled the old lady's heart. Ten days later, walking in the grounds at Herrenhausen, she collapsed and died there, on one of the public walks, and surrounded by weeping servants. She had lost the race for the throne; she was never to be a Queen, and many said it was Anne's letter that killed her. Sophia, for her part, had destroyed Oxford's favour with the Queen and put an end to his hopes of cementing the Tory party.

Bolingbroke had now cast aside all bonds of loyalty and wisdom. He rallied the High Tories like a pack of hounds, and in May they introduced a Schism Bill aimed at dissenters and planned to ban all those excellent academies, one of which was Oxford's own alma mater. It was the voice of naked intolerance, and Oxford could hardly believe that the Queen was prepared to lend her support to the kind of persecution which for years they had been united in resisting. The principles which Oxford had fought for all his life were now threatened. He could no longer associate himself with the Jacobite group; they had now passed out of his control and were making serious preparations for bringing over the Pretender. Oxford threw himself at the Hanoverians; on May 13 he wrote to Hanmer:

I think the crisis at present so particular, that it is easy to save or to plunge our poor country into unforeseen misery; your concern and mine are the same, I shall be glad to unite with you in joint endeavours. . . . I shall be glad to communicate to you my poor thoughts for the public good.

He made a last stand, raising a sad voice in opposition to the government of which he was now a leader only in name.

CHAPTER 21

QUIETUS

OXFORD HAD TRIED TWICE within six months to resign, but the Queen had clung to him, and Bolingbroke had lost his nerve at the thought of being left to act alone. By May, both of them would gladly have let him go, but he perversely refused to surrender the White Staff. 'The dragon holds fast with a dead gripe the little machine,' wrote Arbuthnot. His general health declined, he began to drink heavily, and his customary good humour deserted him. Tact, and the instinct to leave unsaid the wounding remark, became a deadly furtiveness in which everything seemed a secret. The conflict between Hanover and Lorraine, on top of all the routine worries of the Treasurer's office, had reduced him almost to a state of nervous collapse. He knew that his attempt to mediate between the Queen and one of the great parties had ended in failure and that he, like Godolphin before him, had been forced to surrender to the force of faction. And, saddest of all, the Queen had at last been coerced, and seemed to have forgotten those moderate ideals which in the years of friendship they had both openly accepted. But even now, he did not quarrel with her, or try to force his will on her. If she chose to walk in different ways, he could not stop her, for she was a Queen, and he would never try to browbeat her. 'Let thy words be few,' he wrote at the head of notes made before an interview, 'by long forbear[ing] is a Prince persuaded.'

Oxford had made up his mind about the Pretender. 'Our civil rights . . . cannot be under one bred up in French blasphemies,' he noted in some *Considerations*, written on May 11. He was convinced that some of those '*in power*' had designs against the succession, and that the country was in danger. ' 'Tis plain that the public affairs are in great disorder,' he noted on May 22. But he had worked too hard and too long to fight any more. The party system had beaten him. His pages of jottings, figures, names and lists reveal a mind disordered by work and worry. He had been defeated, too, at his own backstairs game, and it was a cruel blow when he realized that Bolingbroke had won over Lady Masham. His notes, strangely, recall Sarah Marlborough's when she was suffering similar frenzied torments. Abigail's name crosses the page with the same kind of insistence as it broke into the Duchess's jealous ravings, entering his thoughts even when he was wrestling with affairs of state. The Queen had once called Abigail an enchantress; it seemed as if she was a torturer as well:

> . . . a misunderstanding between Mrs Masham and R.H.
> That the Queen complained I never came in time.
> Commissioners, excise
> I have had all my faults displayed to the Queen.

He had for so many years given other people the uneasy feeling that he was working behind their backs, and now he had to suffer himself. He knew that Abigail was putting the Queen against him. Nursing a grievance that he had not allowed her profits he had promised in the South Sea scheme, she rounded off their long association with the gracious words:

You never did the Queen any service, nor are you capable of doing her any.

The Queen complained that he neglected all business, was unintelligible in his speech, always came late and often drunk:

Lastly, to crown all, he behaved to her with bad manners, *indecency*, and disrespect.

Many of Oxford's friends had now deserted him. His group of supporters was nothing more than 'a set of people drawn almost to the dregs'. Some had quarrelled with him, others had grown impatient. Dartmouth and Shrewsbury were alienated, Prior was still abroad, waiting for recognition of his services. Lansdowne did not know whether to go in with Bolingbroke or Oxford; Swift, who was still in England, had despaired of reconciling his friends and retired to Berkshire in disgust. On July 3 he wrote to the Dragon:

In your public capacity you have often angered me to the heart, but as a private man never once. So that if I only looked towards myself I could wish you a private man tomorrow . . . I will add one thing more, which is the highest compliment I can make, that I never was afraid of offending you, nor am now in any pain for the manner I write to you in. I have said enough, and like one at your levee, having made my bow, I shrink back into the crowd.

Swift was ignorant of Bolingbroke's machinations. The Secretary, cheered by the Treasurer's look of dumb suffering during the successful passing of the Schism Bill in June, had thrown caution aside. The French agent, who had seen some strange happenings in his time, now had the bizarre task of running between the Ministers while each begged him to reveal what the other was saying about James—'the Chevalier'. '*Le Cte D'Oxford et My Lord Bolingbroke sont plus mal ensemble que jamais*,' he wrote.

Oxford knew better than anybody what Bolingbroke was about. He tried to break back into the Queen's confidence and warn her of the danger she was in. 'See your condition,' he wrote in a Memorandum for July 4. 'Compare now and the time in 1710.' In those days the gentlemen had been 'fervent, united', but there had been no money and no credit. Now, with the lottery and the peace and the improved financial situation, everything, all the improvements made, were threatened by the succession controversy. He wanted to warn the Queen that, if the Jacobites persisted in their preparations, there was a real danger that Marlborough would return and lead an army for the Opposition. But with Lady Masham refusing to carry messages for him, what hope was there of making contact? 'It is for your service that you reconcile L.M. and O.,' he wrote in his notes for a possible interview. 'Tell them both to have them together. O. will put himself in the wrong.' The Queen did not listen to his warnings; she found it pleasanter to listen to Bolingbroke's eloquent assurances.

The force of Oxford's hatred for Bolingbroke astonished his friends. As one of them put it, 'If he would have taken half so much pains to have done other things, as he has of late to exert himself against the Esquire [Bolingbroke] he might have been a Dragon, instead of a Dagon.' By the end of June Arbuthnot knew that there was little hope of reconciling the two leaders. Early in July, Shrewsbury made a vague attempt to bring them together, but Bolingbroke was suspicious of the Duke. Seeing Oxford and Shrewsbury walking up and down together one day, Bolingbroke pointed at Oxford and remarked, 'I know how I stand with that man, but as to the other I cannot tell.' Shrewsbury gave a dinner party for all the Cabinet Council on July 16, but the Dragon failed to attend; the Duke promptly gave up his peace-making efforts. Swift told Arbuthnot on July 17 that Bolingbroke had *rompu en visière* with the Dragon, in other words had made a clean break, but at the same time did not know how to do without him.

Bolingbroke was in a state of heady excitement, working long hours at the office, revelling in the hero worship of the younger Tories and spending what remained of his nights with a choice mistress. On July 24 it was announced that he was to be created an Earl and given the Garter. As far as he was concerned this was far more important than the task of forming a new Cabinet. Everything seemed to be going his way. Oxford's supporters were deserting him. 'The circle of the Dragon's friends seems very narrow,' Swift reported to Arbuthnot on July 25, 'by the loss we were at for healths, we came to yours 6 glasses before the usual time.' Arbuthnot found that he was persecuted for his loyalty. 'I was told to my face . . . that I did not care if the great person's affairs went to entire ruin, so I could support the interests of the Dragon,' he wrote ruefully. Harcourt, summoned to London, published to all the world that he thought Oxford should be dismissed. '*My Lord Chancelier s'est hautement déclaré contre my Lord D'Oxford*,' Torcy was told. Abigail Masham was more distant than ever; she was in an unbalanced state, uncertain of her own future if the Queen should die and, in Swift's opinion, too distraught to be of use to anybody. 'What she said to the Dragon a week ago is in so desperate a strain, that I cannot think her in a temper to be at the head or the bottom of a change; nor do I believe a change accompanied with such passions can ever succeed.' Swift was anxious about her. 'For God's sake do not leave her to herself,' he begged the doctor. The Dragon's state, too, was distressing. 'He visits, cringes, flatters,' wrote Arbuthnot. 'The Dragon dies hard,' the doctor noticed. 'He is now kicking and cuffing about him like the devil.' Oxford himself observed, in front of Abigail, that it was with great difficulty that he kept his friends from pulling him to pieces.

Defoe was indignant about the treatment Oxford was receiving from his former followers. 'I am capable of judging but by outsides of things, and of knowing little but without doors,' he wrote, 'but when I see those who owe their fortunes to you . . . and with what assurance they tell the world how capable they are to act without your help, when I know the time they could not have stood an hour without you, this tells me their folly and treachery at the same time.' The Harley family too was angered by the way Robin was being treated. Because people believed that he would have little influence in the next reign, whoever came to the throne, they had no further use for him. His relations knew that the Queen was being subjected to 'perpetual teasing' from 'some persons who did not think they grew fast enough under his administration' and so wanted her to part with him.

The propaganda did its work, and the Queen resolved to dismiss her Treasurer. At a Council meeting held on Tuesday, July 27, she taxed him with his faults. The Dragon lost all restraint. He accused Bolingbroke of financial corruption. Angrily his rival replied and a furious quarrel broke out between the two men. The Queen stayed long enough to make it clear to the Treasurer that he was finished. Then, ill and agitated, she was helped from the room.

Abigail wrote to Swift without delay. The Queen, she told him, had 'so far got the better of the Dragon' as to take the power out of his hands. Abigail had no doubt that he deserved such treatment: 'He has been the most ungrateful man to her, and all his best friends, that ever was born.' The Queen was less sure. Many believed that she was loath to part with the man who had been her friend for so many years, and only gave in because of ceaseless pressure from Abigail and Bolingbroke. When the Dragon went to the Palace to deliver up the cherished Staff, she granted him an interview and asked him to give an account of the money he had laid out on her behalf, and which she knew was owing to him. For over two hours they sat and chatted together, in a manner that recalled days that had passed.

That night the Dragon sat down and wrote a rhyme 'in imitation of Dryden,' which pleased him so well that he posted it off to Swift:

> To serve with love,
> And shed your blood
> Approved is above.
> But here below
> The examples show
> 'Tis fatal to be good.

Not for a moment did he doubt his own integrity and good faith. He was as oblivious of his mistakes as he was confident that he had acted selflessly and with the best of intentions. When he wrote to his sister Abigail two days later, enclosing the verse, he expressed his blamelessness and clear conscience almost naively. 'It is my comfort I do go out with as much honour and innocency as I came in . . . God preserve my dearest sister . . . I pray God bless all the little ones.'

The Queen had been in better health recently, but the scene at the Council and the strain of dismissing Oxford proved too much for her delicate constitution:

The people about her—the plagues of Egypt fall on them!—put it out of the power of physic to be of any benefit to her,

wrote Dr Radcliffe. On the day after the dismissal she was subjected to a further ordeal when she attended a Council meeting that went on into the small hours. Tired and anxious, she heard the Ministers argue about the new Commissioners of the Treasury without reaching agreement. They noticed that at times she seemed to be wandering and asked the same question several times over. She seemed most agitated when there was any hint that Bolingbroke might succeed at the Treasury. All through her reign she had been served by two Treasurers whose financial probity she could vouch for, but she knew in her heart that Bolingbroke was unreliable. There had been dark hints that he and Abigail Masham had been involved in a doubtful transaction concerning the South Sea Company; his agent Arthur Moore had been accused of corruption in the same connection. Although Oxford had encouraged the House to proceed with an investigation of the South Sea finances, the Queen had hastily prorogued Parliament to defend her Secretary; all the same, the fact that the cautious Oxford had openly accused Bolingbroke of corruption at the Council meeting, had made a profound impression on her. She could not bring herself to hand on the White Staff to such a man.

That night her pulse rate gave cause for concern and Arbuthnot was sent for. To avoid unnecessary alarm the full complement of royal doctors was not called in at once. The Whig physicians were not informed in case they should come and hear any embarrassing fevered ravings about the Pretender.

Bolingbroke, still unaware of the damage the Treasurer's departure had inflicted on the Queen, went about with a gay countenance. He had received his cherished title and routed his adversary, and now he expected to be created Lord High Treasurer after a decent interval. All the coffers of the realm would soon be within his reach. 'Lord Bolingbroke, and the Chancellor are to rule the world,' wrote Roger Kenyon to his brother George. 'It is said they will be swingeing Tories, and not a Whig left in place a month hence.' In spite of such prophecies, Bolingbroke, the great advocate of firmness, soon crumbled when he was unable to shelter behind the much-maligned Dragon. He was never at his best in a crisis. After the Guiscard incident he had made an exhibition of himself, running about the town bareheaded and crying woe. Whenever the Treasurer had threatened resignation or the Queen had fallen dangerously ill, he had flown into a panic.

Six months and more had elapsed since the Queen's Christmas illness, six months in which to make plans and plot for the Pretender. But Bolingbroke had frittered his time away and now that his hour had come, he found himself without a shadow Cabinet and without the means to establish James Stuart. He had been filling key positions in the army with Jacobites, and completing blank commissions for the Pretender's friends in England, but the process had been too slow to be effective, and he knew, as soon as he realized that the Queen was really ill, that his position was precarious. Panicking once again, he made a sudden *volte face*. Some of the younger Whigs—Walpole, Stanhope, Pulteney and Craggs—were astonished to receive invitations to dine at Bolingbroke's house in Golden Square on July 27. They went, and he appealed to their youth, their energy, and their loyalty. He bribed them with immediate benefits. But they were young enough to take the long-term view. They wanted office, but only on their own terms, and they could wait. For weeks now the Whigs had played the waiting game, and they were prepared to play it a little longer. Bolingbroke had hoped to incite the dissenting Whigs to open rebellion with the Schism Bill, so that he could call in France and the Pretender to put them down. But they had refused to rise, only supporting Oxford when he persuaded the Queen to offer a reward to anyone able to seize the Pretender, should he ever arrive. When Bolingbroke, at the dinner party, embarked on some hypocritical cant about his loyalty to Hanover, they were not impressed; he had, after all, been talking openly for months about his partiality for the House of Stuart. They desired deeds, not words; they wanted the Pretender banished from Lorraine and Marlborough re-installed as General of the forces. These things Bolingbroke had no wish to grant. Put off by the frigidity of his dinner-party guests, he threw in his lot with all the full-blooded Jacobites he could find and took panic measures to accelerate the infiltration of the army.

But time was running out. On July 29 the Queen complained of violent pains in her head and was obviously very ill. The cupping administered the previous day by Tory doctors had given temporary relief and no more; they could no longer hide the seriousness of her condition from the Whig doctors and the general public. The full complement of physicians was alerted, including Sir David Hamilton who recorded a trembling of the hands, and nose-bleed. The usual remedies were applied; 'her Majesty had the help of vomiting thrice by the help of cardis,' according to Peter Wentworth. Blisters were tried, and garlic applied to the feet. On the 30th her condition worsened and she suffered a severe seizure, lying 'unsensible' for two hours. Nobody could say that the doctors did not try hard; bleeding, further vomiting and a special concoction made up by a Dr Mead temporarily revived her. But the Duchess of Ormonde, who was in waiting, felt that the end was near, and she sent an urgent message to her husband to tell the members of the Privy Council, who were meeting at the Cockpit, that the situation was serious.

It had been a strange meeting. The Jacobites had arrived in force—Bolingbroke and his friend Sir William Wyndham, Ormonde, his name for ever associated with the Restraining Orders, Buckingham, who had waited a long time for this day, and Lansdowne, still unsure whether he preferred Oxford or Bolingbroke. They were all in the dark about Bolingbroke's plans, if he had any, and Wyndham, for one, was under no illusions. 'It is an impracticable man, and will never be brought in,' he had shocked Lansdowne by saying, as they drove out to Kensington together on the day after Oxford's fall. 'The man of Mercury's bottom is too narrow, his faults of the first magnitude, and we cannot find there is any scheme in the world how to proceed,' wrote Erasmus Lewis, summing up the situation with a detachment which the bewildered Jacobites could not achieve.

The moderates, appalled by the latest turn of events, were determined to avoid having a Jacobite at the head of affairs at the moment of the Queen's death. The Hanoverian 'Whimsicals', Shrewsbury, Robinson, and Dartmouth, all went to the meeting and were joined by Somerset and Argyll who, as members of the Privy Council, had a right to attend. Bolingbroke quailed as he saw them walk in. The political fact which had governed Oxford's whole life dawned on him just at this moment, and he realized that, although the moderates on their own were powerless, they had for years held the balance and they could still hold it now. Frightened by this thought, Bolingbroke did yet another *volte face*, so unexpected that even his own followers were staggered. He made an impromptu speech about the need for the Hanoverian Succession and suggested that Shrewsbury should be made Treasurer forthwith. He was prompted to take this decision by the sudden realization that if the Queen should die before anyone was appointed, Oxford would still be considered Treasurer and as such, *ex officio*, one of the Regents. Anything was better than that. Nobody argued, and the meeting broke up at once, though Bolingbroke himself, according to Defoe, 'rose up expressing himself softly, so as very few heard him to the purpose, "Well, if it must be so!" '

The Lords, headed by Shrewsbury and Somerset, were admitted to the Queen's chamber. Harcourt guided the Queen's hand towards Shrewsbury, who received the White Staff without enthusiasm. The Queen was conscious but unable to say anything except aye or no, and later in the day she relapsed into a coma.

The Council sat all that day and far into the night with Shrewsbury in the chair. 'I resolved,' Bolingbroke later wrote, 'not to abandon my party by turning Whig, or, *which is a great deal worse, whimsical*.' He changed his mind, and abandoned his Jacobites, all within the space of a few days, giving more than passive assent to the hurried preparations being made to proclaim the Elector's accession. The bewildered Lansdowne saw messengers, all ready booted and spurred, waiting in the anteroom for the Queen to breathe her last, before setting off post-haste for Hanover.

The Queen died in the early hours of Sunday, August 1 at the age of forty-nine. 'I believe sleep was never more welcome to a weary traveller than death was to her,' wrote Dr Arbuthnot.

The Jacobites, abandoned by Bolingbroke, were in confusion. Ormonde consulted the Bishop of Rochester, Atterbury, about the best means of proclaiming James King of England. The Bishop, who should have been preaching peacefully in his pulpit on this particular day of the week, offered to proclaim the Pretender at Charing Cross in his lawn sleeves. Spence has it that the more cautious Ormonde wanted to consult the Council before taking such an irremediable step. 'Damn it, sir,' said Atterbury in a great heat (for he did not value swearing), 'you know very well that things have not been concerted enough for that yet, and that we have not a moment to lose.' Fortunately the Bishop was dissuaded from making such a foolhardy gesture. And, in chapels all over the country, dissenters were openly offering up thanks, for this was the very day that the Schism Act was scheduled to take effect, and they realized that under a Hanoverian King they, and their academies, could live in freedom.

The members of the Privy Council summoned to Kensington, as the Queen quietly let go her last hold on life, repaired to St James's Palace and proclaimed the new King, George I of England. The Council, comprised of men of all parties, and united in the emergency, had seen to it that the forces were under the right leadership, that all available troops and trained bands were alerted, and Catholics under strict watch. The five hundred or so extreme Jacobites who had nursed such bold schemes of a Stuart King were incapable of action. As Bolingbroke put it in his *Letter to Sir William Wyndham*:

The thunder had long grumbled in the air; and yet when the bolt fell, most of our party appeared as much surprised as if they had had no reason to expect it. There was a perfect calm and submission through the whole kingdom.

What Defoe called 'the solidity of the constitution' had triumphed. The laws, framed so long ago in the Act of Settlement, automatically guarded the Protestant Succession, and the Regents chosen by George after the death of his mother saw to it that the scene was set for the new King's arrival. And, although Oxford himself took no part in it, he deserved some of the credit for the peaceful hand-over. Many Jacobites, those 'stupefied people', believed, according to Defoe, that 'this damned Staff gave them the *coup de grâce*'. It was his exquisite management that brought the Scottish Jacobites to London, flattered them with false hopes, and lulled them into thinking that everything would come to them if they only co-operated and made no plans. Involved as they were in affairs at Westminster, they had no chance to go to the hills and rally the fierce clansmen. They realized, too late, that Oxford had made tools of them. When their opportunity came, they found themselves unable to move, betrayed, as they thought, by Oxford, and deserted by Bolingbroke.

For a few days after the Queen's death, Bolingbroke went about with a cheerful appearance, hoping that his fervent protestations of loyalty to the House of Hanover would provide a passport to the new King's favour. But he really knew that the game was up, and he wrote to Swift, 'The Earl of Oxford was removed on Tuesday, the Queen died on Sunday. What a world this is, and how does fortune banter us.' He was only thirty-six and his career in politics was over. Soon the Seals were taken from him, and he left London, his marriage broken, his heady flight to fame curtailed. He fell, Defoe wrote, 'unpitied of every side'.

There were many who regretted Oxford's fall. His family was sure that he had been treated with the greatest injustice. The Queen's death restored a sense of proportion in those who had deserted him. Even before she died, many people had written expressing apprehension about the effects of his dismissal. Dr Stratford wrote from Oxford on July 29:

I heartily congratulate your Lordship upon your 'quietus'. My concern is only as to the public consequences of it, in which I hope we shall have our shares in proportion to our stake.

After all the years of friendship, the Dragon might have expected to be at the Queen's side, at the last, but he resisted all appeals to come, though he appeared briefly at the last Privy Council of the reign. Bromley wrote to him and Lord Lansdowne sent a message by Dupplin urging him to come: 'The very worst is to be apprehended. In my opinion your father should not be absent, but he knows best.' Carmarthen, Oxford's widower son-in-law, wrote from Badminton on August 2, 'I am sorry to hear your Lordship is no longer Treasurer, but I assure you you will find me truly dutiful in everything towards the father of my late dear wife.' Paul Foley thought that his kinsman's removal might prove to be 'the alarm bell to the Protestant religion', and the Duchess of Shrewsbury said 'I wish with all my heart you was in still'. Defoe set out to write a searing vindication of Oxford's person and conduct, part of which was already in the press at the time of the Queen's death. Oxford did not altogether welcome the work, which was later published as *The Secret History of the White Staff*, because he felt that his career needed no apology.

All the hangers-on who had depended on the Dragon's largesse for a living were thrown into gloom. The disreputable Mrs Manley, whom Swift had sub-contracted to pen the more horrible attacks on ministerial enemies, lamented the fact that she was unable to save anything from the general wreck. And the literary men who had enjoyed so many pleasant evenings in the presence of their patron, prime minister and friend, mourned for the days that had gone for ever. 'Then it was,' wrote Pope and Parnell from Binfield to Dr Arbuthnot, 'that the immortal Scriblerus smiled upon our endeavours, who now hangs his head in an obscure corner, pining for his friends that are scattering over the face of the earth.' Prior was still in Paris, wondering what was to happen now that the 'sovereign dame' was dead and his two patrons had fallen. 'Am I to go to Fontainebleau? Am I to come home? Am I to be looked upon? Am I to hang myself?' he enquired.

For Abigail Masham, the demise of the monarch was an even greater disaster. She was stricken with genuine grief, heightened by the knowledge that her unique career was at an end. She and her sister, it was said, 'roared and cried enough whilst there was life, but as soon as there was none they took care of themselves'. Lady Masham's apartments were rapidly fitted up for the King's son and his children, and by the end of August that notorious 'she-artist', as Defoe had the kindness to call her, vanished completely from the public scene, taking, it was rumoured, a considerable sum of money with her into obscurity.

As Abigail went, so her old rival returned. The Marlboroughs landed at Dover on August 2; cheering crowds greeted their arrival and their way was strewn with flowers. The General was reinstated, but although he was given command of the army, the new King never forgave him for his spasmodic flirtation with Saint-Germain. The Duchess said that she was ready to go on her knees and beg him not to accept any favours, for she was anxious to spare him the humiliations which are the concomitants of power. In spite of bad health, the General lived to enjoy a few years of retirement, watching the growth of Blenheim and spending leisurely hours at Holywell, the house at St Albans which he had often thought of with longing in the heat and dust of his campaigns.

It was the Duchess of Somerset who watched and waited at the Queen's deathbed, all ready and installed for the next reign. At the funeral, 'Carrots' headed the procession, supported by a barrage of duchesses and at least ten countesses. The sad occasion was postponed until the fourth week in August to allow the ladies to obtain the necessary funeral garments, and was carried out, according to the Queen's own instructions, 'in all particulars . . . like that of the late Prince George'.

There was no harm in trying to start well with the new King, and in August Oxford despatched a letter to Hanover:

August 6–17, 1714. Sire, I beseech your Majesty to accept the most dutiful congratulations [which] can be offered by a faithful subject upon your Majesty's accession to the throne of your ancestors. I had the honour in the two preceding reigns to express my love to my country by promoting what is now come to pass, your Majesty's succession to the crowns of these kingdoms. It remains now that I assure your Majesty I shall study to show the zeal and devotion wherewith I am, Sire, your Majesty's most dutiful, most humble and most obedient subject.

Oxford had flirted with Saint-Germain far less assiduously than many statesmen of the time. Under pressure from Bolingbroke and the Jacobites he had written to James suggesting that he should change his religion—and probably knowing there was little chance that he would ever do so. But these dealings with Saint-Germain had been played up and exaggerated by Oxford's enemies.

In September, when he heard the Tower guns announce the fact that George had landed at Greenwich, Oxford wrote to his son Edward expressing his intention of making his court at the first possible moment. On September 21, as dusk was falling, the King's procession reached the Strand, accompanied by a vast mob. News of appointments and dismissals was flying about the town. 'Zeal for the succession and loyalty will not be extraordinary advocates for any to keep their places,' Oxford wrote on the 23rd to his son Edward. And it was evident that the King had listened to Oxford's detractors and forgotten the helpful letter written to Thomas Harley at the time of the crisis over the Duke of Cambridge's writ. Whatever hopes Oxford may have nursed of success in the new reign were dashed when he came face to face with George I.

Dorset introduced him. 'Here is the Earl of Oxford, of whom your Majesty must have heard,' he said. His Germanic Majesty gave the ex-Treasurer his hand to kiss, followed by a cold, unpromising stare.

CHAPTER 22

AN INSIGNIFICANT OLD MAN

'I DO NOT WONDER at your being out at Court, if you can't slide well, for 'tis very slippery ground,' wrote the Earl of Chesterfield to Matthew Prior. And Oxford soon found out that there was no foothold for him, or for his old 'gang'. It would not have been easy to acclimatize himself to a retinue of Germans, and although he had been adept at whispering pleasantries into the ear of a Queen, to make himself agreeable to a foreign King and the two hideous royal mistresses was hardly in his line. He was anyway worn out with the stress of public life and had little vigour to compete in the battle for power. His remaining friends at court had little influence; Shrewsbury laid down the Treasurer's Staff at the first possible moment, and Dartmouth, Oxford's 'dearest lord', remained faithful but could do little for him. Halifax, who had always liked Oxford and had advised him on financial affairs, was not given the power he expected in the new reign. He wanted to be made Lord Treasurer and felt embittered when he was given nothing higher than the Presidency of the Treasury Commission. The King veered towards the new generation of Whigs, headed by Walpole, those bright young men whom Bolingbroke had invited to dinner in Golden Square. The old Junto, soon to be decimated by the death of several of its members, never came back with its old authority.

Oxford looked forward to retirement, and he let the King know that he intended to withdraw from the fray. He enjoyed the prospect of having leisure to savour life in the country, to attend to his estate and to appreciate the collection of rare manuscripts which his librarian, Humphrey Wanley, had been building up during the years of office. The library, which included three thousand printed books, thirteen thousand charters, deeds and fragments of parchment, and a number of letters of historical interest, was valued at over £4,000, a large sum for those times. Wanley believed that the collection of charters and rolls was one of the largest in the world. Oxford planned to build a special library to house his treasures, perhaps on the land adjoining the Palace of St James, which the Queen had granted to him when she appointed him Housekeeper of the Palace in 1703. The first indication that he was to be actively persecuted in the new reign came when he received hints that the King intended to rob him of this post and of the house and ground which went with it—'after fifty years of public life,' he scrawled bitterly, and with some exaggeration, on a scrap of paper which had notes about the surrender of the house and the salary due to him as Housekeeper. The Queen had granted him the house and land for thirty-one years, but the King went to the lengths of purchasing it back for £7,500 after a special Act of Parliament. Oxford knew then that he was to receive nothing in recognition of his service. He bowed to the King's command, stipulating only that he should be allowed to keep the house until his daughter-in-law, Lady Henrietta, who was to lie-in there, 'be in a condition to remove'.

Reading the signs, and anxious not to cause unnecessary offence, Oxford sold his house in York Buildings and moved his library to Edward's house at Wimpole. This in itself was a formidable task, involving bleak journeys to Cambridgeshire in mid-winter. He caught a bad cold at the coronation and soon afterwards was seized with rheumatism and strangury. In January 1715, when he was still in town, rumours began to circulate that the Ministry had seized the Earl of Strafford's papers relating to the peace negotiations, and everyone knew that this boded ill for 'the men of Utrecht'—Bolingbroke, Oxford and Ormonde.

Bolingbroke tried to appear unconcerned; he continued to make his brilliant witty speeches and hoped that people remembered the outsize bonfire he had lit outside his door in Golden Square to celebrate the arrival of the King he had done his best to keep away:

> And for those who did conspire
> For to bring in James Esquire
> Now hoped to be saved by their own bonfire
> Doctors agree they are never the higher
> Teste Jonathan

as Oxford had put it in his usual bad verse. At the new year, Bolingbroke's nerve, never strong at times of danger, began to weaken; when Marlborough, poker-faced as ever, warned him in a secret interview that the Ministry intended to try him and had enough against him to cut off his head, he made immediate plans to bolt. That same evening, March 26, after appearing at the theatre, he set out for France disguised as a valet in a black bob wig and very ordinary clothes. For once in a lifetime, Bolingbroke was anxious to forget the fact that he was 'out of the common herd'. Safely in France, he established himself as the Pretender's Secretary, until even the exiled Prince grew tired of his tendency to blurt out state secrets to his many mistresses.

Marlborough's ruse had only been a bow at a venture, but Bolingbroke's sudden flight was taken to be an admission of guilt. The more cautious Oxford had less to fear, for he had always been careful not to commit himself on paper, and his obscure style had usually prevented him from saying anything very definite. His letter asking the Pretender to change his religion was safely in France, and there too, if James is to be believed, the sense was so muddled that it would have been useless as evidence.

Oxford was at Brampton when he heard the news of Bolingbroke's defection. His son Edward wrote urging him to come to London at once and to take great care of any papers he had in his possession:

It is very happy that your Lordship was not here before this flight, which will now precipitate their proceedings. They have moved for all the papers relating to the peace to be laid before the House of Commons this day, and it is said they will immediately proceed upon them; I therefore hope this will find you on the road, for your absence now will be of very ill consequence. . . . The Almighty, who has so often delivered, will, I trust, in His boundless mercy, yet protect and preserve you from the rage of violent men.

The Dragon refused to give way to alarm, and he wrote his son a brief but soothing reply:

3 April 1715 Brampton Castle. I received yours this morning, and, though my health and other affairs require my stay in the country, I am making all the haste I can towards you as the roads will permit me. I pray God give us a comfortable meeting.

At Brampton, walking one evening with the Auditor, Robin calmly outlined his plans. 'That which is called common prudence,' he said, 'might prompt me to avoid the storm that I see is falling upon me, but having thoroughly considered this matter, and not being conscious to myself of doing any one thing that is contrary to the interest of my country, I am come to an absolute conclusion to resign myself to the Providence of the Almighty, and not either by flight, or any other way to sully the honour of my Royal Mistress, though now in her grave, nor stain my own innocence even for an hour.' He warned the Auditor that as soon as they returned to London they would be put under pressure to leave the country, but although flight might seem prudent, nothing would persuade him to make a gesture that would convict him of treachery. 'There are but two ways,' he added, 'for a man to die with real honour, the one is by suffering martyrdom for his religion, the other by dying a martyr for his country.'

Robin knew enough about the implacable malice of the Whigs to realize that he was in real danger. Walpole, understandably, felt vindictive towards those who had impeached him so unjustly in 1711; Bolingbroke, his real persecutor, had escaped, so he turned his attention to the man who had never approved of the impeachment, and who had endangered his whole position with the Tory party by refusing to carry out a purge of the Whigs. 'They make no distinction between your Lordship and my Lord Bolingbroke'; one of Oxford's agents had pointed out. Many people, seeing Bolingbroke vanish at the first whisper of trouble, believed that Oxford would fly to the continent too, all the more so as Bolingbroke had kindly offered up his book of letters relating to the Peace.

Lord Coningsby, the Harleys' rival in the border country, announced confidently in the Commons that the Queen's First Minister had absconded. At this, the Auditor rose to his feet. 'The person the Lord means', he said, 'is so far either from absconding or flying, that he came last night to his own house in London, where he is resolved to remain, being determined to justify his conduct, which, if he could not do, he would think his blood too small a sacrifice to atone for anything he had done against the liberties of his country.' The Auditor was advised by 'a certain person,' who handed him a bill drawn on a banker in Paris for unlimited credit, to make his brother vanish over the sea. When he was told this, Oxford simply said, 'I am unalterably fixed in my first resolution.'

The Ministry realized that as yet they had a very meagre case against the ex-Treasurer. Nothing of an incriminating nature had been discovered, and his confidence that nothing ever would be was distinctly unnerving. In April a Secret Committee was formed, with Walpole in the chair. Its brief was to inquire into the Peace of Utrecht, and after two months it produced a bulky report containing 'matters of the highest importance'. On June 9 Walpole acquainted the House that before he read the report he would ask the Speaker to issue a warrant for the arrest of several people, including Prior, who had returned from France in March, and Oxford's cousin Harley.

The news of the forthcoming impeachments, caused a great stir in London. Oxford attended the Lords as usual, 'notwithstanding this affair,' wrote Sir Thomas Cave, 'which I believe will be the worst bout he ever had, for with more warmth was nobody ever followed.' The trained bands were called out to control the crowds and special guards were posted at Westminster.

On July 10 the impatient and irascible Coningsby rose to his feet when Walpole had finished moving the impeachment of Bolingbroke, a motion, incidentally, which was carried without a division. Coningsby— 'the great hangman', as Ned called him—then put into words what many of his colleagues would rather have left unsaid, since they considered the evidence too slender to justify a trial in Oxford's case:

The worthy Chairman of the Committee has impeached the hand, but I do impeach the head; he has impeached the Clerk, and I the justice; he has impeached the scholar, and I the master; I impeach Robert Earl of Oxford and Earl Mortimer of high treason and other crimes and misdemeanours.

Having made his point, the honourable member for Leominster sat down, well pleased. He had hoped to see his enemy's head on the block after the Greg affair, and now felt certain that this time he would achieve his aim.

Foley and the Auditor made courageous speeches in Oxford's defence and there were even Whigs brave enough to say that there were insufficient grounds for an impeachment. 'The Treasurer's [Oxford] letter and history of himself to the Queen made the House exceeding merry,' Addison reported, and he added that Walpole 'humoured' the letters very well as he read them out. Many Whigs pinned their hopes on Prior, believing him to be the one person who might be able to produce damning evidence.

Prior and Thomas Harley were under house arrest for a week before they were called before the Secret Committee. The two men lived within a few doors of each other in Duke Street and even dined with each other during the week before Prior's examination by the Committee. It is almost certain that the Auditor and young Edward, and possibly Oxford himself, visited him, though Prior denied that he conferred with Oxford:

On Sunday going to dine with Mr Harley, I saw my Lord of Oxford at the stairhead, going out; that I asked him if he dined with us. He told me, he was to dine in better company.

Whether he was primed by the Harley family or not, Prior was more than a match for the Committee. He was able to say in all honesty that it was the Queen and not the Treasurer who had sent him to France to conduct the first secret negotiations, and he offered to produce the original note written in the Queen's hand and signed 'A.R.'. He swore that he could not remember whether Oxford had been present at the meeting when the Preliminaries were first discussed. This annoyed the Committee and Coningsby began to lose his temper and demand that letters from Oxford should be produced. 'You know, my Lord,' said Prior suavely, 'that your countryman is no very exact correspondent':

This I said [explained Prior] having known that my Lord Coningsby had troubled great men, if not my Lord Treasurer particularly, with letters, who had never taken care to answer him. I grant this was very foolishly said; for one should never provoke a hedge-hog.

Prior revealed nothing, and was condemned to twelve months' close confinement. 'One of the most villainous outrages that ever were made upon the liberty of an Englishman' was the Auditor's verdict. 'I believe he is the first person in any Christian country,' wrote Swift, 'that ever was suffered to starve after having been in so many great employments. But among the Turks and Chineses it is a very frequent case, and those are the properest precedents for us at this time.'

The Committee realized that it had drawn a blank, but would not give up. Lady Dupplin told Abigail Harley that a longer time than usual was allowed to lapse before the charge was carried up to the House of Lords, to give Oxford another chance to escape. 'Knowing his innocence,' wrote Lady Dupplin, 'he is resolved to stand it; . . . it is a comfort that he is not guilty of any crime, and I hope his innocence will appear.' On June 14, her father dined with her; he seemed well and very cheerful, and she was in hopes that he had at last mended his ways. 'He now keeps regular hours of dining and going to bed, if he would continue that I hope it would be of a great advantage to his health.' But the strain proved too much for his constitution, even though he refused to be frightened, and towards the end of June his wife came hurrying up from Brampton, alarmed to hear that her 'dear Lord' had been obliged to call in Dr Mead— for Dr Radcliffe had died of an apoplexy earlier in the year—and was feeling very ill. She wrote her sister-in-law one of the very few letters in her hand which are to be found among the Harley papers:

I am to return my dear sister thanks for her very kind letter, and for her extraordinary kindness to me at such a time, when I am under the greatest trouble . . . I am told that my Lord doth not fear Coningsby nor [his] pack of bloodhounds. I pray God deliver him out of their hands.

During the last week in June and the first in July, Ormonde was impeached on a charge of treason, for which many people pitied him, and Lord Strafford was accused of 'high crimes and misdemeanours'. Coningsby announced that he would find proof of the Pretender having been seen at Oxford's house, and set about suborning a servant who had once served in the Harley household. 'Sure there never was such wild doings,' wrote Lady Dupplin.

Many Whigs still believed that the most they could do was to accuse Oxford of pursuing a bad policy, and if politicians could be put on trial for that, few would enter such a dangerous profession. Sir Joseph Jekyll, Chief Justice of Chester and a member of the Secret Committee, declared that he thought the proceedings were 'slightly founded and straining the law'. This, the Auditor reported, threw the whole party into great confusion, and provoked such a storm that the Speaker was moved to inquire 'whether they were impeaching the Lord Oxford or Sir J. Jekyll'. Coningsby's motion that the ex-Treasurer should be impeached on a charge of high treason was voted by 280 and 'Mr Walpole swore that if 280 would not make him fly, the Devil was in him, for there was no such man living in the world'. Once again, Oxford's courage caused widespread admiration. 'Sure he is very happy that can be cheerful and easy amidst so much ill usage,' reflected Lady Dupplin.

On the night of July 9, Lord Coningsby carried the Articles of Impeachment up to the Lords. In the long debate that followed, voices were raised in Oxford's defence. The Earl of Anglesey, the Whimsical Hanoverian, said that such cruel proceedings 'would shake the sceptre in the King's hand', at which Sunderland rose angrily and said 'no man dared say that without the House nor none ought to say it within'. The Dragon himself was in agonies from an attack of the gravel

yet was he so supported by the Almighty that, notwithstanding the very great pain of the gravel and rheumatism under which he then laboured, his defence of his Royal Mistress, the liberty of the Peers and his own, was maintained with so much firmness of mind that the speech he then made fetched tears either of rage or compassion from the greatest of his enemies; the Duke of Marlborough himself saying that he could not but envy him that under such circumstances could talk in such a manner with so much resolution.

'I shall lay down my life with pleasure in a cause favoured by my late dear royal mistress,' Oxford finished.

He was acquitted by the Lords, but an order was made for committal into custody, and in view of his illness he was allowed to remain at his house under the care of Black Rod for a few days. He was accompanied from Westminster to his house at St James's by a cheering mob that cried out he was acquitted, which caused consternation in the Whig coffee houses, and so alarmed the King that he left his supper in great confusion.

Many begged Oxford to take this last chance to escape, but he had said in his speech that he was 'unconcerned for the life of an insignificant old man' and he always replied 'I know how to die but cannot fly'. On July 12 an order committing him to the Tower was passed by 80 votes to 55 and it was rumoured that five more articles were being brought against him which even the lawyers would have to accept. He was allowed a few more days at his own house and on July 16, though by no means recovered, he went with Black Rod to the Tower at eight o'clock in the evening. He agreed to go by a quiet route, avoiding the Strand and Fleet Street where a large crowd was waiting to cheer him and insult Black Rod, but even so he was accompanied by a sympathetic mob with many huzzas and cries of 'High Church and down with the Whigs'. His son and son-in-law, Lords Harley and Dupplin, with the Auditor, two doctors and all his servants, went with him to the Tower, but after an hour he was left alone with his wife, a chambermaid and two footmen. At first he lodged with one Mr Tollet, who had been one of his 'dependents' and who looked after him with honesty and gratitude, but his enemies believed that he was too comfortable and prevailed upon the Lieutenant of the Tower, Mr Compton, to have him moved to different lodgings. Although he was still very ill, he was moved late at night to new rooms where 'taking a fresh cold, his pains grew so very severe, that for many months he was neither able to put on his clothes or feed himself". In spite of this, neither his pain nor his imprisonment robbed him of his sereneness and composure. 'Your heroic and Christian behaviour under this prosecution,' wrote Swift, 'astonisheth everyone but me, who know you so well, and know how little it is in the power of human actions or events to discompose you.'

So began the long imprisonment of the last high-ranking statesman to be immured in the Tower. During the first three months he was too ill to put pen to paper, but later he wrote many affectionate letters to his family, with frequent references to 'sweet Peggy', the small daughter of Edward and Harriet. The happy outcome of his supreme stroke of match-making never ceased to give him comfort. 'It is a great pleasure of my life to see you so mutually happy in each other,' he wrote. In October, just as he was gaining strength, he was struck down with a virulent fever. Lady Oxford nursed him through it with great tenderness, sitting up with him night after night until she herself was exhausted. He wasted away almost to a skeleton, but on November 16, for the first time since July, he was able to put on his coat and move about the room. Thereafter, although he still suffered from his old complaint from time to time, and was often so crippled with rheumatism that he was unable to write, his health improved and he was able to enjoy reading the books his son brought for him, and to take an interest in such domestic matters as the teething troubles of 'pretty Mrs Peggy Cavendish'.

The world outside bothered him little. A month after he was imprisoned, the King of France died, bringing a final finish to the affairs of the old era. The crowns of Spain and France were separated, confounding the critics who had gloomily foretold that they would be joined under Philip of Anjou, and justifying the architects of the Peace of Utrecht. 'The powers of Europe had never been poised with so much equality since the dissolution of the Roman Empire,' wrote the Auditor. Safely in the Tower, Oxford was saved from any false accusations of playing a part in the '15, the Pretender's ill-planned and desperate attempt to capture the throne from the uninspiring and unpopular George; but soon the prison was overflowing with friends, including Lord Lansdowne and others taken at Preston. Lord Dupplin was among those seized and sent to the Tower, and Lady Dupplin, about to give birth to her fifth child, suffered 'barbarous treatment' at this time.

Many of those who were imprisoned far more justifiably than Oxford, and who had actively, if ineffectively, plotted for the Pretender, were tried and released in the summer of 1716, but he was destined to stay for a whole year longer. In April 1716 he admitted to Dartmouth that his very great stock of patience was almost exhausted and he complained of 'perpetual imprisonment . . . without remedy either for my liberty, or what is the dearest thing to me, my reputation'. He had been forced out of country retirement to face exorbitant charges and a long refusal by the Lords to listen to his petition or fix a date for his trial. 'Had I absconded, had I tampered with witnesses . . .' he wrote. But there was nothing Dartmouth could do.

Oxford had spent most of his political life fighting the excesses of faction, and by strange justice, it was faction that saved him. The Whigs were soon rent with dissension. In the first rush of confidence, they passed the Septennial Act, thus establishing themselves in power for seven years, and they also voted for a standing army which they felt was called for after the effects of the '15. These were the very measures which the young Robin Harley had opposed so vocally in the reign of William. 'I came late last night from the funeral of the Triennial Act,' wrote the Auditor on April 25, 1716, 'which I wish may not prove the interment of the liberties of England, for what may not be expected from a standing Army and Parliament?' Townshend and Walpole, in the opinion of the Auditor,

QUEEN ANNE AT A GARTER INVESTITURE, 1713

ROBERT HARLEY, EARL OF OXFORD

now looked upon themselves as absolute dictators; 'these two haughty ministers never perceived their approaching fall, till they found the very ground on which they stood beginning to sink under them.' Sunderland, unchastened by the sad death of his wife, was still as aggressive as ever; and he accused the younger Ministers of making trouble with the Prince of Wales while his father was in Hanover. Jealousy of his heir bedevilled the King's life, and once the suspicion was planted, he did not waste much time in removing Townshend and Walpole. In the fury which ensued some of the Whigs were kind enough to take Oxford's side.

As the term of imprisonment dragged on, some people advised Oxford to petition for leave to go into exile, but with exemplary patience he refused to bring his own case for fear of jeopardizing anybody else in custody. It was not until May 1717, almost two years after his committal to the Tower, that he felt able to petition the Lords for his trial. Even now he feared that the Whig majority would vote against him, but he had not been in politics for so many years without being able to recognize a government split when he saw one and he felt that it was time to see what he could do. By an extraordinary reversal, Walpole, Chairman of the Secret Committee, now joined with Tories and Jacobites to secure his acquittal. It would have been too inconsistent on their part to move for his immediate release, in view of all they had said about him in the past, so they resorted to a political ruse so cunning that one is tempted to believe it can only have been suggested by Oxford himself. The Whigs still hoped to succeed with vague charges of 'high crimes and mis-demeanors', even though they had given up hopes of proving him guilty of high treason. Oxford's supporters in the Lords moved that the treason clause should be taken first; the Commons were angered at such a motion coming from the upper house and huffily alleged an infringement of their privilege. It soon developed into the old conflict between Lords and Commons; the Commons refused to maintain the prosecution and when the Lords finally assembled in Westminster Hall for the trial, no prosecutor appeared, no charge was maintained and the prisoner was acquitted, to the joy of his relations and the fury of Lady Marlborough who was 'distracted with disappointment'.

On his release from prison, Oxford received the King's order not to come into the royal presence nor to court. He made this an excuse to absent himself from Garter services and took little part in public life. His library was now catalogued and housed at Wimpole, and he took an active and expert interest in the collection. 'The Dragon, I suppose has convinced your Lordship of the vellum as impracticable, improbable,

K

impossible,' Prior wrote to Ned Harley. Nowadays, however, it was Ned who made most of the new purchases. Robin had time now to enjoy his family, Lord and Lady Dup and the little Dups—'Duppliniana', as Prior affectionately called them:

'Thursday,' says Lady Dupplin in a soft voice, 'we dine with my father, and he will take it very ill if you don't come, for he ordered me to invite you in great form.' And before this dinner is half digested, at that memorable moment when the toasted cheese appears, 'Prior you dine with me to-morrow, for we must to Richardson's before dinner. I'll call you at one, pray be ready.' Friday—that 'one' is three.

Unpunctual as ever, the Dragon still enjoyed good company and was extremely proud of his grandchildren. There was Lord Danby, 'a sweet child', son of 'the glorious Lady Carmarthen', and Tommy Haye, the Dupplin heir, whom Lady Pye considered to be one of the finest youths she had ever seen. He took the part of Cordelio the page in *The Orphan*, acted by the Westminster scholars, and did it 'mighty well' in the opinion of his mother; Erasmus Lewis thought his performance 'much beyond what I thought possible for a child of his age'. Prior wrote a prologue for the occasion which the lordling recited. 'Little mistress Peggy' was the Harleys' only child, but she was a favourite both of her grandfather and of Matthew Prior, who wrote, 'I never saw an angel, though I have read much of them but, I fancy, she is very like one. She has no wings, indeed, but she has legs that carry her so lightly that it is a question if she flies, or no.' The poet wrote a charming verse offering good advice:

> In double beauty say your prayer,
> Our Father first, then *notre Père*.
> And, dearest child, along the day,
> In everything you do or say
> Obey and please my Lord and Lady,
> So God shall love, and angels aid ye.

The inquiry had revealed that Prior was one of Oxford's 'creatures' and in gratitude for his loyalty and skill when facing the Committee, Lord Harley took care of the poet, offering him gifts of turkey, beef, brawn and beer and allowing him the liberty of his house at Wimpole, where he could enjoy 'the best books all the morning and the most desirable company all the afternoon'. Harley also bought Down Hall, a house in Essex, for Matt to live in, and although at first sight the poet thought it nothing more than 'a low ruined white shed', looking as if 'all the cross unmathematical devils upon earth first put it together', he spent many happy hours planning the alterations.

Many friends deserted Oxford at the crisis, including Swallow Poulett, for many years so faithful. Dartmouth, Shrewsbury and Swift were among those who never betrayed him. Swift often talked of visiting the Dragon in Herefordshire, but although they corresponded occasionally, they never met again. With his 'gang' dispersed and no favour at court, a political come-back was obviously out of the question, though he watched affairs with some interest and noted down a few critical comments about current policy:

Loss of trade—fresh war—Acts of Parl. formerly advanced trade, now spoil it—the Prince and his favourites—Secret favourites a burden to his master.

Early in 1718 he made a rough 'Memorandum about coin' prior to speaking in the coinage debate, and a short while after he opposed both the Mutiny Bill and the Peerage Bill; the first he considered an infringement of civil liberty and the second a threat to the constitution. The Peerage Bill laid down that the existing number of peers could not be increased by more than six and also proposed that the sixteen elected peers from Scotland should be replaced by twenty-five hereditary noblemen. The Bill was introduced by Sunderland, and Oxford seemed temporarily rejuvenated as he opposed his hated rival from the past. The Scottish peers showed great gratitude for his support, and many Commoners did too, for it was generally agreed that in the future, should the Bill succeed, very few Commoners would be promoted, and the whole strengthening process of replenishing the peerage from the middle classes would be lost. On April 14, Sunderland announced that the Peerage Bill would be dropped; Oxford had summoned his failing energy to good purpose and it was his last public work.

When the South Sea Bubble burst in 1720, some of Oxford's friends wanted him to return and give everyone the benefit of his financial experience and acumen. But Oxford's nephew Edward, son of the Auditor, warned his uncle that it would be unsafe to come to London, since people might set on him as the originator of the scheme. Besides, there was nothing that he or anyone could do to redress the folly of Sunderland and others in encouraging speculation and avarice. Erasmus Lewis had warned Oxford months before that the company 'your own child . . . since you suckled and nourished the infant, it is grown prodigiously, I had almost said to unnatural bulk'. In March his daughter Abigail, now the Countess of Kinnoull, reported that it was very unfashionable not to be 'in' the South Sea. 'I am sorry to say, I am out of the fashion,' she added, sensibly. The careful-minded Auditor was scandalized by the wild speculation. 'The madness of stock-jobbing is inconceivable,' he wrote in May. It pained him to see the scheme, which he had helped to frame, ruined by ignorant greed. 'Everyone thirsts for more, and all this founded upon the machine of paper credit supported only by imagination.' The Auditor urged his brother not to come up to London. 'I must say that there are none here, except of your own name, that would not sell you or anyone for a South Sea subscription'.

Not that the Dragon showed any keenness now to come to the metropolis. He had suffered too much from the folly and ingratitude of men. Like Prior, who confessed to being tired of the madness of the people, and frightened with the roaring of the South Sea, he preferred to remain at rest with his books and his bowls and to watch the human farce from a distance. As Prior put it:

> Fame counting thy books, my dear Harley, shall tell,
> No man had so many, who knew them so well.

Being a very laborious poet, I made these two verses in a morning in the library, and was never in my life better pleased with my own work than to hear little Mademoiselle Harley repeat them the next morning with the prettiest tone and manner imaginable. God bless that dear child, the excellent good woman her mother, and all of us, and keep us from the foul fiend.

In 1721 Prior died, after a lingering fever, and the Dragon had not long to live. After the South Sea panic had subsided, his friends wanted him to come to London, for they had little faith in country doctors and felt he should be under the care of Dr Mead and Dr Friend. Some of his old supporters, groaning under a 'Walpolish' government, longed for the good pilot to return and give the country the benefit of his 'sagacity and dexterity'. 'Will you see your country ruined?' they asked. It was Bromley's opinion that 'nothing less than your Lordship's genius and abilities can extricate us . . . and prevent a relapse'. But he had done his work and had no wish to rectify other people's mistakes. 'In such a jumble of jarring interests, boundless avarice, necessitous clamours, enterprising quacks,' he wrote, 'it must . . . be a head better than mine, who can pretend to talk reasonably upon so perplexed a subject.' So he stayed in the country and consulted Dr Mead by post, who prescribed 'manna with a little plague water as a purge, asses' milk every morning, and thirty grains of Gassia's powder every night'. Understandably, Oxford's symptoms showed no signs of improvement in spite of this barrage of remedies, and he spent his last years almost entirely in retirement:

> Dext'rous, the craving, fawning crowd to quit,
> And pleased to 'scape from flattery to wit

as Pope put it. Prior had noted the same tendency:

I still heard from Lord Harley that you were well, and from the Auditor that you did not intend to trouble us, having a strange taste of liking your paternal seat, fine woods, good books and what company you please better than Westminster, Change Alley, mistaken politics and the conversation of pickpockets and stockjobbers.

In May 1724, while on a visit to London, Oxford died and his body was borne to Brampton Bryan to be buried with his ancestors. A fine marble tablet to his memory was placed in the church, where it can still be seen, as can the ruined castle in the grounds of Brampton Bryan Hall.

Oxford had dedicated his life to public service without enriching himself from public funds, and after he died Auditor Harley, or 'the Governor' as they called him in the family, had the task of rehabilitating an estate which had been in the hands of an absentee landlord for over twenty years. Papers at Brampton reveal just how much his private affairs had suffered as a result of his political career. But at least his children were well provided for, and Edward inherited the library. The new Earl, charming but somewhat ineffective, and lacking his father's strong will and cunning nature, wasted his substance in expensive purchases and was in debt when he died in 1741. The books were sold, but the manuscripts were bought from the Countess in 1753 by the trustees of the newly founded national library, and it is with this collection that the Harley name is always coupled. Oxford's grandson, Lord Dupplin, made a name for himself in the field of learning, and Margaret Cavendish-Holles, Prior's 'noble, lovely little Peggy', married in 1734 the second Duke of Portland, who gained not only a beautiful wife, but also the estate of Welbeck, and a large part of the Harley correspondence.

Edward Harley as he went through his father's papers, was sad to think that the statesman who had dominated the political scene for so long had left no personal memoirs. Typically enough he has left us with an enigma. It seems that Swift thought of writing his friend's life, and Edward cordially invited him to stay and devote some time to going through the papers. 'I have houses enough,' wrote Ned, 'you shall take your choice.' The invitation was never taken up, and few others have felt tempted to delve into the heart of this most secret man. He has too often been dismissed as an artful schemer; posterity has labelled him 'Robin the Trickster', accepting the testimony of his enemies and neglecting the charm of character that won him the friendship of a Queen and the admiration of many political and literary men. The mass of letters and reports that flowed into his office, and the piles of notes written in his own hand, reveal a man who struggled to master the difficulties which politics imposed on him, who never wavered in his loyalty to the Queen and who through all his strange intrigues kept always in front of him the ideal of the temperate zone between the extremes. His Mecca and mirage was a nation ruled over by a monarch divinely endowed with power, and managed by moderate men of both parties, helped, but not dominated by, the strength of the majority party. His career highlights the difficulties which always beset mild and moderate men in the diamond-hard world of politics. The hazards of building up a middle party can be seen in our own day, and Oxford's attempt to achieve a balance failed because his loosely organized following fell away as soon as it met with success. Moderation, as a binding force, is weak compared to other more clear-cut ideals, and once the common enemy is removed, 'friends fall apart, the centre cannot hold'.

Bolingbroke, with a lifetime to think over the follies of his youth, grew wise in exile, and wrote into *The Patriot King* all those virtues which he had once scorned in his rejected master. And the group of poets and politicians who sat at his feet on his return to England, including Pope and the youthful Pitt, built up the picture of an ideal man resembling the politician who tried to carve a way between the extremes, who fought to the end with the extremes of faction, who maintained a stoic calm in the face of calamity, and who was 'free though in the Tower':

> A soul supreme, in each hard instance tried,
> Above all pain, all passion, and all pride,
> The rage of power, the blast of public breath,
> The lust of lucre, and the dread of death.

His vagueness, his clandestine ways, his involved speech and muddled style made many people distrust and even hate him. But his family loved and admired him, and 'the best of Queens' was his close friend for nearly ten years. 'For my own part,' he said in his last speech in the Lords, 'as I always acted by the immediate directions and commands of the late Queen and never offended against any known law, I am justified in my own conscience.' His piety maddened his enemies, but the religion he inherited was no empty cant, but a real and sincere belief that sustained him in times of stress. 'His friendship and conversation you will ever want,' wrote Swift to Edward Harley, 'because they are qualities so rare in the world, and in which he so much excelled all others. It has pleased me in the midst of my grief to hear that he preserved the greatness and intrepidity of his mind to his last minutes, for it was fit that such a life should terminate with equal lustre to the whole progress of it.'

BIBLIOGRAPHY

In GENERAL, works are referred to in the notes by the author's surname. Exceptions are given in the bibliography in square brackets.

MANUSCRIPT SOURCES

Blenheim Palace: The Marlborough Papers [Blenheim MSS].
Brampton Bryan Hall and Herefordshire County Record Office: Harley family papers [Brampton Bryan MSS].
British Museum: Portland Loan. [B.M.29], Lansdowne MSS, Additional MSS.
Hertfordshire County Record Office: Panshanger MSS, thirteen letters from Harley to Lord Chancellor Cowper 1706–7, and the Diary of Sir David Hamilton, the Queen's physician, a copy in the hand of Mary, Countess Cowper [Hamilton *Diary*].
Longleat: *Correspondence and Letters of the Harley Family* [Longleat MSS].
Shropshire County Record Office: Morgan, (Mill Street), MSS.
Walton: Mordaunt papers [Walton (Mordaunt) MSS] and *Some Memorandums concerning Bishop Hooper*, MSS memoirs by his daughter Mrs. Prowse [Walton (Hooper) MSS].

PRINTED SOURCES

Reports of the Historical Manuscripts Commission [H.M.C.]: Bath (I and III), Buccleuch, Cowper III, Dartmouth, Downshire, Kenyon, Marlborough, Portland (P. II, III, IV and V) and Stuart.
ADDISON, JOSEPH: *Letters*, ed. W. Graham (1941).
AILESBURY, THOMAS BRUCE, EARL OF: *Memoirs* (1890).
AITKEN, G. A.: *Life and Works of John Arbuthnot* (1892).
AYLMER, G. E.: *The King's Servants* (1961).
BALLARD, GENERAL COLIN: *The Great Earl of Peterborough* (1929).
BATHURST, LT-COL. THE HON. BENJAMIN: *Letters of Two Queens* (1924).
BAXTER, STEPHEN: *William III* (1966).
BEATTIE, J. M.: *The English Court in the Reign of George I* (1967).
BICKLEY, FRANCIS: *The Life of Matthew Prior* (1914).
BOLINGBROKE, HENRY ST JOHN: *Letters and Correspondence of Lord Bolingbroke*, ed. G. Parke, 4 vols. (1798).
— *Works*, ed. D. Mallet, 5 vols. (1778).
BOYER, ABEL: *History of the Reign of Queen Anne digested into Annals*, 3 vols. (1703–13).

— *The History of the Life and Reign of Queen Anne* (1722).

BURNET, GILBERT, BISHOP OF SALISBURY: *History of His Own Time*, 6 vols. (1833).

BUTLER, IRIS: *Rule of Three* (1967).

CHURCHILL, WINSTON S.: *Marlborough; his Life and Times* (2-volume edition, 1947).

CLARK, G. N.: *The Later Stuarts 1660–1714* (1934).

CLERK, SIR JOHN: *Memoirs* (1895).

COBBETT, WILLIAM: *Parliamentary History*, vols. VI and VII.

COKE, R.: *A Detection of the Court and State of England*, vol. III (1719).

COWPER, WILLIAM, 1ST EARL: *Private Diary*, ed. E. C. Hawtrey (1833).

COXE, ARCHDEACON WILLIAM: *Memoirs of John, Duke of Marlborough with original correspondence*, 6 vols. (1820 edition) [Coxe].

— *Correspondence of Charles Talbot, Duke of Shrewsbury* (1821) [Coxe Shrewsbury].

DASENT, A. T.: *The Speakers of the House of Commons* (1911).

DEFOE, DANIEL: *Eleven Opinions Regarding Mr. H — y* (1711).

— *Legion's Memorial, The True-Born Englishman*, in Somers *Tracts*, II, 256–65 (1814).

— *Letters*, ed. George Harris (1955).

— *The Secret History of the White Staff* (1714).

ELLIOT, HUGH: *Life of Godolphin* (1888).

EVELYN, JOHN: *Diary*, ed. E. S. de Beer vol. 5 (1955).

EVES, CHARLES KENNETH: *Matthew Prior* (1939).

FEILING, SIR KEITH: *History of the Tory Party* (1924).

FIENNES, CELIA: *Through England on a Side Saddle*, ed. Hon. Mrs Griffiths (1888).

FOOT, MICHAEL: *The Pen and the Sword* (1957).

FREIND, DR. JOHN: *An account of the Earl of Peterborough's Conduct in Spain* (1707). Published anonymously.

GREEN, DAVID: *Sarah Duchess of Marlborough* (1967).

HAMILTON, ELIZABETH: *The Mordaunts* (1965).

HANDASYDE, ELIZABETH: *Granville the Polite* (1933).

HANMER, SIR THOMAS: *The Correspondence of*, ed. Sir Henry Bunbury Bt. (1838).

HARLEY, ROBERT: *Faults on Both Sides*, dictated by Harley to Simon Clement (1710) in Somers *Tracts*, XII, 693 (1814).

— *Plain English*. B. M. Loan 29/10/1.

HART, JEFFREY: *Viscount Bolingbroke* (1965).

Hatton Correspondence, ed. Edward Maunde Thompson. 2 vols. (1870).

HOLMES, GEOFFREY: *British Politics in the Age of Anne* (1967).

— and W. A. SPECK: *The Fall of Harley in 1708 Reconsidered*, E.H.R. LXXX (1965).

KEMBLE, J. M.: *State Papers from the Revolution to the Accession of the House of Hanover* (1857).

KENYON, J. P.: *Robert Spencer, Earl of Sunderland* (1958).

LEGG, L. G. WICKHAM: *Matthew Prior* (1921).

LEVER, SIR TRESHAM: *Godolphin, His Life and Times* (1952).
LEWIS, JENKIN: *Memoirs of Prince William Henry, Duke of Gloucester* (1789).
LUTTRELL, NARCISSUS: *A Brief Historical Relation of State Affairs*, 6 vols. (1857).
MACKNIGHT, THOMAS: *Life of Viscount Bolingbroke* (1863).
MACKY, JOHN: *Memoirs of the Secret Services of John Macky Esq., including Characters of the Court of Great Britain, drawn up by Mr. Macky, pursuant to the Direction of Her Royal Highness the Princess Sophia* (1895).
MACPHERSON, JAMES: *Original Papers*, vol. II (1775).
MALLET, DAVID: *Memoirs of the Life of Viscount Bolingbroke* (1352).
MANCHESTER, THE DUKE OF: *Court and Society from Elizabeth to Anne*, edited from the papers at Kimbolton (1864).
MANLEY, MARY DE LA RIVIÈRE: *The New Atlantis* (1709).
— *The Secret History of Queen Zarah* (1743).
MARLBOROUGH, SARAH, DUCHESS OF: *An account of the Conduct of the Dowager Duchess of Marlborough from her first coming to court to the year 1710*, ed. Nathaniel Hooke (1742).
— *Letters from the original MSS at Madresfield Court* (1875).
— *Private Correspondence*, 2 vols. (1838).
MARSHALL, DOROTHY: *Eighteenth Century England* (1962).
MAYOR, J. E. B.: *Cambridge under Queen Anne* (1911).
MESNAGER, NICOLAS: *Minutes of the Negotiations at the Court of England* (1717). (Authorship suspect.)
MICHAEL, WOLFGANG: *England under George I* (1936).
MILLER, O. B.: *Robert Harley*, Stanhope Prize Essay (1925).
MONTGOMERY, I. and R. GEIKIE: *The Dutch Barrier* (1930).
MOORE, J. R.: *Daniel Defoe, Citizen of the Modern World* (1958).
NICHOLSON, T. C. and A. S. TURBERVILLE: *Charles Talbot, Duke of Shrewsbury* (1930).
Norris Papers, ed. Thomas Heywood (1846).
OLDMIXON, JOHN: *The History of England during the Reign of King William and Queen Mary etc.* (1735).
— *The Life and Posthumous Works of Arthur Maynwaring* (1712).
OMAN, CAROLA: *Mary of Modena* (1962).
PARKER, IRENE: *Dissenting Academies in England* (1914).
PETRIE, SIR CHARLES: *Bolingbroke* (1937).
PLUMB, J. H.: *Sir Robert Walpole*, vol. I (1956).
PRIOR, MATTHEW: *Literary Works*, ed. H. Bunker Wright and Monroe K. Spears, 2 vols. (1959).
— *History of his Own Time*, ed. J. Banks (1740).
QUEEN ANNE: *Letters and Diplomatic Instructions*, ed. B. Curtis Brown (1935).
RALPH, JAMES: *The Other Side of the Question* (1742).
REID, J. STUART: *John and Sarah, Duke and Duchess of Marlborough* (1914).
ROBB, NESCA A.: *William of Orange*, vol. II (1966).
ROSCOE, E. S.: *Robert Harley* (1902).
SHARP, THOMAS: *Life of Archbishop Sharp* (1825).

K*

SHREWSBURY, CHARLES TALBOT, DUKE OF: *Correspondence*, ed. W. C. Coxe (1821).

SOMERVILLE, THOMAS: *History of Great Britain during the Reign of Queen Anne* (1798).

SPECK, W. A.: *The Choice of a Speaker in 1705*. Bull. I.H.R. xxxvii (1964).

STEBBING, WILLIAM: *Peterborough* (1906).

STRICKLAND, AGNES: *Lives of the Queens of England*, vol. VIII (1864).

SWIFT, JONATHAN: *Correspondence*, vols. I and II, ed. Elrington Ball (1911).

— *Journal to Stella*, ed. H. Williams, 2 vols. (1948).

— *Prose Works*, 13 vols. (1953).

TINDAL, N.: *Continuation of Rapin's History of England*, vols. IV–VI (1763).

TREVELYAN, G. M.: *England under Queen Anne*, 3 vols. (1934).

TURBERVILLE, A. S.: *A History of Welbeck Abbey and its Owners*, 2 vols. (1938–9).

— *The House of Lords in the Eighteenth Century* (1927).

Verney Letters of the Eighteenth Century from the MSS at Claydon House, ed. Margaret Maria Lady Verney, vol. I (1930). [Verney].

VERNON, JAMES: *Letters illustrative of the Reign of William III*, ed. G. P. R. James, vol. III (1841).

WALCOTT, ROBERT: *English Politics in the Early Eighteenth Century* (1956).

WARD, A. W.: *The Electress Sophia* (1909).

Wentworth Papers 1705–1739, ed. J. J. Cartwright (1883).

WILLIAMS, BASIL: *Stanhope* (1932).

NOTES

CHAPTER 1 FIRST BEGINNINGS

Quotations concerning the Harley family in Chapters 1 and 2 are from P. III, where they are printed in chronological order.

4 *Ear trouble*: in later life, Harley, like Swift, suffered from deafness in the left ear. His servants and friends knew which ear it was wise to whisper into.

5 *Prior and Harley—'the Grand Monarch'*: Legg 191.

8-9 *Letter from Elizabeth Foley to her sister*: Morgan (Mill Street), MSS Shropshire County Record Office, 783/Box 24.

9 *The Prince of Orange*: Walton (Hooper) MSS 5.

9, 10 *Abigail Pye*: P. III, 437, 444.

11 *Feud with the Coningsbys*: Aylmer, 377-8.
Election petition: P. III, 450-1.

12 *The Commission: £500 to the clerks*: P. III, 459. Wentworth, 132, and Boyer. *The History of the Life and Reign of Queen Anne*.

12-13 *Self-justification*: P. III, 467.

13 *Death of Elizabeth*: P. III, 483-4.

CHAPTER 2 FAIRER FRUITS

17 *The attack in Radnor*: P. III, 543.
Marriage: P. III, 552 et seq.

18 *The chaplains and Princess Anne*: Walton (Hooper) MSS 14.

19 *Sarah Foley's Letters*: Morgan (Mill Street) MSS Shropshire County Record Office 783/Box 24.

20 *Devaluation*: 'A great quantity of coin of base metal is being dispersed abroad', wrote Robert Harley to his brother in April 1693. Brampton Bryan MSS.

21 *Harley's letter to Bromley*: P. III, 575.

22 *Prior's letter*: H.M.C. Bath, III, 204, April 10, 1698.

23 *Boyle*: P. III, 578.
Princess Anne's extravagance: Verney, I, 48.

24 *William and the Junto*: Kenyon, 304.
Shrewsbury: P. III, 580.

25 *The seaman's rabble*: P. III, 615.

26 *Death of Foley*: P. III, 612-14; Verney, I, 51.

27 *Seymour*: Hatton Correspondence, II, 246.

27-9 *Harley and Vernon*: Vernon, III, 20-1, 61, 67, 85, 88, 91, 105.

29 *The pony*: Bathurst, 236.
The Queen and Gloucester: Reid, 95.
Death of Gloucester: P. III, 624.

30–31 *Guy, Harley and Weymouth*: P. III, 634 *et seq.*
32 *Air to a mine*: P. IV, 7.
   References to Brampton: P. III, 494, 514, 544, 566, 586, 598.
33 *Henry Guy*: P. IV, 13.
   John Evelyn: Evelyn, V, 446.
   Bromley: P. IV, 15.

CHAPTER 3   THE GILDED MACE

36–7 *The Kentish Petitioners*: Defoe *Legion's Memorial* in Somers, *Tracts*, II, 256–65.
37 *Death of James*: H.M.C. Bath, III, 257, August 27, 1698; Manchester, II, 191–4.
38 *Election of Speaker*: Norris Papers, 76.
39 *The gilded mace*: P. IV, 33.
   Death of William: P. IV, 35; Evelyn, V, 493.
40 *Prior*: H.M.C. Bath, III, 325.

CHAPTER 4   THE NEW QUEEN

41 *Chesterfield*: H.M.C. Cowper, III, 1.
42 *Godolphin's letters*: P. IV, 34.
43 *Coronation*: Fiennes, 255; B.M. Cavendish Papers 1696–1707, 47;
   Evelyn, V, 498.
44 *Buckingham*: Macky, 41.
   Mary's remark: Bathurst, 158.
   Marlborough and Buckingham: Holmes, 200.
45 *Anne's illness*: *Porphyria—a Royal Malady*, Ida Macalpine and Richard Hunter.
   British Medical Journal booklet.
   Prince George: Macky, 34; Reid, 141; Burnet, V, 10.
46–52 *Godolphin's letters*: P. IV, 43–58.
47 *London in midsummer*: Mayor, 348–53.
49 '*a spice of lethargy*': Vernon, III, 228.

CHAPTER 5   THE TRIUMVIRATE

49 *St. Paul's*: Mayor, 318.
50 *Thanksgiving service*: 'pyramidical illumination', Coke, III, 138.
   John Evelyn and Marlborough: Evelyn, V, 524–5. Churchill puts his income at
   this time at £60,000.
51 *Queen Anne and the Catholics*: Bathurst, 109.
   John Evelyn and the clergy: Evelyn, V, 542, July 1703.
53 '*The habit of a clergyman*': P. IV.
   Godolphin to Harley: P. IV, 53, 58.
54 *Rochester's self-love*: Duchess of Marlborough, *Conduct*, 142.
55 *Abigail Pye about the Duchess*: P. IV, 59.
   '*Never let difference of opinion*': Duchess of Marlborough, *Conduct*, 156.
56 *Letter to Lady Bathurst*: Bathurst, 169.
   Duchess of Marlborough and the Queen: Blenheim MSS G-1-8.
57 '*dear dear Mrs. Freeman*': Duchess of Marlborough, *Conduct*, 157.
   '*the impartial hand*': Coxe, Chapter LVIII.

58 *Duchess of Marlborough and her description of Harley*: Blenheim MSS G-1-9; Green, 117.
   Hooper and Harley: Walton (Hooper) MSS 18–19.
58–9 *Robert Monkton and Newcastle*: P. IV, 59.
60 *Harley and Godolphin, and Defoe's release*: Moore, 145; P. IV, 68.
   Harley's letters to Abigail: P. IV, 64.
61 *St John's letter to Harley*: P. IV, 73.
61–81 *Letters of Marlborough and Godolphin*: Coxe, Chapters XVII and XIX.
61 *'contumelious'*: Swift, *Correspondence*, I, 38.
62 *'calming people'*: Godolphin to Harley, P. IV, 77.
64 *Dartmouth's comments on Kent*: Burnet, V, 142n.
   Vernon: Vernon, III, 239.
   Marlborough: Blenheim MSS A-1-14.
64–5 *Stanley West*: P. IV, 118, August 29, 1704.
65 *'spawn of a Presbyterian'*: Feiling, 421.
   Congratulatory letters: P. IV, 84–6.
   'so united and linked': P. IV, 119.
65–6 *Vernon*: Vernon, III, 239.
66 *Godolphin*: H.M.C. Bath, I, 57, May 21, 1704.

CHAPTER 6   SECRETARY OF STATE

67 *Vernon and Harley*: Vernon, III, 239.
68 *Sir John Clerk*: Clerk, 72.
   'Female Buzz': Defoe, *White Staff*, II, 42.
69 *Abel Boyer*: Boyer, *The History of the Life and Reign of Queen Anne*, 322.
   Mesnager: Mesnager, *Minutes of Negotiation*, quoted Strickland, VIII, 420.
69–70 *Defoe's spy system*: P. IV, 106.
70 *The Ogilvies*: P. IV, 298, October 23, 1705.
71–2 *'Domestick Correspondence'*: B.M. 29/263; *Robert Harley's Letter Book*.
72 *Coke's letter*: H.M.C. Cowper, III, 38.
   Thomas Foley: P. IV, 108.
73 *St John to Coke*: H.M.C. Cowper, III, 49.
73–4 *Hooper*: Walton (Hooper) MSS 25.
75 *Balls at court*: Verney, I, 263, February 1705.
76 *The election*: Hamilton, *The Mordaunts*, 55–7 and for 'New Moderation Principles', letter from the Rev Humphrey Whyle to Sir John Mordaunt, Walton (Mordaunt) MSS II, 87.
   Worcester and Chester: P. IV, 189; Dyer's News Letter, May 29, 1705.
77 *'The Queen will be courted'*: H.M.C. Bath, I, 75.
   The Duke of Newcastle: B.M. 29/237–8, August 18, 1705 (taken from the original MS and not from P. II); P. IV, 226.
78 *Sharp and Godolphin*: Sharp, 365–6.
   Abigail Pye: P. IV, 212.
79 *Harley*: B.M. 29/171.
   Harley to Godolphin: H.M.C. Bath, I, 72.
   Defoe: P. IV, 147.
   Letter to Robert Davers: P. IV, 261, October 16, 1705.
80 *The bear garden*: P. IV, 223, August 14, 1705.
81 *Lady Pye and Robin*: P. IV, 257.
   The value of his relations: Brampton Bryan MSS.

CHAPTER 7 'THE QUEEN IS THE HEAD'

82 *Coke*: H.M.C. Cowper, III.
   Sir Nathan Wright: P. IV, 226.
   Trevor: B.M. 29/237/97–8; Holmes, 204.
83 *The merciless men*: B.M. Additional MSS 28070 12–13.
   'All the care imaginable': Blenheim MSS, quoted Churchill, II, 29.
   Harley to Godolphin: H.M.C. Bath, I, 74.
84 *'Great guns'*: B.M. 29/237/115.
   Electress Sophia: Ward, 181 et seq.
   Hothead and Testimony: Burnet, V, 242n.
85 *'Dear Mrs. Freeman'*: Coxe.
   Cowper: Cowper, *Diary*, 33.
86–8 *The Union*: P. IV, 296; Greg, P. IV, 194.
89 *Newcastle*: P. II, 193.
90 *'oyl and vinegar'*: Cowper, *Diary*, 12.
   Sunderland's temper: Churchill, II, 205.
   The Queen's letters: Blenheim MSS G-1-4, August 30, 1706, copy.
91 *Godolphin's letter*: Coxe.
   The arbitress: B.M. 29/9/38.
   Harley and Godolphin: H.M.C. Bath, I, 111.
92 *Cowper*: Cowper, *Diary*, 35 et seq; P. II, 195.
   St John: H.M.C. Bath, I, 121, November 5, 1706.

CHAPTER 8 THE MALICE OF THE WHIGS

93 *Harley's illness*: P. IV, 384, Manchester, II, 209.
   The debate in the House: Churchill, II, 213.
94 *Defoe's letter*: P. IV, 387.
   Sir John Clerk: Clerk, 69.
95 *Defoe*: P. IV, 403, April 24, 1707.
96–7 *The Duchess and Abigail*: Duchess of Marlborough, *Conduct*, 183–7.
96 *'mightily in the right'*: Duchess of Marlborough, *Conduct*, 204.
97 *Abigail to Harley*: P. IV, 454.
   The Duchess—'I can't prevail': H.M.C. Downshire, I, ii, 855.
98 *Sharp*: Sharp, 301.
   Dawes: Manchester, II, 231.
98–9 *Godolphin, Harley and the Queen*: Coxe, Chapters LXII and LXIII.
99 *Harley to Godolphin*: H.M.C. Bath, I, 180.
   Harley to Cowper: Panshanger MSS, Hertford County Record Office; Cowper
   Letters 15/1, 27/20, September 26, 1706, September 12, 1707.
   Harley to Godolphin: H.M.C. Bath, I, 180–1.
100 *Harley to Marlborough*: Coxe, Chapter LXII; H.M.C. Bath, I, 185–6.
   The Duchess—'strangling': Strickland, VIII, 343.
   Harrow on the Hill and Maidenhead: H.M.C. Bath, I, 180–1.
   Godolphin to Harley: H.M.C. Bath, I, 184.
101 *The Queen, Marlborough and Harley*: Coxe, Chapter LXII.
   Harley to Newcastle: P. II, 200–1.
   Harley to Marlborough: H.M.C. Bath, I, 185.
103 *Harley to Cowper*: Panshanger MSS, Hertford County Record Office; Cowper
   Letters, 15/1.

CHAPTER 9   THE ALTERNATIVE SCHEME

105 *Greg's debts*: P. IV, 401, April 15, 1707. Greg to Harley. 'My uneasy circumstances put me upon thus importuning me sore against my will, for without paying the ten pounds to-night I must expect to be affronted before I get to the office tomorrow morning.'
   The Crosskeys Tavern: B.M. 29/10.
106 *Greg's clipping and coining*: Manchester, 311–12.
   His confession: P. IV, 469.
106–114 *'The Fall of Harley Reconsidered'*: Holmes and Speck, E.H.R. vol. LXXX, October 1965.
107 *Devonshire*: Macky, 40.
   The meeting at Boyle's House, agenda, etc.: B.M. 29/9/51.
108 *The Member for Liverpool*: Norris Papers, 161–2.
109 *Harley to Godolphin*: H.M.C. Bath, I, 190.
110 *Godolphin to Harley*: H.M.C. Bath, I, 190.
   Greg's letter: P. IV, 475.
   St John and the letter, etc.: Swift, *Correspondence*, I, 75.
111 *Marlborough and the Queen*: Churchill, II, 312–13.
   'soft expressions': Burnet, V, 354.
   The Duchess: Duchess of Marlborough, *Conduct*, 212–13.
111–12 *The council meeting*: Cropley to Stanhope. Public Record Office, 30/24/21/150, quoted Holmes and Speck in *The Fall of Harley*; Burnet, V, 354; Coke, III, 323.
112 *Somerset*: Swift, *Correspondence*, I, 75.
   Harley's visit to the House: Vernon, III, 344.
112–13 *The interview*: B.M. 29/9/52.
113 *The whole gang, etc.*: Vernon, III, 343, 349.
   'The great shake': Sir John Cropley to Shaftesbury. Public Record Office, 30/24/21/150.
   Swift: Swift, *Correspondence*, 76.
114 *Harley's apologia*: B.M. 29/10/1.

CHAPTER 10   GREG

115–19 *The Greg affair*: P. IV, 479–88.
115 *'The devil and his necessities'*: Vernon, III, 362.
   Atterbury and the Auditor: P. V, 648–9.
116 *Valière and Bara*: Burnet, V, 357.
   The Auditor and Captain Baker: P. V, 648.
117–18 *The Pretender's expedition*: Trevelyan, II, 342; Manchester, II 297, 331.
117 *Lady Wentworth*: Wentworth, 62.
118 *The Queen and the Pretender*: Burnet, V, 369.
   Lady Wentworth: Wentworth, 62.
   Man proposes: Manchester, II, 311.
120 *Swift*: Swift, *Prose Works*, VIII, 115–16.
   Montagu: Walcott, 149.
121 *Somers*: Swift, *Correspondence*, I, 85; Manchester, II, 329.
   Marlborough, Mrs Masham, Godolphin: Coxe, Chapter LXVII.
   Dinnertime: Coxe, Chapter LXVII, or Blenheim MSS A-2-38.
   Prince George's illness, lethargy, etc.: Churchill, II, 476.
122 *The Queen's illness*: P. IV, 491.

122 *Harley to Bromley*: B.M. 29/128/3.
   Erasmus Lewis: P. IV, 489.
   Letter to Newcastle: P. II, 205.
   Harley to Harcourt: H.M.C. Bath, I, 192.
   St John: H.M.C. Bagot, 341.
   Harley to Monckton: Longleat MSS, *Correspondence and Letters of the Harley Family*, X, 57.
123 *Shrewsbury*: Nicholson, 168; H.M.C. Bath, I, 191.
123–4 *Harley to Abigail*: Longleat MSS, *Correspondence and Letters of the Harley Family*, X, 55.

CHAPTER 11   COUSIN ROBIN AND COUSIN KATE

125 *Swift*: Correspondence, I, 75.
   The Queen to Marlborough: Reid, 275.
   Marlborough's letters: Coxe, Chapter LXVII.
126 *Sarah's anonymous letters*: Green, 216–17.
126–7 *The site at St James's*: Manchester, II, 224.
127 *Abigail to Harley*: P. IV, 495.
   Abigail and the Queen: B.M. 29/38/2.
   The ballad: Green, 322.
   The house at Windsor: Duchess of Marlborough, *Conduct*, 222.
128 *Code*: B.M. 29/38.
129 *Abigail to Harley*: P. IV, 496, 499.
129–30 *Harley's code letters*: Longleat MSS, *Correspondence and Letters of the Harley Family*, X, 51, 55, 59.
130 *Sharp*: Sharp, 332.
   The prince: Coxe, Chapter LXXV.
131 *The Queen and the portrait*: Green, 139.
   Mourning: Wentworth, 82.
   The Duchess and her rooms: Blenheim MSS G-1-9.
132 *Tabby and Ned*: P. IV, 511, 518.
132–3 *Bromley and the Speaker's Chair*: Holmes, 303.
133 *Tabby*: P. IV, 523.
   Coningsby and Harley: Manchester, II, 294.
134 *The matrimonial address*: P. IV, 519; *Wentworth Papers*, 70, 75.
   The Duchess and Somers: Althorp MSS, quoted Trevelyan, II, 391.
   Harley and Harcourt: H.M.C. Bath, I, 193.
135 *'Dreadful bloodshed'*: Tindal, IV, 104.
136 *Erasmus Lewis, Oudenarde*: P. IV, 501, August 19, 1708.
   Marlborough: P. IV, 507.
   Code letter: Longleat MSS, *Correspondence and Letters of the Harley Family*, X, f. 55.
   The Duchess and Harley: Duchess of Marlborough, *Conduct*, 218.
137 *'sordid avarice'*: Longleat MSS, *Correspondence and Letters of the Harley Family*, X, f. 55.
   Berwick: Churchill, II, 500.
   Dethroning the old Monarch: Wentworth, 88.
138 *Malplaquet*: Coxe, Chapter LXXXIII.
   Harley to Newcastle: P. II, 208.
139 *Abigail*: P. IV, 525, September 4, 1709.
   Harley and the Somersets: P. IV.

140 *The Duchess of Somerset*: Blenheim MSS G-1-8.
140 *Shrewsbury*: Vernon III, 108; Nicholson, 184; Wentworth, 51; Feiling, 412.
141 *Haversham*: P. IV, 526.
 Granville: P. IV, 527.
 '*You broke the party*': H.M.C. Bath, I, 191–3, October 11; November 6, 1708.
141-2 *Bromley*: P. IV, 504.
142 *St John*: H.M.C. Bath, I, 191–3.
 Shrewsbury: H.M.C. Bath, I, 197, November 3, 1709.
 Mansell: P. IV, 528, November 10, 1709.
 Swift: Swift, *Prose Works*, VI, 87.

CHAPTER 12 A NONSENSICAL HARANGUE

145 *Maynwaring*: Blenheim MSS E-28.
 The new Atlantis: Private Correspondence of the Duchess of Marlborough, 233–5.
146 '*gogling wildness*': Churchill, II, 661.
147 *Lady Dupplin*: P. IV, 531, February 5, 1709.
 Abigail Harley: P. IV, 532–4.
 Pamphlets: Coke, III, 382; Wentworth, 74.
148 *The scorching fire*: Petrie, 177.
 Worcester: P. IV, 550.
149 *Last interview with Sarah*: Blenheim MSS G-1-9; Duchess of Marlborough, *Conduct*, 238–43.
 The Queen's health: Hamilton, *Diary*, 1–5.
150 *The letter*: Swift, *Prose Works*, VIII, 116.

CHAPTER 13 THE SHAKING SEASON

151 *Kent*: Burnet, V, 142n.
152 *Lady Sunderland's letter*: Churchill, II, 712.
 Maynwaring: Blenheim MSS E-28.
 Dartmouth: Green, 160; Macky, 71; Churchill, II, 890.
 '*All joy*' Burnet, V, 11, Dartmouth's note.
153 *Sunderland*: Churchill, II, 890.
154 *Hanmer*: H.M.C. Bath, III, 437, June 15–26, 1710.
 Dupplin: Feiling, 412.
 Somerset and the Kit-Cat Club: Holmes, 298 (from Stowe MSS).
155 *Sir David Hamilton*: Hamilton, *Diary*, 9.
 Harley to Newcastle: P. II, 211.
 Cresset: Wentworth, 128.
156 *The Electress*: Verney, I, 236.
 '*The emperor cannot be snubbed*': Halifax to Newcastle, P. II, 213.
157 *Shrewsbury to Harley*: H.M.C. Bath, I, 198, July 22, 1710.
 The Queen to Godolphin: Coxe, Chapter XCIV.
157-8 *The dismissal*: Wentworth, 130.
158 '*an old nurse*': Hamilton, *Diary*, 15.
 Harley and the City: Holmes, 174 *et seq.*
 Defoe: P. IV, 546–8, 585.
159 *Newcastle*: P. II, 215.
 Stanhope's victory: Brampton Bryan MSS.
160 *Belasyse's letter*: P. IV, 570, August 20, 1710.
 Halifax to Newcastle: P. II, 216.

161 *Cowper*: P. IV, 556; Cowper, *Diary*, 42–3.
162 *Hanilton*: Hamilton, *Diary*.
　Swift: Swift, *Correspondence*, I, 199.
　Molesworth: P. IV, 613, October 11, 1710.
　Monckton: P. IV, 574, August 23, 1710.
163 *Defoe*: P. IV, 553, July 28, 1710.
　Swift: Swift, *Journal to Stella*, September 9, 1710.
　Swift and Godolphin: Swift, *Correspondence*, I, 194.
164 *The dissolution*: Hamilton, *Diary*, 18.
　Cowper: Cowper, *Diary*, 46.
165 *A pet to Petworth*: Wentworth, 143.
　Weymouth and Prior: H.M.C. Bath, III.
　Harley to Newcastle: P. II, 220, 221.

CHAPTER 14　CHECKS AND HINDRANCES

167 *Beaufort*: P. IV, 599, 611, September 23, October 9, 1710.
　'*Bumkings*': Verney, I, 304, October 26, 1710.
　The Warwickshire address: Hamilton, *The Mordaunts*, 68.
　Atheism: P. IV, 539, March 25, 1710.
168 *The couplet*: Handasyde, 109, 121.
　Sarah Marlborough: Blenheim MSS G-1-8.
　Harley and the election: Brampton Bryan MSS.
　Granville: P. IV, 590, 623.
　'*I hear myself called rogue*': Blenheim MSS E-28.
170 *Abigail*: Wentworth, 66.
　Swift: Swift, *Journal to Stella*, September 22, 1711.
171 *Maynwaring*: Blenheim MSS E-28.
172 *The Marlboroughs*: Blenheim MSS G-1-8.
173 *Swift*: Swift, *Journal to Stella*.
　'*unseasonable hours*': P. II, 211.
174 *Harold Wilson*: *The Times*, October 13, 1966.
　The Whigs: Swift, *Journal to Stella*, January 7, 1711.
　The Auditor: Auditor Harley, *Memoir*, P. V, 651.

CHAPTER 15　GUISCARD

176 *et seq* The account of the assassination attempt is based on Auditor Harley's version, most of which is omitted from the published Memoir in the Portland Papers, vol. V, and is to be found in the British Museum Lansdowne MSS 885. Abel Boyer, in his *History of the Life and Reign of Queen Anne* gives the version that was circulated by St John and his followers. Further details are in Swift's *Journal to Stella* and his *Memoirs relating to the Change which happened in the Queen's Ministry*, and Luttrell, VI, 700–9. Letters from Lady Dupplin and Abigail Harley are in P. IV, 668–70. The Commons resolutions are taken from Luttrell, VI, 669. 'The solemnity of the occasion' is a quotation from an account 'dictated by Lord Oxford November 1721' which tallies with the Auditor's account, and is in Mr Christopher Harley's collection. The tears in the coat also bear out the description, and the penknife in his possession has the tip fastened to the blade with a silver link, and a note attached to it states 'I have ordered a goldsmith some way to contrive how the broken piece of this penknife may appear to those who may be desirous to see it' and on the back '. . . the broken piece of the penknife is fixed by a small silver link'.

176 The description of the Queen's reaction to the news is quoted from Holmes, 197.
   In Swift's *Prose Works* there is an article from *The Examiner*, 33, on the Guiscard affair, possibly written by Harley himself.
183 *Sir Constantine Phipps and Ralph Thoresby*: P. IV, 667–8.
186 *'Harley beware'*: Longleat MSS, *Correspondence and Letters of the Harley Family*, f. 249.

CHAPTER 16 THE WHITE STAFF

187–8 *Harley's re-appearance in the House*: P. IV, 680, April 28, 1711.
189–90 *Poulett*: P. IV, 684, May 4, 1711.
190 *Somerset*: P. IV, 690.
   Lady Dupplin: P. V, 3.
191 *Poulett*: P. IV, 683–4.
   Oxford and Newcastle's death: Brampton Bryan MSS.
192 *Marlborough and Robethon*: Churchill, II, 800.
192–3 *Marlborough to the Duchess*: Coxe, Chapter C; Butler, 250.
193 *Sir David Hamilton*: Hamilton, *Diary*.
193–4 *Maynwaring and Harley*: Blenheim MSS E-28, G-1-8.
194 *Marlborough to Harley*: H.M.C. Bath, I, 205.
196–7 *Prior's Diary*: P. V, 34–42.
197 *Macky*: Macky, 15.
   Swift: Swift, *Journal to Stella*, August 24, 1711.
198 *Matchiavell*: The quotation is from the ballad *Matt's Peace*; Bickley, 177.
   Lady Pye: P. V, 65.
199 *The porter*: P. V, 17; Swift, *Journal to Stella*, August 17, 1711.
200 *The Queen and Jersey*: B.M. 29/10 (two papers).

CHAPTER 17 THE QUEEN'S FRIEND

202 *Mesnager*: Strickland, VIII, 420.
   The Queen's Letters: H.M.C. Bath, I, 207–14.
   The Queen hunting: Swift, *Journal to Stella*, July 31, 1711.
203 *Hamilton and Dr Radcliffe*: Hamilton, *Diary*, 31.
203–4 *The birth and the christening*: B.M. 29/38/2; Swift, *Journal to Stella*, September 7, 1711.
204 *Oxford's peerage*: Harley's grandmother, Brilliana (so-called because her father, Sir Edward Conway, at the time of her birth in 1600, was Governor of the Dutch town of Brill) was connected on her mother's side to Lord Vere of Tilbury, a grandson of the 15th Earl of Oxford. The Harley claim to the title of Mortimer was less tenuous.
   Gallas: Churchill, II, 890.
204–5 *St John*: Swift, *Journal to Stella*, August 24, 1711.
206 *The Electress*: Macpherson, II, 347.
   Marlborough's grandson: Churchill, II, 872.
   Marlborough and Harley: Coxe, Chapter CV.
206–7 *'Tatler'*: No. 191.
207 *The Queen's letters*: H.M.C. Bath, I, 211–15.
208 *Davers*: P. V, 106.
209 *Harley to Somerset*: P. V, 119.
   Swift's 'Conduct of the Allies': Swift, *Prose Works*, vol. VI.
210 *Shrewsbury*: H.M.C. Bath, I, 217.

211 *Swift*: Swift, *Journal to Stella*, 3 December, 1711.
    The Bishop of Exeter: P. V, 117.
    Oxford and Archbishop Sharp: Hamilton, *The Mordaunts*, 106–7.
211–12 *Scottish peers*: P. V, 115, 121.
212 *Poulett and Nottingham*: P. V, 119.
    Poulett and Oxford: P. V, 119.
214 *Halifax and Oxford*: P. V, 132.
    Marlborough's dismissal: Coxe, Chapter CVI.
    Louis XIV: Reid, 363 (a letter purported to be from Louis XIV among the Blenheim MSS).
214–15 *Dartmouth and the peers*: Burnet, VI, 87.
215 *Hamilton*: Hamilton, *Diary*, 38.
216 *Hamilton*: Hamilton, *Diary*, 39.

CHAPTER 18   ROBIN AND HARRY

217 *'Advice to the October Club'*: Swift, *Prose Works*, VI, 67 *et seq.*
218 *orderly men*: Holmes, 308–9.
219 *et seq. Eugene*: Wentworth, 243 *et seq.*; Churchill, II, 921–6.
220 *Defoe*: Defoe, *White Staff*, II, 43.
    'Necessitous lords': Hamilton, *Diary*, January 20, 1711.
221 *Cholmondeley*: Holmes, 295; H.M.C. Bath, III, 438.
221–2 *The Earl of Mar*: Swift, *Journal to Stella*, February 2, 1712.
222 *Levee day*: Swift, *Journal to Stella*, February 27, 1712.
223 *Ormonde*: Clerk, P. V, 157.
224 *Prime Minister*: Holmes (Appendix C) discusses this point fully.
224–5 *Debate about the Peace*: Coxe, Chapter CVIII; Cobbett, *Parliamentary History*, VI, 1132.
224 *Ravings of the Whigs*: Verney, I, 311.
225 *Bromley*: Walton (Mordaunt) MSS III, 15, June 7, 1712.
226 *Bolingbroke and his promotion*: Bolingbroke, *Works*, I, 12.
227 *Defoe*: Defoe, *White Staff*, II, 73.
    Cowper and Oxford: Cowper, *Diary*, 54.
228 *Cowper and Hamilton*: Hamilton, *Diary*, 45.

CHAPTER 19   THE LONGED-FOR PEACE

229 *Abigail and the Queen*: P. V, 223, September 18, 1712.
    Bromley: P. V, 240.
    Abigail's fright: Verney, I, 370, October 19, 1712.
231 *Drummond*: P. V, 250.
    Swift: Swift, *Journal to Stella*, February 21, 1713.
232 *Bolingbroke*: Bolingbroke, *Correspondence*, IV, 19, April 8, 1713.
232–3 *Cholmondeley*: Bolingbroke, *Correspondence*, IV, 30.
233 *Prior*: Prior, *Works*, 402.
    Swift: Swift, *Journal to Stella*, April 8, 1713.
234 *'separate treating'*: Holmes, 79; B.M. 29/12/4, August 16, 1711.
    The Duchess: Green, 183; Blenheim MSS G-1-9.
    The Court of Hanover: Macpherson, II, 388–90.
    Gaultier and James: E.H.R.XIX, 510, July 1915.
    'the wheels of the machine': Defoe, *White Staff*, II, 20.

235 *Oxford and Hooper*: Walton (Hooper) MSS 30.
235–6 *The vote about the Union*: Trevelyan, III, 242.
236 *Bolingbroke*: Bolingbroke, *Correspondence*, Feiling, 451.
237 *Auditor Harley's 'Memoir'*: P. V, 660.
   Bolingbroke's letter: P. V, 311.
   Abigail and Dartmouth: P. V, 315; B.M. 29/38, August 6, 1713.
238 *Lady Harriet*: P. II, 206; Wentworth, 58.
239 *Bolingbroke and Oxford's journey*: P. V, 324.

CHAPTER 20 HANOVER AND SAINT-GERMAIN

240 *Lord Weymouth*: P. V, 325.
   Lord Oxford at Wimpole: B.M. 29/10/12.
   'Ploughing with the heifer': Defoe, *White Staff*, II, 28.
   Abigail and Lady Harriet, P. V, 324.
241 *Interview with the Queen*: B.M. 29/10/11, October 13, 1713.
   Defoe: P. V, 361, November 26, 1713.
241–2 *Bolingbroke*: P. V, 342, 369–70, 373.
242 *The Queen to Oxford*: H.M.C. Bath, I, 243.
242–5 *The Queen's illness*: P. V, 374 *et seq.*; Swift, 'An Enquiry into the Queen's Last Ministry', *Prose Works*, VIII, 154; Hamilton, *Diary*.
246 *'Any, good Lord, any'*: P. V, 341.
   Defoe and the Peace Treaty: P. V, 349, 356, October 19 and 31, 1713.
   South Sea Company: Decker to ? P. V, 385, February 1714.
247 *Hamilton*: Hamilton, *Diary*, 33, 54, 59.
248 *Greek script*: B.M. 29/10.
   The Brothers: Swift, *Journal to Stella*, February 1712.
249 *'friend Mortimer'*: Aitken, 567; Longleat MSS.
   Parnell: Aitken, 79.
   Gay: Roscoe, 217 *et seq.*
   Auditor Harley: P. V, 405, March 29, 1714.
250 *Sir Godfrey Kneller*: P. V, 398, March 15, 1714.
   The Pretender: E.H.R. July 1915, No. XXV, 512–14.
251 *Harcourt and Bolingbroke*: P. V, 400, 404, March 17 and 27, 1714.
   Lady Masham's letter: P. V, 403.
251–2 *Queen's speech*: Holmes, 75
252 *Violence of the Whigs, etc*: Verney, I, 246, April 17, April 24.
253 *Erasmus Lewis*: P. V, 413.
254 *Oxford to Thomas Harley*: P. V, 417–18, April 13, 1714; Macpherson, II, 595.
255 *Queen's Letter to Sophia*: Queen Anne, 413.
   Oxford to Hanmer: Hanmer, 168, May 13, 1714.

CHAPTER 21 QUIETUS

256 *The dead gripe*: Aitken, 68.
   'Let thy words be few': B.M. 29/10/7, June 14, 1714.
   'Considerations', B.M. 29/10/11.
257 *Abigail Masham and the Queen*: Strickland, VIII, 518–19.
   'A set of people': Aitken, 62, June 16, 1714.
   Swift to Oxford: P. V, 469–70.
258 *Gaultier, le Cte D'Oxford etc*: Appendix to Trevelyan, III.

258 *'Memorandum'* etc: B.M. 29/10/6.
   Shrewsbury and Bolingbroke: Nicholson, 208.
   Swift: Bolingbroke, *Correspondence*, II, 185, 190.
258-9 *Arbuthnot*: Aitken, 64-74.
259 *Defoe*: P. V, 475, July 26, 1714.
261-4 *The Queen's last days*: Feiling, 475; Aitken, 75; H.M.C. Kenyon, 456; Wentworth, 407; Hamilton, *Diary*, 68; H.M.C. Downshire, I, ii, 902.
261 *Bolingbroke and commissions for Jacobites*: Hanmer, 166.
262 *Bolingbroke's dinner party*: Swift, *Correspondence*, II, 202; Williams, 146.
263 *The Cabinet meeting*: Defoe, *White Staff*, II, 62; Handasyde, 138; Feiling, 476.
   Bolingbroke, 'the whimsical': Bolingbroke, *Works*, I, 27-8.
264 *Hanover messengers*: Handasyde, 138.
   Arbuthnot and the Queen's death: Aitken, 77.
   Bolingbroke: Petrie, 250 et seq.
   Defoe: Defoe, *White Staff*, II, 32.
265 *Defoe and Bolingbroke*: Defoe, *White Staff*, II, 64.
   Stratford: P. V, 477.
   Lansdowne: P. V, 477.
   Carmarthen: P. V, 481
   Foley: P. V, 481.
266 *Mrs Manley*: P. V, 491.
   Pope and Parnell: Aitken, 79.
   Prior: Prior, *Works*, 408 and Bickley, 216.
   Abigail: Wentworth, 416, August 20, 1714.
   'she-artist': Defoe, *White Staff*, II, 39.
267 *The funeral*: Addison, 289, August 12, 1714.
   Oxford's letter: P. V, 484, Letters in the Brampton Bryan MSS show that Oxford
   was ill in September.
   Arrival of the King: P. V, 495, 496.

CHAPTER 22   AN INSIGNIFICANT OLD MAN

268 *Chesterfield to Prior*: H.M.C. Bath, III, 447.
268-9 *The house at St. James's*: B.M. 29/10/1.
269 *Oxford's illness*: H.M.C. Dartmouth, 321-2.
   Bolingbroke's flight: Churchill, II, 1023; Petrie, 254; *The London Gazette*, March
   30, 1715.
270 *Edward Harley's letter*: P. V, 509, March 31, 1715.
   Oxford's letter: P. V, 509. In March Oxford wrote to the Auditor 'I am under
   great difficulties in my affairs' Brampton Bryan MSS.
   Conversation with the Auditor: Auditor Harley's *Memoir*, P. V, 663-4.
271 *'No distinction'*: P. V, 499, October 16, 1714.
   Cave's letter: Verney, I, 338, June 11, 1715.
272 *Coningsby*: Roscoe, 175, Cobbett, *Parliamentary History*, VII, 67.
   Addison: Addison, 338, 342.
272-3 *Prior's description of his examination*: History of His Own Time, 417-60.
273 *Swift*: P. V, 561.
273-4 *The impeachment*: P. V, 511-14; Auditor Harley's *Memoir*, P. V, 664-5, and
   B.M. 29/10/24.
274 *'I shall lay down my life with pleasure'*, and *'an insignificant old man'*: Mallet 191-2;
   to his brother Edward Oxford wrote, in one of his letters from the Tower, 'I will

274 never sacrifice my own reputation, or the liberty of my country, to save a poor perishing life', Brampton Bryan MSS.

275 *Illness in the Tower*: Brampton Bryan MSS.

276 '*Had I absconded . . .*': H.M.C. Dartmouth, 322–3.
The Triennial Act: P. V, 522, Auditor Harley, *Memoir*, P. V, 667.

277 *The trial*: Coxe, Chapter CXV.

277–8 *The library*: Prior to Lord Harley, H.M.C. Bath, III, 450.

278 '*Duppliniana*': H.M.C. Bath, III, 450 *et seq.*
'*Glorious Lady Carmarthen*': P. V, 514.
Tommy Haye: P. V, 592, 593, 601.
Catalogue of grandchildren: P. V, 521–2.
'*in double beauty*': Prior, *Works*, I, 527.
'*the best books*': P. V, 470.
Down Hall: H.M.C. Bath, III, 483.

279 *Memorandum*: B.M. 29/10.
The Peerage Bill: Cobbett, *Parliamentary History*, VII, 533, 618; Roscoe, 190.

279–80 *South Sea Bubble*: P. V, 592–3, 597–9, 610.

280 *Oxford's retirement*: P. V, 604–7, 634.
Pope: '*To Robert, Earl of Oxford*'.

281 *Prior to Oxford*: H.M.C. Bath, III, 491, 1720.
The ruined castle: 'the ruins of the castle give me great trouble', Oxford wrote, December 26, 1723, Brampton Bryan MSS. Papers relating to the debts, etc. left by Oxford in connection with the Brampton Bryan estate, are to be found in Bundle 6, Packet 7 of the Brampton Bryan MSS.

282 '*Friends fall apart*': W. B. Yeats, *The Second Coming*.
'*A soul supreme*': Pope, *op. cit.*
Last speech: Mallet, 291.
Swift's letter: P. V, 639.

INDEX